The Economics of
the Industrial Revolution

The Economics of
the Industrial Revolution

Edited by

JOEL MOKYR

London
GEORGE ALLEN & UNWIN
Boston   Sydney

First published in Great Britain by George Allen & Unwin in 1985

This book is copyright under the Berne Convention.
No reproduction without permission. All rights reserved.

George Allen & Unwin (Publishers) Ltd
40 Museum Street, London WC1A 1LU, UK

George Allen & Unwin (Publishers) Ltd
Park Lane, Hemel Hempstead, Herts HP2 4TE, UK

George Allen & Unwin Australia Pty Ltd
8, Napier Street, North Sydney, NSW 2060, Australia

© 1985 by Joel Mokyr

British Library Cataloguing in Publication Data

The Economics of the Industrial Revolution.
  1. Great Britain—Industries—History
  I. Mokyr, Joel
  338.0941   HC254.5

  ISBN 0-04-330347-1
  ISBN 0-04-330348-X Pbk

Printed in the United States of America

Dedicated to my wife
Margalit B. Mokyr
Scientist, mother, companion

Contents

Tables and Figures

TABLES

FIGURES

Acknowledgments

I would like to express my gratitude to Mr. Spencer Carr, economics editor at Rowman & Allanheld, for his unflinching support for this project. All authors reprinted below have been generous and cooperative. In particular, Donald N. McCloskey and Jeffrey G. Williamson have provided me with good advice and faith without which this volume would not have been published.

On the technical side, the work on this book would not have been completed were it not for the inexhaustible ingeniousness and diligence of John Nye, who has carried out the thankless and underpaid chores of editorial assistant, typist, and indexer with cheerfulness and verve. In these labors he was assisted by Mrs. Ann Roth with her usual cool-headedness and efficiency.

Evanston, Ill.
November 1984

1

The Industrial Revolution and the New Economic History

JOEL MOKYR[1]

Almost a century has passed since the publication of Arnold Toynbee's famous *Lectures on the Industrial Revolution* (1884).[2] Historians of all persuasions have since come to the conclusion that the Industrial Revolution in Britain constituted a new point of departure in human history, an event of such moment to daily life that it compares to the advent of monotheism or the development of language. Consequently, a vast literature has emerged dealing with its various aspects, written by historians, economists, and sociologists, both left wing and right wing, English and foreign. Little agreement has emerged among the experts about the fundamental questions. There is, first, the mere question of definition: what exactly *was* the Industrial Revolution?[3] Of the many attempts to sum up what the Industrial Revolution meant, Perkin's is perhaps the most eloquent. In his words, it was "a revolution in men's access to the means of life, in control of their ecological environment, in their capacity to escape from the tyranny and niggardliness of nature . . . it opened the road for men to complete mastery of their physical environment, without the inescapable need to exploit each other" (Perkin, 1969, pp. 3–5). More changed in Britain than just the way in which goods and services were produced. The nature of family and household, the status of women and children, the role of the church, how people chose their rulers and supported their poor, what they knew about the world and what they wanted to know—all of these were transformed. It is a continuing project to discover how these noneconomic changes affected and were affected by economic change. The Revolution was, in Perkin's irresistible phrase, a "more than industrial revolution." By focusing on economics we isolate only a part, though a central part, of the modernization of Britain.

Difficult and ambitious questions have been posed. What were the causes of the Industrial Revolution? Why did it occur when it did? What were the effects on the economic and social welfare of the population? What were the roles played by agriculture, population growth, political elements, transportation, and foreign trade? No consensus had emerged on any of these questions by the early 1960s.[4] Those who seek definitive answers should not venture into economic history. The inherent importance of the subject matter, however, has kept scholars and students interested and the literature dealing with the Industrial Revolution has grown extensively in the last decade. The topic has attracted many lively controversies. This tendency to generate debates is no drawback; the mortal enemy of economic history is not error but boredom. As long as the subject can generate vigorous discussions among some of the finest minds working in economics and history departments, it should consider itself alive and well.

In the past two decades, economists have played an increasing role in the historiography of the Industrial Revolution. A New Economic History, eager to apply its tools to new subjects, looked on the Industrial Revolution as an easy target of scholarship. Some scholars indeed have expressed the hope that economic analysis and quantitative models would resolve some of the controversies (Hartwell, 1971, pp. 133–34). The articles reprinted in this volume contain a sampling of the work of economists and economic historians familiar with economic analysis on subjects related to the Industrial Revolution. It should be pointed out that this collection does not pretend to be a systematic "New Economic History of the Industrial Revolution." It is not a complete coverage of the subject, but it addresses a number of important and well-defined aspects of it. The New Economic History has shown itself best qualified to answer questions that it itself poses, often well-defined questions that yielded clear, refutable hypotheses. Indeed, the very definiteness of the new methods has confined them to a narrow range of problems.

An important contribution of economists has been a more sophisticated and imaginative use of statistics to test hypotheses about causal relations in the Industrial Revolution.[5] The New Economic History has used existing statistics in new and imaginative ways and has added significantly to the body of quantitative information concerning England during the Industrial Revolution.[6] But most important, the New Economic History has imposed certain standards of economic logic upon the field. Economists are not less prejudiced and politically biased than other social scientists, and they certainly do not monopolize common sense (the strong beliefs of some members of the profession notwithstanding). But economics allows at least fewer logical lapses than other social sciences and when an economist commits them, he or she can count on other economists to point them out mercilessly.[7] Although disputes continue, they are fought with sharper and more accurate tools than before. Arguments can be—at least in principle—proven wrong. For example, it is still argued at times that population growth led to economic growth (Boserup, 1981, p. 112) and was an important causal factor in the Industrial Revolution in Britain. Economic analysis can lay bare the assumptions under which this theory holds. What has to hold is either a direct relation between population growth and technological change (a nexus which is difficult to document), or that economies of scale were strong enough to offset the negative effects of diminishing returns. These conditions can be tested, and although such tests by their very nature cannot be absolute, they are the key to distinguishing between the possible and the probable.

Some Problems of Definition

It has been said that revolutions are not events, they are processes. The Industrial Revolution was, as revolutions go, a rather drawn-out thing. Most scholars would date it approximately between 1760 and 1830. There were some years of feverish activity such as the *annus mirabilis* of 1769 when within five months James Watt and Richard Arkwright patented two of the most important inventions ever made, but the Industrial Revolution lacked the dramatic climaxes of political revolutions. Some of the best historians of the period have shunned the term altogether (Clapham, 1926–38; Heaton, 1948). Those who claim with Hartwell (1971) that the Industrial Revolution was a "great discontinuity" are opposed by the gradualist school, whose point of view was well expressed by Hughes (1970, p. 45). He finds it difficult to think of anything that lasted so long as abrupt: "We cannot think of the events of the last seventy years as sudden. Seventy British years [in the period 1760–1830] passed no more rapidly."

But the term has stuck and not only because, as Ashton put it, it is now so widely used that it would be pedantic to propose a substitute (Ashton, 1948, p. 4). The main reason why we think of the Industrial Revolution as a "revolution" is that its effects were so profound that even if we divide it by seventy, the per annum change was far-reaching enough to dwarf any economic change in Britain since the Black Death. Mantoux (1928, p. 25) noted that the term *revolution* is apt even though "few political revolutions had such far-reaching consequences." Economic change and productivity growth were not new in 1760. But unlike earlier periods, such as the wave of technical change that swept Britain in the century after 1540, growth was sustained and indeed accelerated. And it is this acceleration which is embodied in metaphors of discontinuous and abrupt growth such as W.W. Rostow's "take-off" and Alexander Gerschenkron's "great spurt."

Four different schools of thought about what really mattered during the Industrial Revolution can be distinguished. They differ in their emphasis on different areas of change, although many of the significant works defy such classification.[8]

1. *The Social Change School.* The Industrial Revolution is regarded by this school to have been first and foremost a change in the way economic transactions between people took place. The emergence of formal, competitive, and impersonal markets in goods and factors of production is the basis of this view. Toynbee (1884, p. 58) wrote that "the essence of the Industrial Revolution is the substitution of competition for the medieval regulations which had previously controlled the production and distribution of wealth." Karl Polanyi (1944, p. 40) judged the emergence of the market economy as the truly fundamental event, to which everything else was incidental.

2. *The Industrial Organization School.* Here the emphasis is on the structure and scale of the firm—in other words, on the rise of the factory system. The focus is on the emergence of large firms, mills, mines, railroads, and even large retail stores, in which workers were usually concentrated under one roof, subject to discipline and quality control. Mantoux (1928) is the classic example of this school, but Karl Marx's interpretation of the rise of "Machinofactures" also belongs here as do some modern writers in the radical tradition (Marglin, 1974–1975). A modern work discussing the Industrial Revolution from this point of view is Pollard (1965). Related to this

interpretation is the one that emphasizes the distinction between circulating capital and fixed capital. Some economists have defined the Industrial Revolution as a shift from an economy in which capital was primarily of the circulating kind (e.g. seed in agriculture and raw materials in domestic industry), to one in which the main form which capital took was fixed capital, e.g. machines, mines, structures (Hicks, 1969, pp. 142–43; Ranis and Fei, 1969).

3. *The Macroeconomic School.* The Macroeconomic School is heavily influenced by the writings of Simon Kuznets. Here the emphasis is on aggregate variables, such as the growth of national income, the rate of capital formation or the aggregate investment ratio, or the growth and composition of the labor force. Rostow (1960) and Deane and Cole (1969) are important examples of this school, and their influence has extended to non-economists (e.g. Perkin, 1969). Some writers, such as Gerschenkron (1962), aggregate on a sectoral level, preferring to deal with the rate of growth of the manufacturing sector rather than the growth of the entire economy. Most of the New Economic History tends to belong to this school, because by its very nature it tends to ask questions about large collections of individuals rather than about single persons (Fogel, 1983a, p. 29).

4. *The Technological School.* This school considers changes in technology to be primary to all other changes and thus focuses on invention and the diffusion of new technical knowledge. Technology is more than just "gadgets," of course: it encompasses organization of labor, consumer manipulation, marketing and distribution techniques, and so forth. The most influential book in this school is Landes (1969a).

The exact chronology of the Industrial Revolution differs depending on which school is teaching. From a technological point of view, the most dramatic changes occurred in the period 1760–1800, while the years 1800–1830—some major inventions notwithstanding—should be considered a period of consolidation. On the other hand recent research (Harley, 1982; Crafts, 1983) has shown that the aggregate effects of the Industrial Revolution on the economy or the total industrial sector before 1820 were not overwhelming. Two industrial revolutions can thus be distinguished: the wave of gadgets which occurred in the last third of the eighteenth century, and the economy-wide changes accompanied by rapid growth of the industrial sector which became dominant after 1815. Although the latter would not have taken place without the former, recent authors have insisted that any aggregative changes were both slower and later than has hitherto been believed, questioning the timing of the beginning of the Industrial Revolution in the 1760s and 1770s.[9]

This new view of the Industrial Revolution is in part based on the simple arithmetic truth that the rate of growth of national income or industrial output is equal to the weighted average of the growth rates of its components. While a few industries like cotton grew at a dazzling rate, these industries were initially small and their effect on the aggregate was quite modest. The proper reweighting of the more dynamic industries has thus led to more conservative estimates of the rate of aggregate industrial growth. Moreover, the critical years of the Industrial Revolution happened to overlap with the French and Napoleonic Wars, the economic effects of which contaminate the long-run story of the Industrial Revolution (Hueckel, 1973; Mokyr and Savin, 1976; Williamson, 1984). In terms of income per capita and other economic aggregates, the Industrial Revolution was at first relatively small and localized. Only a small minority was affected in a significant way. No wonder then that the entire affair looked less auspicious to contemporaries than to historians, including political economists who should have known better. As McCloskey (essay 2 below) and North (1981, p. 160) have noted, neither Adam Smith nor Ricardo (let alone Malthus) had more than an inkling of the revolution occurring around them.[10]

The finding that the macroeconomic effects of the Industrial Revolution are not overwhelming before 1820 is not really surprising. It is useful to regard Britain during the Industrial Revolution as a dual economy in which two economies coexisted. One was the traditional economy which, although not stagnant, developed gradually along conventional lines, with slow productivity growth and slowly rising capital-labor ratios. This sector contained agriculture, construction, domestic industry, and most traditional "trades" which we would now clasify as industrial but which in the eighteenth century and before were partially commercial: bakers, millers, tailors, shoemakers, blacksmiths, tanners, and other craftsmen. The modern sector consisted of cotton, iron, engineering, mining, transportation, and some consumer goods such as pottery and paper. At first, however, only segments of these sectors underwent modernization, so that dualism existed within as well as between various products, which makes calculations about the performance of the modern sector rather tricky.[11] According to McCloskey's computations in chapter 2, the traditional economy was large, though shrinking. The average size of agriculture and "all others" between 1780 and 1860 was 79 percent of the British economy, meaning that in 1760 it was likely to have comprised close to 90 percent of the British economy. Productivity growth in this sector is estimated by McCloskey at about .6 percent per annum. During the same period productivity in the modern economy grew at a rate of 1.8 percent per annum.

Two-sector growth models imply that abrupt changes in the economy *as a whole* are a mathematical impossibility. Even if changes in the modern sector itself were discontinuous, its share in the economy would grow only gradually, while the traditional sector would lose ground only slowly. In the long run the force of compound growth rates was such that the modern sector swallowed the entire economy. How long was the long run? A numerical example is illuminating here. Assume two sectors in a hypothetical economy, one of which (the modern sector) is growing at the rate of 4 percent per annum, while the other (the traditional sector) is growing at the rate of 1 percent per annum).[12] Suppose that initially the modern sector produces 10 percent of total output. After 30 years of "dual growth" the share of the modern sector will have increased to 21 percent, and after 50 years to one third. Only after 74 years will the two sectors be of equal size, and a full century after the starting point the traditional sector will have shrunk to about 31 percent of the economy. The British economy as a whole was changing much more slowly than its most dynamic parts, because growth was diluted by slow-growing sectors (Pollard, 1981, p. 39). These numbers fit the actual record well, and they indicate that it is hardly surprising that it took until 1830 or 1840 for the economy-wide effects of the Industrial Revolution to be felt.

In reality the modernity of industries and enterprises was a continuum rather than a dichotomy, and the example is thus highly simplified. It also abstracts from what actually happened in its failure to allow the growth of the modern and the traditional sector to affect each other. The co-existence of the old and the new is important, and the interaction of the two sectors greatly affected the growth of the aggregate. Although technological change in the traditional sector was slow by comparison, its production techniques were affected by what happened in the modern sector. For instance, construction technology may have changed slowly, but the rapid improvement in transportation technology allowed the shipment of bricks throughout Britain, which made cheaper and better buildings possible. Agriculture benefited in countless ways from technological developments in manufacturing including the production of clay and, later, metal drainage pipes and various agricultural machines and implements. Gaslighting, one of the most neglected of the "great inventions," allowed many artisans and craftsmen in the traditional sector to work longer hours and reduced the cost of night work (Falkus, 1982). These intersectoral spillover effects imply that the distinction between the traditional and modern sectors is to some extent arbitrary. The interaction of the two sectors was, of course, reciprocal. From the point of view of the modern sector, the traditional sector was important because it determined the socio-political environment in which the new industries operated. And although the modern sector was largely self-sufficient in raw materials and capital, it depended on the traditional sector for its labor supply.

In a sense, the inclusion of the concept of duality in our analysis of the Industrial Revolution answers Hartwell's (1971, p. 169) query as to whether it was "industry" or "the economy", i.e., whether the Industrial Revolution should be regarded as a change in the economy as a whole or whether its analysis is best confined to the manufacturing sector. The modern sector was more than industry, but not all of industry. The Industrial Revolution can thus best be thought of as a three-pronged development in which (a) one sector of the economy underwent very rapid change (b) this sector grew more rapidly than the rest of the economy, so that its proportion in total output and employment grew (the former faster than the latter) and (c) the modern sector eventually affected the rate of development in the traditional sector as well. The economy grew, but its sectoral composition also changed. It was "growing up" (Mokyr, 1976b). It was, of course, not the economy though eventually it would become it. Measuring aggregate growth rates in the tradition of Kuznets is therefore perhaps not the best strategy in trying to understand the Industrial Revolution, although it has its uses. Historians of the Industrial Revolution should recall Schumpeter's (1939, p. 144) warning that relations between aggregates are entirely inadequate in teaching us anything about the nature of the processes which shape their variations. Taken literally, this warning is certainly false; but it serves to remind us of the rapidly diminishing returns to highly aggregative analyses of the Industrial Revolution.

The Causes of the Industrial Revolution

Why was there an Industrial Revolution? In this crude form the question is unanswerable. In more focused versions of the question some answers have been provided, and while full agreement is still remote, the discussion is one of the more lively in the historical literature. Examples of more focused formulations are: why did the Industrial Revolution occur in Britain and not in France (or the Netherlands, Germany, Spain)? Why did it start in the last third of the eighteenth century rather

than, say, a century earlier? Can we find factors that should be regarded as "necessary preconditions" for the Industrial Revolution to have taken place?

To start with the last question, the notion that certain changes were a *sine qua non*
for the Industrial Revolution has become increasingly difficult to maintain (Gerschenkron, 1962, pp. 31–51). Some factors which were present in Britain facilitated the
Industrial Revolution and in this sense can be said to be causal. Others impeded its
progress, and the Industrial Revolution proceeded in spite of them. After all, factors
which were neither necessary nor sufficient for the outcome can still be thought of as
causal. For instance, heart attacks cause deaths, though not all deaths are caused by
them and not all heart attacks are fatal. Economic historians have come to concede
increasingly that the positive effect that factor X had on the Industrial Revolution
does not entitle factor X to the status of "necessary factor." Counterfactual analysis
has to be resorted to, at least implicitly, to assess the indispensability of the various
elements.[13]

It is not clear that the question "Why Britain? " is necessarily a good way to make
sense of the Industrial Revolution. Two of the articles reprinted below launch powerful challenges to the approach. Prof. Pollard (essay 8 below), as well as in his more
recent book *Peaceful Conquest* (1981, p. 41), has insisted that the question "Why Britain" is inappropriate. Rather than the customary division of Europe into economies
which correspond more or less to national entities, Pollard prefers a finer grid of
"regions." The Industrial Revolution was not an affair that took place in certain
national economies, it was primarily a regional affair. To be sure, Britain had a relatively large endowment of regions favorable to industrialization, but by no means all
or even most of Britain was in an advantageous position. Some areas in Continental
economies such as the provinces of Liège and East Flanders in Belgium, the northern
départements of France, Alsace, parts of Switzerland, the Rhineland in Germany, and
the industrialized region in the eastern United States lagged only a little behind Britain in industrial development, although the surrounding economies (with the possible exception of Belgium) were *on average* less developed than Britain.[14]

A different criticism of the "Why was Britain first" question is expressed by Crafts
in Chapter 5. Crafts maintains that there is a strong element of randomness in
Britain's supremacy, and that conditions in France on the eve of the Industrial Revolution were as favorable as they were in Britain. The ultimate success of Britain is
thus largely inexplicable. A good analogy is the tossing of a fair coin: once it is tossed
and heads comes up, there seems little point in explaining why that has occurred.
This approach, too, has been criticized, and one of these critiques (by Prof. Rostow) is
reprinted below. As Hicks (1969, p. 5) wrote, "though there is a sense in which the
Industrial Revolution is an event, it is itself a statistical phenomenon; it is a general
tendency to which theory is unmistakably relevant." The "randomness" which
exasperates Crafts is in part a reflection of the inability of economists to build models
which explain big events like the Industrial Revolution.[15] Nevertheless, we have to
ask how Britain differed from Continental economies so as to gain a headstart in the
race for industrial leadership.

GEOGRAPHICAL FACTORS

The availability of mineral wealth, particularly coal and iron, has traditionally been a
popular and seemingly persuasive explanation of Britain's success, as well as the

failure of some tardy industrializers like the Netherlands or Ireland.[16] The importance of coal and iron location is logically correct but of a secondary importance.[17] Coal, although it eventually became the main source of energy in Europe, had good substitutes in peat and timber (for thermal energy) and water power (for kinetic energy). Iron was much less easy to replace, but it was already an internationally traded good before steam power reduced the costs of ocean shipping to a fraction. In 1794–96, Britain imported an average value of 852,000 pounds of iron and iron ore, mostly from Sweden. The later reliance on British iron obviously was a convenience, but in its absence Swedish ores could have continued to be imported. After the invention of the Bessemer process, Britain imported large amounts of haematite ores from Bilbao. Sweden's rich iron ores did not help it to attain much success in modernizing its industry before 1850. The most dynamic industry in Britain (cotton) was wholly dependent on imports for its raw materials. Switzerland, Flanders, and Alsace are examples of regions which were not abundantly endowed with coal and iron yet were successful in modernizing their industries.

Such criticisms of the geographical explanation should not be exaggerated. A region or an economy had to have *something* going for it to produce goods and services at competitive costs. Surely geography cannot be absolved for the lack of industrial development in, say, Greenland.[18] In a static analysis, however, the importance of raw materials and fuel cannot exceed its share in total manufacturing costs times the extra cost involved of shipping in a substitute.[19] When more dynamic models are considered, the importance of mineral wealth is less easy to assess. Cardwell (1972) has written that "it is probably true that . . . European material culture has been based on mining . . . the mining areas of Europe in medieval times were centers of technology and science as well as financial organization and business enterprise", and lists the inventors and businessmen whose careers were associated with mining (p. 73). Wrigley (1962) has emphasized the importance of coal mines in the development of coastal shipping, canals, and later the railroads. Furthermore, coal mining generated more technical innovation than any other industry before the Industrial Revolution (Mason, 1962, p. 272). Problems encountered in mining led to the development of the steam engine, as well as pumps, iron rails and other inventions in hydraulic and civil engineering. Natural resources not only supplied cheap fuel and raw materials, but also created technological externalities which affected other activities that were not dependent on location. Britain enjoyed an additional advantage thanks to the availability of coastal shipping, although this form of transportation eventually was found to be inadequate and was supplemented, by canals and highways and later by railroads.

Another way in which geography singled out Britain to become the first workshop of the world was by virtue of being an island and thus a natural fortress. Since 1066 Britain has not been successfully invaded by hostile forces, and the only military devastations in the country were self-inflicted. Although some of the ravages caused by civil wars were severe, Britain was never as abused by incessant warfare as Belgium, Poland, northern Italy, and large portions of Germany. Consequently, it never had to spend exorbitant sums to protect itself from foreign invaders, and a comparatively small proportion of Britain's best and brightest citizens wasted their talents and energies on unproductive military careers. Above all, Britain managed to remain insulated from the actual fighting during the crucial years between 1792 and 1814.

True, the French and Napoleonic Wars proved expensive to Britain in that they slowed down the rate of capital accumulation compared to what it could have been. Nevertheless, the gap between Britain and the Continent widened during these years. Whether or not France and Britain were at comparable levels of industrialization in 1780 as maintained by Crouzet (1967b) and Crafts in essay 5 below, by 1815 Britain was far ahead. Taxation, conscription, direct war damages, trade disruptions, and the siphoning off of energy and talent into the military and politics cost the Continent at least a quarter century of industrial development despite Napoleon's attempts to encourage the modernization of French industry. Britain escaped this quite simply because Napoleon's army at Boulogne never managed to cross the channel.

SCIENCE AND TECHNOLOGY

In the view of most historians, the role of technological progress as one of the prime engines of the Industrial Revolution stands undiminished after a century of debate. Whether economic analysis can be of much help in understanding the process of technical progress will be discussed below. At present, we have to deal with the question of whether the British were, for some reason, better at adapting the laws of nature to economic needs. A large number of important inventions made elsewhere found their most successful application in Britain. Among these were chlorine bleaching, invented by the Frenchman Claude Louis Berthollet (1785); the soda making process, invented by the Belgian Nicholas Leblanc (1787); gas lighting, co-invented by the Frenchman Philippe Lebon and the Scotsman William Murdock (around 1798); the mechanical linen-spinning process, invented by Philippe De Girard (about 1810); the famous Jacquard loom (patented in 1802); the technique of the preservation of fresh fruits and vegetables, invented by François Appert (in 1795); and the continuous paper mill, invented by N.L. Robert (1798). French inventors toyed with steamboats in the 1780s, invented the balloon in 1783 (two Frenchmen were the first men ever to leave the earth), and were the recognized world leaders in the engineering of bridges. Still, it is noteworthy how easily many of these foreign inventions found uses in the industries of Britain. Going in the other direction, the export of British technology to the Continent encountered many obstacles. Some of these were artificial, created by the British government in an attempt to prohibit the export of machinery (revoked in 1843), although recent research suggests that the prohibition was not very effective (Jeremy, 1977). But most of the delays in the diffusion of British technology were caused by the industrial backwardness of the Continent. British engineers and technicians were usually required to operate and maintain the machines in the first stages, and most successful entrepreneurs on the Continent had to resort to the advice of British experts (Henderson, 1972).

While the British thus did not monopolize the generation of new technological ideas, they demonstrated an amazing ability to put these ideas to good use. There was a certain hard-nosed practical knack among British inventors, engineers, and businessmen that is harder to spot on the Continent at this time. Men like Smeaton, Brindley, Boulton, Arkwright, the Darbys, and the Walkers had not only the ability to generate new ideas but, equally important, the ability to recognize and value somebody else's. If inventors for one reason or another were unable to exploit their invention, many others were always waiting to grab the opportunity. A good example is the rolling and puddling technique of producing wrought (bar) iron developed by Henry Cort in 1784, arguably the most important single invention made during the Industrial Revolution. Cort was a naval contractor who succeeded in solving a puzzle many others had challenged unsuccessfully before. As a businessman, however, he was not a success, and as the result of the suicide of one of his partners his patent lapsed and ironmasters like Richard Crawshay who previously had to lease Cort's patent from him could now use it freely. Although Cort failed, within a very short time, his technique was used throughout Britain.[20]

Still, we should not draw rash conclusions about the acumen and talent of British businessmen active during the critical stages of the Industrial Revolution. Although examples of successful entrepreneurs are easily found, entrepreneurial history can be misleading, because the historical record is made up of survivors, who typically tended to be the best and the luckiest. The history of the Industrial Revolution is littered with the cadavers of businesses that failed, inventions that did not quite work, bankruptcies, and disappointments.[21] Many firms whose initial success constituted the bread and butter of the Industrial Revolution failed in subsequent stages (Payne, 1974, pp. 35–38). However, we only know about failures when firms were at first successful; firms who never did well at all are hard to trace. The resources—both physical and entrepreneurial—used up by these firms are one of the hidden costs of the Industrial Revolution not usually discussed. These costs should not be exaggerated: the equipment and plant of firms that went bankrupt were usually not wholly lost to society but were returned to productive use under different ownership.

A different set of explanations of Britain's success centers around the possibility that education, and in particular scientific education, was more advanced in Britain than elsewhere. Britain was a literate society but not significantly more so than Holland, France, or Sweden (Cipolla, 1969, pp. 62–99; Sandberg, 1979). Sanderson (1972) has shown that few occupations made use of literacy and that literacy did not play an important role in the Industrial Revolution. A number of issues here should be kept separate. One question is factual: did literacy rise during the Industrial Revolution? Schofield (1973) has denied that it did, but E.G. West (essay no. 11) disputes this. Given that literacy rose between 1780 and 1840, there is no certainty in which direction causality ran. Some of these issues are dealt with by Mitch (1982) who discusses in detail the demand and supply of literacy. Mitch concludes cautiously that increases in demand explain most of the increase in literacy. In any event, there is little in his work to suggest that literacy was a major causal element in industrial growth. Industrialization affected the nature of education, but not all literacy was acquired by formal education, and not all formal education was aimed at teaching the three R's. Education was aimed more at establishing certain moral attitudes that were regarded as important to the labor force (Field, 1979).

On the other hand, R.A. Houston (1982a, 1982b) has found that literacy rates increased substantially in the Scottish Lowlands and northern England between 1650 and 1750. He points out that there was no necessary connection between literacy and industrialization, but that increasing literacy amongst artisans and merchants may have increased indirectly the productivity of industrial workers.

So far as science is concerned, Britain had its share of eminent scientists and mathematicians in the seventeenth and eighteenth centuries. Students of the history of science know the names of the great British scientists alive during the Industrial

Revolution such as Priestley, Cavendish, Black, Herschel, Dalton, Davy, and Faraday. But Britain by no means had a monopoly on scientific discovery, the contributions of Frenchmen, Germans, and Americans to the progress in the natural sciences between 1760 and 1850 being at least as important as the British. There is no systematic difference between British science and Continental science corresponding to the gap in economic achievement.

Moreover, the impact of pure science on technological progress in this period was modest and indirect at best (Cardwell, 1972; Mathias, 1972; von Tunzelmann, 1981). Simply put, not much of what scientists knew could have led to major breakthroughs in technology. From the list of the fifty most important inventions made between 1760 and 1830, only a handful would qualify as having any direct connection with science or scientists, and even in those cases the relation was tenuous. Still, it may be premature to dismiss the importance of science and the scientific community altogether. Compared with scientists elsewhere, the British scientist tended to have strong practical interests. In Britain more than elsewhere the interaction among scientists, engineers, and businessmen was regular and embodied in such institutions as Birmingham's famed Lunar Society.

French science by comparison tended to be abstract, formal, and at times aloof from the real world. The motives of scientists were different: in France science was pursued for its own sake or served military purposes; in Britain many of the great scientists were constantly looking out for some economically useful and, if possible, profitable application to industry. An interesting example is provided by the Glasgow chemist Joseph Black. It has been maintained—following a claim made by Black himself—that James Watt's crucial insight of adding a separate condenser to Newcomen's steam engine was inspired by Black's teachings. The claim has been refuted. But Black was a lifelong friend of Watt's and his influence extended to other key figures in industry such as James Keir, a pioneer of the British chemical industry and John Roebuck, founder of the Carron ironworks. That Black attempted to take credit for Watt's invention is in itself significant in that it demonstrates the desire of scientists to be associated with industrial progress. British science differed from Continental science in that its traditions were derived from Francis Bacon rather than from the more mathematical and formal methodology of Descartes. Bacon and his most important followers such as Robert Boyle and Robert Hooke stressed the fact that "Natural Philosophy" had to be useful to society, and that Baconian empiricism was the natural medium to achieve such results.[22]

It is perhaps too simple to argue that scientific progress "caused" the Industrial Revolution or vice versa. Scientists and engineers shared and mutually reinforced a "rational faith in the orderliness and physical processes" [and] "a rejection of all that could not be personally seen . . . and made available to others" (Parker, 1979, p. 55). Engineering may not have been able to make direct use of any basic scientific principle, but it learned from scientists the importance of accuracy in measurement, rigorous experimental method, and the use of calculation and mathematics. In Britain scientists were eager to give and technicians were eager to receive. At the same time, it should be stressed that science was not the sole mainspring of accuracy and the technology of transmitting power. Clock- and instrument-making trained many of the engineers who played key roles in the Industrial Revolution (Cardwell, 1972, p. 16).

POLITICS AND THE STATE

British political institutions differed much from those of most European countries. Recent thinking by economists has tended to place considerable emphasis on political elements. Douglass C. North (1981, pp. 147, 158–70) has argued that the British Industrial Revolution was facilitated by better specified property rights, which led to more efficient economic organization in Britain. The link between property rights and economic growth consists of the greater efficiency in the allocation of resources resulting from the equalization of private and social rates of return and costs. Property rights in innovation (patents and trademarks), better courts and police protection, and the absence of confiscatory taxation are examples of how the same phenomenon could raise the rate of innovative activity and capital accumulation. North points out that well specified property rights are not the same as laissez-faire. The former were by far more important because they reduced transaction costs and thereby allowed more integrated markets, higher levels of specialization, and the realization of economies of scale.

North argues that the efficient specification of property rights resulted from the victories of Parliament over the Stuarts in 1650 and again in 1688 (p. 156). Parliament was able to stop the Crown from taxing the population in an arbitrary and unpredictable fashion by granting monopolies and taxing privileges to individuals. "Had such a shift [of power from the Crown to Parliament] not occurred, the economic history of England would have been much different" writes North.[23] Different in emphasis but equally unequivocal in its certainty about the role of politics in Britain's Industrial Revolution is the view advanced by Mancur Olson (1982). Olson's theory of economic growth is based on the idea that political bodies are subject to pressure groups who are pursuing the economic interests of their members, even if it comes at the expense of society as a whole. Olson is thus led to associate periods of economic success such as the Industrial Revolution with the comparative weakness of such pressure groups. Britain during the Industrial Revolution, maintains Olson, was relatively free of class differences, and by comparison a socially mobile society, so that loyalty to a particular pressure group was not yet very strong. The Civil Wars of the seventeenth century, moreover, had created a stable nationwide government, which made Britain into a larger jurisdictional unit, in which it was more difficult to organize pernicious pressure groups (Olson, 1982, pp. 78–83, 128).[24]

Was Britain a laissez-faire economy, and does the Industrial Revolution therefore stand as a monument to the economic potential of free enterprise? Perhaps, but some qualifications should be kept in mind. In absolute terms Britain was not a pure laissez-faire economy. But absolutes are not very useful here. Compared with Prussia, Spain, or the Habsburg Empire, Britain's government generally left its businessmen in peace to pursue their affairs, and rarely ventured itself into commercial and industrial enterprises. Mercantilism in Britain never took the extreme forms it took in France under Colbert and in Prussia under Frederick the Great, where the State simply deemed private enterprise to be incompetent and stepped in to do its job—usually without success. During the heyday of the Industrial Revolution even social-overhead projects which in most other societies were considered to have enough public advantages to warrant direct intervention of the State were in Britain left to private enterprise. Turnpikes, canals, and railroads were built in Britain without direct state support and schools were private. Even the more enlightened forms of state support, like the policies of William I of Orange in the Low Countries, or the Saint-Simonians in France during the Second Empire, were notably absent in Britain. Before the end of the nineteenth century, the British government clearly eschewed invading what it considered to be the realm of free enterprise.

Regulations and rules, most of them relics from Tudor and Stuart times, remained on the books, but the general consensus among historians today is that the regulations were rarely enforced. As the economy became more sophisticated and markets more complex, the ability of the government to regulate and control such matters as the quality of bread or the length of apprentice contracts effectively vanished (Ashton, 1948, p. 95). The central government was left to control foreign trade, but most other internal administration was left to local authorities. Internal trade, the regulation of markets in labor and land, justice, police, county road maintenance, and poor relief were all administered by local magistrates. While in principle these authorities could exercise considerable power, they usually elected not to. This *de facto* laissez-faire policy derived not so much from any libertarian principles as from the pure self-interest of people who already had wealth and who were making more. By ignoring and evading rather than abolishing regulations, Britain moved toward a free market society. Except for its strictures against the State's intervention in foreign trade, *The Wealth of Nations* was a century out of date when it was published: what it advocated had already largely been accomplished (Perkin, 1969, p. 65). Some regulations were more difficult to ignore than others. The usury laws, which set a ceiling on all private interest rates are thought by some historians to have had considerable impact on the allocation of resources (Ashton, 1955, pp. 27–28; Williamson, 1984). There is however, evidence indicating that the usury laws were widely evaded.[25] The Calico Act, passed in 1721 and repealed in 1774, which is sometimes credited with stimulating technical change in the cotton industry, had important loopholes which exempted fustians from the prohibition. Because fustians looked much like calicoes, the prohibition was widely evaded, although it remained a nuisance. The Bubble Act, passed in 1720, required a private act of Parliament to establish a common stock corporation. However, modern scholars have increasingly realized that this impediment, too, was more an inconvenience than a real obstacle to business activity (Cottrell, 1980, p. 10). The same appears to be true for the restrictions on the exports of textile machinery and the emigration of artisans (Jeremy, 1977). A few government monopolies such as the East India Company survived well into the nineteenth century. Moreover, free trade remained a far cry from reality. During the Napoleonic Wars, tariffs were raised to unprecedented heights (peaking at 64 percent of the value of imports in 1822). A slow trend toward lower tariffs began in 1825, culminating in the abolition of the Corn Laws in 1846 and the repeal of the Navigation Acts, which had severely limited foreign freighters from carrying British goods, in 1849–54. To be sure, tariffs and navigational restrictions were widely evaded, too.[26]

Another area in which government intervention was important and the law far from a dead letter was poor relief. Here the difference between Britain and the Continent is striking. Nowhere in the world can one find a well-organized, mandatory poor relief system like the English one. The Old Poor Law, sometimes erroneously referred to as "Speenhamland" (in fact, the Speenhamland System of allowances in aid of wages was used in a minority of counties) has had a notably bad press. Two major criticisms have been raised against it. One was the Malthusian complaint that outdoor relief reduced the incentive to work and increased the birth rate. The other criticism, already mentioned by Adam Smith (1776, p. 157), was that the Old Poor Law (and particularly the Settlement Acts) encumbered the free movement of labor and thus hindered its allocation in a society in which labor markets played an ever increasing role (Polanyi, 1944, pp. 77–102; Ashton, 1948, p. 111).

These criticisms have not fared well in recent years. Indeed, it seems likely that the effects of the Poor Laws on the Industrial Revolution were not nearly as negative as used to be thought. The demographic argument against them has been effectively demolished by the work of James Huzel (1969, 1980). As to the work incentive effect bemoaned by the Malthusians, research carried out by Blaug in the 1960s has recently been reinforced by the work of Pollard (1978, pp. 109–110) and George Boyer (1983). They argue that the causality runs the other way: wage-support payments were made in areas which suffered from seasonal unemployment, which explains the association of Speenhamland with the agricultural areas of England. Whether the Old Poor Law was somehow responsible for the creation of an army of able-bodied paupers is still unclear and awaits further research.[27] As to the geographical immobility imposed by the Settlement Acts, these were to some extent alleviated by the Poor Law Removal Act of 1795 [(35 Geo. III (1795) c. 101)], which expressly forbade the ejectment of poor immigrants unless they actually became chargeable to the parish. Even before 1795 the system was "by no means such a check on mobility of labour as some of the older writers . . . supposed" as the option to evict was exercised in a haphazard and casual way (Styles, 1963, p. 62). Some contemporary opinion agrees with this finding. Sir F.M. Eden, whose opinion according to Redford was "as weighty as that of Adam Smith", thought that the Settlement Laws were too weakly enforced to constitute the hindrance to mobility alleged by Smith (Redford, 1964, p. 85).[28] Perhaps the primary mechanism by which the Settlement Acts discouraged migration was by their sheer complexity and the uncertainty that irregular enforcement implied for anyone contemplating migration. Since migration was, however, a risky undertaking under any circumstances, it is far from obvious to what extent the Old Poor Law made things worse.[29]

Indeed, it could be maintained that the Poor Laws, despite their obvious flaws (in particular their non-uniformity), may have had some overall positive effects on the Industrial Revolution. A comparison with Ireland, which had no formal system of poor relief prior to 1838, bears this out (Solar, 1983; Mokyr, 1983). The social safety net provided by the Poor Laws allowed English individuals to take risks that would have been imprudent in Ireland where starvation was still very much a possibility. In societies without such laws, self-insurance in the form of large families and liquid assets were widely held, whereas in England even the "worst case" rarely implied actual starvation. The Speenhamland system assured a regular labor force during the busy seasons in agriculture. A similar argument may be made for manufacturing: workers could be laid off during periods of business slumps without fear of having the labor force emigrate or starve. Irish employers, on the other hand, complained about having to continue to pay their workers during slumps or risk losing them (Mokyr, 1983, p. 227). In addition, the practice of pauper apprenticeships and the recruitment of factory workers from workhouses run by local Poor Law Guardians provided an important source of labor to the factories, especially in rural and small-town mills before 1800.[30] All this is not to argue, of course, that the Poor Laws somehow "caused" the Industrial Revolution. But it seems that a case can be made that their net effect was not nearly as negative as has been maintained, and that they may have had hitherto unsuspected beneficial effects.

Another political difference between Britain and most other European countries was the lack of centralization of political power. Britain's system of government left most of the power of the day-to-day management of affairs to local magistrates, most of whom were respectable residents for whom administration was a form of leisure activity. Whether this government by amateurs was an effective way of providing government services is another matter, but one effect was the relative unimportance of London as an administrative and cultural center when compared to Madrid, Paris or Vienna. In France, for example, Paris traditionally drained large amounts of talent from the provinces, and local centers of learning and technology like the Manchester Literary and Philosophical Society or the universities of Glasgow and Edinburgh, located near centers of industry, did not exist. This rural-urban brain drain would not have mattered, of course, if industrialization could have been concentrated near the capital of the country. Interestingly, this seems to have happened nowhere. Neither Brussels, nor Paris, nor Berlin, nor St. Petersburg, nor any other major capital city in Europe became a center of modern industry. While some manufacturing activity developed around the capitals, the main centers of modern industry usually were elsewhere. As a result a highly centralized state in which the capital city drained the countryside of ambitious and able men, strongly attracted to "where the action is" operated at a disadvantage compared to a decentralized state like Britain.[31] Wrigley (1967) has argued more or less the opposite, ascribing to London a major role in creating the conditions leading to the Industrial Revolution. The size of London relative to England's population and its enormous needs in terms of food, fuel, and other products seem to support his claim. Sheer size, however, is not necessarily an advantage. A top-heavy capital might just as well be viewed as imposing a major cost on the country. Wrigley's argument seems better suited to explain commercial development before 1750 than industrial development thereafter. During the Industrial Revolution, indeed, the demographic predominance of London declined somewhat. Between 1650 and 1750 London's share of English population rose from about 7 percent to 11.8 percent. By 1800 this percentage had declined to 10.5 percent.[32]

Some historians have argued that the British government stimulated the Industrial Revolution by creating a demand for military products which led to rapid technological change in some industries (McNeill, 1982, pp. 210–12). It is true that some of these externalities can be identified. Cort's rolling and puddling technique was completed when its inventor was working on a contract for the Admiralty. Wilkinson's lathe, which bored the accurate cylinders needed for Watt's steam engines, was originally destined for cannon. Nevertheless, most scholars seem to agree that these effects were relatively small, and the effects of the Wars between 1756 and 1815 were negative on balance (Trebilcock, 1969, pp. 477–478; Hyde, 1977, pp. 112–116). Not only that the evidence for the hypothesis is not strong, it also runs into the dilemma that if military efforts created major technological externalities, why did France and other continental countries not benefit from them in the same degree that Britain did?

To summarize, most economic historians would agree that politics was a positive factor working in Britain's favor, although the exact magnitude of the effect as well as its *modus operandi* is still in dispute. The appropriate standard of judgment should be a comparative one, and it seems hard to disagree with the proposition that the form of government in Britain created an environment which was more conducive to economic development than elsewhere. Some oppressive mercantilist laws were on the books, but most were successfully evaded. Britons were heavily taxed, but taxation was never allowed to become arbitrary and confiscatory. Most important, the right to own and manage property was truly sacrosanct, contrasting sharply with the confiscations and conscriptions of the French Revolution and the Napoleonic era. Personal freedom—with some exceptions—was widely accepted in Britain. True, the Acts of Settlement remained on the books until 1834, but they were by no means as restrictive as the harsh requirements on the books in France and in Prussia, where workers were required to have "cahiers" or "Wanderbücher" in which their employment was recorded and which required them to ask for passes for journeys within the country. Serfdom was still very much in existence east of the Elbe in 1815. Only the cathartic revolutionary medicine administered to the Continent between 1789 and 1815 by the French prepared the rest of Europe for the modern age. But the medicine's immediate side-effects were so painful that most of the Continent required many years and maybe decades to recover from the treatment and start to threaten Britain's lead. Britain did not need this harsh shock treatment, since it alone had learned to adapt its institutions to changing needs by more peaceful means, and the channel sheltered it from undesirable political imports.

Britain's political stability contrasts sharply with the history of France, with its four major revolutions in the eight decades following 1789. But was political stability always an asset in the path toward modernization? Common sense suggests that investors will be wary of investment in politically unstable environments. It is likely that political stability was an asset and that its absence had a negative effect on industrialization. But how important was that effect? And how do we judge the economic performance of powerful autocratic regimes in Russia and Prussia? Moreover, Olson (1982) has insisted that political stability is in fact a rather mixed blessing, because it permits the crystallization of pressure groups whose activities are, in Olson's view, the archenemy of economic development. It is thus unclear how much of the difference in economic development can be attributed to this difference.[33] Still, it is no exaggeration to say that nowhere in the world was property *perceived* to be more secure than in Britain.

SOCIETY AND ENTREPRENEURSHIP

Perhaps the most controversial hypothesis is that England's miraculous performance resulted from the special features of British society, which were conducive to economic growth. Invention, capital accumulation, the sacrosanct nature of private property, the willingness of the regime to alter the environment to adapt to changing needs, and the interest of scientists and engineers in applications of science to industry, are all considered "endogenous to the system," that is, consequences of deeper social conditions. In the center of the stage, in this view, stands that controversial figure, hero in some opinions, sidekick in others: the entrepreneur.

The New Economic History has felt uncomfortable with explanations of economic success and economic failure based on entrepreneurial acumen or individual success. Entrepreneurship, the pivotal element in Schumpeter's (1934) scheme of economic development, seems to fit poorly in modern economic theory, which assumes that economic agents (at least most of them) try to do as well for themselves as possible. Opportunities to make a profit selling in a newly opened market, using a new machine, mining in a newly found seam, or lending money to a reliable government will not remain unexploited for long. If one businessman will not do so, others will take his place. Other economic historians, however, led by David S. Landes (1969a) have insisted on the importance of the supply of entrepreneurship as a determinant of the divergent economic experiences of industrialization. It would be rash to conclude that one approach has carried the day. Still, the Schumpeterian tradition, which views the entrepreneur as crucial, is not really incompatible with neoclassical theory. The implicit assumption of some Cliometricians is not so much that entrepreneurship was unimportant as that its supply was highly elastic and available at the same price world-wide. In this view, one might think of entrepreneurship in a similar way as we treated raw materials before: if an economy does not have adequate supplies of them, they can be created or imported.

Persuasive explanations of long-run economic change require some causal element which is exogenous, i.e., does not need an economic explanation itself. It is thought that differences in the quality of entrepreneurship is a weak explanation of economic differences between nations because economic conditions determine the quality of entrepreneurship. Therefore it is necessary to discover whether there were non-economic determinants behind differences in such entrepreneurial qualities as willingness to bear risk, resourcefulness, initiative, perseverance, and similar elements thought to be part of successful entrepreneurship.

A well-known and highly controversial theory of entrepreneurship is the one somehow linking businessmen to religion. Originally proposed by Weber, the argument is more successful in explaining the differences between Western Christianity and the rest of the world than in explaining differences within the West (White, 1978). Some modern social scientists have nonetheless displayed considerable ingenuity in an attempt to explicate and justify the link between religion and economic development. Thus McClelland (1961) defines the personal need for success, or n-Achievement as the prime mover of development. The nonconformists in England, because of their higher n-Achievement, were "more responsible for the increased entrepreneurial activity that sparked the Industrial Revolution from around 1770 on" (ibid., p. 146). In particular, McClelland points to the Wesleyan Church as placing much stress on personal excellence and success, and thus promoting the type of motivation which led to entrepreneurial behavior. Unfortunately for this thesis, however, few entrepreneurs belonging to the Wesleyan Church can be found. Wider definitions of non-conformism are more promising. Everett Hagen (1962) has shown that nonconformist entrepreneurs did indeed play a disproportionate role in the Industrial Revolution. Whereas they constituted 7 percent of total population, they provided almost half of the major innovators in manufacturing. Hagen rejects Weber's thesis that the causal link operated through dogma, and instead focuses on a psychological model of entrepreneurial behavior. In this model entrepreneurship was facilitated by a reaction of children to "retreatist" fathers who had been rejected by society because of their dissent. While Hagen's theory has not gained many adherents, it is a bold attempt to infuse the question with original interdisciplinary thinking, and it is a pity that no further attempts have been made to apply psychological theory toward a deeper understanding of the men who made the Industrial Revolution.

The most complete and persuasive attempt to provide a social explanation of the Industrial Revolution has been provided by Perkin (1969). Perkin dates the creation of the type of society which was most amenable to an Industrial Revolution to the Restoration of 1660 and the social and political changes accompanying it.[34] He points out that the principle upon which society was established following the Civil War was the link between wealth and status. Status means here not only political influence and indirect control over the lives of one's neighbors, but also to which houses one was invited, what partners were eligible for one's children to marry, which rank one could attain (that is, purchase) in the army, where one lived, and how one's children were educated. In Perkin's view, the quality of life was determined not just by "consumption" as usually defined by economists, but by the relative standing of the individual in the social hierarchy. Whether this social relativity hypothesis is still a good description of society is an open question, but a case can be made, as Perkin does, that it is an apt description of Britain in the eighteenth century. Perkin cites a paragraph from Adam Smith's *Theory of Moral Sentiments* which economists—always a bit eclectic in what they learned from the Master—have been ignoring at their risk:

> To what purpose is all the toil and bustle of the world . . . the pursuit of wealth, of power, and preeminence? Is it to supply the necessities of nature? The wages of the meanest labourer can supply them . . . what then is the cause of our aversion to his situation . . . Do the rich imagine that their stomach is better, or their sleep sounder in a palace than in a cottage? The contrary has so often been observed . . . What are the advantages [then] by that great purpose of human life which we call bettering our condition? . . . It is the vanity, not the ease of the pleasure, which interests us. But vanity is always founded upon our belief of our being the object of attention and approbation. The rich man glories in his riches, because he feels that they naturally draw upon him the attention of the world . . . Everybody is eager to look at him . . . His actions are the objects of the public care. Scarce a word, scarce a gesture can fall from him that is altogether neglected. In a great assembly he is the person upon whom all direct their eyes . . . It is this, which . . . renders greatness the object of envy and compensates . . . all that toil, all that anxiety, all those mortifications which must be undergone in the pursuit of it [Smith, 1759, pp. 50–51].

In Perkin's own words, "To the perennial desire for wealth, the old society, [i.e., Britain after 1660] added more motivation which gave point and purpose to the pursuit of riches. Compared with neighbouring and more traditional societies it offered both a greater challenge and a greater reward to successful enterprise . . . the pursuit of wealth *was* the pursuit of social status, not merely for oneself but for one's family" (Perkin, 1969, p. 85).[35] Perkin's insight is important because it underlines a basic point often overlooked by economists trying to understand entrepreneurial behavior. It is almost always true that an easy opportunity to earn money will not be passed over by a rational individual. Moreover, if there is a divergence of opinion about the expected profitability of an opportunity, one should expect the optimists to replace the pessimists. Unexploited opportunities to quick gains will rapidly disappear. There were opportunities to make money during the Industrial Revolution, but few were quick and easy. Almost all major entrepreneurial figures took enormous risks, worked long and hard hours, and rarely enjoyed the fruits of their efforts until late in life or enjoyed them vicariously through their descendants. Entrepreneurship will be more forthcoming if the rewards of money exceed the costs of risk-bearing, hard work, and postponed gratification. Perkin's thesis stresses the benefit side in this equation: in Britain money bought more than just comfort. It is perfectly consistent with economic logic and should be regarded as complementary to the New Economic History.

Still, some empirical questions have to be answered before it can be accepted as one explanation of England's success.[36] Was the correlation between wealth and social status stronger in Britain than elsewhere? At least in one case, Holland, this is probably false, and this case indicates that having the "right kind of society" is not a sufficient condition for a successful Industrial Revolution.[37] But what about France? In the eighteenth century aristocratic titles could be bought, and much of the nobility was a *noblesse de robe*, i.e., of bourgeois origins. Was the aversion to parvenus among the upper class stronger in France than in England? While the latter question cannot readily be answered, there were two important differences between the two countries in this respect. First, in France money could enhance social status, but the respectable local country gentleman who ran the affairs of the parish was a wholly British institution. Secondly, in France social status was often literally bought. The price of a noble title reflected a tax-exemption, so that the sale of titles was not a one-way street in which the crown soaked up wealth. But nobility implied high standards of consumption in the noblesse oblige tradition. In England, by contrast, wealth was correlated with influence and respect, but one did not have necessarily to part with the former to attain the latter.

Furthermore, Perkin's logic implies an almost dialectical dynamism of the supply of entrepreneurship. If merchants and manufacturers made money in order to buy themselves or their descendants the good life of the country squire, the ranks of the entrepreneurial class would be constantly depleted. Upward mobility by means of wealth thus also led to the eventual destruction of the entrepreneurial class. Having arrived at their new status, the new elite tended to slam the door shut to further entrants. This "gentrification" of the commercial and industrial class, which has been blamed for the decline of Britain's leadership in the Victorian age (Wiener, 1981), seems a logical extension of Perkin's thesis. As the debate on the "failure" of Victorian Britain lies outside the scope of this volume, this implication cannot be pursued here.

Agriculture, Foreign Trade, Population Growth, and Technology

There have been many attempts to write the history of the Industrial Revolution in terms of certain necessary preconditions which have to be satisfied prior to successful industrialization. For instance, the "agricultural revolution" is still held by some to have to precede or occur simultaneously with an Industrial Revolution. This hypothesis is then tested by pointing to the improvements in British agriculture which took place in the eighteenth century. A different approach is the view that the acceleration in population growth which occurred after 1750 was instrumental in triggering the Industrial Revolution in Britain. A third view considers foreign trade to be the "engine" of the Industrial Revolution, and the rapid increase of exports—which included a more than proportional share of goods produced in the modern sector—to be essential for the subsequent development of industry. All these approaches suffer from an application of the *post hoc ergo propter hoc* principle. It is more appropriate to start by searching for the exact causal links between events exogenous to industry and the Industrial Revolution, and then to ask if one can show that these "preconditions" were indeed indispensable.

AGRICULTURE

The ability of the economy to generate enough food for an expanding non-agricultural sector was one of the greatest concerns of the political economists witnessing the Industrial Revolution. Indeed, the fear of food scarcity led the two most prominent thinkers of the time, Ricardo and Malthus, to take a far more pessimistic view of the economy than Adam Smith, although Smith wrote at the dawn of the Industrial Revolution while Ricardo and Malthus had an opportunity to witness the full swing of technological innovation and rising productivity in manufacturing. The Malthusian fear of insufficient food production is one of the most egregious mistakes in the history of economic thought as far as the West is concerned. The economic history of the western world in the past two centuries has been plagued most of the time by *over*production of agricultural goods. From the British Corn Laws (first introduced in 1670 and updated repeatedly in the eighteenth century) to the Common Agricultural Policy of our own time which has led to the notorious "mountains" of agricultural surpluses, European governments had to be more concerned with guaranteeing adequate prices for their farmer constituencies than ensuring adequate food supplies for their populations. The only exceptions were the periods of major war and the "hungry forties," both unusual cases.

Europe's success in feeding itself could be interpreted as providing support for the importance of the Agricultural Revolution. But matters are not that simple. For one thing, if one looks at Britain, the timing of the "two revolutions" creates some doubt. Agriculture in Britain started to change as early as the sixteenth century, and progressed at first very slowly. After 1640, with mixed farming spreading through the light soil regions, productivity growth accelerated (Kerridge, 1969; Jones, 1974, pp. 66–81). During the years of the Industrial Revolution, however, agricultural production fell short. After 1760, and especially after 1793, the rate of growth of supply was outstripped by the rate of growth of demand. Food prices rose and famines became a real threat. This reversal was due in part to fortuitous factors (weather, the disruption of foreign trade) and in part to the unprecedented rate of population growth after 1750. Moreover, the shortfall was not large. Jones (1974, p. 98) concludes that agriculture had supplied the country's wants more than adequately until the mid-eighteenth century and that it failed to do so afterward only "by the slenderest margin."

The question is whether, had the rate of growth of agricultural supply been lower, the rate of industrialization would have been slower. In a closed economy, agricultural stagnation would indeed lead to ever-worsening terms of trade for the non-agricultural sector, rising money wages, rising rents, and declining profits and accumulation—exactly what Ricardo feared and Malthus hoped for. But because Britain was an economy open to trade, relative prices changed much less. Part of the error of the Malthusians is attributable to the unique circumstances between 1790 and 1815 when their ideas were shaped, since during these years the Napoleonic Wars disrupted the world economy leading to theories which do not take full account of the open-ness of the British economy. But these years also mark the closer integration of the Irish and British economies, which provided Britain with a nearby and politically secure source of grain and animal products. These issues are discussed in greater detail by Brinley Thomas in Chapter 6, who poses an explicit challenge to the view that the Agricultural Revolution was crucial to the Industrial Revolution.

If we widen the definition of the Agricultural Revolution, the paradox of classical political economy in part disappears. Food production and distribution used non-agricultural inputs, many of which underwent major progress in this period. In this view then, the Industrial Revolution largely fed itself. For example, the modernization of transportation affected the supply of agricultural products in a way similar to improvements in agricultural productivity properly speaking. What is known as the "transportation revolution" (canals and turnpikes, then improved ships and railroads) was nothing but the application of ideas and principles from industry to transportation, and should be regarded as part and parcel of the creation of the modern sector. The decline in transport cost helped Britain to feed itself during the nineteenth century. Moreover, as noted above, the Industrial Revolution also produced better and cheaper inputs for agriculture, so that productivity increases in that sector were in part caused by the Industrial Revolution itself. It is therefore quite unreasonable to think in terms of a necessary sequence of agriculture first, industry next.

Another argument links agriculture and the Industrial Revolution through the supply of labor. It is often thought that rising productivity in agriculture made it possible not only to produce more output but, in addition, to dispense with parts of the agricultural labor force which then became available to manufacturing. The enclosure movement after 1760 was thought to have been instrumental in this process of "labor release". Chambers (1953) has shown that enclosures did not release much agricultural labor. But, as Crafts shows in Chapter 7, accelerating population growth and declining labor requirements of agriculture jointly allowed a significant reshuffling of the labor force toward industry.

"Agriculture," writes Eric Jones, "contributed in real, if complicated, ways to the emergence of industrialism in England" (Jones, 1974, p. 119). Phrased in this cautious manner, this view will encounter little criticism. But it is far from clear whether differences in agriculture explain why the Industrial Revolution occurred when and where it did. It is certainly unwarranted to infer that because agricultural growth affected industrialization, the latter could not have taken place without the former.

FOREIGN TRADE AND EMPIRE

For the historian, foreign trade is one of the most visible forms of economic activity. Import and export statistics are a prime source of quantitative information, going back in time far beyond any statistics of aggregate production. It has therefore been tempting to use foreign trade data to learn something about other aspects of the economy. But inferences can be misleading: in the 1780s, total net imports amounted to about 19 million pounds which was less than 10 percent of national income in current prices. This proportion grew during the Industrial Revolution, and was about 25 percent in the 1850s.

The precise function of foreign trade in the Industrial Revolution has two aspects. The first and most obvious is that foreign trade made it possible for Britain to import certain commodities which it could not produce as efficiently (or at all) at home. Raw cotton from North America, sugar from the Caribbean, grains and timber from the Baltic area all played important roles in the British economy, and some of them were critical inputs in British industry. Economists delight in teaching that the gains from trade are *real* gains: an open economy can consume more than a closed economy. Thus trade creation resembles technological change, leading to higher incomes. The other aspect of foreign trade which in some views was equally important was that foreign demand provided the necessary markets for industrial output.

The argument that foreign markets were essential in creating the demand for British products is less plausible than the straightforward gains-from-trade argument, and is dealt with in some detail by Mokyr in essay 4 below. Britain exported goods and services, but from the point of view of British consumers these exports were a necessary evil. After all, every yard of cotton cloth sent abroad was no longer available for domestic consumption. Exports *as such* were not a good thing for the British economy. What *is* true is that a buoyant foreign demand will lead to more favorable terms of trade, all other things being equal. Yet, from 1790 on Britain's net barter terms of trade worsened (Thomas and McCloskey, 1981, p. 101). It is likely that Britain's single factoral terms of trade (in which prices are weighted by the productivity of domestic factors of production) improved over the same period. Thus the ability of Britons to buy foreign goods may well have improved. In any event, demand expanded, but it did so at a slower rate than British supply.

Was international trade in some sense the engine of the Industrial Revolution? Thomas and McCloskey (1981, p. 87) start their essay by citing Deane and Cole to the effect that overseas trade was of central importance to the expansion of the economy; they then add an ominous "we shall see," arriving ultimately at the conclusion (p. 102) that "the commercial revolution had some small role in industrialization...As began to be apparent in the late eighteenth century, the strongest effect between commerce abroad and industry at home was from industrialization to commerce, not the reverse. Trade was the child of industry." The same conclusion is reached by Findley (1982).[38] A somewhat different conclusion, based on an econometric analysis of eighteenth-century trade statistics, has been reached by Hatton, Lyons, and Satchell (1983). They find that there was indeed an exogenous element in export demand, although they warn that this finding does not allow them to suggest that the Industrial Revolution can be described in terms of export-led growth.[39] The attack on the theory that regards exports as the "engine" of industrialization has not been limited to Cliometricians. More traditionally inclined economic historians, too, have been having second thoughts. For example, Ralph Davis (1978, pp. 9–10) has expressed his agreement that overseas trade did not have an important direct role either in bringing about the Industrial Revolution or in supporting the first stage of its progress, although he insists that after 1800 home demand became inadequate and foreign markets became "absolutely vital."

Foreign trade expanded considerably faster than output throughout the Industrial Revolution. Between 1700 and 1800 the volume of foreign trade grew sixfold. Although the expansion was studded with leaps and bounds followed by sharp retreats, it was on the whole much faster than output and population growth. Perhaps this has led many historians to conclude that foreign markets were indispensable to British industrial growth. They were not. In some markets, of course, exports accounted for a large part of sales. Especially in the cotton industry, the proportion of total output destined for the overseas market was large. Deane and Cole estimate that approximately half the total cotton output was exported between 1819 and 1841, a proportion that rose to 60 percent in the late 1840s and to 70 percent in the mid 1870s (Deane and Cole, 1969, p. 187).[40] Cotton was one of the industries with the fastest productivity growth, so export markes were to some extent responsible for the rate of productivity growth of the modern sector as a whole. But how much cotton would have been produced in Britain if export markets had not been available? In the absence of foreign markets production would have been smaller, but by less than the quantity exported. At lower prices the domestic market would have absorbed some part of output that was in actuality exported.

To summarize, international trade can create higher incomes inasmuch as international division of labor generates gains from trade. But this is not the same as saying that the growth of exports was "vital" to the Industrial Revolution, since the growth of international trade and specialization and productivity growth were substitutes rather than complements. To put it differently, the gains accruing to the British economy from international trade were not necessary to achieve the gains from productivity growth. Given that technical progress occurred, however, its beneficial effects were enhanced by the expansion of trade.[41]

What is true for international trade as a whole holds *a fortiori* for individual markets. The assertion that the British Empire was an important element in the Industrial Revolution is by now discredited. In 1784–86, Asia (that is, primarily India) absorbed 13.3 percent of total British exports. This share remained more or less constant throughout the period, reaching 13.1 percent in 1854–56 (Davis, 1978, pp. 96, 100). To be sure, India absorbed an ever-increasing share of Britain's exports of cotton goods, but its share was never dominant. In 1854–56, Asia (without China) bought 22.5 percent of Britain's cotton exports. Europe, the Near East, and Latin American remained equally important, and in these markets Britain competed on an equal basis. For those who believe that imperial control over foreign markets is somehow critical for the development of modern industry, it should suffice to cite the example of the Netherlands, which, in spite of great efforts, failed to produce a modern cotton industry to supply the demand for cotton in the Dutch Indies, while Switzerland, landlocked and without any overseas possessions, succeeded.

POPULATION GROWTH

Agricultural progress and export growth may not have been necessary or sufficient conditions for the Industrial Revolution, but they were unambiguously positive factors. Not even that much can be said about population growth, which nevertheless has been heralded as determining the timing of the Industrial Revolution (Eversley, 1967; Perkin, 1969). Population growth will usually lead to a faster increase in the demand for food than for manufactured products, because food has a lower income elasticity. Since technology in pre-modern manufacturing or even in the early stages of the Industrial Revolution was still labor-intensive, population growth will also cause the supply curve of non-agricultural goods to shift to the right faster than that of agricultural goods. The net result is a rise in the price of agricultural goods relative to non-agricultural goods, but changes in the composition of total output depend on the various elasticities of demand and supply.

Those who place demographic change in the center of the stage have to take recourse to a dynamic argument which explicitly relates technological change to population growth (Boserup, 1981). If such a causal link could be established beyond doubt, we would indeed have a powerful theory of the Industrial Revolution since the growth of population in Europe after 1750 was more or less independent of the Industrial Revolution (at least initially). The theory of induced innovation, inchoate as it is, lends little support to the Boserup view. Population growth tended to lower the relative price of manufactured goods and real wages, and thus was not likely to have stimulated a "search" for labor-saving innovations. It is more persuasive to relate population growth to labor supply. If cheap labor was an important factor in the Industrial Revolution, population growth may have had a positive effect in insuring a large labor supply. In that way, the surge in population growth after 1750 may have been a positive factor in the growth of modern industry. Nonetheless, population growth also meant that the transition to a more capital-intensive, mechanized technique required more saving to accumulate the capital necessary to employ more workers. The labor supply question is discussed in some more detail in essay 5 below.

North (1981) analyzes population growth in a more static model of economic growth. In his view population growth led to the opportunity to create better-defined property rights. The enforcement of property rights was subject to economies of scale, that is, as population increased, it became easier to administer justice, maintain law and order, and enforce contracts, and thus to create a more efficient society. This argument is an application of Adam Smith's theory of specialization being limited by the size of the market. But North raises more questions than he answers: is this scale effect powerful enough to offset the diminishing returns to labor resulting from population growth? And do not the economic gains due to more efficient property rights run into diminishing returns themselves? What was the "minimum size" needed for a political unit to have sufficiently effective property rights to generate an industrial revolution? And can one show that Britain—and no other economy—crossed that threshold between 1740 and 1770?

In any event, the historical record has been particularly unkind to the demographic explanation of "Why was Britain first". Population growth resumed almost everywhere in Europe at some point around 1750, and it is reputed to have led to a bewildering host of phenomena, from the adoption of the potato in Ireland (Cullen, 1969) to the political revolutions which swept Europe after 1789 (Langer, 1969, pp. 10–11; Goldstone, forthcoming). While the timing of industrial growth and population growth in Britain seems superficially consistent with a positive causal connection between the two, neither theory nor cross-section comparisons lend it much support. In short, while population change and the Industrial Revolution changed British history after 1750, their simultaneity does not warrant any conclusions about mutual causation. One could do worse than to view them as more or less independent forces.

One interesting conclusion that the New Economic History has tended to come up with repeatedly is that there are few necessary conditions in economic history. No single element seems to satisfy what Fogel has called "the indispensability axiom." Agricultural progress was important, but it could have been—and ultimately was—replaced by imports. Foreign trade was a major element in the demand for British goods, but in its absence domestic markets could have played an even larger role than they already did. Of course, *jointly* these factors were more important than the sum of each separate factor. In the absence of *both* agricultural progress and foreign trade, the fears of the Classical Economists would in all likelihood have materialized, and the process would at some point have ground to a halt.[42]

TECHNOLOGICAL CHANGE

Much recent work, including Feinstein (1978) and McCloskey (essay 2 below), suggests that residual productivity growth, not capital accumulation, was the principal cause of the rise in labor productivity and per capita output during the Industrial Revolution. Although the respective importance of capital formation and total productivity increase is still a matter of some controversy, recent research has focused attention on technological change as one of the main elements behind rising labor productivity. The sources and effects of technological change in the Industrial Revolution are discussed in greater detail in essays 4 and 5 reprinted below, as well as in von Tunzelmann (1981). Comparatively little has been added to the literature since Musson's (1972) magisterial survey of the literature. The most common approach utilized by economists (e.g. Crafts, 1981, 1983; Feinstein, 1981) is to compute total productivity growth. These estimates of the residual are useful, but have obvious limitations which are fully acknowledged by the scholars who use them. They do not, in any event, have anything to say about how and why technology changes.

Historians of technology have noted that technical progress tends to be an autocorrelated process, that is, nothing generates technological progress like earlier technological progress. Landes (1969a) has referred to this mechanism as "challenge and response," and Rosenberg (1969) has called it "compulsive sequences." In more common parlance it is tempting to call it the "one thing leads to another" theory. A model of technical change of this type requires two assumptions. One is that some activities are almost complete complements, such as spinning and weaving, coalmining and iron casting, and so on. The second is that there are costs in making radical changes in the existing allocation of resources. The process is set into motion by an exogenous (not necessarily random) event, which increases productivity in one of the processes. This improvement creates a bottleneck in the complementary process and thus generates a more intensive search there than would be the case otherwise. Because the "output" of technological change cannot be set at a high level of accuracy, however, it often happened that the improvement in the second process overshot its target, and a new bottleneck was created. The rapid succession of inventions in the textile and iron industries during the Industrial Revolution fits this leapfrogging model of innovation. But as Parker (1972) and others have pointed out, this is not a satisfactory explanation of what happened. The disturbance of the original equilibrium can be corrected either by further technological progress or by reallocating resources from the industry which underwent innovation to the complementary industry. The entire concept of a technological bottleneck depends on some rigidity in the system which hinders the quick reallocation of resources. It follows that such rigidities should be made explicit and investigated further.[43]

The decline in the cost of a complementary good or process is one possible stimulant to technological progress, the rise in the cost of a substitute is another. Much has been made of Britain's good fortune to deplete its reserves of the most important natural resource of the pre-industrial era, wood. The scarcity of wood, it is alleged, forced Britain to use coal for smelting and later for puddling and rolling, and metal as a substitute for wood as a raw material (Boserup, 1981, pp. 105–111; Brinley Thomas, 1980). The problem with this interpretation is that we cannot predict when such pressures will lead to invention and when they will simply lead the economy into stagnation. The timber scarcity argument also has a serious timing problem. Rosenberg (1976, pp. 250–51) reminds us that the scarcity of wood in England began in Elizabethan times. Nef and others showed long ago that the substitution of iron for wood was drawn out over centuries. The use of timber in glassmaking was prohibited in 1615, four years after Edward Zouch was awarded the first patent for making glass in a coal-burning reverberatory furnace which was later used for lead and steel making as well. Coal was also widely used in brickmaking, salt- and soapboiling, and the manufacture of alum, lime, and saltpeter. Nevertheless, John Nef's view that for those reasons the second half of the sixteenth century should be regarded as the beginning of the Industrial Revolution has gained little support. The "good fortune" of high timber prices may have induced the switch from charcoal to coke smelting but as Hyde (1977, pp. 32–41) has shown, coke pig iron was at first more expensive than charcoal pig iron. Moreover, the coke-smelting process discovered by the Darbys of Coalbrookdale was long kept a tight industrial secret, and the process spread slowly: as late as 1760, half a century after its discovery, there were only 14 coke furnaces in Britain. The same is not true for Cort's rolling and puddling process, but Cort's invention was so vastly superior to anything used earlier that it seems farfetched to attribute it to high timber prices.

The economic logic of the argument which seeks to turn a resource disadvantage into a technological advantage should be spelled out more explicitly. The argument assumes the existence of a "learning curve" in the use of coal. A learning curve shows how costs decline over time as a particular technique is used and as experience makes it more efficient. If it is argued that the scarcity of timber was beneficial in the long run, it has to be assumed that the learning curve for coal-using techniques was steeper than charcoal smelting. When the price of wood and charcoal rose, industry switched to a previously unprofitable technique (coal), but as it "learned," it discovered to its surprise that the new technique was becoming more efficient than the old one ever was. Even if the forests grew back, nobody would return to the old wood-using techniques. This scenario is not implausible, but many of the assumptions on which it depends remain to be demonstrated. Some techniques which fell into disuse were perfectly capable of major technology improvements. Cort's forging techniques used charcoal in areas where coal was expensive relative to wood (Derry and Williams, 1960, p. 480). The charcoal wrought iron industry made impressive gains, especially in the all-important area of fuel economy (Landes, 1969a, p. 93). Water power, in many areas replaced by steam power, witnessed important engineering breakthroughs in the period after 1750 (Cardwell, 1972, pp. 102–06). Thus, unless there was a significant difference in the slopes of the learning curves of the old and new techniques, running out of a resource was what common sense dictates it should be: a setback, not a stroke of good fortune. It did not have to be a fatal setback, since most resources had substitutes. But it is one thing to argue that ingenuity and inventiveness could reduce the effects of such a setback and quite another to maintain that ultimately such scarcities were all for the good and that they brought about the Industrial Revolution.

The concept of "learning by doing" is quite useful to the understanding of how technological change really occurred. The idea of "local technical change," first proposed by Atkinson and Stiglitz (1969) and used ingeniously by David (1975), has some radical implications for how rapid technological change is likely to be and where it is likely to take place. The assumption behind these models is that technical progress does not take place across all possible production techniques, but only in the neighborhoods of techniques already in use, through learning by doing and similar mechanisms. When the learning curves are not known in advance—and how could they be? —major differences among the rates of technological (and hence economic) progress between nations could be explained by the fortuitous event that one economy happened to have picked a specialization in an industry with strong learning effects, while another selected a "loser." An example is the three main textile industries, wool, linen, and cotton. The physical properties of cotton made it much more amenable to technological change, so areas which happened to specialize in it, in particular Lancashire, ended up becoming foci of industrial growth, while areas which specialized in linen (Northern Ireland for instance) grew more slowly. Here, too, the argument should not be pushed too far. Once a "winning" industry or technique has been identified, economies or areas which had previously bet on the wrong horse could switch to the better technique, although this was often costly and slow.

One of the main sources of productivity growth was the institution with which the Industrial Revolution will forever remain associated: the factory or "mill" as contemporaries called it. The factory was not entirely new in 1760, of course. The Lombe brothers' silk-throwing mill in Derby and Ambrose Crowley's ironworks in Newcastle were large factories already in operation in the first half of the eighteenth century. The Mercantilist Manufactures on the Continent were also proto-factories (Freudenberger, 1966). Nevertheless, the factory in which large firms concentrated their workers under one roof and subjected them to rigid work rules has become the symbol of the Industrial Revolution. It separated the household (the unit of consumption) from the firm (the unit of production) and thus profoundly changed the life of every person involved.

There are two views of this transformation. One is that the factory system was inevitable because of technical economies of scale. The new equipment needed central sources of power, such as the large water mill and the steam engine. Somewhat later in the nineteenth century, the chemical and steel industries were subject to important scale economies in the production processes themselves. The development of continuous flow processes, assembly-line production, and other forms of the division of labor led to larger and larger units of production.

The alternative approach considers the factory system as a solution to the monitoring problem (Millward, 1981). Under the putting-out system, the entrepreneur had little control over the *inputs* to the production process. He did not know how many hours his workers were active or how hard they worked, and embezzlement of raw materials was a common complaint. As a result, he compensated the workers according to *output*, not input, by paying them a piece wage. In the factories the workers were in many cases paid by the day, because the factory owner could observe the inputs directly. He controlled the number of hours worked, controlled the flows of raw materials and fuel, and his foremen tried to control the efforts made by the workers. There were advantages in this system, especially in quality control of the final product. More important, it seems, was the advantage that in more sophisticated production systems it is often very difficult to measure the output of a given worker since it depends on the productivity of other workers. In such systems it is also inevitable to pay the workers according to input, not output. There were also serious costs involved, both from the point of view of the manufacturer, who after all had to provide the building, and on the part of the worker (Smelser, 1959; Pollard, 1965, Ch. 5). In some industries, like cotton spinning, metallurgy, potteries, and chemicals, the benefits exceeded the costs. In others, in which the the small workshop survived for many more decades, they apparently did not.

Little research has gone into the question which of the two explanations of the rise of the factory is more powerful in the early stages of the Industrial Revolution. Recent writers as diverse as North (1981, p. 169) and Cohen (1981) have supported the monitoring hypothesis and rejected the technical scale-economies. But doubts linger. Consider the cotton industry. While spinning, dyeing, carding, printing and later weaving, all became concentrated, the production of apparel before 1850 remained primarily a domestic industry. Perhaps quality control is easier with apparel, but it stands to reason that the main obstacle for the concentration of tailoring in factories was the absence of technical scale economies in the production of the final output. Something similar must have been the case for the iron industry: puddling and casting were carried out in factories, but cutlery and nails continued to be made in small workshops until well into the nineteenth century. It is of some significance that when workers produced an identifiable output, such as in the cotton-weaving industry, they continued to receive a piece wage. Piece wages apparently provided a better incentive to efficient work than any control of supervisory personnel.

Is it possible to analyze technological change with the traditional tools of the economist, the rules of supply and demand? Property rights in new techniques were protected, albeit imperfectly by British patent law. Some inventors who failed to capture any of the social benefits of their work were rewarded directly by society.[44] The motives of the great inventors, professionals as well as amateurs, are far from well-understood. It is possible, moreover, that these motives mattered very little. Technological change and inventive activity were by no means identical. The cumulative effect of small improvements made by mostly anonymous workers and technicians was often more important than most of the great inventions. The question of economic vs. noneconomic motives in technological change goes further than that, however. At the secondary, entrepreneurial, level of technological change, economic motives must be regarded as primary. It is precisely on this point that the explanation of technological change finds useful support in the sociological theories of Perkin and others. The higher desirability of the monetary rewards of successful enterprise relative to security and leisure in Britain may have been instrumental in the faster rate of technical change in the British economy.

To summarize, the research carried out by economists has reduced but not eliminated the importance of two elements which traditionally had been viewed as central to the understanding of the Industrial Revolution. Agricultural progress and foreign trade have been somewhat diminished in significance in explaining why the Industrial Revolution occurred when and where it did. Population change seems in some danger of losing its position altogether as an explanatory variable. Technological progress, in its widest definition, has remained as the basis of the Industrial Revolution, and it still poses a challenge to economists whose understanding of it has thus far been limited.

The Inputs: Labor and Capital

Economic change can be decomposed into increases in the quantities of inputs and changes in the way inputs are utilized. Essay 3 by Solow and Temin below discusses the many difficulties encountered by economists trying to carry out this exercise. A related question, equally controversial and studded with theoretical pitfalls, is the effects of initial factor endowments on the rate at which the modern sector grows. A satisfactory model would allow us to approach the question "Why was Britain first?" from a different angle. How crucial was the supply of factors to the Industrial Revolution?[45] Where did the inputs come from, and how did market mechanisms channel them where they were needed?

There are two competing views of the role of labor in the Industrial Revolution. One of them sees labor as a scarce resource, in fact as *the* scarce resource, and therefore the Industrial Revolution had a better chance of succeeding in areas in which it was abundant and cheap. The second view, most closely associated with the work of H.J. Habakkuk and Deane (1962) maintains that inventive activity in the nineteenth century was mostly labor-saving and that scarce labor stimulated waves of technical change. Recent work has not done much to determine which view is more "correct," but some of the assumptions on which the two alternative theses are based have been made explicit.[46] As David (1975) has pointed out, the Habakkuk view implies that localized technological change has to be stronger in the capital-intensive range of techniques than in the labor-intensive range. In that case a high-wage economy will naturally have chosen a less labor-intensive technique, and will experience faster technological progress as the unintended by-product of this choice.

The first model (Habakkuk, 1963; Mokyr, 1976) assumes that technological change was more or less independent of factor prices. This would be the case if there was little choice in the range of techniques, i.e. the "best practice" techniques at the onset of the Industrial Revolution were the most efficient for any realistic set of factor prices. The transition from the old to the new technique required capital accumulation in the modern sector, which enabled the new techniques to be implemented. Steam engines, mule-jennies, blast furnaces, paper mills, chaff cutters, and threshers, are all examples of a new technology requiring a large capital expenditure. Above all, there were factories which had to be built, maintained, heated, lighted, and guarded. The modern sector was physically located, by and large, in large buildings. And in contrast with France and Belgium, in Britain there were no more monasteries to confiscate and convert. Given the reasonable assumption that the earners of profits in the modern sector are more likely to reinvest in the modernized firms, it follows that, all other things equal, lower wages (and thus higher profits) led to faster accumulation of capital and therefore more rapid modernization.

The *ceteris paribus* clause in this model did not always hold. For instance, it is important to ask *why* labor was cheaper in one place than another. If it was purely a matter of opportunity cost, the model holds. But if labor was cheaper in one place because it was less productive, the model encounters a difficulty, though not a lethal one.[47] Labor could vary in its productivity for a variety of reasons.[48] Differences in education seem to have made relatively little difference in productivity (Sanderson, 1972). Another interpretation emphasizes diet: low-wage workers could not buy enough food, and their malnourishment caused their work to be of low quality (Freudenberger and Cummins, 1976). This view too has some attractive features, since the so-called "efficiency-wage" model seems quite promising in explaining the failure of premodern, poor societies to develop. Unfortunately the evidence produced thus far to support this promising idea is less than convincing.[49] Differences in productivity, in the early stages of the Industrial Revolution were also likely to arise from differences in workers' attitudes. Concentrating large numbers of workers (of both sexes) in one room, and subjecting them to discipline, regularity, and the increasing monotony of the more advanced technique was one of the most difficult problems encountered by early factory masters (Thompson, 1967). Cheap labor was no advantage unless it could be effectively transplanted from the traditional to the modern sector. Sidney Pollard (1965, chapter 5) has pointed to the central paradox of the labor supply question during the Industrial Revolution: "the lack of employment opportunities... existing simultaneously with a labour shortage is in part explained by the fact that the worker was averse to taking up the *type* of employment being offered, and the employer was unwilling to tolerate the habits of work which the men seeking work desired" (ibid., p. 196).

How a rural, mostly self-employed labor force was enticed to work in mostly urban mills is one of the most interesting questions in the debate on the Industrial Revolution, and yet it has not received much attention in the literature produced by economists. One answer is given, ironically, by the social historian Perkin: "By and large, it was the prospect of higher wages which was the most effective means of overcoming the natural dislike for the monotony and quasi-imprisonment of the factory" (Perkin, 1969, p. 130). Plausible enough, but is it true? Pollard (1965) and Thompson (1967) suggest a variety of ways in which the factory owners educated their workers in their own image, trying to imbue them with an ethic which made them more docile and diligent. Here, too, more research would have a very high marginal product in understanding the economics of the Industrial Revolution.

Aside from the question of the productivity of labor, the wages the factory masters had to pay were determined by the other forms of employment open to the worker.[51] The opportunity cost of labor was determined by its productivity in the traditional sector, which still dominated the economy. Before 1850, the modern sector was small and thus close to a price taker in the labor market. Crafts's essay no. 7 below discusses the flow of labor from agriculture. But there was more to the traditional sector than agriculture. The domestic weavers, spinners, nailers, frame knitters, and cutlers, whether they were in the putting-out system of working for their own account, found their economic position increasingly threatened as the Industrial Revolution progressed. After all, the goods they produced were close substitutes for, and at times identical to, the manufactured goods produced by the factories. Slowly at first, but with increasing force, domestic industry was transformed by the Industrial Revolution. Ultimately it was doomed, but during the Industrial Revolution its relation with the modern sector was complex.

In many industries, mechanized factory production and manual home production were complementary and while the type of industrial commodities produced in domestic industry changed substantially, the outwork system showed a remarkable tenacity in its struggle with the factory system. The mechanization of spinning led to a short-lived boom in domestic weaving, and some domestic industries like tailoring, frame knitting, nail making, boot and shoe production, and tailoring remained domestic until well into the second half of the nineteenth century (Bythell, 1978). The wage rate in these "sweated trades" was very low. Since domestic industry was open to anybody, it set the lower bound on the opportunity cost of labor. True, the wage rate in the modern sector was higher and rose faster than that in the traditional sector. Still, they were not independent of each other unless the labor market was subject to extreme segmentation. Thus the growing modern sector produced its own labor force, and while real wages ultimately could not be kept down, the slowness of their rise in spite of rapidly increasing labor productivity has to be seen as part of the interaction of the modern and the traditional sectors.[51] This sheds an important light on the role of cottage industry prior to the Industrial Revolution. The pre-existence of cottage industries was neither a necessary nor a sufficient condition for the modernization of industry (Coleman, 1983). But as Jones (1968) and others have noted, cottage industries catering to distant markets tended to arise in areas where agriculture paid low wages. These were not necessarily areas in which agriculture was backward. In the English Midlands the heavy soils were not suitable to the new husbandry based on mixed farming and stall-fed livestock. This left these regions at a comparative disadvantage in agricultural production, and they increasingly specialized in nonagricultural goods. In other areas cottage industries emerged because high population/land ratios reduced average farm size.

While the transition from domestic industry to modern industry was at times difficult and varied from region to region, the conclusion that the former was a positive factor in the establishment of the latter has been widely accepted.[52] A number of factors have been proposed as possible explanations of this nexus, including the supply of entrepreneurship by the domestic system, the pre-existence of skills, and technological bottlenecks within the domestic sector which led to further innovations. Some of these, like the flying shuttle, increased the productivity of domestic workers. Others, like the power loom, were feasible only in a factory setting. Here, too, more detailed research is needed.

It is thus misleading to view the Industrial Revolution solely as the transition of labor from rural and agricultural occupations to urban and industrial occupations. The critical event was not the creation of an industrial labor force as such, but its transformation. In the domestic system workers toiled at their homes, but they were usually only part-time industrial workers, cultivating small plots and hiring themselves out as seasonal wage workers during harvest time. In the modern sector the existence of a large fixed investment implied that part-time operation was uneconomical. In addition to discipline, therefore, there was a need for regularity. The factory worker lost his freedom to allocate his time as he wished: either he wholly submitted to the requirements of the employers and worked the days and hours prescribed by the mill owner, or he did not work. Although cottage industry in various forms supplied a portion of the labor force needed by the Industrial Revolution (Redford, 1964, p. 41; Bythell, 1969, pp. 257–263), there were workers, especially in rural areas, who hesitated to make the great leap. Only their sons and daughters realized the hopelessness of the situation and moved (Redford, 1964, p. 186; Lyons, 1979).

In Ireland, where the collapse of domestic industry in the 1830s was swift and brutal, migration of workers to England and Scotland was widespread (Collins, 1981), and these immigrants were an important supplement to the British labor force during the Industrial Revolution (Redford, 1964, pp. 132–64). As Pollard (1978, p. 113) puts it: "[Irish emigrants] were, in many aspects, the mobile shock troops of the Industrial Revolution, whose role consisted in allowing the key areas to grow without distorting the labour market unduly." Whether Ireland actually functioned as a reservoir of cheap labor, as Pollard suggests, remains to be seen, but it may be no coincidence that the destruction of the Irish laboring classes in the Great Hunger also marks the beginning of an unprecedented rise in real wages in Britain.

Besides the question of the reallocation of labor from the traditional to the modern sector, there are many other loose ends in the area of labor supply during the Industrial Revolution. One question is what happened to participation rates. We have no clue about these rates for the eighteenth century, and scholars have used population growth rates as a proxy for labor force growth rates. After 1801 the census provides figures for total occupied population which allow us to compute some very approximate participation rates. For what they are worth, the participation rate shows an initial decline from 1801 to 1831 and then rises until 1851 (Deane and Cole, 1969, pp. 8, 143). These changes are small and reflect primarily the changing age structure and measurement error.[53] The concept of a participation rate is perhaps something of an anachronism, as it requires a worker to be able to declare himself as either being in the labor force or not. In a society in which a large if declining percentage of the labor force was economically active in households (farms or workshops) this might not be simple to do even if we had better data. It is thought that the Industrial Revolution mobilized a large part of its labor force by turning part-time workers into full-time workers and transferring workers from "disguised unemployment" to regular work, (Pollard, 1978). Recent work has revived the interest in children as a strategic source of labor during the critical stages of the Industrial Revolution (Nardinelli, 1980; Crane, 1983).

Changes in the amount of labor performed per worker were possibly of greater importance to the labor supply than changes in participation rates. It is also a variable on which aggregate information is the hardest to come by. Labor input per worker could increase by lengthening the laboring day and the number of days worked by an employed worker, and by a reduction in involuntary unemployment.[54] Did workers in 1830 work more than in 1760? This view is certainly part of the conventional wisdom. Pollard (1978, p. 162) has no doubt that this is the main explanation of the rise of family income before 1850. Jones (1974, pp. 116–17) and Freudenberger (1974, pp. 307–20) are equally clear that workers toiled longer hours during the Industrial Revolution. This account sounds plausible enough, but can it be sustained by evidence? We simply do not know with any precision how many hours were worked in Britain before the Industrial Revolution, in either agricultural or non-agricultural occupations. Most workers in the traditional economy started the week slowly, then picked up steam as the weekend approached, often working very long days toward the end of the week (Thompson, 1967, p. 50; Hopkins, 1982, p. 61). The decline of "St. Monday" (Reid, 1976) may therefore have been less of a net increase of the working week than a rearrangment to distribute the effort more evenly. McKendrick (1974) has derided the idea that longer hours explain higher incomes labeling it a "prelapsarian myth of the golden past", and asserted that premodern labor was "grinding toil", as bad as factory labor but less remunerative. It is easy to document many cases of long and hard hours in cottage industries, and days of 14 to 16 hours were common (Rule, 1983, pp. 57–61). It is not clear, however, how common such long days were, and to what extent they did not make up for the customary long weekend or for unusually low wage rates. Much of our information comes from nineteenth-century sources, which may be biased because economic conditions were deteriorating for cottage industry. If labor supply curves were downward sloping, as is widely believed, the declining wage rates in domestic industry in the nineteenth century led to longer working days. Still, the idyllic picture drawn by some (Thompson, 1967; Medick, 1981) of working conditions in domestic industry in the eighteenth century is probably unrepresentative of premodern labor conditions.

One reason the comparison of factory to domestic work may yield misleading conclusions is that the representative industry discussed for the nineteenth century is often the textile industry, and especially cotton spinning. The laboring days of workers in the cotton mills before the mid-1840s were long even by the standards of the time. The labor day was extended by as much as two hours, the number of weekly days was set at six, resulting in working weeks of 76 hours, compared to about 60 hours in most other industries. Official holidays were few, and unofficial leaves had to be made up with overtime (Bienefeld, 1972, pp. 30–49). In mines, too, labor hours were increased during the Industrial Revolution. These extensions were, however, far from universal. A recent study of Birmingham and the Black Country has found no evidence of longer working hours, and the traditional work-day of 12 hours including meals remained the most common practice (Hopkins, 1982). Only a small proportion of the labor force was actually employed in Satanic Mills or mines by 1840: most British workers were still employed in agriculture, domestic service, construction, and small workshops, where employments work habits changed very little.

Another possible source of labor was the reduction of involuntary unemployment. On the one hand, the amplitude of business fluctuations gradually increased after 1760, and as slumps became more severe, short-time and layoffs became more common. On the other hand, improved transportation and communication allowed a more efficient organization of the economy, thus reducing the problem of seasonal unemployment. The notion of large reserves of unemployed workers awaiting a rise in labor demand is quite ahistorical. Whatever the Industrial Revolution was, it was not a "secular boom" which increased aggregate demand along long-run Keynesian lines. Of more interest is the question to what extent modernization reduced the multitudes of unemployables: vagrants, beggars, prostitutes, and other persons on the fringes of society. A glance at Mayhew's description of London in the late 1840s suffices to warn us that the Industrial Revolution did not eliminate these people and possibly increased their proportion of Britain's population during the period.

The role of capital is not less controversial than that of labor. Recent work has concentrated on the speed at which capital accumulated, as well as on changes in its composition and on the sources of its supply. Our knowledge has been increased on the first of these issues by Feinstein (1978) who has created a data base to investigate the quantitative aspects of capital formation in this period. Feinstein's data permit us to test two hypotheses which have dominated the literature on capital in the Industrial Revolution. One hypothesis is the Lewis-Rostow claim that the investment ratio doubled during the Industrial Revolution. The other is the Hicks-Ranis-Fei view that the truly fundamental change was the shift from predominantly circulating to fixed capital. Both hypotheses have been criticized vigorously, and we are now in a position to assess these criticisms.[55] Feinstein's data imply that the contemptuous dismissal of Rostow's hypothesis was premature. The ratio of total gross investment as a proportion of GDP rose from 8 percent in 1761–70 to 14 percent in 1791–1800, and after a temporary set-back in 1801–11 returned to 14 percent for the half-century after 1811 (Feinstein, 1978, p. 91). More recently, Crafts (1983) has revised Feinstein's estimates, criticizing in particular the price deflators that Feinstein used. Crafts's figures still show a doubling of the investment ratio from 5.7 percent in 1760 to 11.7 percent in 1830, which reproduces the Lewis-Rostow prediction of its doubling with dead accuracy, though somewhat more gradually than Rostow thought, which is hardly surprising in view of the highly aggregative nature of this ratio. As to the other hypothesis, fixed capital rose from 30 percent of national wealth to 50 percent between 1760 and 1860, while the corresponding ratio of circulating capital declined mildly from 11 percent to below 10 percent. In industry and commerce the ratio of total circulating to total fixed capital fell from 1.2 in 1760 to .39 in 1830 and .30 in 1860 (Feinstein, 1978, p. 88). The absolute amount of circulating capital increased as well during the Industrial Revolution, but its growth was dwarfed by the rise in fixed capital. In this sense, then, the Hicks-Ranis-Fei view is corroborated. The economic reasons for the change in the composition of capital have not been fully specified. Improved transportation, communications, and distribution reduced the need to hold large inventories of raw materials, fuel, and finished products. There are well-understood economies of scale in the holding of inventories and cash, so that it is clear that larger firms needed less circulating capital per unit of output than domestic industry. This may have been partially offset by the requirements of new inputs such as fuel and spare parts. A second factor in the relative decline of circulating capital is the decline of output prices due to productivity growth, which reduced the value of goods in progress and raw materials relative to that of buildings and equipment.

Oddly enough, Feinstein's estimates also seemingly imply that capital formation was a comparatively minor factor in the Industrial Revolution. His computation of the "residual" (Feinstein, 1981, p. 141) implies that the rate of growth of output per worker was about 0.9 percent per annum of which only 0.2 percent was attributable to capital accumulation and 0.7 percent to productivity increase. For the period 1760–1830 the contribution of capital was almost nil. Feinstein himself wisely rejects this interpretation, and points to the importance of capital as the "carrier" of technical progress. One can also quibble about the procedures which Feinstein employs to arrive at his residual, such as the lumping of capital with land, which tends to bias the contribution of capital downward.[56] Still, the apparent dominance of invention over abstention suggested by total factor productivity analysis stands out as one of the most striking findings of the New Economic History.

Regarding the supply of capital, little work has been carried out since Crouzet (1965, 1972). The smallness of the modern sector relative to the entire British economy meant that its demand for loanable funds did not loom large relative to the needs of the economy. The Industrial Revolution did not crowd out much investment in agriculture or commerce, although private investment (including capital accumulation in the modern sector) was crowded out as a whole during the Napoleonic Wars

(Mokyr and Savin, 1976; Williamson, 1984). Dealing with the supply of savings on an aggregate level, however, is even more misleading than an aggregate analysis of labor markets. Such an analysis assumes the existence of "a" capital market which allocated funds to competing users, presumably on the basis of an expected rate of return and riskiness. There were capital markets in Britain during the Industrial Revolution, and it is important not to neglect them. Certain developments, especially the growth of transport networks, would have been slowed down considerably and possibly aborted, had it not been for capital markets. In the early stages of the Industrial Revolution, however, they played a secondary role in the process and certainly were far removed from the naive well-functioning market which allocates resources efficiently in neo-classical growth models.

The capital needs of the modern sector during the Industrial Revolution were met from three sources. First, internal sources in which the investor borrowed, so to speak, from himself using his private wealth (or that of his family) for start-up, and plowing his profits back into the firm. Second, there were informal or "personal" capital markets in which borrowers turned to funds from friends, relatives, or partners. Third, there was the formal capital market (banks, insurance companies, stock markets), in which the borrower and the lender did not meet and in which financial institutions fulfilled their classic functions of intermediating between lenders and borrowers, concentrating information, and diversifying portfolios. The questions to be faced are how important were these three forms of finance in the Industrial Revolution, and how can we explain this complex and seemingly inefficient mechanism. Students of the Industrial Revolution agree that most industrial fixed capital originated from internal finance. Crouzet (1965) concludes that "the capital which made possible the creation of large scale 'factory' industries came . . . mainly from industry itself . . . the simple answer to this question how industrial expansion was financed is the overwhelming predominance of self-finance . . . this fact is so obvious as to be almost a cliche (ibid., pp. 172, 188)." In a later paper he qualified this conclusion somewhat but insisted that it remained "broadly valid" (Crouzet, 1972, p. 44).[57] The pure reinvestment model has certain interesting implications. One, in its extreme form, is something of a paradox, since if capital produces more capital, at inception "some capital had to exist in the first place" (Mathias, 1969, p. 149). While some curious mechanisms have been proposed to solve this problem such as the Williams (1944) thesis, which attributed the "original accumulation" to profits generated in the slave trade, the difficulty seems a bit overstated, since in the early stages of the Industrial Revolution the fixed-cost requirements to set up a minimum-sized firm were modest and could be financed from profits accumulated at the artisan level (Crouzet, 1965, p. 165). As technology became more sophisticated after 1830, the initial outlays increased, and it became increasingly difficult to rely on internal finance to start a business. For existing firms, retained profits remained usually central to the accumulation of capital.

The second source, the informal capital market, can easily be illustrated with examples, but it is not known how important this form of finance was relative to other sources. Capital, as Postan (1935) has pointed out, was still a very personal thing, which most people wanted to keep under control. If one was to lend it out, it was only to an intimate acquaintance or to the government. Even partnerships, which were frequently resorted to in order to avoid the costly road of forming a joint-stock company, were usually closely tied to family firms, and the taking in of strangers as sleeping partners merely for the sake of getting access to their wealth was rare (Heaton, 1937, p. 89). This caution slowly dissipated during the Industrial Revolution, but it was still very much a part of British society in 1800. Many of the most famous characters in the Industrial Revolution had to resort to personal connections to mobilize funds. Richard Arkwright got his first loan from a publican friend, and James Watt borrowed funds from, among other, his friend and mentor, Dr. Joseph Black. While the phenomenon was thus widespread (Mathias, 1969, pp. 150, 162–63; Crouzet, 1965, p. 184), personal loans are more of interest as a symptom of how the system operated than as a major channel through which funds were mobilized. As the modern sector grew, intrasectoral flows of funds between firms became more important, usually within the same industry. Insofar as these mechanisms only reallocated funds among different industries in the modern sector, the upper bound that the rate of profit imposed on the rate of accumulation did not disappear. Instead of constraining the individual firm, the supply of funds now constrained the modern sector as a whole.

The formal credit market operated primarily through merchants, wholesalers, and banks. The consensus on the role of the banks is that, with some exceptions, they rarely figured in the financing of long-term investment. Their importance was mainly in satisfying the need for working capital, primarily by discounting short-term bills and providing overdrafts (Flinn, 1966, p. 53; Pressnell, 1956, p. 326). Pollard has made a case for the re-examination of the importance of the banks on these grounds. Given that banks provided much short-term credit, firms short of capital could use all their internal funds on fixed investment (Pollard, 1964, p. 155; Crouzet, 1965, p. 193). Pollard, however, assumed that fixed capital grew at a rate much lower than implied by Feinstein's figures. His own earlier estimates imply a rate of growth of fixed capital of 2.5 percent per annum, whereas Feinstein's fixed capital estimates grew at 4.2 percent per annum. In manufacturing and trade the discrepancy is larger: according to Feinstein, fixed investment grew at 7.7 percent per annum, as opposed to Pollard's 3.4 percent between 1770 and 1815. Thus, financial constraints on capital accumulation were more stringent than Pollard presumed. Moreover, as industrial output increased, the demand for circulating capital increased, too. Feinstein shows that between 1760 and 1830 fixed capital in industry and commerce increased from 5 percent of domestic reproducible capital to 18 percent, while circulating capital in industry and commerce increased from 6 percent to 7 percent in the same period. Was the activity of banks enough to finance an increase of 164 percent over 70 years in working capital? Cottrell (1980, p. 33) has concluded cautiously that there are indications that industrial growth before 1870 may have been blunted by shortages of circulating capital. A study by Honeyman (1983, pp. 167–68) maintains that small businessmen found banks unreliable, and that even for circulating capital kinship and friendship groups were preferred. The difficulty in obtaining funds led to the selective weeding of the industry of entrepreneurs of humble origins who did not have access to these informal sources of funding and thus failed to survive crises during which working capital was hard to obtain. From a different point of view, Cottrell has speculated that short-lived firms had better access to formal capital markets than firms that survived. The sharp fluctuations in the financial sector dragged into bankruptcy many industrial firms, and this effect may result in an under-estimate of the true importance of the plow-back of profit, as a source of investment, because the firms which left records would tend to be *less* dependent on external finance (Cottrell, 1980, pp. 35, 253–55). Yet it remains to be seen whether enough evidence can be produced to jeopardize the widely held belief in the predominance of internal financing in this period. Thus capital scarcity and biases in the capital markets were possible factors in slowing down the rate of accumulation and in limiting social mobility. In spite of these qualifications, it is still true that if credit markets had not existed at all, the accumulation of fixed capital would have been somewhat slower, though the rehabilitation of the banking system does not go far enough to allot it a truly strategic role in the Industrial Revolution.[58]

To what extent can economic theory explain this complex picture and assess its consequence? The limited willingness of commercial banks to finance long-run projects is understandable. Banks needed their assets in liquid form to be able to pay depositors on demand since there was no lender of last resort.[59] Yet this constraint was merely a result of the nature of commercial banks. Investment banks and other forms of financial intermediaries did not have to maintain such liquid portfolios. Why such institutions were relatively unimportant in Britain is still an unanswered question.

Indeed, for an economist, the prevalence of self-finance presents something of a puzzle. The use of retained profits to finance expansion in the United States today is explained by the double incidence of the corporate income tax. But its importance during the Industrial Revolution suggests that there is a deeper reason for the phenomenon as well. In an age in which fewer and fewer persons produced their own food and built their own houses and fewer and fewer worked for themselves, why should the most advanced segment of the economy be self-sufficient in capital to such an extent? As it happens, most theoretical recent work carried out seems little concerned with imperfections in the capital market. The modern theory of finance and its proudest product, the capital asset pricing model, essentially exclude any intelligent discussion of situations in which the expansion of a firm is constrained by limited access to finance, and in which rates of return are not equalized among firms. In earlier theoretical work such as Hicks (1946) and Scitovsky (1971) firms were perceived to face upward sloping supply curves of loanable funds. These models were not pursued, however and their microeconomic foundations were never quite made clear. Recently, Mayshar (1983a, 1983b) has taken up this problem again. Mayshar's point is that it is not risk per se which causes real-world capital markets to deviate from the theoretical constructs, but divergences of opinions among potential lenders with respect to the rate of return. Such divergences would of course gradually disappear in a stationary world in which no new information was created. But in a world of rapid technological change, shifting demand patterns, and a changing political environment, they were not only possible, but in fact inevitable. Thus rapidly changing conditions during the Industrial Revolution effectively precluded the efficient operation of capital markets. Only after the rate of change slowed down somewhat after 1830, could capital markets become more important. Mayshar shows that under certain assumptions the rate of divergence of expectations among potential investors is positively correlated with the rate of interest that the borrower has to pay. Moreover, the capacity of the firm to borrow is, up to a point, independent of the characteristics of the contemplated investment projects. Mayshar pictures savers as forming concentric circles around the entrepreneur, with his own funds in the center and those closest to him (friends and relatives) being most likely to lend to him. The farther one gets from the center, the more the expectations tend to diverge from the entrepreneur and the higher the rate of interest that he has to pay.

How important to the course of the Industrial Revolution were the failings of the capital market? Crouzet has concluded that

> the eighteenth century capital market seems, to twentieth century eyes, badly organized, but the creators of modern industry do not seem to have suffered too much from its imperfection . . . English industry, compared with that of the Continent, seems to have overflowed with capital [Crouzet, 1965, pp. 187–88].

This conclusion may be ripe for some re-examination. First, while the comparison with the Continent is probably accurate on the whole, there were important exceptions (Mokyr, 1975). On the Continent, too, self-finance was the norm, and it is not quite clear whether England was so much better supplied with capital than, say, Belgium. Moreover, the question should be whether the Industrial Revolution in Britain would have occurred faster and more efficiently if financial constraints had been less stringent. Given that the modern sector was at first rather small compared with the rest of the economy, the capital market's imperfection meant that from the outset the rate of profit set a ceiling on the rate of accumulation. The existence of *some* capital markets does not necessarily refute this argument. If these markets channeled savings from one firm to another in the modern sector, the constraint on the modern sector remained in force, and fixed capital had to grow by pulling itself up by the bootstraps. Postan put it well in his classic article:

> By the beginning of the eighteenth century there were enough rich people in the country to finance an economic effort far in excess of the modest activities of the leaders of the Industrial Revolution . . . what was inadequate was not the quantity of stored-up wealth but its behaviour. The reservoirs of savings were full enough, but conduits to connect them to the wheels of industry were few and meagre [Postan, 1935, p. 71].[60]

The Consequences: The Standard of Living Debate

Between 1760 and 1830 four events profoundly affected economic life in Great Britain: the string of poor harvests which occurred between the middle of the eighteenth century and the end of the Napoleonic Wars; the state of war in which Britain found itself during most of this period; the resumption and then acceleration of population growth after the middle of the eighteenth century; and the combination of technological change, capital accumulation, sectoral shifts, and related changes which we commonly refer to as the Industrial Revolution. Of these four, the first three tended to depress standards of living. Poor harvests raised the price of food and reduced real incomes. The wars reinforced nature's punishments. Especially during the Napoleonic Wars British living standards were depressed because the country had difficulty making up food deficits as wars and blockades reduced Britain's export earnings and foreign exchange scarcities limited food imports. Higher taxes reduced disposable income even more, and the continuous shocks and dislocations caused by the wars threw the economy into a succession of slumps which slowed down industrial growth and created unemployment in the new industrial centers in the midst of continuous inflation (Mokyr and Savin, 1976). As far as the effect of population growth on per capita income is concerned, the economist's first intuition is to appeal to the law of diminishing returns. In the present context, diminishing returns simply means that when population grows, living standards will be lower than they would have been in its absence, unless some very unusual conditions obtain.[61]

If we are to assess the effect of the Industrial Revolution, we must somehow "net out" the effects of the other events. As von Tunzelmann points out (essay 10 below), following Hartwell and Engerman (1975), there are two debates. One, the "factual debate," is about what actually happened: what was the trend in living standards between 1760 and 1850? The other, the "counterfactual debate" concerns what might have happened in the absence of the Industrial Revolution, considers its effect in isolation from those of extraneous events. The factual debate is biased against the pessimists in the sense that it is difficult to prove that the Industrial Revolution caused standards of living to decline. The reason for the bias is that the three other effects affecting the economy before 1815 all operated to hurt it. Thus a finding of falling living standards between 1760 and 1815 would not be proof of the negative effects of the Industrial Revolution, whereas a rise could only be attributed to it. The critical period for the standard of living debate is therefore after 1815 or 1820. At that point the wars and the harvest failures were over and, while population continued to grow, the crude rate of natural increase peaked in 1822 and the dependency rate in 1826. Moreover, by that time the relative size of the modern sector was large enough to affect the economy at large.

It is therefore particularly noteworthy that the New Economic History has reached something of a consensus on the actual course of living standards after Waterloo. Lindert and Williamson (essay 9 below) show that real wages start to rise substantially after 1819 whereas they made little progress between 1760 and 1819. Similarly, Feinstein (1981) has estimated that real private consumption per capita which had increased negligibly until the 1810s, rose from £11.3 in 1811–20 to 14.6 in 1821–30 and 17.9 in 1831–40 (p. 136). Crafts (1983, p. 198) has revised these numbers somewhat, but nevertheless joins Feinstein in his conclusion that after 1820 a marked progress in the standard of living is undeniable. The differences between these estimates are mostly in the dating of the rise in living standards. Craft's computations suggest that the improvement was more evenly spread over the period 1780–1851, with the improvement after 1819 being less of a sudden leap upward than earlier computations suggest. The differences stem primarily from differences in the weighting of the various commodities in the price index used to deflate the nominal wage series.

Whether these findings are definitive remains to be seen. One interesting issue raised (but not pursued) by Taylor (1975, pp. xxix–xxxi) is the evidence of consumption per capita of some key commodities. There are annual series for the consumption of some imported consumer goods such as sugar, tea, and tobacco. These series show no secular rise before the mid 1840s. For instance, sugar consumption, according to Taylor's figures, averaged 18.12 lbs. per capita in 1800–09, 17.83 in 1820–29, and 18.45 in 1840–49, and then leapt to 30.30 lbs. in the 1850s and 68.09 in the 1870s.

The stability before 1850 is not necessarily inconsistent with a rise in living standards after 1819 (since relative prices or tastes may have changed), but doubt lingers over whether the rise in living standards after 1820 may not be somewhat overstated[62]

The reason why the factual debate is so difficult to resolve, aside from the methodological difficulties, is the ambiguity of the reference group. On one hand, aggregate income or consumption statistics are inadequate because the reference group is too large and information about the distribution of income is required before we can infer anything about the standard of living. On the other hand, the real wage series reflect the living standards of a reference group which is too small, because it omits large "silent" groups of self-employed craftsmen, outworkers, and Mayhew's *lumpenproletariat* whose living standards may have moved in opposite directions.[63] The appropriate reference group shoud be the bottom 80 or 85 percent of the income distribution, whether they were self-employed, wage laborers or outside the labor force. In spite of much recent progress, some unsettled questions in the factual debate remain.

What happened to the distribution of income in Great Britain during the Industrial Revolution? Following the conjectures of Kuznets (1966, p. 217) it has been thought that in the first stages of growth the distribution of income, on balance, became more unequal, but that at a later stage this trend was reversed. Lee Soltow (1968) has computed British income inequality and found that inequality in 1867 was about the same as in 1801–03. More recent research has found more support for the Kuznets hypothesis. Lindert and Williamson (1983b) have revised Soltow's data and have estimated the Gini coefficients to be around .49 in 1759, .52 in 1801–03 and .55 in 1867. As they point out (ibid., p. 100), the trends they discern confirm Kuznets's hypothesis. Williamson (1980) has examined the inequality trends in the earnings of adult male workers. He found a sharp increase in inequality in a relatively short period (1827–1851). The Gini coefficient estimated by Williamson rose from .293 to .358, and the share of the 10 percent best-paid workers increased from 27.9 percent to 34.3 percent. Moreover, Williamson had to assume inter-occupational stability for most workers in this comparison, so that these estimates still underestimate the increase in inequality.

All the same, a worsening of income distribution can only go so far in explaining the slow rise in living standards. If income per capita rose at a rapid rate, a constant income of the lower 80 percent would imply a rapidly falling share of the poor. This logic is behind O'Brien and Engerman's (1981, p. 174) conclusion that even if income distribution had become considerably more unequal in the first half of the nineteenth century, it is impossible for the worsening to have been so severe as to exclude the bottom 80 percent of the income earners from the benefits of growth. O'Brien and Engerman assume that the bottom 83 percent of income earners in 1850 received 41.3 percent of income. Since income per capita, according to them, grew by "about 1.2 per annum" (so that 50 years before it would have been only 54.9 percent of its 1850 level), the poor's share in 1800 should have been 41.3 percent of 54.9 percent, or about 75.2 percent of total income. This being patently absurd, the entire possibility of a worsening income distribution affecting the standard of living debate is dismissed. Unfortunately, O'Brien and Engerman's facts are not quite as good as their logic: the critical assumption of a rise of 1.2 percent in real income per capita is weak. Presumably it was derived from Deane and Cole's table 72 (1969, p. 282), which implies precisely that rate of increase in national product per capita. With the general revision of Deane and Cole's figures, that estimate too has become a casualty. Crafts (1983) reduces the per capita national product growth rate to 0.52 percent per annum for the period 1801–31. Assuming that the Deane and Cole estimate for 1831–51 is closer to the mark than that for 1801–31, income per capita for the entire half-century 1800–50 grew at about .7 percent per annum. At those rates the share of the bottom 83 percent that O'Brien and Engerman examine would have been about 58 percent of national income in 1800, which, while high, is not "inconceivable," as they term it.[64] According to Lindert and Williamson's recent estimates, the share of the bottom 90 percent in income fell from 54.6 percent (1801–03) to 47.3 percent in 1867. If inequality peaked around 1850 (after which year two decades of undisputed rises in real wages occurred), the sharpening of inequality may indeed have been a more powerful factor than O'Brien and Engerman give it credit for.[65]

A somewhat different approach to the issue of the standard of living and the distribution of income is taken by Church (1980). Church is concerned primarily with business, not with consumers, but his work is pertinent to the standard of living debate. Church maintains that the first stage of the Industrial Revolution, which came to an end at around 1825, was characterized by feverish innovation and disequilibrium. As economic theory suggests, disequilibria created unprecedented opportunities to earn high profits. As the rate of innovation slowed down after 1825, the economy began to resemble more and more the standard textbook economic model, in which relentless competition eroded all "supernormal" profits and quasi-rents. This finding is of course consistent with the Lindert and Williamson finding of rising real wages, because declining entrepreneurial profits meant higher wages and lower prices for consumer goods. Because entrepreneurial profits are rarely observed directly, testing the Church thesis is difficult. An indirect and rather crude way to examine it is by confronting it with Feinstein's (1978) data on capital formation. Such a confrontation (Mokyr, 1982) yields mixed results. First, if we believe that there is a strong correlation between the rate of profit and the rate of capital formation, Feinstein's figures raise a difficulty for the Church thesis. The rate of growth of fixed capital accelerated during the Industrial Revolution, from 1.0 percent per annum in 1761–1800 to 1.6 percent per annum in 1801–30 and 2.3 percent in 1831–60. If, as Church suggests, the rate of profit may have fallen in 1830–60 to half its previous level, the reinvestment propensity of capitalists must have tripled, or the functional relation between the rate of accumulation and the rate of profit changed dramatically. A third of the growth of fixed capital after 1830 was in transport, which relied heavily on capital markets, so that such a shift is not wholly inconceivable, but still seems rather unlikely. An alternative way of testing the Church thesis is to compute the change in the incremental capital-output ratio. The heroic assumption behind this computation is that the marginal product of capital, which is approximately the reciprocal of the incremental capital-output ratio, is a rough proxy to the profit rate. If we compare the period 1800–1860 to 1760–1800, Feinstein's figures imply an annual rise of 1.4 percent in the marginal product of capital, but a comparison of 1830–60 to 1800–30 shows a decline of .66 percent per year. However, Feinstein uses Deane and Cole's estimates of output growth, which are 2.8 percent per annum for 1800–30. If we accept Crafts's revisions downward of that figure to about 2 percent per annum, the conclusion is reversed, and the marginal product of capital was rising by .47 percent per annum between 1800–30 and 1830–60, contrary to what Church implies.[66] At this stage we have to conclude that the evidence for sharply declining profit rates and rising wages before the middle of the century is still too weak to be wholly convincing.

The factual debate is complicated by the insistence of the pessimists that certain nonpecuniary variables ought to be considered. Economists cannot object to this demand on a priori grounds: the debate is, presumably, about economic welfare or utility, and real income measures economic welfare with accuracy only if all markets are complete, i.e., if all goods which convey economic welfare are traded in the market. Four types of variables have been discussed in this literature: leisure, education, health, and environment. In some modern industries, especially textiles, the consumption of leisure of workers in 1830 was reduced compared with corresponding workers in 1760. Moreover, the factory system and its regularity of working hours reduced the worker's freedom to control his time allocation as he or she pleased. To the extent that the preferred allocation differed from the one imposed by the mill-owner, there was some loss in economic welfare. It should be emphasized, however, that until the middle of the nineteenth century, the number of individuals affected by these trends was comparatively small, and that whatever increase in working hours had occurred was offset by the decline in working hours in the second half of the century. As far as education is concerned, there seems to be little dispute that literacy increased between 1760 and 1840, but it would be rash to view that as strong support for an improvement in welfare. If literacy were purely a consumer good and its increase reflected higher incomes, it could serve as a counterexample to the stability in the consumption of sugar and similar products. But insofar as literacy was desired because it was regarded as a key to higher earning in the future, or because it was required by one's employer, the connection between rising literacy rates and economic welfare requires further exploration.

It is also sometimes maintained that the Industrial Revolution was responsible for a decline in health. Once more, it is difficult to disentangle the effects of the Industrial Revolution from those of other, unrelated, events.[67] To complicate matters further, the Industrial Revolution was accompanied by urbanization, and cities were notoriously unhealthy. It is possible that *both* countryside and cities were becoming healthier places to live in, but because people moved from the former to the latter, the aggregate may well show stability or even deterioration. The evidence on the question of health is ambiguous. Wrigley and Schofield (1981, p. 529) present calculations according to which life expectancy at birth gradually crept upwards from 34.6 years in the 1760s to 37.7 in the 1810s and 39.6 in the 1820s. For the next half century, it remained at about 40 years. Their data do not lend themselves to compute infant mortality rates, generally a good guide to the quality of life. The family reconstitution studies summarized by Flinn (1981, p. 92) show a clear-cut decline from 187 infant deaths per 1000 live births before 1750 to 161 in 1740–90, and 122 in 1780–1820. On the other hand, the infant mortality rates reported by the Registrar General's *Annual Report*, which start in 1839 (reproduced in Mitchell and Deane, 1971, p. 36) show that the rate was 153 in the 1840s, 154.5 in the 1850s, and 153 again in the 1860s.

Controversy has been especially lively on the issue of the "disamenities" of urban factory life. The power of this argument extends into the real-wage debate. It is argued that the quality of life in the squalid, crowded, noisy towns and the discipline and monotony of factory work represented a substantial decline in welfare compared to the life led by these individuals in the traditional rural or suburban environment. It was therefore necessary to pay workers a compensating differential for this loss, which took the form of higher wages. This implies that examining the trends of real wages alone involves some double-counting. Plausible enough, but is it true? And if true, was the effect of significant magnitude? Only in recent years have economists applied their tools to this question, generating not surprisingly more controversy (Williamson, 1981, 1982a). Williamson maintains that the compensating premium was only 7 to 13 percent of the wage, which would not seriously deflate the impressive gain in real wages which he claims took place after 1820. The debate between Williamson and Pollard in the Dec. 1981 issue of the *Journal of Economic History* highlights many of the problems in the economist's approach to these issues: Were labor markets efficient? Were workers rational and well-informed? Were there substantial costs in moving which prevented equalization at the margin? Williamson's analysis certainly has some questionable—though inevitable—assumptions in it, but his main conclusion, that urban disamenities cannot negate the improvement in real wages which he and Lindert present below, is not seriously imperiled by Pollard's critique. All the same, few would disagree with his final concession that "the jury is still out on British capitalism's trial (Williamson, 1982a, p. 238)."

The factual debate has thus not been wholly settled. Oddly enough, the counterfactual debate has. There are no longer serious scholars who maintain that Great Britain would have been better off without the Industrial Revolution, even if it is possible (as von Tunzelmann points out in essay 10) that under a different set of policies living standards would have been even higher. Hartwell and Engerman (1975) point out that T.S. Ashton was the first to make a clear distinction between the factual and counterfactual issues. In spite of his obvious sympathy to the optimist case, Ashton (1948, p. 110) pointed out that the years 1760–1830 were "darkened by wars and made cheerless by dearth," which is an elegant way of saying that the net effects of the Industrial Revolution on the standard of living were contaminated by the influence of extraneous events. The counterfactual case can be proven in two ways. The first is to apply the methodology of the New Economic Historians, that is, to estimate approximately the effects of the various other forces affecting living standards, then recalculate the living standard series with the values of the disturbing variables set to their normal levels. The other test consists simply of looking at other economies which did not industrialize and assume, implicitly, that Britain's fate would have been the same were it not for the Industrial Revolution. The latter approach is of course the one taken by Ashton in his famous final paragraph, in which he wrote of the men and women living in China and India, "plague-ridden and hungry" living execrable lives little better than animals, which is the fate of those who increased their numbers without going through an Industrial Revolution. One could choose examples closer to home: in 1845–46 the potato crop failed in Europe. In Ireland, where apart from a small enclave no serious industrialization had occurred, the Famine brought unimagined horror. In Scotland, the industrial and sophisticated economy of the Lowlands was successful in organizing and paying for a relief program which prevented a similar event in the hard-hit Highlands (Smout, 1978, pp. 29–30). In the Low Countries, industrialized Belgium was better willing and able to save its starving poor than the Netherlands, where the traditional structure of the economy had remained largely intact in the first half of the nineteenth century (Mokyr, 1980). In England, where potato consumption was much smaller, the resilience of the economy was not really tried in the 1840s.

An Assessment

Examining British economic history in the period 1760–1830 is a bit like studying the history of Jewish dissenters between 50 B.C. and 50 A.D. What we are looking at is the inception of something which was at first insignificant and even bizarre, but destined to change the life of every man and woman in the West, and strongly affect the lives of others even though the phenomenon remained confined primarily to Europe and its offshoots.

The analogy should not be driven too far. But it is worth pointing out that economic development was not invented in Britain in 1760 any more than monotheism was invented by the early Christians. The beginnings of modernization can be traced to the sixteenth century and even earlier, and are not necessarily rooted in British soil. Moreover, economic growth properly speaking did not start in earnest before 1830. What is unique about the years of the Industrial Revolution is that a small segment of the economy began to expand and spread at an unprecedented rate, and eventually supplanted the traditional economy altogether.

History did not repeat itself. The Industrial Revolution in the Continental economies differed in many ways from the British prototype. Each found its own path to the twentieth century, and judging other nations by criteria based on the British experience may be misleading. Yet the industrialization of the European Continent is unthinkable without the British example. All other countries were followers, borrowing and stealing British blueprints, emulating British techniques, relying on British engineers and advisors for assistance, watching Britain to decide where to go next. Britain, the pioneer, had to grope and find its way alone.

For the Western world, therefore, the British Industrial Revolution remains of unique interest. Economists regard the history of the West between 1760 and 1914 as the textbook case of successful economic development. What ultimately matters most is the irreversibility of this development. Other cases of economic change based on technical progress and the widening of markets can be found in history, but they ultimately led to dead ends. The British Industrial Revolution, viewed from 1983, was irreversible. Britain's position in the world may have weakened and its leadership lost, but it has remained an urban, sophisticated society, wealthy beyond the wildest dreams of the Briton of 1750. Britain taught Europe and Europe taught the world how the miracles of technology and efficient management can break the shackles of poverty and want. Once that lesson is learned, it is unlikely to be forgotten. The teaching process is yet far from complete, and the vigor and energy which astonished the world in the first half of the nineteenth century are long gone. But even if the center of the stage has been taken over by others, Britain's place of honor in the history books is assured: it will remain the Holy Land of Industrialism.

Notes

[1] Many colleagues commented on an earlier version of the manuscript, which led to major improvements in both style and substance. They are Louis Cain, Carolyn Crane, Stefano Fenoaltea, Jack Goldstone, Jonathan Hughes, Eric L. Jones, Peter Lindert, John Lyons, Joram Mayshar, Donald N. McCloskey, Jacob Metzer, and Jeffrey Williamson.

[2] As is by now well-known, the first use of the term "Industrial Revolution" was made by the French economist Jerome Adolphe Blanqui (1798–1854) in his *Histoire de l'economie politique* (1837, p. 389). One year later the term was used, probably independently by the Belgian journalist and publicist Natalis de Briavoinne (1838, Vol. I pp. 185ff.). A third landmark in the use of the term was the translation into English of the classic book of Paul Mantoux (1961, first English edition 1928, first French ed. 1905).

[3] In a recent article Fores (1981) has surveyed the differences among scholars about the subject. He documents the semantic confusions in the literature and concludes from those that the concepts of "industrial" and "revolution" have meant different things to different scholars. While this conclusion is undoubtedly correct, his suggestion to drop the use of the term altogether for that reason is not likely to find much support. Other conkepts in economic history— think of "capitalism", "feudalism", and "imperialism"—have been used in different ways by different scholars, but it would be folly to abandon their use for that reason.

[4] The July 1961 issue of *Past and Present* presented the proceedings of a conference held to deal with these issues. R.M. Hartwell (1967, p. 5) laconically summarizes the outcome as "unsystematic and inconclusive, and did nothing to further understanding of the causes of the Industrial Revolution."

[5] Some of these data have been around for many decades (e.g. the wage data collected by Bowley in the 1890s), others created more recently (Hoffmann, 1955; Gayer, Rostow, and Schwartz, 1953; Davis, 1978). Above all, the work which has provided the Cliometricians with both the ammunition and the targets to practice their trade has been Deane and Cole's *British Economic Growth, 1688–1959* (1969). Among the articles criticizing Deane and Cole's interpretations while relying freely on the data base they created, are Crafts (1976, 1983), Williams (1966), and Hatton, Lyons, and Satchell (1983).

[6] For papers which utilized existing data see in addition to the papers reprinted below, especially Blaug (1961), Harley (1982), and Von Tunzelmann (1978). Examples of new material are the article by Williamson and Lindert reprinted below and Feinstein (1978).

[7] Thus, for instance, one economist (Engerman, 1972) has debunked the myth that profits from the British slave trade were a causal factor in the Industrial Revolution. Similarly, O'Brien (1982) has reduced to quantitative dust the notion that the Industrial Revolution in Britain was the result of the parasitical exploitation of a non-European periphery by the European core. See also the exchange reprinted below between Crafts and Rostow.

[8] The following is inspired by Hartwell (1971, pp. 143–154), although the classification here differs considerably.

[9] The earlier view, proposed by Deane and Cole (1969) which dated the starting point of the Industrial Revolution to 1740 has been rejected by most other writers.

[10] The picture changes once we turn away from the "superstars" of Classical Political Economy. In 1814, for instance, Patrick Colquhoun wrote about "the accumulation of property, extensive beyond all credibility and (during a war of unexampled expense) rapid in its growth beyond what the most sanguine mind could have conceived . . . the prosperity of the British nation has been rapid beyond all example, particularly within the last sixty years" (Colquhoun, 1815, p. 49).

[11] Some approximate idea of the differences between the two sectors can be obtained from comparing pre-1760 rates of output growth to those between 1760 and 1800. Real output in cot-

ton, for example, grew at 1.37 percent per annum in 1700–60 and 7.57 percent in 1760–1800. In iron output, the growth rates were respectively 0.60 percent and 4.10 percent. In two traditional industries the acceleration is far less marked: in linen the growth rates were 1.25 percent and 1.44 percent, and in leather 0.25 percent and 0.57 percent respectively (all data from Crafts, 1983, pp. 6–7).

[12] Note that these rates differ from the ones McCloskey presents, since what is relevant here is *total* output growth, not productivity growth. The average rate of growth of "manufactures, mining, and building" in 1801/11–1851/61 was 3.57 percent, while that of "agriculture, forestry, and fishing" grew at the rate of 1.5 percent per annum (Deane and Cole, 1969, p. 170). For the closing decades of the eighteenth century, industrial output grew according to Crafts's calculations at a rate of 2.11 percent per annum and agricultural output at .75 percent. Crafts has also revised Deane and Cole's figures for the nineteenth century, but the differences are not large enough to affect the point made here. As was noted above, the rate of growth of the "modern sector" must have been faster than that of "industry". For instance, the consumption of cotton— the raw material of the modern industry par excellence—increased at the annual rate of 10.8 percent between 1780 and 1800 and at the rate of 5.4 percent between 1800 and 1840.

[13] Counterfactual analysis involves constructing a hypothetical world that never was. It is helpful in testing the hypothesis that factor X was a necessary conditon in bringing about outcome Y, i.e., that in the absence of X, Y would not have taken place. Although the New Economic History is often credited with or blamed for introducing this mode of analysis, it has always been a staple tool of traditional historians. Thus Craig (1980, p. 1) begins his magisterial survey of German modern history: "It is certainly unnecessary to apologize for introducing Bismarck's name at the outset. If he had never risen to the top of Prussian politics, the unification of Germany would probably have taken place anyway but . . . surely not in quite the same way ."

[14] Pollard's criticism of the national economy as the unit of analysis is not likely to remain unchallenged itself. The best arguments in the choice of the nation-state as the appropriate unit of analysis is still in Kuznets (1966, pp. 16–19), who points out that nations share common heritages and histories, and thus people tend to be interested more in their national history than in regional histories. Moreover, nation-states shared a common government which is the major policy-making body, and insofar as it affected economic development, the unit under its jurisdiction should be the unit of analysis. The fact that most of our data come on the national level (e.g. foreign trade statistics, fiscal returns, price and wage figures) reflects these arguments.

[15] There is a difference between tossing a coin only once and having to explain why a head came up, and tossing a coin one hundred times and explaining why a head came up ninety times. In the latter case, the scholar should take a closer look at the fairness of the coin, i.e., search for systematic forces which determined the outcome. To be sure, this analogy is not quite exact, since the outcomes observed (Britain's successes in various industries and enterprises) were— unlike the tossing of a coin—not mutually independent.

[16] Wrigley (1962) has placed the supply of raw materials at the center of the stage, but it is unclear whether he believes in geographical determinism in explaining the Industrial Revolution in Britain. For him, the crucial change was the switch from wood to coal and iron. While this is an interesting view, it is not an analysis of the Industrial Revolution since these changes started long before 1750, and in the mining of coal proper there was comparatively little technical progress, as noted by Wrigley himself.

[17] Some of the arguments made here are derived from Mokyr (1980).

[18] It should also be pointed out that geography may have been of much greater importance in explaining the development of Europe as a whole, compared with the rest of the Eurasian Continent. This thesis is expounded in a brilliantly original work by Jones (1981b).

[19] As pointed out in Mokyr (1980, p. 441), this number is actually an upper bound, because it does not allow substitution away from a factor which rises in price.

[20] See Ashton (1968), pp. 94–103. Hyde (1977, pp. 98–102) has shown that Crawshay introduced some important improvements into the puddling process, which reduced costs substantially.

[21] Some famous examples of failures include the abovementioned case of Henry Cort, the duo inventors Lewis Paul and Charles Wyatt, who produced the first cylindrical carding machine, and John Roebuck, the famous ironmaster. There is some uncertainty as to the series of bankruptcies, but there is no doubt that hundreds of firms failed each year. The *London Gazette* series, cited by Ashton (1955, p. 254) averaged 495 bankruptcies in the 1780s and 753 in the 1790s. For a discussion of bankruptcy records and their pitfalls, see Marriner (1980).

[22] See in particular Musson and Robinson, 1969, pp. 10–59; Cardwell, 1972, pp. 30–36.

[23] North's views will not remain unchallenged. The development of efficient property rights in Britain is closely related to the gradual development of common law, and the role of political change in it is debatable. After 1688 British Parliament raised taxes in any way it could, at times imposing highly unpopular taxes such as the income tax of 1799. On the other hand, few would dispute that successful industrialization requires some form of political regime congenial to economic modernization, although it is unnecessary to have one similar to the Britain's.

[24] Some of Olson's historical statements invite controversy. He writes (p. 128) that the English Civil Wars "discouraged long-run investment" (a possible but wholly undocumented inference), but that "within a few decades after [the Civil War] it became clear that stable and nationwide government had been re-established in Britain [and] the Industrial Revolution was under way." "Under way" is, of course, an ambiguous phrase, but between the restoration and the beginning of the Industrial Revolution, as commonly defined, a century or more (and not "a few decades") had passed. Hence, Olson's model of the Industrial Revolution might require some further research. Nevertheless, the originality of his approach and the sweeping ambitiousness of his model certainly add a welcome political dimension to the historiography of the Industrial Revolution.

[25] While the usury laws were not capable of holding down private interest rates to 5 percent at all times, they distorted the capital market to a substantial degree. A Parliamentary Select Committee concluded in 1818 that "the laws regulating or restraining the rate of Interest have been extensively evaded and have failed of the effect of imposing a maximum on such rate . . . Of late years, from the constant excess of the market rate of interest above the rate limited by law, they have added to the expense incurred by borrowers on real security (Great Britain, 1818, Vol. VI, p. 141)." See also Pressnell (1956, pp. 95, 318, 368, 428) and Cottrell (1980, pp. 7–8, 13).

[26] Smuggling was widespread as can be verified from the fact that at times, when tariffs were reduced substantially, imports increased by a much larger proportion. For example, when the tariff on coffee was reduced by two thirds in 1808, imports into Great Britain increased from 1.07 million to 9.3 million lbs. in 1809.

[27] McCloskey (1973) has shown that the wage-supplements paid under the Old Poor Law were likely to have reduced the supply of labor and thus may have raised wages, though the magnitude of this effect is unclear.

[28] Taylor (1969) who launches a broadside against the New Economic History of the Old Poor Law disagrees with Styles, but the lack of evidence renders his attack ineffective. His complaint that the 1795 law was not an impetus to better mobility of labor ("the law may have been easier to change than habits of mind") is equally unsubstantiated.

[29] In 1832 out-migration was more important in Speenhamland parishes which paid allowances in aid of wages or child allowances in Kent than in non–Speenhamland parishes (Huzel, 1980, pp. 375–78).

[30] Some of the transactions between Poor Law authorities and mill owners resembled nothing as much as slave trade, e.g. the purchase of seventy children from the parish of Clerkenwell by Samuel Oldknow in 1796 (Mantoux, 1928, p. 411). Pollard (1965, pp. 194–95) cites the sanctimonious claim by some notorious users of child labor that these pauper apprentices were

"more expensive" than paid labor and that they were employed out of civil duty. For a similar view, see Collier (1964, p. 45). Recruiting agents were often sent to scour the surrounding countryside in search of workhouse labor, and some of these children were brought in from the other end of the country, which indicates that for some industrialists pauper apprentices were indeed a cheap and satisfactory form of labor.

[31] See Cardwell (1972), p. 126 for a similar argument. Interestingly enough Ireland, with it centralized government in Dublin, conforms more to the Continental than the British example.

[32] The London population estimates are from Wrigley (1967, p. 44). English population data (less Monmouth) are from Wrigley and Schofield (1981).

[33] The revolutions in France may have increased the perceived insecurity of property and inhibited capital formation. Similarly, the continuous struggle between landlord and peasant in Ireland before the Famine reduced the attractiveness of Ireland as a site for industrial capital (as is the case today in Ulster). The Civil War in Spain (1832–39) and the Miguelite Wars in Portugal (1828–1834) had similar effects in the Iberian Peninsula.

[34] Some social historians argue that the changes started much earlier. Alan MacFarlane (1978, pp. 199–201) explicitly dates the beginning of English "modern society" to some point before the Black Death.

[35] Perkin anticipated here the interesting work of Fred Hirsch (1976) who, although not concerned with history, sets up a framework which complements Perkin's. Hirsch distinguishes between material goods, i.e., ordinary commodities, and positional goods of which there are by definition a constant amount. Examples of the latter are social prestige, political power, and symbols indicating one's relative position. Markets for material goods tend to be well-developed so material wealth provides easy access to them. Markets for positional goods are less well-developed. The more efficient the markets for positional goods, the easier it is to acquire them by the means of acquiring wealth or to lose them by the lack thereof. Therefore, relatively efficient markets for positional goods should strengthen the incentive to get rich (increase the marginal utility of income) and make the toil and risks of entrepreneurship more worthwhile.

[36] Perkin's further attempts to explain the timing of the Industrial Revolution in terms of population growth and demand are far less successful. Some of these issues will be dealt with below.

[37] For economic explanations of the Netherland's failure to industrialize see Mokyr (1976) and Griffiths (1979).

[38] Among the authors who view foreign trade as a central factor in the Industrial Revolution are Berrill (1960), Minchinton (1969), and Habakkuk and Deane (1962).

[39] Crouzet (1980) has attempted to resurrect the claim that exports played a crucial role in driving the Industrial Revolution. His findings have been criticized by Crafts (1983), who has shown that Crouzet's 1780 income figures are too high, leading him to understate the proportion of extra output going to foreign markets in the subsequent decades.

[40] The figures for the period before 1819 are more dubious but they also indicate the central role of exports in the early stage of the cotton industry, disrupted at times by the dislocations caused by the wars. Cotton output, the denominator in the Deane and Cole estimate may be somewhat too low for the earlier period and too high for the later one (Blaug, 1961, p. 376), which implies that the importance of exports in the 1820s and 1830s may have been less than is implied by Deane and Cole, whereas toward the middle of the century it may have been somewhat greater.

[41] The finding that the role of trade as an "engine" of growth is exaggerated is not limited to Britain during the Industrial Revolution. As Kravis (1970, p. 850) has maintained, "Export expansion did not serve in the nineteenth century to differentiate successful from unsuccessful countries. Growth where it occurred was mainly the consequence of favourable internal factors, and external demand represented an added stimulus which varied in importance from country to country and period to period . . . Trade expansion was a handmaiden of successful growth rather than an autonomous engine of growth."

[42] Other examinations of the indispensability axiom yield similar results. For example, Von Tunzelmann (1978) has shown that the steam engine was not nearly as crucial as many have supposed. For most purposes water power was a feasible substitute. However, if we consider steam and water power *together* the concept of a "necessary condition" resurfaces. Production always involves energy consumption, and complete absence of cheap energy could thwart the entire process. However, more than one road led to cheap energy and the Industrial Revolution, and the one actually taken by Britain was not necessarily the only feasible one.

[43] One source of rigidity was the sexual division of labor between men and women: with few exceptions, in preindustrial Europe, women spun and men wove. The invention of the fly shuttle in 1733 increased the productivity of labor in weaving, but created a bottleneck in spinning, which could be overcome only by changing this custom. Such reallocations were not impossible, of course. After the mechanization of cotton spinning around 1790, women and children were increasingly employed in the weaving of calico and coarse linen goods in Lancashire (Collier, 1964, p. 3). A fruitful research program would be to examine various technical bottlenecks and classify them according to the costs involved in solving them by reallocating resources as opposed to the possibilities of searching for a technical solution.

[44] For example, Thomas Lombe (the inventor of the silk throwing machine) and Edmund Cartwright (the inventor of the power loom) received financial settlements from Parliament. Nonetheless, the financial rewards for inventive activity remained extremely uncertain. Another famous inventor, Richard Trevithick, applied repeatedly to Parliament for a similar grant and was turned down.

[45] Since we have already discussed natural resources, the discussion here will be confined to labor and capital.

[46] The literature stimulated by Habakkuk's pathbreaking book is quite extensive. See for example Saul (1970); Landes (1965); Rosenberg (1963, 1967). Most of the debate is carried out in the context of Anglo-American differences. A comparison between Britain and the Continent during the Industrial Revolution would be worthwhile, but so far this has not been attempted seriously. The two views are not necessarily logically incompatible. Cheap labor facilitates the widening of the capital-labor ratio, while high wages stimulate the search for labor-saving inventions thus *deepening* the capital-labor ratio (Habakkuk, 1963). It is not clear, however, whether that distinction is helpful in the context of the Industrial Revolution in Britain.

[47] If labor is not of uniform quality, a conceptual solution is to redefine it in terms of efficiency units, in which a "unit" of labor is weighted by its productivity. The model then predicts faster accumulation if the wage per efficiency unit of labor is lower.

[48] For a survey of contemporary thinking about the "cheap labor is dear labor" issue see Coats (1958).

[49] Freudenberger and Cummins (1976) provide little hard evidence in support of their contention that English workers were undernourished before the Industrial Revolution. There is little support for any substantial improvement in average food intake after 1750, although periodic famines gradually disappear. Fogel (1983B, p. 480) concludes on the basis of his study of heights that "England appears to have been at least a half century into its Industrial Revolution before witnessing a material improvement in the height or nutrition of its laboring class." In Ireland and in the Netherlands, both late industrializers, food intake appears high before 1845, and attempts to use the efficiency wage in prefamine Irish economy have not proved very successful (Mokyr, 1983, pp. 223–26).

[50] The exact alternative is not clearly defined, which makes the notion of opportunity costs, so beloved by economists, somewhat tricky. By 1815, for instance, emigration has to be considered as a possible factor in setting a floor to the real wage. In Ireland this lower bound was reached by more people than in Britain, and thus Irish migration became already quite substantial before 1850.

[51] See Mokyr (1976) for an algebraic representation of this interaction and some further implications.

[52] For some reflections, see Kriedte (1981), especially pp. 152–154; Mokyr (1976), pp. 377–79.

[53] Occupied population as a percentage of total population went from 44.86 percent in 1801 to 43.90 percent in 1831, and then rose to 45.28 percent in 1841 and 46.46 percent in 1851.

[54] We shall ignore the concept of disguised unemployment, since changes in disguised unemployment are in effect changes in the productivity of labor and not changes in labor input.

[55] The Rostow hypothesis was criticized, among others, by Deane and Habakkuk (1963); for a critique of the importance of fixed capital in the Industrial Revolution see Pollard (1964).

[56] Crafts (1981) separates capital from land and consequently finds a much larger contribution of capital to the growth of output per worker for the period 1760–1800. These estimates are extended to 1830 in Crafts (1983).

[57] For similar statements see for example Mathias (1969, p. 149) and Cameron (1967, p. 39). Cameron goes so far as to assert that "the rate of growth of capital is therefore a general guide to the rate of profit" though he concedes that alternative investment opportunities for the factory master could upset that correlation.

[58] See Cameron, 1967 and Crouzet, 1972. It is possible that further work on the asset composition of British banks may revise this conclusion for the period after 1844 which might explain Good's (1973) finding that the ratio banking assets to GNP was relatively high in Britain, compared to later industrializers (see also Collins, 1983).

[59] The necessity of banks to preserve liquidity was made into a virtue by the so-called real-bills doctrine, which stipulated that if banks confined themselves to short-term, self-liquidating loans (such as discounting commercial bills), the price level would remain stable. Regardless of whether there was any merit in this theory in the short run, in the long run it confined commercial banks to supply almost exclusively circulating capital.

[60] Crouzet's statement that the early factory masters "did not suffer" seems oddly incompatible with his own evidence. Two paragraphs below this statement, Crouzet cites the cases of two highly successful firms, the Walker brothers and McConnel and Kennedy, who paid themselves miserably low salaries in order to maximize the income available for plowing back (Crouzet, 1965, pp. 188–89). Some of the most famous inventors and entrepreneurs (Cartwright and Roebuck immediately come to mind) foundered for lack of working capital, and Richard Arkwright's success is often attributed not to his technical skills but to his virtuoso ability to remain afloat in the treacherous currents of finance in the early stages of the Industrial Revolution.

[61] We can get an approximate notion of the magnitude of this effect by postulating the existence of an aggregate production function, in which labor has an output elasticity of approximately one half. Under those conditions a rise in population of 1 percent will reduce income per capita by .5 percent, all other things equal. Between 1761 and 1831 the population of England less Monmouth increased from 6.14 million to 13.28 million, and we may assume that the rate of increase (116 percent) is close to the rate of Great Britain as a whole. According to the assumptions of the crude classical aggregate model, the effect of this increase should have been a decline in income per capita, so that by 1841 incomes would be only 42 percent of what they were in 1761. Moreover, this estimate is biased upward, because it does not take into account the effect of population growth on the age composition of the population. Since most of the population growth resulted from higher birth rates, the dependency rate increased considerably, from 852 in 1761 to 986 in 1831 (1826 = 1000) (Wrigley and Schofield, 1981).

[62] See Mokyr (1984) for details.

[63] According to Lindert and Williamson (1982, p. 101) there was a massive decline in pauperism during the first two thirds of the nineteenth century. Their figures show a decline from 19.9 percent (1801–03) to 14.8 percent (1812) and 6.2 percent (1867). The latter estimate is derived from a figure produced by Perkin (1969, p. 420), who estimated the number of pauper families at 610,000. This figure is pure guesswork: Perkin took the *average* of paupers in 1866, multiplied by two to account for those paupers who lived off private charity, and then divided by three to get

families instead of individuals. It might have been preferable to turn to the opinion of Henry Mayhew, who estimated that 14 percent of the population of England and Wales in the late 1840s were destitute, a figure which Hughes (1969) feels to be acceptable.

[64] O'Brien and Engerman appeal to Deane and Cole (1969 p. 301) for support that the share of employment income in 1801 was 44 percent. This ignores Deane and Cole's warning that the 37 percent of income accruing to "profits, interest and mixed incomes" contains a component received by the self-employed which, properly speaking, should be attributed to labor. The percentage of income in this category was almost unchanged (38 percent) in 1860–69, but that constancy conceals a considerable rise in profits and interest coupled with a decline in income of the self-employed.

[65] It should be added that Lindert and Williamson's figures are for the population exclusive of paupers. If paupers are taken into account, the increase in inequality is somewhat reduced. As noted, however, their treatment of paupers may be somewhat inaccurate.

[66] The procedure is outlined in Mokyr (1982, p. 868).

[67] The research carried on about male height seems to indicate little improvement before 1815, followed by some improvement between 1815–40. Between 1840 and 1900, however, this measure of physical health is quite stable, which indicates that physical height and economic welfare were following quite different courses (Fogel 1983b, 1984 and references cited there). In addition, we may add the control of smallpox, which occurred more or less simultaneously with the Industrial Revolution.

2

The Industrial Revolution 1780-1860: A Survey

DONALD McCLOSKEY

The Quiet Revolution and Its Historians

In the 80 years or so after 1780 the population of Britain nearly tripled, the towns of Liverpool and Manchester became gigantic cities, the average income of the population more than doubled, the share of farming fell from just under half to just under one-fifth of the nation's output, and the making of textiles and iron moved into steam-driven factories. So strange were these events that before they happened they were not anticipated and while they were happening they were not comprehended. In 1700 a percipient observer of Britain looking towards 1780 might have anticipated its enlarged foreign trade and more active workshops (as, in fact, Daniel Defoe had); in 1860 he might have anticipated the competition of new industrial nations or the application of science to factory and farm during the half-century to come, and by 1900 he would at least have comprehended these events happening (as, in fact, the economist Alfred Marshall and others did). Yet in 1776 Adam Smith predicted a Britain of merchants, farmers, and artificers increasing their incomes at a moderate pace through specialization and trade—after which national income increased in eight decades by a factor of nearly seven. In 1817 David Ricardo predicted that landlords would swallow whatever the increase would bring—after which rents as a share of national income fell, 1801 to 1861, from about 17 percent to about 8 percent. And in 1848 Karl Marx, in the midst of economic events belying his prediction, predicted that monopoly capital would swallow all—after which the share of labor in income rose, and the real wages of the exploited classes increased in ten or fifteen years by some 15 percent and in fifty years by 80 percent. The British economy from 1780 to 1860 was unpredictable because it was novel, not to say bizarre.

By analogy with the political revolution in France in the 1790s the transformation of economic life in Britain was called, after it had happened, an "industrial revolu-

Reprinted with major revisions from Roderick Floud and Donald McCloskey, eds., *The Economic History of Britain since 1700*, Vol. 1 (Cambridge: Cambridge University Press, 1981), pp. 103–27. Reprinted by permission of Cambridge University Press.

tion." Its impact on the way people lived was greater, if slower, than most political revolutions. True, its immediate impact on culture or politics was slight. Although some novelists (sociologists before sociology) depicted industrial characters, poets and painters locked their gaze on marigolds, the odd "satanic mill" aside. A contemporaneous rationalization of methods of government had perhaps as much impact on the Reform Bill of 1832 or the crumbling of mercantilist restrictions culminating in the repeal of the Corn Laws in 1846 as did the new economic power of Manchester. Landed wealth purchased Parliament and staffed its governments until well after commercial and manufacturing wealth had come to exceed land in economic weight. The agricultural poor and their revolutionary potential exercised the thoughts of militia officers well after factory hands had come to outnumber farm hands.

The Industrial Revolution then, dominated modern history, more in memory than in happening. The British example of the early nineteenth century, inspired frantic emulation in the late nineteenth century, and myths of how Britain did it influence economic policy to this day. Poor countries now are fascinated by industrialization on the British pattern, complete with exports of manufactures in an age of ubiquitous skill in making them, puffing railways in an age of cheap road transport, and centralized factories in an age of electric power. Their policies would seem odd without the historical example in mind. British ghosts of grasping capitalists, expropriated small farmers and exploited factory workers still haunt political economy.

The economic transformation of Britain from 1780 to 1860, in short, is strange and important. Although explaining it has been the preoccupation of a battalion of scholars for a century or more, the explanations are still uncertain for several reasons. The history was not a simple experiment. The growth of cities, the increase in population, the rise in national income per head, and the shift from farm to factory happened all at once. Britain could have industrialized without expanding her population or urbanised without enriching herself. Yet in fact she did all these things together, confounding the effects of one with the effects of the other. Nor was the experiment controlled. Britain fought, for example, an expensive war against Napoleon in the middle of the period, and her governments, reacting to this and other vicissitudes, repeatedly altered the import duties, monetary arrangements, taxes and regulations of economic life. The evidence is thin. It is there, waiting to be mined from archives in large quantities, but the proportion of miners to consumers of the ore has been low. Oddly, much of the quantitative evidence of Britain's industrialization has been uncovered by foreign scholars. Until Deane and Cole produced their pathbreaking estimates of national income for the period (Deane, 1955, 1957, 1961; Deane and Cole, 1969), the statistics of industrial output (Hoffmann, 1955), the balance of payments (Imlah, 1958), foreign trade (Schlöte, 1952), prices (Rousseaux, 1938), and the business cycle (Gayer, Rostow, and Schwartz, 1953), were imports to Britain. Finally, evidence has often been mishandled. To interpret history is to assign metaphors to it. The metaphors assigned to the industrial revolution, however, have not been apt. Some are merely vacuous, such as "the process of industrialization" or "primary growth sector"; some are short-cuts to unwarranted conclusions, such as the assertion that the British people "depended" on foreign trade or that foreign trade was "an engine of growth"; and some, such as W. W. Rostow's famous assertion (1960) that Britain in this period experienced a "take-off into self-sustained growth" summarize a grand if empty theory with the merit, at least, of stimulating controversy but the demerit of turning the controversy off the trail.

More and Richer People

The cure for flabby metaphor is counting:

> BOSWELL: Sir Alexander Dick tells me, that he remembers having a thousand people in a year to dine at his house . . .
> JOHNSON: That, Sir, is about three a day.
> BOSWELL: How your statement lessens the idea.
> JOHNSON: That, Sir, is the good of counting. It brings everything to a certainty, which before floated in the mind indefinitely.

Boswell's *Life of Johnson*
vol. 2, p. 456
Everyman edition, London, 1949

The most important count, made difficult by the absence of a census until 1801, is of heads. For all the difficulty it is plain that from 1780 to 1860 the population increased at a rate without precedent. It increased in England and Wales by about 1 ¼ percent per year, with a rising rate in the first half of the period and a falling rate in the second. One and a quarter percent per year does not sound large, but it was in fact near the highest in Europe at the time and among the highest rates of growth observed in settled communities before the twentieth century. Like Johnson's calculation, the percentage lessens the idea, but that is the good of counting. The result was that for each Englishman in 1780 there were in 1860 2.7; for each in 1760 there were 3.0.

The histories surrounding this statistic are rich. Population grows when births exceed the total of deaths and emigrations, posing the question of which one changed and why. From what statistics have been gathered so far it would appear that from 1780 to 1860 the main change was a fall in the death rate. Whether and why this was so is still uncertain, because the work of recording births and deaths was not taken over by the state from the Church of England until 1838, well after nonconformity and a deterioration in the quality of parish registers had introduced biases into the figures. In any case, as T.H. Marshall remarked fifty years ago, "a horizontal line on a graph may be as dynamic as a diagonal; the forces that prevent a birth-rate from falling may be as significant as those that make it rise" (1929, p. 107). What one feels must be explained depends on what one expects. What one expects is altered if British population is viewed from other countries at the time rather than from Britain earlier, for the growth of population was great elsewhere in Europe as well. Until the famine of the 1840s, for example, it was great in Ireland. In 1801 a hostile Catholic island off the coast of Britain had a population over a third of the new United Kingdom; in 1861 after the famine, it had fallen to just over a fifth and, as O'Briens and O'Connors raised fewer children and sent large numbers of them to New York, Liverpool and Glasgow, the proportion fell further.

The cities grew faster than other places, and the choice of explanation depends once again on what one has come to expect. The arithmetical reasons for the relative growth of cities were of course continued migration from the countryside. Less obviously, there was a fall in the urban death rate that by around 1800 (judging from the statistics for London) allowed cities for the first time to grow more people than they killed. London was by far the largest city, as always, but grew slower than the rest. In

1801 one in seven Englishmen lived in cities larger than 50,000 people, and three-quarters of these were Londoners; in 1860 over one in four did, and less than half were Londoners. The list of cities growing fastest—Liverpool, Manchester, Birmingham, Leeds, and Sheffield among the largest ones in 1861; Bradford, Salford, Oldham, Preston, and Wolverhampton among the second rank—tells its own story. These were all in the North and the Midlands. The population in the four most industrial counties (the West Riding of Yorkshire, Staffordshire, Warwickshire and—above all—Lancashire) increased from 17 percent of the population in 1781 to 26 percent in 1861 (Deane and Cole 1969, p. 103, column for 1781; Mitchell and Deane, 1962, p. 22).

The increase and redistribution of the population was accompanied by its enrichment, contrary to all reasonable expectations. This is the conclusion of the second piece of counting, the counting of national income. The work of Deane and Cole and others implies that the amounts of bread, beer, trousers, shoes, trips to London, warmth in winter, and protection against conquest increased from £11 per head in 1780 to £28 in 1860 (Feinstein, 1978, p. 84, col. 5; Deane and Cole, 1969, p. 78, last column). It was a real increase, no monetary trick: the money income is measured in the prices of the 1850s. Because he produced two-and-a-half times more than his great-grandfather produced in 1780, the average person in 1860 could buy two-and-a-half times more goods and services. If the wheat grown per farm hand or houses cleaned per maid did not increase by two-and-a-half times (they did not), the output of cotton yarn per spinner or tons of freight shipped per sailor would increase by more than two-and-a-half times (they did). The average worker was a great deal more productive than he had been before.

The halving of the population in fourteenth-century England had increased income per worker by a third; in the other direction the doubling of the population in sixteenth-century England had halved income per worker. The expectation warranted by the experience of earlier centuries, then, would have been a fall, not a rise, in income per head after 1780 as the number of heads increased. The expectation is confirmed by economic reasoning. The reasoning is not that a fixed income of the nation was in 1860 to be divided among nearly three times more people than it had been in 1780. Pleasing though such arithmetic may seem, it is incorrect: it involves the elementary if common fallacy of supposing that a nation's output is unrelated to the number of people producing it. The correct reasoning, embodied in the dismal predictions by Ricardo and Malthus of the immiseration to come, is that more people do produce more (not the same amount, as in the arithmetical reasoning), but less *in proportion* to their increase if the tools and land they work with do not increase as well. The proposition is known as the law of diminishing returns: growth bumps against inputs that are not reproducible.

Land, in particular, was not reproducible. True, landlords could and did increase the effective amount of land by fertilising and hedging it, and freeing it of ancient customs—or, for that matter, by creating new land from swamps or the sea, as on the Somerset Levels and the Fens. But the source of much of the value of the land was irreproducible and unaugmentable. An owner of the "original and indestructible powers of the soil," as Ricardo described them, earned from them "pure rents." The very fact that the tenants were willing to pay him the rents indicate that these powers of the soil were useful in production. How useful is measured by the share of pure rents in national income—before 1815 some 17 per cent. Unlike ploughs and engines, the "free gifts of nature" could not grow in proportion to population. Strictly speaking, they could not grow at all. In other words, Britain was agricultural (albeit less so at the time than any other country except perhaps Holland); pure rent was a large part of agricultural income (albeit diminishing); and, therefore, a large share of national output depended on a factor that could not grow.

In the 80 years after 1780 the other tools with which Englishmen worked did in fact grow. By setting aside each year a portion of the nation's resources to invest in repairing old shovels, ships, roads, spindles, and docks, and in making new ones, Britain increased her panoply from 1780 to 1860 by about 1.6 percent per year. The number of workers using these tools increased somewhat slower (at 1.3 percent per year), which is to say that Britain somewhat increased the value of tools per worker. On this count she offset diminishing returns a little.

She offset them much more by using inputs better. What was extraordinary about the Industrial Revolution is that *better* land, *better* machines, and *better* people so decisively overcame diminishing returns. Had the machines and men of 1860 embodied the same knowledge of how to spin cotton or move cargo that they had in 1780, the larger number of spindles and ships would have barely offset the fixity of land. Income per head would have remained at its level in 1780, about £11, instead of rising to £28 by 1860 (see the final table in the appendix). The larger quantities of capital did make some difference. Had the effort of investment in new capital from 1780 to 1860 not been made—that is, had the Englishman's tools in 1860 been the same in quantity as well as quality as they had been in 1780—income per head would have fallen to £6.4. The possibility was remote, for the rate of savings to be used for new capital changed little in the period, and there is no reason to suppose that it would have fallen to zero. But the larger part of the difference between this dismal possibility and the £28 per head actually achieved by 1860 was attributable to better technology. In short—and this is the main point—ingenuity rather than abstention governed the Industrial Revolution.

The Location of Ingenuity

Great inventions have usually symbolized ingenuity. In textiles, first in cotton and then with a lag of a few decades in linen and wool, the inventions harnessed non-human power first, the power of falling water, and then with a lag of few decades the power of steam, as a team of horses is harnessed to a plough. In the 1770s and 1780s water-driven spindles allowing one factory worker to produce rapidly and simultaneously many strands of cotton yarn initiated the obsolescence of the root meaning of the word "spinster." Steam power for weaving the yarn into cotton cloth began in the early years of the new century (although its massive application awaited the 1820s and later). If cotton cloth is the symbolic consumers' good of the Industrial Revolution, iron is the symbolic producers' good, and was similarly transformed: in the last two decades of the eighteenth century steam and water power were applied to the bellows in the furnace that melted ore into iron and to mills that rolled out useful shapes as a cook rolls out a pie crust. The culinary metaphor applies also to the premier innovation in iron, "puddling," in which, from the 1780s on, a hand process of stirring a soup of iron and boiling off carbon (which weakens the metal) replaced the smith's method of making "wrought" iron, i.e., hammering it in little pieces (or large pieces: power had been applied to the hammering as well). With the introduction in the 1830s of preheating the air from the bellows, the iron industry took the technical form it retained until the introduction in the 1860s of cheap steel (steel is purified and lower-carbon iron). Cheap iron gradually replaced wood in the construction of bridges, ships and, eventually, buildings; with the adaptation of wood drills and lathes to iron—no easy task—it replaced wood in machinery as well, allowing machines to run faster and with more precision. The steam engine, of course, was the characteristic iron machine: the steam pump, the steam locomotive, the steam factory, the steam ship, the steam tractor, the steam this and that allowed Britain to substitute her large endowment of coal for men, horses, wind, and water.

The list of inventions could be extended without limit: clay drainage pipes made by machine and chemical fertilizer in farming from the 1840s on; lathes for making metal bolts and screws from the 1800s; the safety lamp in mining from the 1810s and the wire rope (permitting very deep working) from the 1840s; and scores of others. Few of these ideas were entirely novel, for scientific history is not the same as technological history. Steam engines had existed as toys in classical times, and "atmospheric engines" (in which condensing steam created a vacuum against which atmospheric pressure pushed) were raising water from mines from the early eighteenth century. Agricultural crops that came to prominence in the Industrial Revolution, most notably the potato, were novelties only in their new extent. Rails carried coal from the face to the ship long before they carried passengers behind a locomotive.

A list of inventions, furthermore, is not a list of adoptions, for technological history is the not the same as economic history. The contrary view was expressed to the historian of the Industrial Revolution, T.S. Ashton, with unconscious brilliance by a student: "About 1760 a wave of gadgets swept over England" (Ashton, 1948, p. 59). The gadgets came more like a gentle (though unprecedented) rain, gathering here and there in puddles. By 1860 the ground was wet, but by no means soaked, even at the wetter spots. Looms run by hand and factories run by water survived in the cotton textile industry in 1860, as in wool, linen, and silk. Around 1860 more shipping capacity was built of wood than of iron, and new sailing ship capacity was two-and-a-half times larger than new steamship capacity, not to speak of exisiting ships—overwhelmingly wood under sail.

The rain left much of the ground entirely untouched. Down to 1860 the places in the economy that the new techniques could touch were manufacturing, mining and building—what usually springs to mind when one thinks of "industry"—and trade and transport. From 1801 to 1861 about half of the economy's resources were allocated to these sectors, but within them many of the old ways persisted. The allocation of one resource, labor, is known from the decennial census in greater detail and permits a more subtle calculation. In 1861, at the end of the customary dating of the Industrial Revolution, only about 30 percent of the labor force was employed in activities that had been radically transformed in technique since 1780: railways, ships, mining, metal and machines, chemicals and textiles, and a handful of smaller industries (such as pottery). Britain was not in 1861 a cotton mill. By 1911, by contrast, it is easier to list the classes of employment that had *not* been transformed: public administration, the professions, commerce (but consider the typewriter), roads, fishing and, the largest of these, domestic service, taking together the same 30 per cent of the labor force as had in 1861 been taken by partially modernized industries. (Mitchell and Deane, 1962, p. 60, removing from the denominator the unclassified "All others occupied"). Agriculture acquired its reapers, clothing its sewing machines, food its steam flour mills and refrigerators, building its steam shovels well after the novelty of an accelerated pace of economic life had worn off.

If so much remained to be done in 1860, the great rise in productivity during the 80 preceding years would seem to be a puzzle. But the history of the adoption of new techniques is not the history of their economic impact. A steam locomotive pulling coal trucks over rails is, from the technological point of view, radically different from a horse pulling a coal barge in a canal. The adoption of the new technique, however, may or may not have had a large impact in reducing the cost of transporting coal: that the new technology was revolutionary in form and was adopted is consistent with both a trivial and a significant advantage over the old technology. The advantage must be measured directly, not inferred from the outlandishness of new machines or the rapidity with which they superseded old machines.

And, in fact, many of the few novelties adopted between 1780 and 1860 had great advantages. The most spectacular case is cotton cloth. A piece of cloth that sold in the 1780s for 40 shillings was selling in the 1850s for around 5 shillings. Some of this decline was attributable to declines in the prices of the inputs to cloths, especially raw cotton after the introduction of the cotton gin (picking out the seeds in the raw cotton) and the consequent extension of cotton growing in the United States. But most of the decline was attributable to innovations in preparing, spinning, and weaving the cottons that enormously decreased the cost of the resources to produce a piece of cloth. From 1780 to 1860, on average, these technological changes appear to have reduced the materials, labor, and capital per piece by over 2.6 percent each year, or, to put it in alternative but equivalent words, they raised by over 2.6 percent per year the amount of cloth producible from a given bundle of resources. A number rising at over 2.6 percent a year reaches nearly eight times its initial level in 80 years. By 1860 the new techniques permitted cloth to be produced at a cost about one-eighth what it would have cost in 1780: that is, a given bundle of cotton, labor, and machines in 1860 produced eight times more cotton cloth than it did in 1780.

Most of this accomplishment (and all of it before 1812–15) can be attributed to the mechanization of combing out (carding) the raw cotton and twisting (spinning) it into yarn, rather than to the mechanization of weaving. By 1860, as Table 2.1 indicates, the price of cloth would have fallen to a quarter of its level in 1780 even had weaving not moved out of the weavers' cottages and into factories. Although the power loom was invented in the 1780s, its application awaited later improvements in design and materials, and only after the Napoleonic War did it contribute to productivity change (albeit for a decade or two massively: nearly all the 50 percent decline in real costs 1815–40 is accounted for by innovations in weaving, concentrated in the late 1820s and 1830s). The same point applies to carding and spinning machinery, and, indeed, to innovations in most industries. The heroic age of invention in cotton had ended by the late 1780s, yet the bulk of the resource savings promised by the inventions of Hargreaves, Arkwright, Kay, Crompton, and Cartwright required the ingenuity of later, lesser men—lesser, at least, in glory. By 1799, which may be taken as the end of the first harvest of inventions, the real price of cloth compared to its level in 1780 had halved; but it was to halve twice more by 1860.

Other industries, such as other textiles, had a similar experience of slow perfection of bright ideas. The devices applied to cotton were applicable to any fiber, but between this obvious conception and the actual creation fell a long shadow of adaptation, adapting machinery to silk, flax, and, most important, wool. Wool weavers in Scotland with their hand looms could still sing in the 1840s:

> There's folk independent of other trademen's wark,
> For women need no barbers and the dyker's need no clerk;
> But none of them can do without a coat or a sark . . .
> So the weaving's a trade that never can fail,
> While we aye need a clout to hold another hale.

Though they would very soon join their Lancashire colleagues:

> Come all you cotton weavers, your looms you may pull down,
> You must get employed in factories, in country or in town,
> For our cotton masters have found out a wonderful scheme,
> These calico goods now wove by hand they're going to weave by steam.
> [Dallas, 1974, pp. 97, 119]

The railway is another case among many. The dates of opening of the first railway, the Stockton and Darlington (1825) and of the Liverpool and Manchester (1830) stick in the mind as emblems of the dawn, but in the perspective of what followed the charming little engines and trucks were mere experiments. Further developments reduced the resource cost of railways by at least half by 1860.

The impact of the novelties, then, was spread through many years. Their significance depended on the sizes of the industries they transformed. If cotton had been used only for kerchiefs and iron only for nails, the speed with which their productivity grew would perhaps be interesting in itself (as is the cheapening of clay cups and plates in this period) but not vital to the history of the nation. The appropriate measure of size must be a money measure, for the brute fact that in 1800 Britain produced about 50 million pounds of cotton yarn to be woven into cloth and about

Table 2.1   The Fall in the Real Cost of Cotton Cloth, 1780–1860

	Real cost index	Percentage rate of growth of productivity
c. 1780	100	
c. 1812–15	32(32)	3.4(3.40)
c. 1860	13(24)	2.0(0.65)

() = without weaving productivity growth.
Source: Table 2.2.

200,000 tons of pig iron to be made into castings and wrought iron is uninterpretable. The cloth and the iron must be brought into a unit of account—pounds sterling—that allows them to be compared. And the money measure must be compared with national income as a whole. That cloth sold for about £17 million and the products of iron for about £2.7 million makes the important point that the characteristic consumers' good of the Industrial Revolution in fact dwarfed the characteristic producers' good, but beyond this the figures are by themselves unintelligible.

The ratio of cotton output to national income in 1800 was about 0.07, the ratio of iron about 0.01. In other words, even very great changes in the productivity of ironmaking would have had little effect on national productivity in 1800 (although more by 1860, when the ratio for iron reached about 0.03). Cotton is quite another story. The 2.6 percent of the resources it (had) used that were freed by technical change each year for alternative uses in the economy amounted nationally to $(0.07) \times (2.6 \text{ percent}) = 0.18$ percent per year. The calculation can stand for the whole period, because the size of the industry was smaller when (1780 to 1800) its rate of productivity growth was larger, and its size larger when (1800 to 1860) its growth was smaller. Now the rate of growth of productivity in the economy as a whole 1780 to 1860 was about 1.2 percent per year. Cotton alone, therefore, accounted each year on average for 0.18/1.2 percent or 15 percent of the total. With five or six more such industries as Lancashire cotton, Britain's fortune would have been made.

The location of ingenuity was not in fact so concentrated as this. Nonetheless, a relative handful of other industries with large and easily measurable changes in "productivity" account for a good deal of the fortune's history. Productivity, recall, means the efficiency with which inputs of *all* kinds, not only the labor, are used. Statistics of the prices of products and of the human inputs and materials used to make them can be employed to measure productivity in this sense. The reasoning involved has already been used in describing the innovations in cotton. It is simple and is at this point worth making explicit. To put it in a sentence, the reasoning is that better ways of making things will result in those things becoming cheaper. To put it more fully, in the absence of changes in productivity, the price of, say, cotton cloth will move with the prices of raw cotton, labor, and capital employed, with each input carrying a weight in the total equal to its share in the costs of cloth. A weighted average of the price of inputs is a measure of changes in the price of cotton cloth that would have occurred in the absence of productivity change. The prices of inputs, and thus of this "productivity-absent" price, was falling rapidly, for example, in most of the 20 years after the Napoleonic Wars. If the actual price of cloth was falling even faster (as it was), then the relative fall is evidence that savings were being achieved *over* those from the fall in the prices of inputs. That is, cloth was being made with fewer inputs: productivity was increasing. The difference between the rate of fall in the cloth price and the rate of fall in the input prices is the measure of the increased productivity. This is the central piece of reasoning.

A peripheral piece of reasoning is necessary to extend productivity to the history of national income. The industry's productivity change is to be multiplied by the value of the industry's output divided by national income: 0.07 in the case of cotton. The 0.07 is a measure of the importance of cotton to the nation. It can be understood as follows. In the four years from 1826 to 1830, at the height of the introduction of power looms, the industry saved through productivity change 13 percent of its costs.

If all its costs (equal, of course, to the value of its output) were in 1828 £V, then it released over the next four years £0.13V worth of resources to serve other demands in the economy. The value of its output in 1828 as a ratio to national income (called £I) is £V/£I, and multiplying the ratio by the percentage productivity change in the industry (i.e., £0.13V/£V) will give £0.13V/£I, that is, the resources saved in cotton as a percentage of all resources in the economy. In other words, applying the ratio to the industry's rate of productivity change will give the contribution of the productivity change to national productivity change. And this is what is wanted: a way of gauging the significance of power looms, potteries, and puddling to British economic growth.

The measure is not the usual one, although it is the correct one. Happily, it is typically easy to calculate. National income is divided into the whole value of the industry's output (output multiplied by its price), not merely (to give the more usual measure of importance) into its value *added*. Value added is the portion of the whole value paid directly to labor and capital in the industry, as distinct from payments for material or services from other sectors of the economy (for example, the importing of raw cotton for the material or the mining of coal for the powered machines). It is customary to think of the size of incomes earned *directly* in an industry such as cotton as the appropriate measure of the "contribution" of the industry to national income, and therefore as the appropriate measure of its importance. The arithmetic of this custom seems plausible, for the sum of all direct earnings (values added) is indeed national income. But for present and most other purposes the raw materials cannot be left out. For measuring productivity change it matters that prices of raw materials are often known with fair precision when prices of value added (labor, capital, and land) are not. For understanding and assessing the productivity change it matters that an industry's innovations often save materials, and thereby save the nation's labor and machinery and land indirectly. And for applying the understanding to the history of the industry itself it matters that the cost of materials as well as of labor and the rest determine the supply price of its product.

Applying such thoughts to what is now known of the prices and outputs of Britain's economy during the Industrial Revolution yields Table 2.2, the "contributions" of each of eight parts of the economy to national productivity change. The figures are very crude approximations, and are to be viewed as first attempts. The statistics of "All other sectors" (Line 8) are calculated from what is left over from the whole (1.41) ratio value of output to value added and from the whole (1.19%) national growth in productivity per year. The other seven parts are based on evidence about the part in question, although it should be emphasized again that the evidence is sparse. The best way to appreciate the sparseness is to read the footnotes to the table. One must leap over gaps in the data. The leaps are necessary, but each student of the subject makes them in a personal style: the statistical and the literary approaches to history are not so very far apart.

The result can be looked at in two ways, depending on whether one sees the glass as half-full or half-empty. The half-full way of looking at it is to note with wonderment how very rapid productivity change was in the six "modernized sectors" distinguished in the table, and how wonderfully large a share of national productivity change these sectors can explain—0.52 percent per year for them alone out of a total

Table 2.2   Crude Approximations to Annual Productivity Change by Sector, 1780–1860

		(1) Rates of growth of productivity (percent per year)	(2) Value of output divided by national income (1780–1860 on average)	(3) Contribution to the national growth of productivity = (1) × (2) (percent per year)
1	Cotton	2.6	0.07	0.18
2	Worsteds	1.8	0.035	0.06
3	Woollens	0.9	0.035	0.03
4	Iron	0.9	0.02	0.018
5	Canals and railways	1.3	0.07	0.09
6	Coastal and foreign shipping	2.3	0.06	0.14
	Sum of these modernized sectors	1.8 (Average weighted by share in col. 2)	0.29	0.52
7	Agriculture	0.45	0.27	0.12
8	All other sectors	0.65	0.85	0.55
	Total		1.41	1.19

Sources: For sources and methods of calculation see the Appendix.

of 1.19 percent per year for the nation. The half-empty way of looking at it is to note with equal or greater wonderment how much was left over for sectors unaffected by steam and iron before 1860 to contribute. Their productivity change was slower but their importance was larger, with the result that their contribution to the explanation of national productivity change was larger than that of modernized sectors. Ingenuity in the Industrial Revolution was either wonderfully concentrated or wonderfully dispersed, depending on what excites one's sense of wonder.

The wonder of cotton textiles (Line 1) has been discussed already. The industry of Line 2, worsteds—long-staple wool spun into thin, compact yarn and woven flat, with no nap to the cloth—was similar to cotton in technique, and was quick to adopt the advantageous novelties invented in cotton. The productivity change given in Line 3 for the other wool product, woollens, is a mere guess, but probably of the right order of magnitude. Its relative lowness fits, at any rate, the narrative evidence.

That iron's productivity (Line 4) grew at about the same rate, high nationally but low by comparison with the other modernized sectors, does not fit the narrative evidence. So much the worse for the narrative evidence. Spectacular though they were in a technical sense, puddling and the hot blast were able to cut the price of bar iron (and its raw material, pig iron) only in half from the 1780s to the 1850s, in the face of little change in the prices of raw materials, especially coal. Coal itself is not included in the table because it is difficult at present to know even the few facts the method requires: the pithead price of coal, wages, owner's royalties, and their shares in costs at the beginning and end of the period. In view of the stable price of coal shipped to London it would be surprising if its productivity change were great, though apparently sufficient to offset the higher costs of deeper mines. The large factor of multiplication from the 1780s to 1860 in the output of coal—eleven, when national income was increased by a factor of seven (Clapham, 1926–38, vol. 1, p. 431; Mitchell and Deane, 1962, p. 115)—and the truly stupendous one for iron—fifty-six (ibid., p. 131)—were achieved not by producing a great deal more output from the same inputs, but by drawing inputs from other industries and setting them to work in mine and furnace.

Transport, on the other hand (Lines 5 and 6), had rapid productivity change. Transport rates fell to a third of their former levels on the routes of canals, and if the railway had a less spectacular immediate effect it was less confined by the need for water in its choice of routes and continued to cheapen down to 1860 and beyond. Productivity change in ocean transport was still more rapid. Especially on long hauls the improvement is attributable not to the application of iron and steam to shipping (which came on a large-scale later), but to bigger sailing ships with smaller crews per ton of cargo (North, 1968). Textiles and transport figure heavily in the explanation of national productivity change from 1780 to 1860. Together they account for over two-fifths of it.

Agriculture is more typical of the other sectors of the economy. Productivity change did occur, but at a modest 0.45 percent per year instead of the 1.8 percent per year average in cotton and the rest. All the other sectors—commerce as distinct from transportation, the making of clothes as distinct from the making of cloth, food processing (bread-making, beer, canning, and so forth) as distinct from food growing, the making of machinery and implements as distinct from the iron raw material, together with domestic service, building, and the professions (having little or no technical change) and chemicals, pottery, glass, gasworks, tanning, furniture (having a good deal of technical change)—experienced productivity change at 0.65 percent per year, on average.

Small though it is by comparison with textiles or transport, 0.65 percent per year is no trivial achievement. Had agricultural productivity grown as it did (i.e., at 0.45 percent per year) and had all other sectors grown at this 0.65 percent per year (instead of some at 1.8 percent per year), national income per head would still have grown substantially: it would have doubled from 1780 to 1860, rising from £11 to £22 per head (rather than from £11 to £28 as it actually did). The Great Inventions—mule spinning, power weaving, steam traction, and behind these the steam engine—deserve special attention, for their effects were indeed out of proportion to the sizes of the industries in which they flourished. But the doubling of income that would have occurred even had they been ordinary inventions serves as a warning: ordinary inventiveness was widespread in the British economy 1780 to 1860.

Explanations: Supply

The chronology of growth so far established sets limits on explanations of it. There is something to be explained, something unexpected, namely substantial growth of income per head in the face of a sharp rise in the number of heads. British growth from 1780 to 1860 was not uniquely fast. The rate of growth of income per head was equal or greater in later periods of comparable length. And by comparison with countries industrializing after Britain and having therefore the benefit of techniques perfected in Britain, the rate was not spectacular. Yet these very facts are notable. That Britain's experience from 1780 to 1860 was the prelude to modern economic growth at home and abroad, with real incomes per head routinely doubling every half-century, demands explanation.

The explanation cannot, it would appear, rely on the accumulation of capital. True, there was a new enthusiasm for projects such as canals and enclosures involving large investments and large but distant returns, whether from a fall in the interest rate (Ashton, 1948) or, more fundamentally, from a rise in the national propensity to save (Rostow, 1960). As was shown above, however, rises in income that are not explicable as more machines per man dominate the story. This is a bitter disappointment to economists. The scientists of scarcity delight in the thought that more consumption later can come only from abstinence now. As it is put in the mildly comical jargon of the discipline, there is no such thing as a free lunch. Yet indubitably Britain from 1780 to 1860 ate a massive free lunch. The normal return on investment was 10 or 15 percent per year, the return that would bring the benefits from investment into that equality with costs so pleasing to economists. Yet in fact the nation was earning 12 percent or so in addition to this on the investments with no corresponding costs, if one attributes all a year's productivity gain to capital. The story that might be called vulgar capitalism—more savings produces more capital which produces more income which produces savings and so again in a "self-sustained virtuous spiral" (the usual tired witticism)—lacks force for this reason, among others. The higher income was attributable largely to something outside the spiral, namely, technological change.

The significance of capital accumulation for British economic growth can be rescued in various ways, none wholly persuasive. It can be argued that better technology was embodied in new capital equipment, and therefore that the nation could not have had the advantage of the better technology without the new investment. Old spindles and ships, it is said, could not simply be sped up or enlarged or redesigned as the knowledge of how to do so became available. The persuasive sound of the argument, however, springs from the element of tautology embedded (not to say embodied) in it rather than from any great logical or empirical power. Of course better weaving technology, say, required new looms. But this does not imply that productivity change in weaving required a rise in the nation's savings. Replacement investment provided an occasion, a frequent one, for introducing the better technique. And were this not fact enough to suit businessmen, they could divert saving from sectors with low rates of embodied technical change (buiding and agriculture, for example) to those with high rates (textiles and transport), as did early cotton manufacturers who set up business in disused warehouses rather than spend on buildings money

better spent on primitive machines (Crouzet, 1972, p. 38), or as did landlords invest-
ing agricultural income in canals.

A deeper argument is that investment is undermeasured. Knowledge is not free, as
Faust could testify, and apprenticeship, schooling, and inventive effort might be
viewed as payments to the devil of scarcity. The educational portion of the argument,
the only portion that is easily measureable, is not strong on the face of it: although
literacy at marriage did increase from 1780 to 1860, especially women's literacy (from
an appalling 38 percent to 65 percent), the increase was no revolution, and the low
(and sometimes falling) rates that persisted in industrial areas down to the end of the
period confirm the natural supposition that the ability to read was unimportant to a
factory hand (Schofield, 1973). Still, it has been estimated tentatively that the cost of
maintaining the literacy there—literacy, alas, is not inherited—was as high as 1 percent of national income in the 1830s (West, 1970 and 1978, reprinted, below; but see
Hurt, 1971, and West, 1971) or 7 percent of total investment in more conventional
forms of capital. Admitting the desirability of counting all the costs of achieving
higher income, however, the size, and what is more to the point the rate of increase,
of nonmeasured capital would have to have been impossibly large from 1780 to 1860
to account fully for the change in productivity (Deane, 1973).

The rejection of capital accumulation makes it necessary to search the menu of the
free lunch. If great inventions were most of the story the search could narrow to great
inventors, proceeding by a reduction to individual biography. This is the style of
much industrial history, still more of business history, and for the task of explaining a
handful of definite innovations it has merit. But it was shown earlier that contrary to
much thinking on the matter, innovation was widespread. The Industrial Revolution
was not the Age of Cotton or of Railways or even of Steam entirely; it was an age of
improvement.

Although widespread consequences do not invariably have widespread causes, the
betting would have to be on that side. Resources were being allocated better in many
places. A favorite focus of improved allocation, for example, is the capital market, for
the notion that accumulation governed the Industrial Resolution dies hard. In the
simplest form it is believed that if merchants or landlords can be shown to have
invested heavily in railways or coal mines (as they can be), then the original
accumulation of industrial capital, in Marx's phrase, will have been identified.

Reallocations of capital, however, are ill matched to the task of explaining a doubling of income per head. The reasoning is simple and distressingly decisive, applying
with equal force to reallocations of labor: it can be shown that the potential gains
from eliminating misallocation were small. Too much capital is applied to, say, agriculture if capital earns less in agriculture than elsewhere, perhaps 5 percent a year
rather than (to take a generously high figure) the 15 percent to be earned in manufacturing or transport or other projects. The net gain to the nation of moving £1 worth
of agricultural capital into the other projects is clearly $(0.15 - 0.05) \times (£1) = £0.1$
per year. As more £1 worth is so moved, however, the differential return narrows
(capital becomes relatively less abundant and therefore more valuable in agriculture
and more abundant and less valuable elsewhere), being zero when capital is allocated
correctly. The total gain to national income is the area, as it were, of a triangle with a
height equal to the amount of capital (in pounds) to be reallocated, a base of
0.15–0.05, and an apex at the point of zero differential. If the percentage allocation

of the nation's capital to agriculture in 1860 (25%) is taken as the correct allocation in 1780 (when it was in fact 50%), the correct allocation would require the movement of a quarter of the nation's total capital stock of £670 million. The height of the triangle of gain to reallocation is therefore $(1/4) \times (£670) = £168m.$, and the area of gain is $(1/2) \times (£168m) \times (0.10) = £8.4$ million. This is only 8½ percent of British national income in 1780, as against an increase to be explained of 150 percent per capita down to 1860.

No doubt this argument and its conclusion will appear strange at first, but on second thought they can be seen to be in accord with common sense: were differentials in returns to labor or capital very large, the laborers or capitalists could be expected in so developed an economy as Britain in 1780 to have exploited them already; and the reallocations that in fact took place between 1780 and 1860 involved no very large portion of the nation's labor and capital. The upshot is a moderate gain on a moderate portion of the nation's resources, not the stuff of revolutions in economic life.

The explanation of the revolution must be sought in less definite reallocations, of human effort and spirit, and in the luck of invention. These are old and obvious notions, although they have not been tested persuasively. Studies of individual enterprise and invention are less conclusive than they are numerous, for what is wanted is general evidence rather than doubtfully representative cases in point. A much-traveled path to general evidence is by way of comparisons, most fruitfully between successful and unsuccessful parts of the country (for example, the vigorous industrial North versus the sleepy agricultural South), although more usually between Britain and France. There is growing evidence that the contrast with France has been overdrawn, that if France was for much of the period a country with less freedom for enterprise and more rigid social stratification, this did not long retard the development of new techniques in industry and agriculture (O'Brien and Keyder, 1978; Roehl, 1976). The industrialization of northern England was merely a little earlier and a little faster than the industrialization of northern France, Belgium, and the Prussian Rhineland.

Whatever the seed, the ground in these places was fertile. Farmers do not debate whether it is the seed or the soil that causes their crops, nor perhaps should historians, though recognizing that both were present. Nothing very definite can be said about the "preconditions" for British growth, which leaves room for unrestrained speculation on what they were. Security of property, peace, an acquisitive and inquisitive mentality among the people, a hostility to governmental monopolies, and the ability of the occasional ploughboy to rise to a seat in Parliament are all candidates, and for each an opposing candidate can be found. As to peace, the first half of the period consisted largely of French wars, albeit not on British soil. As to laissez faire and security of property against government, the new interventionism of factory acts replaced the old interventionism of wage regulation (though both were at this time ineffective), and the same French wars left taxes high (though smaller than they were to become in the twentieth century). And so forth.

Fixed backgrounds, by definition, do not move, making it difficult to detect their contribution to the play. Moving them in the imagination is delicate work. One is free to imagine a Britain of lazy businessmen, say, but it is hazardous to infer from the mental comparisons that vigorous businessmen were a prerequisite for British growth.

The most that economic reasoning can offer at present is the valuable thought that one condition for growth can substitute for the lack of another. To return to the comical jargon of the field, there is more than one way to skin a cat, and more than one way to grow in wealth (Gerschenkron, 1962). How exactly the cat was skinned in Britain from 1780 to 1860 remains uncertain: we know less what it was than what it was not.

Explanations: Demand

One thing it probably was not was a response to demand. It is proper to treat demand symmetrically with supply in explaining the growth of iron output or wheat output, but for the nation as a whole it is improper. The demand for things-in-general is income itself, which is determined by the resources and technology supplied to the nation. In the aggregate (with some exceptions to be mentioned below) demand is not an independent factor causing income to grow (Mokyr, Chapter 4).

If we judge from the frequency with which it has eluded writers on the Industrial Revolution, the point is an elusive one. The simplest way to grasp it is to think of Britain as that favorite of economic exposition, Robinson Crusoe (before Friday). Obviously, if Crusoe decides to demand more wheat (from himself) his total product, taking wheat and fish together, does not *ipso facto* grow, for he must give up fish to acquire the time to grow more wheat. Still more obviously, if he decides to eat more with his left hand than with his right his total product does not grow, for what goes into one hand must come from the other. Britain, likewise, could (and did) demand more iron from itself, but only at the expense of other things, the factors of supply being given. An expansion of the iron industry caused by a rise in the demand for iron did not "generate" income, either in the iron industry itself nor, through what are wisely known as "backward linkages" and "multipliers," in the mines and factories that supplied inputs to the iron industry: it merely redistributed the income. Similarly, like left and right hands, an enrichment of one group (say, producers of grain during the Napoleonic Wars) and the consequent increase in their demands for manufactured good comes at the expense of impoverishment of another (consumers of grain) and a decrease in their demands (Hueckel, 1973).

There are two conditions under which demand in the aggregate can nonetheless have an effect on the size of national income. Neither was important. The first is a large foreign trade, which can again be made clear by reference to Crusoe. If Crusoe trades with someone, say Friday, then demand—Friday's demand, not his own—does affect his income. The increase in population and wealth abroad undoubtedly did increase British national income, but the increase attributable to this cause was small (see Thomas and McCloskey, 1981, pp. 99–102; Harley and McCloskey, 1981, pp. 53–56).

The second condition under which aggregate demand would have a role of its own is mass unemployment. If Crusoe behaved like another shipwrecked sailor

> . . . my grandfather knew
> Who had so many things which he wanted to do
> That, whenever he thought it was time to begin,
> He couldn't because of the state he was in.

he would be behaving like a modern economy in depression. For reasons that are still unclear, the business cycle in virulent form appears to have begun during the Industrial Revolution (Gayer, Rostow, and Schwartz, 1953). Crop failures in an agricultural economy evoked prayerful resignation: business failures in an industrial economy, man-made as they were, evoked social criticism. The social disease at which the diagnoses and cures were directed, however, was an episodic one, not a chronic. This is the critical and frequently overlooked point for the role of aggregate demand in British economic growth. Crusoe can overcome his indecision and end his involuntary idleness, raising his income by the amount of the increase in demand, but from one episode of full employment to another his income is constrained by supply, not demand. And at the peaks of the business cycles Britain was near full employment. The force of the argument can be made plain in a simple calculation. The increase in income to be explained is an increase from £11 per head in 1780 to £28 in 1860. Suppose, to take the most favorable case, that 1780 to 1860 was one long secular boom, with previously unemployed resources set to work by a rise in aggregate demand; it does not matter whether the rise was itself a consequence of external demand (more foreign trade) or internal demand (less hoarding of money or more creating of money by the government). To sustain the interpretation, unemployment in 1780 would have to have been at least $(28 - 11)/28 = 61$ percent. The figure is absurd—the most enthusiastic believer in open or disguised unemployment as a factor in economic life would not advance a figure above, say, 20 percent at this time—and therefore the premise that aggregate demand dominated the industrial revolution is absurd as well.

Demand is a more plausible cause of growth if its effects are constrained to work through the composition of output. The verdict is not decided, but possibilities may be offered. The oldest argument, a neglected fruit of Adam Smith's thinking, is that the division of labor is limited by the extent of the market. It could well be that a rise in the demand for, say, cotton allowed the industry to exploit economies of scale, to train a highly differentiated and specialized work force, for example, or to support specialized sub-industries, such as cotton marketing or machinery-making.

Any economies of scale initiated by increases in demand, therefore, would have been economies of a whole industry's scale. In this form the argument is at least logically cogent. But whether it is significant in the Industrial Revolution remains to be seen. The increase in one demand, to repeat, must be achieved at the expense of a decrease in another. If potential economies of scale were scattered about the economy at random, then what was gained on the wings might be lost on the roundabouts. If they were located in the sectors made relatively larger by demand, then there may have been a net gain to the nation. We do not know.

Nor do we know the significance of another and related argument from demand. It is that disproportionate rises in the demand for one or another product induced technological change. Ignorance has not forestalled confident assertion that it was or was not significant. To return to an earlier line of argument, if technological change is costly then one can expect technological change to occur in those industries in which demand is rising rather than falling, just as any costly factor of production is allocated to expanding industries. Like economies of scale, however, the effect must be asymmetrical to lend significance to demand. It is entirely plausible that the textile industries were ripe for technological resolution from the middle of the eighteenth century on, but it must be shown that some other industry—furniture, say— whose demand languished because textile grew was not thereby robbed of its own technological revolution. In any case, the notion of technological ripeness turns attention back to supply, to the initial supply of technological knowledge and the supply of vigor to exploit it.

A more mechanical argument capturing the effects of demand is available, and has the merit of being possible to implement. Suppose that technological change descended on industries for reasons unconnected with their sizes. In that case the national rate of technological change would depend on the importance of the various industries, that is, on the composition of demand. A smaller cotton industry would have the same rate of technological change but would contribute less to national growth than a larger one. The argument has in fact already been tested: it was found earlier that had the modernized industries mentioned in Table 2.2 experienced productivity growth at 0.65 rather than 1.8 percent per year (which is equivalent to reducing their size to about 40 percent of their actual size), income per head would nonetheless have doubled between 1780 and 1860, not far short of its actual increase. And so the circle is complete. The pursuit of effects on income related to demand has come back to supply, that extraordinary flowering of ingenuity in many sectors of the British economy known as the Industrial Revolution.

The causes of the Industrial Revolution are uncertain, then. But they are not therefore mysteries beyond knowledge. If many of the explanations proposed can be shown to fail the tests of economic fact, the failures themselves are increments to knowledge. To know what one does not know is the first, large step to true wisdom. True wisdom about the Industrial Revolution is that little is known, and much more can be known.

Appendix
Sources and Methods of Calculation for Table 2.2

Except for Line 8 (which is discussed below), the sources are arranged by rows. Column A is the estimate of productivity, usually estimated by subtracting the rate of growth of output price (e.g., cotton cloth) from the rate of growth of input price (e.g., spinning labor and raw cotton). Column B is the ratio of the industry's value of output to national income averaged over 1780–1860. As explained in the text, Column C is the product of these two, i.e., the industry's productivity growth per year weighted by the industry's importance in national product.

Line 1: Cotton

Column A: Because raw cotton is an import its price is well known (Mitchell and Deane, 1962, pp. 490–91). As such things go, the wage of labor is also well known (Wood, 1910) and can be extrapolated back to 1780 by Gilboy's Lancashire wages in Gilboy (1934, p. 282). The crucial and difficult statistic is the price of the output, i.e., yarn and cloth of average quality. The sources were Sandberg, 1974, pp. 239–48; Edwards, 1967, pp. 240–42; and Ellison, 1886, pp. 55, 61. The calculations in the text of productivity change in spinning and weaving separately use cost shares of the two processes in the final product.

Column B: Deane and Cole (1969, pp. 185, 187) estimate the gross value of cottons produced, and on p. 166 they estimate British national income from 1801 on by decades. The estimate of 0.07 is, if anything, an understatement of the ratio of the two 1780–1860 (making due allaowance for the low ratio likely before 1800).

Lines 2 and 3: Worsted and Woollens

Column A: The best estimates, so to speak, are the worsteds. The essential fact is that around 1805 a worsted piece cost four times the value of the raw wool, around 1857 only two times (Deane and Cole, 1969, p. 198). In the meantime the price of raw wool had fallen at 0.7 percent per year (ibid., p. 196, column B divided by column A). These two facts together imply that the price of a worsted piece fell 1805–57 at 2.0 percent per year. Labor's wage did not change much (Mitchell and Deane, 1962, p. 348, note 3 to table). The fall in the output price minus the fall in the price of raw wool weighted by its share in costs (the latter being the average of 0.25 and 0.50) yields 1.77 percent per year, or about 1.8. The woollens productivity is a mere guess—half the worsted, on the grounds that the mechanization begun in cotton came next to worsteds and only tardily to woollens.

Column B: Deane and Cole (1969, pp. 196, 198) estimate woollens and worsted as roughly equal in size, and some 7 percent of national income together (e.g., p. 196, col 4 for 1805 divided by p. 166, last column, for 1801–11 averaged equals 8.4 percent; likewise for 1855–64 and 1861 equals 6.4 percent).

Line 4: Iron

Column A: Pig iron prices (made with coke) for 1780 are from Charles K. Hyde, 1973, pp. 401–14. For 1860 they are from Mitchell and Deane, 1962, p. 493. Prices for wrought iron are from Ashton (1924, p. 101), which is a mere remark on the fall in price from £20 to £12 down to 1812. Birch (1967, p. 42) reports a price of £16 a ton in 1787, which lends credence to the estimate of £20 in 1780. The price for 1860 is taken to be the £8 a ton figure for the 1850s given in Mitchell and Deane (1962, p. 493). With equal weights on cast and wrought iron the price falls at about 1.0 percent per year 1780–1860. Coal prices fell somewhat in the period, making 1.0 percent an overestimate. The estimate of 0.9 percent for a modest fall in the prices of inputs into iron.

Column B: The figure is an average of 1 percent around 1800 and 3 percent around 1860. Numerators are tons of pig iron (Mitchell and Deane, 1962, p. 131) in the two years multiplied by its price (ibid., p. 492f) multiplied by two to allow for fabrication into wrought (much fabrication) and cast (little fabrication) products.

Line 5: Canals and Railways

Column A: The railway estimate of 2.2 percent per year is Hawke's (1970, p. 302, col. 10), assumed to apply back to 1830. Before 1830 the source of productivity change is assumed to be canals, cutting overland transport costs by perhaps two-thirds on the perhaps half of the transport experiencing improvement down to 1860. The implication of these guesses is a rate of 0.8 percent per year from 1780 to 1830, the end of substantial canal building. The entire productivity-experiencing sector, then, had productivity growth at $(50/80) \times (0.8) + (30/80) \times (2.2) = 1.3$ percent per year over the entire period 1780 to 1860.

Column B: Railway receipts were only about 4 percent of British national income in 1861 (Mitchell and Deane, 1962, p. 225; Deane and Cole, 1969, p. 166). The rest of the productivity-experiencing portion of transport might add another 3 percent for 7 percent in all.

Line 6: Coastal and Foreign Shipping

Column A: D.C. North (1968) estimates productivity change in Atlantic ocean shipping 1814 to 1860 at 3.30 percent per year. He estimates it at 0.45 percent per year from 1600 to 1784; a guess of 1.0 percent per year 1780–1814 is perhaps reasonable. The resulting average for the entire period would be $(35/80) \times (1.0) + (45/80)$ $(3.3) = 2.3$ percent per year.

Column B: Imlah's estimates for the balance of international payments of Net Credits from Shipping (1958, pp. 70–2, col. F) divided by British national income (Mitchell and Deane, 1962, p. 366) give 3.2 percent for 1820 and 4.5 for 1860. Foreign earnings, which these are, were probably growing faster than coastal shipping. The figure of 6.0 percent for both makes a crude allowance for this fact.

Line 7: Agriculture

Column A: The figure is the rate of change of labor and land prices (weighted 0.75 for labor, 0.25 for land) minus the rate of change of output prices. Labor's wage (England and Wales) is from Mitchell and Deane (1962, p. 348f); land's rent from Norton, Trist, and Gilbert, "A Century of Land Values: England and Wales" (1891), reprinted in E. M. Carus-Wilson, ed. (1962, vol. 3, p. 128f). Output price is the Gayer, Rostow and Schwartz index of "Domestic Commodities" (largely agricultural) in Mitchell and Deane (1962, p. 470), extrapolated to 1860 by relation to Rousseaux's index of total agricultural products (ibid., p. 471f) for 1840–50. The resulting productivity change was assumed to apply to the 1780–95 period as well.

Column B: The share is from Deane and Cole (1967, p. 166), average share 1780–1861 of agriculture in national income (agriculture has very few purchased inputs), with 1780 and 1790 assumed to be the same as 1801.

Line 9: Total

The total requires estimates of national productivity, which in turn requires estimates of national outputs and inputs. The basic source is Feinstein (1978). The initial date used here is 1780 instead of 1760, which necessitates some interpolation. The principle in interpolation is that 1760–1780 was a time of war, in which income and capital per man could be expected to remain constant. Therefore, Feinstein's estimate (based on those in Deane and Cole) of gross British domestic product per head of population in 1760 (i.e., £11—Feinstein's table 25, col. 5) is used for 1780 as well; so too is his 1760 estimate in constant prices of domestic reproducible capital (cited in col. 1, 1760 level blown up by change in number of workers 1760–80). The number of workers in 1780 is derived by applying the 1801 participation rate (0.44) to the 1780 population of Britain (as Feinstein did for 1760). The 1780 population is derived by calculating the Scotland/England and Wales ratio for 1761 and 1791 (Deane and Cole, 1967, p. 6), using Feinstein's implied figure for Scotland in 1761 of 1.3 million; then interpolating this ratio by a straight line to 1780; then applying the interpolated rate to the (allegedly known) population of England and Wales in 1781 to get Scottish population. Interpolating the Scottish growth rate 1761–91 gives very similar results. To do productivity calculations one needs shares.

Land's share: This is meant to comprise pure rents alone, not returns on capital. Feinstein (1978, part V, section 5, p. 72) gives estimates of the unimproved value of farmland at his four benchmark dates and also the year's purchase applied to all rents (not only pure rents). Dividing the years' purchase into the unimproved value should give annual pure rent: 1760 = £15.2 m., 1800 = £22.5 m., 1830 = £29.3 m., 1860 = £45.0m. These appear to be reasonable in relation to agricultural income. Feinstein uses 20 years' purchase to capitalize urban rents (p. 73). Applying this, as with farmland, to his estimates of the capital value of urban land rent (1978, table 15, p. 68, line 6) and then removing his deflation to 1851–60 prices (table 5, p. 38, col. 1) yields annual urban rents of 1760 = (15.2 + 0.9)/90 = 0.18; 1800 = (22.5 + 1.0)/140 = 0.17; 1830 = (29.3 + 1.9)/310 = 0.10; 1860 = (34.0 + 21)/650 = 0.085. The arithmetic average, presumably typical of 1780–1860, is 0.13.

Labor's share: The estimate by Deane and Cole of wages and salaries in 1801, 1831, and 1861 (1967, p. 152) was divided by their estimate of gross national income minus income from abroad (p. 166), as shown in Table A2.2.

The 1780 share was supposed to be equal to the 1801 share. The average is [2(0.45) + 0.44 + 0.49]/4 = 0.46.

Appendix Table A2.1   Basic Statistics of Income, Labor, and Capital

	Income per head (in £)	Labor	Capital (£)	Capital laborer (£)
1780	11	3.93m.	670	170
1860	28	10.8m.	2770	256

Appendix Table A2.2

	Wages and Salaries	GNI	Share
1801	104	232	0.45
1831	148	336	0.44
1861	315	648	0.49

Capital's share: As usual, a residual. The simplest calculation is: $1.00 - 0.46 - 0.13 = 0.41$. The result is shown in Table A2.3.

The assertions about diminishing returns earlier in the text derive from recombinations of these facts.

Appendix Table A2.3

	Growth rate (percent per year)	Share	Contribution to "explaining" change in income per head (percent per year)
Income/head	1.17	—	—
Capital/labour	0.35	0.41	0.14
Land/labour	−1.26	0.13	−0.16
Residual	1.19	—	1.19

3

The Inputs for Growth

ROBERT M. SOLOW and PETER TEMIN

I

The purpose of this essay is to advance our understanding of industrial development by describing the progress what economists call the "factors of production," i.e., the inputs out of which food, clothing, and shelter are made. It is by no means clear, however, that the increase in our ability to produce food, clothing, and shelter that we call "the industrial revolution" was a direct result of an increase in the factors of production. In fact, the relation between the traditional factors of production—land, labor, and capital—and the ability of an economy to produce is far more complex than the use of the words "inputs" and "outputs" might suggest. We therefore introduce the discussion of the factors of production by an attempt to set forward the relations between these factors and industrial development that is the subject of this book.

It is a great abstraction to talk of the economy as a whole and of only a few factors of production. The uses of such an abstraction are obvious: it enables us to make generalizations, to compare countries with each other,and to direct our research into areas of potential usefulness. But there are also limitations to this usefulness, limitations that are directly related to the ability of this abstraction to tell us something interesting about a complex world. The relationship between the factors of production and the process of industrialization to be described shortly holds good only under a variety of restrictive assumptions. If one agrees that these assumptions are roughly true, then the relation and the resultant discussion will appear useful. But if these assumptions appear less appropriate than some others, the limitations of this relation may be more apparent than its uses. We cannot here enter into the technical discussion of alternative assumptions; instead we simply assert that they are a useful and informative set.[1]

We need, first of all, some index to tell us when an industrial revolution takes place, how fast it is progressing, and how far it goes. Some index of human welfare

Reprinted from Peter Mathias and M.M. Postan, eds., *The Cambridge Economic History of Europe*, Vol. 7 (Cambridge: Cambridge University Press, 1978), Pt. I, pp. 1–27. Reprinted by permission of Cambridge University Press.

might seem appropriate to indicate the existence and extent of such a revolution, but an index of welfare is too broad for our present purposes. There are many things that affect the happiness of people, and the state of the economy is only one of them. People who have eaten to satiety are not always happier than those who eat more lightly. We are all familiar with discontent in wealthy societies and with unhappiness coming from non-economic causes. There are even those who say that the overall psychological state of mankind is not susceptible of alteration by economic means. Each man, this theory says, will worry according to his nature. If he is poor, he may worry about his poverty. But if he is rich, he will find something else to worry about.

It is not necessary to hold to this extreme theory to see that a measure of welfare is too broad for our present concerns. It is enough to realize that we do not have the means to disprove such a theory to know that the link between the industrial revolution and welfare is quite tenuous. For example, historians have been debating for many years whether workers were better off in the early years of the industrial revolution than they had been previously.[2]

Another possible measure is an index of structural change. The terms "industrial revolution" and "industrialization" are often used interchangeably, and the place of industry in the economy would tell us something about the process to which these terms refer. It is a valid measure, however, only if there is some fixed relation between the industrial revolution and the place of industry in the economy, i.e. if there is a pattern which every country must follow to achieve its revolution. The diversity of historical experience has disabused us of this simple notion, and while industry plays a more important role in societies that have had an industrial revolution than in societies that have not, the extent of this role is determined by many as yet unknown factors, and today lies more in the different economies than in the relative sizes of these sectors (Kuznets, 1957). Just as a measure of welfare is too broad for our purposes, a measure of structural shifts within the economy is too narrow.

Since we have found one bowl of porridge to be too hot and one too cold, it is obvious that the third will be just right. Looking into one well-stirred bowl, we find the following: "The characteristic which distinguishes the modern period in world history from all past periods is the fact of economic growth" (Cole and Deane, 1965). Economic growth, or the ability of the economy to produce ever more goods and services of value to its members, is a more restricted measure than changes in welfare, because it looks only at the goods and services produced by the economy. We presume that, all other things being equal, an increase in these goods and services would increase welfare, but we do not know that other things remained the same when economic production was increased. On the other hand, economic growth is a broader measure than structural change, for an economy can grow in many ways and with many different types of structural change. It is the results of structural change that concern us, and we use them as our index of industrialization.[3]

Many people have seen the progress of industrial development in the expansion of railways, the growth of coal production, and other such activities. We have to decide if our measure of production is to be the simple sum of these activities. The problem is that some of the coal production of the nineteenth century was used to fuel railways. If we count both activities separately, therefore, we are counting some of the coal production twice: once when the coal was mined and again when it was used to power locomotives. We have phrased this problem in specific terms, but a similar problem arises whenever the output of one industry is the input of another.

It is obviously preferable not to count the same activity twice. To avoid doing so, we do not count the total production of the economy in constructing our measure of economic growth; we count only the production of those goods destined directly for use by consumers. We call these goods "final goods" to distinguish them from the "intermediate goods" that are inputs to further production.

The distinction between intermediate and final goods is easier to make in theory than in practice. We cannot discover the disposition of everything produced by the economy, and we must make rules that allow us to deal with groups of commodities and services. The most widely used rule is that goods and services bought by consumers are final goods, while those bought by business firms are intermediate goods.

This rule, like any general rule, has implications that must be recognized. For instance, it costs more to live in the city than in the country. Food must be brought to the city; people must travel to work; living space is more expensive. If people like to live in cities and would choose to live there even if there were no economic incentives for them to do so, then these extra expenses are part of consumption, i.e., final goods. On the other hand, if people do not like to live in cities and live there only because they need to be near places of employment, then these extra expenses are a cost to them of working in the cities. They are then part of the cost of production of goods made in the cities, and they should be classified as intermediate goods and not included in our measure of economic growth. We have no way of discovering the preferences of all urban dwellers; our rule assumes that they work in the city in order to live there, as opposed to living in the city in order to work there.

Consider another example. Flour that is used to make bread in a bakery is clearly an intermediate product. Is flour that is purchased by housewife to make bread at home the same? We conventionally consider housewives as consumers, and this flour therefore is considered a final good. As with the costs of urban living, we assume implicitly that housewives bake bread at home because they enjoy doing so and not because this is a necessary part of maintaining a family. This assumption is appropriate to industrialized twentieth-century societies where housewives have the option of buying bread; it is less relevant for pre-industrial societies. It has the added implication that as activities get taken out of the home and incorporated into businesses that sell their services, our measure of economic growth increases, even though the volume of goods produced may not have changed.[4]

Finally, let us take a somewhat esoteric problem. How should we treat the consumption of slaves? From the point of view of the slaveowner, slaves were part of his capital, and their consumption was the cost of maintaining this capital. Clearly, the consumption of slaves was an intermediate good to the slave owner, similar in all respects to fuel for locomotives. To the slave, on the other hand, his consumption represented a final product of the economy, and he would have thought that it should be counted as such. In addition to deciding how to treat goods and services bought by consumers, consequently, we have to decide who are consumers. A slaveowner in the American South before the Civil War may well have had a different index of economic growth than we—believing that all men are equal and to be counted as consumers—would construct today.

This rule tells us how to construct our measure, but it does so in a method that is not suitable for all uses. The coal mines, to return to our original example, sell most of their products to other firms, and their output does not appear directly in this measure of total output. If we wish to integrate our measure with studies of coal production we need to construct our measure in a way that allows us to make the transition from industry to nation.

A railway buys the coal that it uses. If we attribute to the railway the total value of its product used by consumers, we are counting the value of the coal in this product, even though it was not produced by the railway. To avoid this, we talk of something called "value added," which is the value of an industry's products less the value of the intermediate goods purchased by that industry, i.e., the value of the industry's services over and above the cost of the materials it purchased. Since we derive the value added by subtracting all the intermediate products from each industry's total, we can add the value added in different industries to get our total measure. We get the same total as before because the value of the bread purchased in a store equals the value added by the farmer, the baker, the wholesaler, and the retailer. And we can see the amount added to our total by each industry, whether or not it produces goods for final consumption.

This method also gives us a way to connect our total with the factors of production. If we subtract the intermediate goods purchased from the firm's receipts, we are left with the firm's value added. This equals the firm's payments for inputs other than intermediate goods, i.e., for labor, for capital (including profit and depreciation), and for raw materials not produced by other firms. A firm's value added, in other words, equals the sum of its payments to the factors of production. And our measure of an economy's output can be seen as either the sum of the final goods produced, the sum of the value added in different industries, or the sum of the payments to the factors of production. This measure, of course, is called national product or national income by economists. (These terms have slightly different meanings but can be used as synonyms here.) We measure economic growth by changes in national income, and these changes are equivalent to changes in the payments to the factors of production.

II

We said earlier that the relation between the national product and the factors of production used to produce it was complex. And so it is. For while payments to the factors of production have to rise with the national product, the quantities of these factors used may not rise in exact proportion to the rise in output. And the national product itself might rise because of a rise in the value of the commodities and services being produced, and not because of an increase in the quantity produced. If we wish to talk of the volume of production and its relation to the quantities of factors used, we must first find a way to transform the sum of values that we have called national product into a measure that is independent of price, i.e., into "real" national product.

Were there only one unalterable commodity, and consequently only one price, the problem would be trivial: dividing the value of production at different times by the price at that time would give a measure of the quantity produced. Similarly, if all prices changed together, one price would be as good as another to use for deflation, and the problem would be solved. But when there are many goods, and when prices do not move together, it is necessary to choose what price or combination of prices to use for deflation. The measure of the goods and services produced—i.e., of real national product—that will emerge will depend on the choice made; obviously, there is no unique measure of real national product.

The problem may be restated as follows: when prices and quantities do not move together, it is necessary to choose a scheme whereby the changes in the various quantities are weighted to produce an average change. Various weighting schemes have been named after nineteenth-century investigators. A Paasche index is one that uses prices of the current year as weights; a Laspeyres index is one that uses prices of the initial year of the series as weights. In other words, a Paasche index uses the weights of the observer looking backward; a Laspeyres index uses the weights of a man at the start of the historical period being considered looking forward. (These gentlemen actually computed price indexes, but the problems are the same. Reading this discussion with "price" substituted for "quantity" and vice versa will show the problems as they encountered them.) As each observer uses the prices of his period as weights, each observer will give heavier weight to those industries with the higher relative price, i.e. the higher price relative to the prices of other industries. If there is a systematic relationship between the movements of relative prices and the growth of industries, there will be a consistent difference between the two measures.

Some writers have seen the industrial revolution as a result of spontaneous innovations. According to this view, the pattern of demand stayed relatively stable. Innovations in some industries lowered the price of their products, and people consumed more of them. (Expansions took place primarily by shifts of supply curves and movements along demand curves.) There was thus a negative correlation between price and quantity changes; those industries whose relative prices fell the most were also the industries whose output rose the most. An observer looking forward into the future would have seen rapid expansion in the industries he associated with relatively high prices; an observer looking back would see relatively slow expansion in the industries he associated with relatively high prices. The Laspeyres index would show a higher rate of growth than the Paasche index.

Is this a realistic—albeit simplified—view of industrialization? The reader is referred to the essays in volume 6 of the *Cambridge Economic History of Europe* for informed opinion (particularly the chapter by David S. Landes). Tests of this proposition by the use of index numbers have shown that the discrepancy anticipated from this theory can be found in indexes of machinery output, but that it may not be present in indexes of consumer-goods industries (Gerschenkron, 1962, chap. 9; Scott, 1952, pp. 386–87). We may hypothesize that in the production of capital goods, shifts of supply curves were more important in the expansion of production than shifts of demand curves, while shifts of both types of curves were equally important in the expansion of consumer-goods production. But this is not the place to analyse the industrial revolution; we want only to point out the possibility of systematic differences between index numbers.

The important question now arises of whether the story of the growth of real economic output can be translated into a story about the growth of the conventional productive inputs. Do the historically observed increments in the supply of labor, capital goods, and land (or natural resources) "explain" economic growth? The very notion of an industrial revolution suggests not; historians would presumably be surprised to discover that all that happened in the second half of the eighteenth century was that the supplies of labor, capital, and natural resources began to grow more rapidly than they had done before. But even if there is more to the story than that, it is still a matter of some interest and importance to discover what part of the growth of output can be explained by the growth of inputs, and what part remains to be explained in other ways.

We must first state what we mean by "explain." It is not a matter of "ultimate" explanation, of asking whether land is the mother of output and labor the father, or vice versa. If we were to say that a factor explains output if it is indispensable to the process of production, then to all intents and purposes we could explain output thrice over. Our notion of explanation is incremental. We want to account for changes in output by changes in the various inputs, to the extent that we can. "Account for" is perhaps more descriptive than "explain." We wish to account for changes in output by changes in input much as one would account for changes in the area of a rectangle by the historical changes in the lengths of its sides. The differences are, first, that we have no prior definitional relation between output and inputs as we have between the area of a rectangle and the lengths of its sides; and, second, that we do not even know that changes in output can be accounted for completely by changes in inputs, and indeed we suspect the reverse.

In order to perform this accounting, we need to know something about the historical time-paths of what economists call the "marginal products" of the factors of production. We need answers—approximate answers—to questions like this: In such and such a year, if employment had been higher (or lower) by 1,000 average workers and everything else had been the same, how much higher (or lower) would output have been? It is plain that such questions can have only rough answers, if they have answers at all. How are "average workers" defined? Are we to imagine them appearing or disappearing in London, in Bristol, or all over the country in proportion to the existing supply of labor? Is everything else to be unchanged—even the stock of houses, which after all are capital goods? We will recur to some of the difficulties of principle and practice later; but some such estimates have to be produced if any analytical connection is to be made between the growth of inputs and the growth of output.

If the marginal product of a factor is known or knowable, then knowing it is almost equivalent to knowing a slightly more convenient quantity, the "elasticity of output with respect to a particular factor of production," a kind of proportional marginal product. It answers in principle the question: In such and such a year, if employment had been higher (or lower) by 1 per cent and everything else had been the same, what percentage increase (or decrease) in output would have been registered? These elasticities are natural concepts in the kind of acccounting that we are trying to do. To be precise, over some interval of time, the appropriate measure of the contribution of a particular input to the average annual rate of growth of output is given by the product of the average annual rate of growth of the input and the elasticity of output with respect to that input.[5] To ask whether the growth of productive inputs "explains" the growth of output is simply to ask whether the sum of such products is equal to the rate of growth of output itself. Following Domar (1961), we call the excess of the rate of growth of output over the sum of these products—if it exists—the "residual." It is significant that the residual does exist and is sometimes of substantial size; and the significance is more than merely descriptive. We mentioned earlier that the national product is so defined as to be equal to the national income (apart from minor discrepancies arising primarily from the tax and subsidy operations of government). All that the economy produces in any year is necessarily recorded as the income of one of the factors of production, as wages, rent, interest, or profits—although it is not always clear which, as in the case of the family-owned and family-operated business. Now consider the rates of return for the various factors of production: the annual wage per man, the annual rent per acre of land, the annual rate of profit on capital. If there were no residual, any increase in the rate of return to one or more factors of production could come about only at the expense of a fall in the rate of return to one or more of the remaining factors of production. The wage cannot rise unless the rate of profit, say, falls.

In other words, if in fact the growth of output were fully accounted for by the growth of inputs, then history could not record simultaneous increases in the real wage rate of a given grade of labor and in the rate of profit, nor even an increase in one while the other remained constant. The importance of the residual is that it provides the output, so to speak, out of which can come all-round increases in the rewards to factors of production.

There are exceptions to this rule, the most important of which derives from increasing returns to scale. If an economy automatically grows more efficient as it grows in absolute size, so that for instance a 10 per cent increase in all the factors of production generates a larger percentage increase in total output, then the increment over and above 10 per cent is available to support an increase in all rates of return to factors of production. The status of increasing returns to scale in contemporary industrial economies is still an unsettled question; but we would hazard the guess that in the large modern economies increasing returns to scale is probably considerably less important than the residual as a source of increased output. For the time and circumstances of the industrial revolution, however, there seems to be no basis for such a presumption, and the importance of economies of scale is an open question for research.

It is worth emphasizing, in this context, that "internal" economies of scale, such as would be connected with an increase in the size of the individual factory, are only part of the problem. "External" economies, i.e. reductions in cost connected with the finer specialization made possible by an increase in the size of the economy as a whole, may be at least as important, especially at early stages of industrialization. The part of economic growth that can be attributed to increasing returns to scale is assimilated, after a fashion, to a story about the growth of conventional inputs.

III

It is time we commented on the practical difficulty of carrying out this sort of analysis. We have mentioned that two kinds of numbers are required to make the connection between the growth of output and the growth of inputs. They are estimates of the rates of growth of real output and of the supplies of the various factors of production, and estimates of the elasticity of output with respect to each of the factors of production.[6]

We have already discussed some of the problems encountered in measuring the growth of real output. The problems of measuring the growth of inputs are similar but not identical. We now turn to a consideration of their unique characteristics.

It is easy to provide definitions of the three traditional factors of production—land, labor, and capital—but hard to translate these definitions into workable rules for use. There are many factors of production, and this triad represents only a particular way of separating these myriad factors into distinct groups for analysis. The first problem is how to determine where any particular factor belongs.

"Land" consists of the sum of all natural resources possessed by an economy, i.e., those earning assets not created by man. "Labor" includes that part of the population able and willing to contribute to economic production. And "capital" is the sum of earning assets created by man; it is often called "reproducible capital" to distinguish it from land ("nonreproducible capital").

Business units of the economy employ the services of these three factors to produce goods and services. The definitions have been given in terms of the stock of the three factors, i.e., the amount of the factors available to the economy, but the entire stock of land, labor, and capital is not used to produce goods and services in any one year; the services of these factors are used instead. In addition to defining the stock of these factors, therefore, we must provide a means for evaluating the input of each factor to production.

We begin our discussion with labor. Labor differs from the other two traditional factors of production in at least one important way. People can improve their level of well-being by working to increase their income—i.e., their ability to purchase goods and services produced by others—but they can also increase their well-being by abstaining from work. The alternative to using land or capital is to let them stand idle, which does not increase anyone's happiness. But the alternative to working is leisure, which provides pleasure directly to the workers involved.[7]

The market for labor, therefore, is unlike the market for other factors of production. Competing against the various "productive" uses of labor is the additional demand for time for leisure. In general, when the price of a commodity rises, it becomes profitable for firms to substitute the production of the now higher-priced commodity for other production (or at least it never becomes profitable to switch the other way). When the price of labor rises, this effect is present: workers are inclined to substitute labor for leisure, as they can buy more of the goods they desire for a given quantity of work. However, there is also another influence at work. A higher wage means that a man doing the same amount of work as before has a higher income than before. He may want to spend this income on goods he can buy, but he may also wish to consume all or part of it in increased leisure. A rise in wages therefore may actually decrease the amount of labor supplied, if what we may call the "income effect" increasing the desire for leisure offsets the "substitution effect" by which labor is made more attractive. In this case, we talk of a "backward-bending" supply curve of labor, because the quantity of labor supplied falls as the price rises. A backward-bending supply curve can be an obstacle to industrialization, for increases in the productivity of workers can be offset by declines in the amount of labor supplied. This is an obstacle that cannot be present with either of the other factors; it is a historical question whether it was present for labor.

The historical question is compounded because the distinction between work and leisure is itself comparatively modern. Religious ritual appears as a leisure-time activity in modern life, but it was far more serious in pre-modern society. It is doubtful whether men who believed in the active intervention of supernatural beings in human affairs viewed religious observances as recreation. Similarly, the domestic worker producing cloth or other articles would have been hard pressed to say when the "productive" activity stopped and the duties of being a housewife or the recreation of sitting and talking began. The process of fixing a work week is distinct from the process of varying it—they may involve entirely different forces and have quite dissimilar effects on production.

Let us start our discussion of how to measure the services of labor by considering the services of a single worker, or alternatively a set of identical workers.

The simplest index of labor services is the size of the labor force. This index is often the only one permitted by the data. In fact, the labor force itself often is not observed but instead derived from demographic data by assuming stable participation rates, either for the population as a whole or for groups within the population. As the limitations of the data will remain severe, this measure will continue to be used. But let us ask, as we did with the measure of the national product, what is being measured.

To count the number of people who can work is to measure the potential labor input rather than the actual input: no account is taken of unemployment. It is virtually impossible to find reliable data on unemployment before the twentieth century, and no correction for unemployment is possible. Consequently, the measure of potential input that we use does not quite match a measure of actual output. (On the other hand, if output is estimated by using data on capacity, as is common in industry studies, the two measures do match.)

Similarly, no account is taken of the different amounts that people work when they do work. This implicitly assumes that the output to be associated with a man's labor is independent of how long he works: a man working an eight-hour day is assumed to produce as much as one working a ten- or twelve-hour day. The question about the backward-bending supply curve raised above disappears; we do not care how much a person works, because he always produces the same amount. In addition, the history of the nineteenth century becomes very hard to understand. Starting early in the century, workers demanded shorter working hours. They were adamantly and consistently opposed by their employers (excepting a few aberrant inustrialists like Robert Owen). If the employers stood to lose nothing by reducing the hours of work, why did they object? It seems unlikely that their fear of workers' vices was strong enough to explain their actions.

There are several factors that could cause output to remain the same when the length of the working day changes. If people work harder when they work shorter hours, if they damage fewer machines and make fewer mistakes when they are working less and are less tired, if their morale improves when their hours fall, their productivity in any given time may rise. The hypothesis that the intensity of work rises when the duration of work falls poses a problem like the problem of the backward-bending supply curve. In that case, there were two offsetting influences affecting the amount of labor offered at a given wage rate. There is no theoretical way to tell which was stronger at any moment of time; it is an empirical question. Similarly, the extent to which the increased intensity of work offsets a reduction in its duration is an empirical question. And, as often happens, several answers have been proposed (all by investigators studying the twentieth century).

No investigator thinks that the change in intensity is exactly the same as the change in duration for all conditions. On the other hand, they seem to agree that there is a maximum output attainable from any individual and that this maximum is obtained well before complete physical exhaustion sets in. Lloyd G. Reynolds asserted that the maximum ouput came when a person was working between forty and fifty hours a week. Edward F. Denison, in his study of economic growth in the United States, said that a person produced his maximum output when he worked about forty-nine hours a week (the normal working week in 1929). In his later, more comprehensive study, Denison (1967) assumed that the point of maximum output was reached for non-farm workers when they were working ten hours a week more than they worked in 1960, or about fifty-four and fifty-nine hours a week for the United States and northwest Europe respectively. (Denison assumed that the output per man-year of agricultural workers was independent of the hours worked, i.e. that the offset was exact and complete throughout the reported range.) Finally P.J. Verdoorn asserted that an individual produced the most when he worked sixty hours a week.[8]

Even though these findings vary in detail, there is general agreement that a man working more than sixty hours a week is producing less than a man working fewer hours. It is probable that the ability to sustain long hours has increased over time as nutrition and factory experience have grown, making this conclusion valid for the nineteenth century as well. These findings imply, therefore, that a ten-hour day probably was not the most efficient use of labor in the nineteenth century, and that longer working days definitely resulted in smaller total output than the same workers would have produced had they worked shorter hours. Should we believe this inference, or should we re-examine our method of dealing with changes in hours today? The essays in this volume may suggest some answers.

We have switched easily from talking about the intensity of effort to talking of hours per week, but there are many ways of reducing the hours that people work. Hours per day, days per week, and weeks per year are all subject to change. Does it make any difference which way the change is made? The preceding discussion assumed that all changes took place within the unit of a week, but longer weekends and vacations may also increase the efficiency of workers while on the job. We know even less about the effects of vacations than we do about the effects of variations in the length of the work week; historical judgments may help us out.

For example, it has been estimated that there were 111 feast days a year under the *ancien regime* (Rude, 1953–54). Workers in eighteenth-century France consequently worked, on average, a five-day week (assuming that whatever they did on feast days was not work). This may have represented fewer hours of work than the more ususal nineteenth-century six-day week, or it may simply have represented a different allocation of hours within a week. In any case, did it affect the productivity of labor?

The discussion so far has treated the problem of a homogeneous labor supply, whether composed of a solitary worker or of many identical laborers. Let us now consider the problem of diverse workers. The labor force will no longer be an adequate index of labor services, because it does not show changes in the quality of labor. There are many ways in which workers differ from one another; we must ask if these differences are likely to change the rate of growth of the labor force and, if so, how we can adjust our data.

First, workers differ in intelligence. In the absence of any evidence or reason to the contrary, we may assume that the distribution of intelligence among people remains constant over time. When the size of the labor force increases, the quantity of intelligent—and of less intelligent—people rises in exact proportion to the labor force. Similarly, although intelligent people can be expected to earn more than less intelligent ones, the distribution of salaries based on intelligence alone may be expected to remain constant, and the changes of any one wage can be used as an index of the movements of all wages. Therefore, we do not have to take explicit account of differences in intelligence among workers.

Second, workers differ in the skills they possess. (We distinguish here between skills learned on the job and those that are the results of formal education.) If these skills were purely the product of experience, if everyone acquired them as he aged, and if the age composition of the work force remained constant, then job skills could be treated in exactly the same way as intelligence. There would always be a pool of job skills, and this pool would increase with the size of the labor force: no specific account would need to be taken of it. Although everyone does not acquire skills at the same rate, we could assume that aptitudes are constant and ignore these differences as we have ignored differences in intelligence. If the age structure changes, a simple correction could be made.

But the relationship between skill and experience cannot be treated so simply. As jobs changed, the importance of experience changed. As traditional apprenticeship programmes were abandoned, the communication of skills was altered. As education became more widespread, the aptitude for on-the-job instruction undoubtedly rose. As workers became more used to factory discipline, their willingness to learn probably also increased. And as workers became more adapted to urban life, their ability to focus on their jobs probably rose too. An adjustment should be made in the measure of labor input to account for these changes. The method could follow that for education—to be described shortly—but the size is not clear. Empirical work must precede an explicit measure.

Third, workers differ in their educational backgrounds. The main problem with education can be seen by making a few extreme assumptions. Let us assume first that people learn nothing of economic value in school that they would not have learned in any case. The economic function of school then would be to sort out the intelligent people, those who finish school, from less intelligent people, those who do not finish—even though the intelligent people would have been as productive as they actually were even if they had not attended school. We would observe that the people with the most schooling earned the highest salaries, but we would not want to increase our estimates of labor input when the level of education rose as a result; the distribution of salaries in this case would be the distribution caused by differences in intelligence, which we have seen remains constant over time. (It may still be rational to have schools even if they teach nothing of economic value. Their sorting function may be worth their cost, and people may enjoy school as they enjoy leisure.)

Now let us assume the reverse, namely that there are no differences in native intelligence and that differences among workers are produced purely by education. Then any salary differentials would relate not to the constant distribution of intelligence but to the fruits of schooling. As the educational level of the population increased, we would want to show the quality of labor services being used as increasing with it. Or, to use current terminology, we would want to show an increase in "human capital" along with the increase in the labor force. (The valuation of this capital would pose the same problems as the valuation of any kind of capital—to be discussed shortly—although it is normally included with labor in discussions of production.)

It is fair to assume that one man earns twice as much as another because he produces twice as much (subject to qualifications to be mentioned in connection with labor mobility). It follows that the high wages of a university-educated worker reflect his high productivity, which comes in turn (by our assumption) from his education. We can construct an index of labor services, therefore, in the same way that we constructed an index of real national product. We find that the wages of workers with different educational levels in some base period, and we use these wages as weights to combine the numbers of workers with these educational levels at each point in time. We will not have valued the stock of "human capital," but we will have an index of the extent to which it augments the services of uneducated labor. It will be recalled that we constructed this index under the assumption that there are no differences in native intelligence, only differences in education.

Clearly, neither this assumption nor the alternative extreme assumption that education teaches nothing is valid. The true condition lies somewhere in between, wage differentials reflecting differences in both education and intelligence. The question then is how much of the differences to ascribe to education—a question to which no satisfactory answer has been given. Denison assumed that three-fifths of the wage differentials were due to education, measuring differentials from the wage of a worker who left school at the age of fourteen. In other words, Denison assumed that the salary differentials that would have been observed had all workers been exactly as intelligent as actual workers with eight years of schooling would have been three-fifths as large as the actual differentials (Denison, 1967, chap. 8). There is no good way to test this assumption, because we have no way to separate the results of education from intelligence: our tests for intelligence are being revealed increasingly as tests of education. It is not clear how much historical work can contribute to the resolution of this dilemma.

However, unless we use an ad hoc assumption like Denison's, we cannot show educational investment as an element in the increase in national product. For if we do not use such an assumption, we have no way of separating the return to education from the fruits of native intelligence.[9] Either we must omit this important input from our discussion or else enter it according to a conventional method whose value has yet to be tested.

The preceding discussion has treated differences among workers, but there can also be changes in the character of the labor force coming from changes in the nature of the labor market. For example, there are many barriers to labor mobility. A worker may have to travel to find the best job, and he may be unwilling or unable to do so. He may refuse to leave a traditonal occupation for one he is more suited for. He may not be able to enter into the social class that is needed to fill a job he could otherwise ably perform. As a result, the labor force may not be used to its fullest capacity. If the relationship between the actual productivity of the labor force and its perfect-market potential remained constant, we would not have to worry about it; like differences in intelligence, it would remain internal to the analysis. On the other hand, if the geographical and occupational mobilty of labor increased—as it did during the industrial revolution—then there would be an increase in labor services in addition to the growth in the size of the labor force.

In general, we do not have to take account of the characteristics of the labor force that stay constant over time. We are interested in measuring changes in the services of labor supplied, and if all components of a disparate aggregate move together, we can use any one component as an index of change. On the other hand, if different components are changing at different rates, then we are faced with an index-number problem exactly analogous to the problem we faced in measuring the national product. Of course we have to determine the nature and identify the causes of the differences between workers before we can tell which is which. We have to decide in each case if an attribute is inborn and immutable—and will therefore vary with the size of the labor force as a whole—or is the result of changing circumstance—and will change at a rate all its own.

IV

These problems, however, pale to insignificance compared to the complexity of valuing the services of capital and land. We have a naive measure of labor services in the labor force. There are many difficulties with this naive index, and we try to improve upon it; but it represents a fairly advanced starting point. We do not have this advantage when we discuss reproducible and non-reproducible capital, and we must start from scratch.

We must first distinguish the two kinds of capital from intermediate goods. We stated above that goods and services bought by business firms were intermediate goods. We now amend that definition to say that of the goods and services purchased by business firms, those that are used up within one year are intermediate goods. Goods or services that last longer than a year we will classify as capital, including them with "capital" or with land depending on whether or not they are reproducible. Coal bought by a railway is an intermediate product, but rails are capital because they last more than a year.

The distinction is important. We measure the national product on a yearly basis, and we want to have a measure that treats all years symmetrically. A railway typically uses most of the coal it buys within a year, and it is left at the start of the next year in the same position that it was in originally. On the other hand, a railroad that buys rails in one year has them on hand in the next. It is better off at the start of the second year than at the start of the first, and if we classified rails as an intermediate good we would observe an unexplained increase in the production of railroad services. To avoid this, we classify the rails as capital, and only their depreciation, i.e. the amount by which they are used up, is subtracted from output to get value added. The undepreciated portion of the rails is carried over from one year to the next as capital, and the excess of the production of capital over its depreciation is defined as investment and is added to consumption to give national income or product.[10]

This discussion points to two ways of formulating a measure of the reproducible capital stock. We could add together all the undepreciated capital existing in the economy at any one time; or we could add together the investments from past years, discounting them to allow for the intervening depreciation. The two measures are conceptually the same; the problem—as always—is that prices change. The cost of building a brick factory in 1840 differs sharply from the cost of reproducing that same building today and also from the cost of a modern pre-stressed concrete building that could serve the same purpose. At which price should we value the factory?

This question is of great theoretical importance, for the very nature of capital is at stake. In choosing a price by which to value the factory built in 1840, we are selecting its contemporary equivalent. This might be a modern reproduction of the 1840 factory, duplicating in every detail the nineteenth-century construction, or it might be a modern concrete and glass factory with the same floor space. In the one case, it is the physical characteristics that define the unit of capital; in the other, the economic.

The theoretical importance of this question, however, is matched by the difficulty of applying it in historical studies. We have enough data for recent years to make a choice between alternative concepts of capital, but we do not have enough data for the eighteenth and nineteenth centuries to use price indexes based on either of the choices just outlined. Let us therefore examine the assumptions implicit in the measures that can be used.

The worst—but not unusual—situation is where there is no separate price index for capital at all. Investment is then deflated by a wholesale price index to get a value for real capital formation. Without a standardized commodity, no price index is possible, and most wholesale price indexes concentrate on uniform commodities such as agricutural products and cloth. They do not generally include the prices of many capital goods, and we will not go too far wrong in this discussion if we make the slightly inaccurate assumption that wholesale price indexes measure the prices of consumption goods.

Deflating investment by the price of consumption goods denies that there is any separate commodity called "capital." Investment is then the act of putting aside consumption goods for future years, of accumulating inventories of consumption goods as opposed to consuming them. This can be seen by the following argument. Prices at any one time measure the relative costs of producing different commodities. If a country chooses to invest one pound or one franc less this year than last, it can thereby produce one pound's or one franc's worth of extra consumption goods. By extension, if a country chooses to invest nothing at all, it could then produce more consumption goods equal in value to the investment forgone.[11] Investment therefore represents consumption forgone, and we can measure it by the amount of consumption forgone, i.e. by valuing it as we value the past production of consumption goods.

A slightly better situation exists when we have a price index especially constructed to value investment which measures the prices of inputs to capital formation: wood, bricks, iron (steel for the late nineteenth century), and the labor used to combine these elements into capital. This situation is better because it opens another alternative to us, but this new price index has many of the characteristics of the old. It too denies the existence of capital goods, valuing the investment of the past by the resources used as opposed to the capital produced. It is as if the economy used its resources to accumulate inventories of intermediate goods, raw materials, and labor, whose work could be measured by the value of these items at a later date.

We initiated this discussion of capital by differentiating capital from intermediate goods. Capital, we said, consisted of inventories—goods produced in one year but not used till a later year. To value the capital stock we need to know what kind of goods comprise these inventories, and the choice of price indexes is the same as the choice of assumptions on this very question. Using a wholesale price index assumes that the inventories are composed of consumer goods (or their equivalent); using the prices of inputs, that they are composed of these inputs. In either case, investment is simply the accumulation of inventories. There is no form of production recognized as capital goods and valued separately from other goods.

This is a theory of investment popular among Austrian economists at the end of the nineteenth century, and it is more appropriate to agricultural than to industrial societies. Wine and trees improve with age, and an economy can productively use its resources by holding inventories of these commodities. Generalizing from these and similar examples, the Austrians concluded that postponing consumption was in itself productive. Capital formation became inventory accumulation, and capital became the ability to wait.

No one denies that the ability to postpone is an important aspect of capital, but few people today would agree that this ability is the only aspect of capital worth considering. It is not enough just to accumulate inventories; it matters what goods you inventory. And we do not just store consumer goods or inputs to production. We construct special goods to store, goods distinguished by their usefulness in production over time. We call these goods "capital goods," and it would be nice to value our inventory of these goods in a way that takes account of our changing ability to produce them. The construction of a price index suitable for this use poses many problems, but the nature of the available data limits the relevance of these problems to the topics dealt with in this volume, and we shall not consider them here.[12]

Instead we turn to a qualitative distinction that can be made between different kinds of capital formation. As the size of the labor force—measured by one of the methods already discussed—changes, the size of the capital stock must change in order to keep constant the ratio of capital to labor. Capital formation that accompanies a rise in the labor force and serves only to maintain the existing capital-labor ratio is called "capital-widening." On the other hand, capital formation that increases the ratio of capital to labor is called "capital-deepening." Capital-deepening can take place whether or not the labor force is increasing, and capital-widening and -deepening can take place simultaneously.

We have suggested that a rise in the national product is a hallmark of industrial development. It is reasonable to go further and to say that a rise in the national product per capita should be the appropriate measure. This measure has the disadvantage of ignoring any increases in the population caused by industrial development, but it has the advantage of focusing attention on the increase in a typical individual's ability to consume.[13] And if it is used, the distinction between capital-widening and capital-deepening is very important. In an economy with a growing labor force, some investment is required simply to maintain the existing output per capita, by maintaining the existing capital per worker; and investment to increase the output per capita must be in addition to this capital-widening. A given amount of investment, there-fore, will cause a smaller increase in the national income per head in a country with a rapidly growing population than in one with a less rapidly growing or stable popula-tion. Even if we cannot discover the exact rate at which the capital stock grew, there-fore, it is often illuminating to know how capital formation was divided between capital-widening and capital-deepening.

We turn our attention now to the remaining factor of production: land, by which we mean raw materials or "non-reproducible capital." Countries differ in their endowments of natural resources, and it is appropriate to take account of this fact in the explanation of economic production. But the problems of measurement encountered in the discussion of labor and capital are as nothing when compared with the difficulty of measuring raw material. As with capital, there is no naive meas-ure of land similar to the labor force for labor. But unlike capital, natural resources were not produced and are not reproducible, and there is consequently no easy way to value them or the cost of their production.

The problem is further complicated by the capricious nature of technology. The value of the minette ores of Lorraine was vastly increased by the discovery of the Thomas process for using ores containing phosphorus in the Bessemer converter. The value of palm oil and related products was raised by their substitution for tallow and other animal products in the manufacture of soap. Similarly, deposits of oil, alumi-num, uranium, etc., were valueless before technology advanced to the point where they could be used in the production of goods or services.

And as if these problems were not enough, there is also the problem of discovery. The New World was composed of many riches, but what was its value to the Old before it had been discovered? The United States paid $15,000,000 for the Louisiana Purchase; it is hard to know what deflator would translate that price into the present value of the American Great Plains. The lands surrounding the Persian Gulf gave no evidence for many years of the liquid wealth lying beneath them; for all we know, the land we stand on may have similar undiscovered treasures beneath it.

It is interesting and useful to chronicle the discovery and exploitation of these resources, but we would like to know the total amount of natural resources available to each country to unify our discussion of land with that of the other inputs. For the reasons just listed, however, we can only find a measure of the resources in use at any given time—the value of those not in use or not even yet discovered being impossible to know. Half a loaf is better than none, and we turn to a measure of this type.

The crudest measure—but by the same token the easiest to use—is the area of a country, or alternatively its population density. This measure assumes that resources are spread evenly over the earth and is consequently of little help except in extreme cases, such as a comparison of nineteenth-century Australia with twentieth-century India. The quantity of one particular resource, like arable land or coal, is an alterna-tive measure, but it is too restrictive a measure for use in any but specific, narrowly defined inquiries. And if we say that the sum of several different resources should be used, we are faced with the index-number problem deriving from the different valua-tion of different resources over time.

Some functions of exports can also be used as an index of resource endowments (Chenery, 1960). Countries tend to export the products whose production depends on the utilization of resources they possess in relative abundance, and the ratio of exports to the national product gives an index of the resource endowment. The measure, however, is seriously flawed. The United States is obviously well endowed with natural resources, yet its exports are much smaller in relation to its national product than the exports of many less well-endowed but smaller countries. British foreign trade was large in the nineteenth century as a result of Britain free-trade policy. And all exports fell in the 1930s, even though the world was not deprived of its natural resources by the depression in world trade. The size of a country, the nature of its mercantile policies and the state of international affairs—as well as natural-resource endowments—affect the volume of a country's exports. Nevertheless, a better index of resource endowments is hard to find.

V

Suppose that, somehow, estimates are constructed of the rates of growth of real output and of the employment of the main factors of production. Without those estimates there is no possibility of even posing the quantitative question about the extent to which the growth of inputs accounts for the growth of output. Even with them, the calculation of an answer requires another ingredient, the marginal products or output-elasticities of each of the inputs, or at least their average values during the period of time in question.[14] These elasticities have a status quite different from that of the rates of growth. They are not at all directly observable quantities but must be inferred.

There are essentially only two ways in which this can be done. One is by direct statistical inference from observations on output and input quantitites, as one might estimate a demand curve from observations on price, quantity, and related variables. There are many advantages to this approach, but it has the substantial handicap of requiring a large number of observations over a fairly wide range of independent variation in input quantities. No such statistical record is likely to be available for periods more than a century in the past; indeed, even with contemporary data it is not easy to fulfill the requirement for independent variation in input quantities. Perhaps the most that can be expected of historical data on input and output quantities is that they serve as a check on conclusions derived by indirect methods.

The indirect approach to the estimation of marginal products and output-input elasticities rests on the proposition from economic theory that, under competitive market conditions, the return to a unit of each factor of production (measured in units of output) will approximate its marginal product. This is equivalent to saying that the fractional share of the return to a factor of production in the distribution of the output it has helped to produce will be an estimate of the elasticity of output with respect to that factor.

The great advantage of this approach, of course, is that it requires only data on factor returns—wage rates, rents, profits—or the proportional distribution of the product of the economy or industry among the various inputs. This sort of information may be available even in the absence of usable data on the quantities of inputs and outputs. The disadvantages of the indirect approach is that its validity depends on strong assumption: that the markets for land, labor, and capital are approximately competitive, and that they are approximately in equilibrium (i.e., that factor returns do not differ from marginal products as a signal that the organization of production is in the process of adapting to change). These assumptions are not easy to swallow in ordinary times; they may be misleading in times of extraordinarily rapid and thoroughgoing change. If that is so, the data themselves may provide a warning by moving sharply or systematically. Suitably checked, this is probably the only way that the accounting exercise can be done, if it can be done at all.

Even if it can be done and if part of the growth of output can be imputed to the growth of inputs and the remainder segregated as a residual, the result can have only the rough validity of a parable or abstract model, a relation among statistical aggregates. When one says that over two decades the increase in labor input accounted for a specified part of the growth of output, one is saying that if employment had grown a bit more slowly than in fact it did, output would have grown a bit more slowly than in fact it did, and one is saying by how much. Now "labor" and "output" (and "capital" and "land") are particular statistical constructs. At the level of detail there are many ways, perhaps infinitely many ways, in which a small difference in the rate of growth of the aggregate "labor input" might have occurred: the geographical balance, the industrial composition, the occupational structure might each or all have been different. Corresponding to each of those ways, the fine detail of output might have responded in alternative ways. And while some statistical "stock of capital" remains constant, particular capital goods are ageing and are being replaced by new varieties. Only under the most special circumstances will there exist any exact relation among the aggregates so that one could say: Had the rate of growth of one input been greater or less by so much, the other inputs growing as they did, the rate of growth of output would have been so much higher or lower.

Nevertheless, one has the notion that there are times when the residual contribution to the growth of output is very large, and times when it is relatively small. It is probably possible, with available data and more or less aggregative methods, to distinguish one set of circumstances from the other. Suppose, then, that one is able to estimate the rate of growth of output over some interval, and the contribution of each broad input to that rate of growth (i.e., the product of the rate of growth of the input and the estimated elasticity of output with respect to the input). Suppose the sum of the calculated contributions falls short of the rate of growth of output and leaves a residual.[15] If Nature abhors a vacuum, accountants abhor discrepancies. Can we say anything about the sources of the residual, even if we cannot account for it in quantitative terms?

Some of the things that can be said have already been mentioned, but it is well to gather them together here. Generally speaking, the residual is made up of two kinds of items. The first we can call measurement errors, though that name is misleading. The errors in question are not merely statistical (there will be plenty of those, but they might be expected to be unbiased) but rather systematic conceptual errors that tend to underestimate the rate of growth of inputs. The second sort of component that goes to make up the residual consists of genuine increases in productivity, and these can happen in any of several ways.

Among the measurement errors—or "specification errors," as an econometrician would call them—the most important has already been figured in our discussion. Over historical time, the supplies of the factors of production change both in quantity and in quality. Labor becomes better educated, healthier, more skilled, more or less adapted to industrial work. Capital goods become more or less durable, more accurate, more efficient; and eventually they are utterly transformed. In principle, one should count each grade of worker, each physically different piece of equipment, as a separate factor of production. In practice one lumps them together as labor and capital.

The effect of lumping these disparate inputs together into a few large aggregates—even if one distinguishes between educated and uneducated labor—is to disregard much if not all of the increase in the quality of the inputs. The growth of the inputs used in production is consequently underestimated; and the proportion of output that cannot be explained by the growth of these inputs is overestimated. The size of this overestimate in contemporary data is a matter of some dispute.[16]

It should be remarked that inadequate allowance for improved quality of output may cause the rate of growth of output to be underestimated also. Correcting this bias has the reverse effect of adding to the unexplained residual. On the other hand, in economies at that stage of development in which self-sufficiency and local barter are giving way to the market, the coverage of statistical series is likely to widen, and the rate of growth of output to be overestimated. This sort of error verges on the merely statistical and suggests that even statistical errors may impart a bias to measured rates of growth for intervals of time long enough to make a difference.

Even after the best possible adjustment is made for quality changes in inputs and output, a positive residual is likely to remain as a reflection of a genuine increase in the productivity of the economic system. It is this increase in productivity that is available for all-round increases in the rewards to factors of production of constant quality. (Some part of the apparent increase in wage rates, however, is a result of the rise in the average quality of labor input; it is not part of a general rise in wages, as would be apparent if each grade of labor were accounted as a separate factor of production.) This true increase in productivity can be sub-classified according to its source. The three main sources are increasing returns to scale, improved efficiency in the allocation of resources, and technological progress, but it is exceedingly difficult to get any idea of their relative importance.

We have already mentioned the possible importance of economies of large-scale production as a source of economic growth. The economist distinguishes between internal economies that have to do with the scale of the individual producing unit and external economies that have to do with the possibility of extended specialization of function as the whole economy grows in scale. The exploitation of economies of scale is often, perhaps usually, accompanied by changes in technique of production. In principle, increasing returns to scale should be distinguishable from genuine technological progress, because the changes in technique that merely accompany changes in scale should be reversible. Let an economy experience prolonged contraction and, in the absence of technological progress, techniques should revert to what they were before. But in fact, of course, one does not observe prolonged decay of whole economies (though studies of individual industries might throw light on this question). Increase in scale and increase in technical knowledge occur together, so that even sophisticated statistical analysis will have a hard time separating the effects of one from the effects of the other.

A second source of higher productivity is the achievement of a more efficient allocation of existing resources among industries and localities. In most industrial economies, even those that have been industrialized for a long time, there appear to be industries and occupations where the marginal products (and the earnings) of labor

and other factors of production are lower than elsewhere. These are usually contracting industries (agriculture, especially small-scale agriculture, is of course the main
example), but they are not contracting fast enough to keep the returns to factors from
falling below those available elsewhere in the economy. In these circumstances, any
transfer of resources from low-productivity employment to high-productivity
employment has the effect of increasing real output as measured, with no corresponding increase in the total of inputs. Gains of this kind may be most available at times of
rapid industrialization, or whenever the composition and location of economic
activity are changing substantially. The immobility that holds resources in low-
productivity employment need not be exclusively a matter of habit or non-pecuniary
advantage or lack of information. It may be, for instance, that the pace of movement
of labor from agriculture to industry is limited by the rate of capital investment in
industry (and in housing). In this case, there is a sense in which the whole increment
of output accompanying the shift of resources might be attributed to the capital
input. But, equally, there is a point in distinguishing this kind of output gain from the
kind that occurs when additional capital investment increases the productivity of
other resources already engaged in industry.

Potential gains from the improved allocation of resources can be realized in other
ways: from the elimination of monopolistic restrictions of output, for example, or from
the end of discriminatory practices in the employment of women, Negroes, or others.
These are likely to be smaller, if only because their incidence affects a small fraction
of the labor force.

The last major component of the residual growth of output is, of course, technological progress itself. One rather expects this to be a big component most of the time
and especially at the times that tend to be labelled as First, Second, or Third Industrial Revolutions. For this reason, much attention has been lavished on the pure
theory of technological change. No way has been found, however, to measure directly
the contribution of technological progress to the growth of output. Studies of patent
statistics and the like have been inconclusive (Schmookler, 1966). The usual routine,
in the absence of anything better, is to treat technological progress as the ultimate
residual. One identifies as many of the components of economic growth as one can,
and what is left provides at least an upper limit to the contribution of technological
change.

This is particularly unsatisfying to the historian, who is aware of technological
change primarily as a concrete phenomenon taking place in particular industries in
particular localities. It is clear that neither extreme will do. The aggregative method,
apart from its excessive indirectness, has the defect of concentrating all the errors of
measurement of all the other factors into economic growth in the residual one, technological change. The wholly microeconomic approach has the defect that while a
particular invention can be described with accuracy, its implications for economic
growth are to be found not only in the industry in which the invention occurs but dif-
fused through the whole economy. The contrast between the two ways of describing
and analysing technological change suggests an experiment. The method of isolating
the contribution of inputs to the growth of output, leaving a residual component of
productivity increase, can be applied to the outputs and inputs of a single industry as
well as to a whole economy. It would be interesting to conduct such an analysis for an
industry and to compare the results with the economic historian's record of actual

concrete changes in technology, in the same industry. One would hope for some correspondence.

If the object is to account for the growth of output, it is clearly the application of an invention in production rather than the invention itself that counts. To the extent that a particular innovation requires, for its application, labor with special skills or major investment in capital equipment of a novel kind, these requirements may govern the pace at which the innovation is introduced into production. This is another example of interaction among sources of economic growth that is much harder to handle in practice than in theory. Should the addition of this novel kind of capital be recorded as a rise in the input of capital or in the residual?

Since the statistics of inputs and outputs can reveal the consequences of technological changes only as they are applied, no distinction appears between the application of newly created knowledge and the diffusion or imitation of technical knowledge already in existence for some time. The distinction is an important one, but it has to be made extra-statistically. The point of the preceding paragraph is that the story of diffusion of new technology may be in many cases part of the story about inputs.

In any case, the relation between inputs and outputs that we have been discussing is a relatively mechanical one. It has to do with the evolution of productivity, and in that formal sense it explains the increase of output that we call economic growth. There are other, at least equally important, things to be said, but this method cannot say them. It can say that the growth of employment accounts for so much growth of output, and so much more when the improved quality of labor is given appropriate weight. It cannot say why the supply of labor did not increase faster or slower, or why it was not more or less mobile from place to place, from country to city, from farm to factory. Nor does it cast any light on the reverse influence: the extent to which, for instance, the evolution of the labor force was a response to the rise in wages, or a matter of demography, or something more complicated.

Analogously, it is important to know how much of the growth of output is attributable to capital investment. But it is at least as interesting to ask how that investment was motivated and financed. Was the willingness to invest primarily a reaction to the emergence of profit opportunities in industry? Or was it motivated otherwise? Or was the supply of saving the main limitation on the achieved growth of capital? In any case, a question arises about the sources of saving, whether the appearance of wholly new ones or the expansion of the old.

It seems, then, that economic development can be viewed in terms of the evolution of the main inputs, but it is a partial view, with something left out at either end. At one end, when the contributions of the broad factors of production to the growth of output have been evaluated, there will be something left over. This residual, or a substantial part of it, may be identifiable with technological progress. The difficult job remains of coordinating that indirect measure with a more circumstantial account of the course of invention and innovation.

At the other end, the evolution of inputs itself needs to be explained, with neither quantity nor quality slighted. The explanation will no doubt run in part in economic terms, as a response to changes in prices and incomes, output and its distribution. This reflex is what makes the economy an interrelated system. There will also be part of the explanation that runs in terms of attitudes and beliefs, chance and force. This is what keeps the economy from being an isolated system.

Notes

[1] For a contrary view, see Robinson, 1953–54. The technical literature on this question is surveyed in Harcourt, 1969.

[2] See Hobsbawm and Hartwell, 1963–4, and references cited there, particularly the early work of the Hammonds and Clapham. See also Flinn, 1974.

[3] The relations between economic growth and welfare on the one hand and structural changes on the other are of great interest. They are considered more fully in volume VIII of *The Cambridge Economic History of Europe;* we are now asking about the inputs that produce economic growth.

[4] We have adopted the convention of treating housewives as consumers for two reasons. First, the measure was evolved for modern use, and we are merely trying to be consistent. Second, the activities of housewives represent a stable part of the economy that is normally not available for alternative uses, and excluding them does not affect the estimates of changes in output—that is, in economic growth. It should be noted, however, that in the Second World War, housewives were used as factory workers in many countries. This appeared as an increase in output rather than as a transfer of resources from one use to another.

[5] It is a mathematical result that in an economy with no economies or diseconomies of scale (i.e. an economy in which a doubling of inputs produces a doubling of outputs, all other things being equal), output equals the sum of the quantities of each of the inputs multiplied by its marginal product. It follows from this that the rate of growth of output is the sum of the rates of growth of the inputs multiplied by the elasticity of output with respect to that input. It must be emphasized that this is a mathematical result; the rate of growth of output in actuality may or may not be equal to the sum just described. It all depends on whether all other things are equal.

[6] Many refinements of this process have been worked out and applied experimentally; they have somewhat different data needs. It would be out of place to discuss them here.

[7] It should be clear that we are discussing voluntary abstention from work by workers. Involuntary unemployment is not a source of pleasure to most people. It should also be noted that idle land can be a source of pleasure to some people—conservationists, for example—but this is the exception rather than the general rule.

[8] Taken from the discussion in Denison, 1967, chap. 6.

[9] We cannot estimate the return to education by time-series analysis—using our assumption that intelligence levels have not risen—since increases in educational levels have been associated with increases in other investment, urbanization, and industrialization, and it is impossible to disentangle their individual effects.

[10] We are talking here of *net* national product and *net* investment. Owing to the difficulty of getting data on depreciation, it is often neglected, giving what are called gross national product and gross investment.

[11] This extension involves the assumption that the marginal rates of transformation in the economy are constant over the relevant ranges, i.e. that the production-possiblities curve is flat. This assumption was used often by John Stuart Mill and others but is less favoured now. If we abandon the assumption, the extra consumption goods capable of being produced would be less than the investment forgone because the efficiency of resources would vary in different uses. The argument in the text would then only be approximately true.

[12] A brief discussion of these problems can be found in Kendrick, 1961.

[13] See Deane and Cole, 1962, for a discussion of these matters in eighteenth-century Britain.

[14] See section II above.

[15] This is the typical result for the twentieth century. See Solow, 1957.

[16] See Jorgenson and Griliches, 1967; Denison, 1969.

4

Demand vs. Supply in the Industrial Revolution

JOEL MOKYR[1]

The intelligent application of the formal principles [of economic theory] is . . . chiefly significant negatively rather than positively, for showing what is "wrong" rather than what is "right."

Frank Knight (1940)

In the process of what could best be called "making sense of the Industrial Revolution," few articles have been more influential than Gilboy's eloquent plea to view demand as an equal partner in bringing about the most profound economic change in human history (Gilboy, 1932). The notion that *both* sides of the demand and supply equation come into play in the explanation of the crucial questions, such as "why England first" or "why the eighteenth century," has made sense to more than a generation of economic historians better trained in handling Marshall's scissors than Occam's razor. The appearance of Keynes's *General Theory* a few years later lent additional support to the notion that demand was somehow important.

This chapter reexamines what may be termed the "Gilboy thesis." The concept of demand itself is too vague without additional clarification. What I shall therefore attempt is to reformulate the Gilboy thesis in consistent and testable form.[2]

I. Did the Demand Curve Shift?

It is possible to interpret the Gilboy thesis as a shift in aggregate demand, or as a shift in the market demand curve for industrial goods. Leaving the former for section III, we first consider whether the Industrial Revolution could be triggered by an outward shift of the industrial demand curve.

In her original article, Gilboy maintained that

The factory could not become typical until demand had been extended . . . throughout the entire population to consume the products of large scale indus-

Reprinted from the *Journal of Economic History*, Vol. 37, No. 4 (December 1977), pp. 981–1008. Reprinted by permission of the trustees of the Economic History Association.

try. . . . In order that a shift in the demand schedule may occur, individuals must be able to buy more units of a commodity at the same price, or the same amount of the commodity at a higher price . . . the entire schedule must shift upward, indicating a greater buying power [Gilboy, 1932, pp. 122–26].

In this simple form the demand thesis is based on circular reasoning. A shift *of* the demand curve for manufactured goods can occur only if income rises, the price of nonmanufactured goods falls, or if a change in tastes occurs. Ruling out the latter for the moment, the shift in the demand curve must be caused by a rise in real income, and can therefore not serve at the same time as an explanation of it.

It is obvious that if a shift in the demand curve for industrial goods is to be used for the explanation of the rise of industrial output, the shift in the demand curve must be caused by factors other than the rise of output itself. Three alternative theories have been presented in the literature in this context, namely agricultural growth, expansion of foreign demand, and population growth (Cole, 1973). It is worthwhile to examine these theories in more detail. The first and in many ways the most attractive hypothesis is agricultural progress. A decline in prices of agricultural goods will lead to an increase in the demand for nonagricultural goods if, ceteris paribus, the demand for agricultural goods is inelastic, as is usually assumed. While unimpeachable on a priori grounds, the theory runs into a timing dilemma: whereas agricultural prices fell in the first part of the eighteenth century, they started to rise after 1750, a trend that persisted until the end of the Napoleonic Wars both in Great Britain and on the Continent.[3] Moreover, it is not always sufficiently emphasized that there should be a decline in the price of agricultural goods *relative* to the price of nonagricultural goods. The movements of relative prices are less clear-cut.

What was the contribution of falling agricultural prices to the rise in demand for nonagricultural goods? The order of magnitude of the impact of changing relative prices on demand can be estimated approximately following a procedure outlined in a 1975 study by R.A. Ippolito.[4] Since the price elasticities as well as the actual movement of prices are subject to large margins of error, the procedure followed has been to estimate a lower and an upper bound of the expansion of industrial demand due to the fall in relative prices.[5] The upper bound of the estimate is 26.1 percent for the entire period 1750–1850, or .26 percent annually, while the lower bound is −.25 percent annually.[6] The average rate of growth of individual output for the entire period can be estimated conservatively at 3 percent annually. The changes in relative prices thus account for, at best, 8 percent of the industrial expansion, while it is quite possbile that their net effect was on the whole negative.

Some efforts have been made to rescue the argument by maintaining that rising agricultural prices due to an exogenous decline in supply (for example, harvest failures) could, under certain conditions, stimulate industrial demand. The mechanism supposedly responsible for this is that a bad harvest raises agricultural prices. Since the elasticity of demand for farm products is usually thought to be less than unity, farm income would rise. If the farmers have a very high propensity to spend on manufactured goods, a harvest failure could allegedly cause a net rise in the demand for nonagricultural goods (Landes, 1950, pp. 200–201; Deane and Cole, 1969, p. 93; Post, 1974, pp. 338–39). In a simple general equilibrium framework it can be proven that if both goods are normal, this cannot occur. Only if agricultural goods—taken as a whole, including both consumption and investment goods—are inferior goods (that is, the income elasticity for them is negative), demand for nonagricultural goods may (but does not have to) expand as a result of harvest failures. For all practical purposes, this version of the demand thesis can thus be ruled out. (The proof of the theorem will be found in Appendix A.)

Eversley has maintained that the post-1750 rise in agricultural prices was not caused by a decrease in supply but by a rise in demand (1967, pp. 240–46). The absence of detailed output data precludes a direct test of this argument, but the work of Eric Jones and others demonstrates that agricultural productivity followed an upward secular trend throughout the eighteenth century, including the period 1750–80. But it does not help to explain the growth in industrial production. If the increased demand for agricultural goods came at the expense of industrial goods, say through a change in tastes or income distribution, it runs directly counter to the Gilboy thesis. If it did not come at the expense of the industrial goods, where did it come from? Surely, in this case rising aggregate income must be the underlying mechanism. To the extent that a higher aggregate income resulted from population growth, it will be dealt with below. But if higher income per capita is the source of the expansion of demand, we are back in the same circular argument as before.[7]

A more convincing rationalization of the apparent paradox is provided by Eric Jones.

> It is unlikely that higher food prices after 1750 ever seriously eroded the expansion of the home market for consumer goods by eliminating the margin for such spending among the working population. Agriculture constantly demanded more labor. The "golden age" of the laborer in the second quarter of the eighteenth century apparently engrained in him tastes for manufactured goods which he was willing to work harder thereafter to gratify [Jones, 1974].

In other words, there seems to have been a shift of the labor supply curve due to a reduced leisure preference. Following this argument, it can indeed be maintained that demand factors mattered insofar as the supply of labor, the demand for leisure, and the demand for goods are simultaneously determined. If there was an increase in the "demand for income," economic growth would occur, but only at the expense of leisure.[8] Possibly this change in attitudes may have been of importance in the initial stages of the Industrial Revolution, but it can hardly account for sustained economic growth. It should be added that others have attributed the lengthening of the labor day to different factors such as coercion (for example, Marx and the Hammonds) or improved diets (Freudenberger and Cummins).

The second exogenous source of demand which allegedly was a necessary condition for rapid industrial growth in Britain in the last third of the century—and, by implication, Belgium, Switzerland and France in the half-century following Waterloo—was exports (Habakkuk and Deane, 1962, pp. 77–78; Minchinton, 1969). It is important, however, to phrase the question precisely; it is not sufficient to state that a "leading" nation had an export sector which pulled the entire economy behind it. In the case of early industrial Europe, if export demand was a main determinant of the patterns of industrialization and growth, it is necessary to show that the successful industrial nations were somehow favored over other potential sellers for whom the expansion of world demand did not lead to rapid industrialization. Moreover, as Kindleberger has pointed out (1964, pp. 264–66), the coincidence between exports and growth is not self-evident. It is necessary to specify in which way foreign expansion brings about growth over and above the simple gains of trade.[9]

The issue of export as a critical component of industrial demand is complicated by the continuous improvements in the productivity of international trade. These had the effect of reducing the transactions and transportation costs, which led to increased international specialization along the lines of comparative advantage. The proportion of national product exported thus rose, and at the same time national income itself grew as the gains from international trade were realized. It could thus be argued that the ultimate causes of growth were changes on the supply side, even though from the point of view of the economy in question the changes were perceived as shifts of the demand curve. More substantial than this taxonomy is the objection that exports may have increased as a result of supply shifts which caused prices to fall, resulting in rapidly growing exports. Unless the shifts in demand and supply curves are separated, it is impossible to attribute rising exports to growing foreign demand.

How important was export in the demand for British industrial output? A well known remark in MacPherson's *Annals of Commerce* dismisses the importance of exports altogether, estimating the ratio of exports to home consumption at 1:32 (Deane and Cole, 1969, p. 42; Minchinton, 1969, p. 38; Ashton, 1972, p. 63). This number is obviously too low, but it illustrates the fact that some contemporaries were skeptical of the preponderance of exports in the expansion of industrial demand. The available data support that impression. Schlote's index of the relation between total overseas trade and industrial product displays a striking stability in the period in which export is supposed to have led industrialization. The index, which moves slightly above 50 (1913 = 100) in the first half of the eighteenth century, leaps to 65 in the 1760s, but averages only 54 for the rest of the century and 55 for the period between the Napoleonic Wars and 1850 (Schlöte, 1952, p. 51). Eversley stresses the powerful counterexample provided by the events of the 1770s: while exports collapsed, industrial output kept growing (Eversley, 1967, pp. 247–49). The aggregate data for the eighteenth century may be deficient, but data for individual goods display the same features.[10] Even in the case of cotton in Great Britain it appears that the relation between exports and total output is not very pronounced. One crude test of the export-led hypothesis would expect to find a positive correlation between the rate of growth of the cotton industry and the proportion of total output exported. But the correlation coefficient between the quinquennial rates of growth of cotton goods production (approximated by raw cotton consumption) and the proportion of total output exported is not statistically significant for the period 1750–1829.

Turning to the nineteenth century, we have access to somewhat more aggregated data, which are inconsistent with an "export pull" or staple theory of growth. Total domestic exports as a percentage of national income fell from 18 percent in 1801 to 11 percent in 1841, and then rose to 14 percent in 1851. The corresponding ratios of exports to industrial output are 76 percent, 32 percent, and 42 percent (Mitchell and Deane, 1962, pp. 282–83; Deane and Cole, 1969, p. 166). Had export demand been the one factor that singled out Great Britain as the economy most suitable to industrialization, one should observe that the role of exports increased when industrial growth was fastest, that is, after the Napoleonic Wars. Quite clearly, this version of the Gilboy thesis fails the test.[11]

Furthermore, it is clear that the British Empire, where expansions in demand would benefit British manufacturing more than other countries, providing a small proportion of total industrial demand. From the Peace of Paris on, the share of the colonies fluctuates above 35 percent of total exports, although the data for 1793–1814 are not easy to interpret. After Waterloo the British Empire accounted for less than 30 percent of exports. In 1846–50, total exports to India were only 87 percent of total exports to Germany and only 30 percent higher than exports to the Low Countries. The demand exerted by colonial markets is thus not a very persuasive explanation of why Britain became the "workshop of the world."[12]

The third source of demand cited as important to the Industrial Revolution is population growth.[13] England's rapid population growth is supposed to have created a large market for industrial commodities, while France's slow population growth is viewed as a cause of retardation. As a matter of economic logic it simply is false that population growth, all other things held equal, will invariably increase the demand for industrial goods. Demand, after all, depends on consumers' income, not merely their numbers. Population growth will increase the number of consumers but decrease income per capita due to diminishing returns. The net effect is indeterminate. It can be shown that, in general, the following proposition holds: all other things equal, a rise in population will lead to an increase in demand for any good if and only if the income elasticity of the demand function of that good is less than the reciprocal of the elasticity of non-labor in the production function. (The proof of this proposition is straightforward and is found in Appendix B.) The implications are quite striking. Assume that the economy was sufficiently competitive to approximate the elasticity of non-labor by its share in national income. Deane and Cole estimate the share of labor in national income in 1801 at about .45, which implies that all goods with an income elasticity of 1.8 and higher would experience a decline in demand as a result of population growth.[14] It can also be seen from equation (6) in Appendix B that if we assume that the income elasticity for agricultural goods was about .5, which implies that the income elasticity for nonagricultural goods was about 1.25, a 1 percent increase in population would lead only to a .31-percent increase in the demand for nonagricultural goods as a whole. Thus population growth *alone* increased demand for nonagricultural goods by 14 percent between 1751 and 1801 and by another 29 percent between 1801 and 1851. The increment of population increased demand by *less than 10 percent of* total output growth for the first half of the nineteenth century, and probably by even less than that for the period 1751–1801. Even if it is assumed that population growth was fully exogenous, its significance in generating the demand for increased industrial production was marginal.

It thus appears that cost-reducing and factor-increasing changes occupy the center of the stage: supply rules supreme. Technological change, capital accumulation, improvements in organization and attitudes all made it possible to produce food, clothing, pots, and toys cheaper and better. But the skeptical reader may still be unconvinced. Will these goods be sold? Will it be "possible to find people with income and demand schedules capable of absorbing this increased output?" (Eversley, 1967, p. 211). Is it not true that "the growth of industry has to be explained in terms of its markets, the reasons why increasing quantities of its products could be sold" (Davis, 1973, p. 304)?. Contrary to the first intuition, when considered in a competitive, multiproduct economy these questions are meaningless. As John Stuart Mill put it: "The demand for commodities determines in what particular branch of production the labor and capital shall be employed; it determines the direction of the labor, but not the more or less of the labor itself, or of the maintenance or payment of that labor" (1929, pp. 79, 87, emphasis in original). Nothing has since been added to the body of economic theory that could refute this view—at least as long as the economy is in full employment. After all, the decisions on how, what, and how much to produce are made by the firm. And the individual firm always faces a demand curve which is elastic, irrespective of the demand elasticity for the industry as a whole.[15] An inelastic demand curve facing an *industry* will not affect the impact of a cost-reducing innovation on the rate of growth of the economy. In this case the income effects of the falling prices will simply be siphoned off to other industries.

II. Induced Technological Change and Economies of Scale

One interpretation of the Gilboy thesis maintains that the supply curve shifts outward as a result of increases in demand. We now turn to this issue.

The idea that technological change is demand-induced is far from new, although its full impact on economic theory has not been felt until relatively recently.[16] The precise meaning of demand-induced innovation is more difficult to formalize if we keep in mind that historians have to deal—often simultaneously—with both process and product innovation. In any event, the theory that the intensity of technological change depends on demand factors is different from the Kennedy concept of "induced innovation." The latter shows how market conditions affect the location of an economy on a *given* "innovation possibility frontier." But for the Gilboy thesis in its dynamic version to be true, it is necessary that demand conditions should be capable of causing a shift *of* the frontier outward. This implicitly assumes that there is a "market" for inventions.[17] The demand for technological progress becomes essentially a derived demand, dependent on the demand for the final good. An increase in the demand for the consumption good will generate more inventions precisely in the same way as it will generate increased employment of other inputs. But in the present context that hardly resolves the dilemma first encountered in section I: whence the initial shift in demand?

Moreover, formidable doubts have been expressed concerning the "market" for inventions (Nadiri, 1970, and the references he cites). If such a market existed at all, it was plagued by at least three sources of market failure, namely the preponderance of externalities, the uncertainty surrounding all stages of innovative activity, and the fact that, often, new knowledge rapidly becomes a public good.[18] Most damaging, however, to the view that the "quantity" of technological progress will respond to shifts on the demand side is that the price on the vertical axis of this supply and demand model is not precisely specified. Since each invention is, by definition, produced only once, the producer has no firm basis on which to estimate his returns. It is often argued, moreover, that financial gain is only a minor consideration for many inventors: scholarly achievement, desire to improve, and pure love of inventing are often cited as prime motives of inventors (Rossman, 1931, p. 152). This does not imply in itself that inventors are unaware of or indifferent to the economic needs of the society they live in. But a distinct possibility of market failure exists all the same. The material needs of society as reflected by the structure of market prices, and the same needs as viewed by an inventor in search of fame or satisfaction can diverge enormously. Often the full potentialities of major inventions were not recognized initially by the progenitors.[19]

Furthermore, as Rosenberg has stressed (1974), it is misleading to assume that the supply of new technology was very elastic so that demand conditions set the "output" of technological change. It is tautological that cost-reducing innovations will be sought after and adopted irrespective of the size of the market; competition forces firms to minimize costs. But is there strong evidence that an increase in demand will result in an increase in inventive activity? Schmookler's results seem to bear this out, but his dependent variable is patenting, not invention nor adoption of an innovation.[20] In fact, there is some evidence indicating increased efforts on technological improvement in times of reduced demand (see Schöller, 1948; Brown, 1957; Rosenberg, 1969). While this line of reasoning has its problems as well and the entire debate is highly speculative, it underlines the weakness of a theory that associates technological change with increasing (or simply "large") demand. Even if the supply of new knowlege were highly responsive to changes in demand, the basic problem of the *primum mobile* remains. If technological change occurred when "demand conditions were ripe" (as Lilley has put it), what changed in this respect in the late eighteenth century? As was shown in section I, most of the traditional sources of demand expansion were of negligible size.

If necessity was indeed the mother of invention, surely the conception was no case of parthenogenesis. A frequently employed notion in this context is that of "bottlenecks" or "challenge and response." To the extent that what is meant here is technology's "responding" to demand, it has been discussed above. But there is a more sophisticated interpretation of this idea in terms of "technological bottlenecks" (Hughes, 1959, pp. 335–36; Rosenberg, 1969; David, 1975, pp. 82–83). Some find it useful to distinguish between external bottlenecks which pass through the market mechanism, and internal imbalances which take place at the level of the firm, but this is immaterial for the present purpose. The essence of the argument can be sketched as follows. Suppose a firm or an industry produces a good X by means of two perfectly complementary processes, a and b. The factors employed are L_a and K_a in process a, and L_b and K_b in process b. Total initial output is thus given as

$$X_0 = \min[a(L_a, K_a), b(L_b, K_b)] .$$

Now suppose that a technological breakthrough occurs which increases the productivity of both factors in process a by a factor of $1 + \alpha$. Due to the strict complementarity of the two processes, however, output will not rise initially at all; a bottleneck in process b has emerged. Obviously any innovation that will raise the productivity of the factors in b by a factor of $1 + \alpha$ or less will be translated directly in an equiproportional growth in output. One could surmise that in this case the incentive to innovate would be especially high, whether the bottleneck is external or internal. But one should not forget that an alternative solution exists to the "imbalance" created, namely the reallocation of labor and capital from process a to process b. In the present example, simple calculations show the reallocated amount, R, to be:

$$R = \frac{\alpha L_a L_b}{L_a + (1 + \alpha)L_b}$$

for labor and a similar quantity for capital. When will a "bottleneck" result in a technological breakthrough and when will it result in a reallocation of factors? Unfortunately we have no good theory that will predict this. It seems reasonable that the ultimate result will depend on the supply side of technology, that is, whether and at what cost the existing stock of scientific and technical knowledge is capable of solving the bottleneck.[21] In addition, it is likely to depend equally on the cost and time involved in reshuffling the factors of production. As reallocation is, by comparison, a relatively continuous process, whereas inventions are more or less discrete events, it is reasonable to suggest that the more time passes without a technical resolution, the more actual reshuffling of resources will take place, gradually lessening the extraordinary pay-off of a technical breakthrough. Many cases can be cited in which apparent "bottlenecks" were solved by reallocation of resources before technological changes altered the required input ratios again. Those "bottlenecks" that were resolved by a spectacular masterstroke such as Eli Whitney's or William Perkin's are likely to receive better coverage in the literature than resource allocations, which tend to be more gradual and evolutionary. An example of the latter is the production of energy in the second half of the nineteenth century. Output of coal increased at an annual rate of 2.5 percent in Great Britain between 1854 and 1911, and even faster in the United States and Germany. The increased demand for energy generated by rapid growth created a bottleneck in coal mining, which was highly labor-intensive. Yet there were few major technological breakthroughs in coal mining, especially in England.[22] The mining of coal continued to depend on arduous manual labor under exhausting and perilous conditions. The "bottleneck" was resolved by a reallocation of resources (Taylor, 1960, pp. 62–64). The proportion of male workers in mining and quarrying in Great Britain rose consistently from 4.2 percent in 1841 to 9.2 percent in 1911. In the United States the proportion of miners in the labor force rose from 1.2 percent to 2.8 percent between 1850 and 1910; in Germany the proportion rose from .9 percent to 2.8 percent in the same period. About two thirds of all mine workers were employed in coal or lignite mines. Another example is cotton, often cited as the prime case of an industry in which technological change occurred in "compulsive sequences." It is rather arbitrary to cite the technological solutions of the "bottlenecks" in dyeing, carding, weaving, and spinning, while ignoring that similar problems existed in the planting and picking of cotton at one end of the process, and the tailoring of clothes at the other end. Bottlenecks here were resolved by reallocation, not invention.

Repeating the words "challenge and response" endlessly constitutes no more of a theory of technological change than Oscar Wilde's parrot's "supply and demand" constituted a theory of prices. As long as challenges occur without a forthcoming response, while other major developments occur without discernible stimuli, the "bottleneck theory" ought to be treated with utmost caution. In any event, the "challenge and response" or "compulsive sequence" mechanism is a weak defense of the Gilboy thesis. After all, even if technology did respond positively to the emergence of "bottlenecks," such a pattern of technological progress is essentially a description of the precise operation of the supply side rather than a "link" between supply and demand.

More powerful in the present context is the argument that views the new technology as a shift in cost curves in such a way as to reduce average cost only at a given level of output; that is, the new technique is subject to economies of scale. The Industrial Revolution implied a manifold increase in plant size in manufacturing and transportation. Central power sources, a more sophisticated division of labor, and efficient supervision and discipline imposed on factory workers brought about an unprecedented increase in firm scale. Hence demand conditions *could* have been important in determining where and when the shift to the new technique occurred, and whether its full potentialities were exploited. What is necessary for this line of reasoning is that the optimal plant size is large with respect to the extent of the market. More precisely, the crucial variable is the ratio of the horizontal distance of the demand curve from the vertical axis at the minimum cost price to the output at which this minimum cost is attained. If this ratio is less than one, the scale economies are not fully realized on account of insufficient demand. Even if the ratio is larger than unity but still small, insufficient competition may slow down growth by reducing overall efficiency. The question whether demand factors could have operated in this fashion is particularly complicated because Europe was, comparatively speaking, a well-integrated economy, so that economies of scale could lead to specialization of large economies in goods in which increasing returns were important. In other words, if country A produced goods under conditions of economies to scale, country B would experience growth, too, if it could import the goods from A at a cheaper price.

It is not an easy task to substantiate the case for increasing returns in manufacturing anywhere before, say, 1870.[23] Rigorous empirical tests of microeconomic data for early European industry are unavailable. But most econometric studies for American data seem to indicate that the hypothesis of no increasing returns cannot be rejected (David, 1975, pp. 142–43; Weiss, 1976, pp. 39–41). There are simpler ways to measure increasing returns than estimating production functions. An early study by G.T. Jones (1933) assigned a very modest role to scale economies in Britain for the period 1850–1920, and there is no reason to believe that before 1850 the situation was any different.[24] The alleged existence of economies to scale in the Lancashire cotton industry is criticized in a 1977 article by Gatrell, who concludes that "size in itself guaranteed neither efficiency in good times nor viability in bad . . . one may be most impressed by the ability of small, not to say middle-sized, units to exploit their opportunities in an increasingly competitive industry" (p. 125). A suggestive but not entirely unambiguous procedure is to argue that if there had been industries in which potential scale economies were present but in part unrealized due to inadequate demand, a process of concentration should have taken place in these industries, possibly resulting eventually in the emergence of "natural" monopolies. There is very little evidence for such phenomena anywhere in Europe before 1850—and certainly none before 1760. One—admittedly rough—indication is simply to look at the number and size of firms active in manufacturing. In 1834, there were 1134 cotton mills in

Britain, which rose to 1932 in 1850, stabilizing around 2500 in the 1860s.[25] In Ghent there were 29 cotton spinning firms in 1817 (a crisis year), which rose to 48 firms in 1826 and 78 in 1839 (Heuschling, 1841, p. 96n; Coppejans-Desmedt, 1962). Lévy-Leboyer (1964, pp. 170–71) has observed the proliferation of small firms in the textile industry in France. In the iron industry, similarly, there is little evidence of concentration; as late as the mid-1850s British iron works were small and dispersed.[26]

It seems unwarranted to rely on scale economies to rescue the Gilboy hypothesis. Scale economies were prominent on the level of the firm, and yet could be relatively insignificant for the economy as a whole if most firms operated on the horizontal segments of their cost curves. The most significant exception to this rule is inland transportation, especially canals and railroads. Here a combination of large fixed costs and non-tradeability would be consistent with the argument that in the absence of a high level of demand there would have been much less reduction of transportation costs. Some gains might have been made on account of increased interfirm specialization, but evidence for such vertical disintegration is not strong. Stigler's rash assertion that England's early start was because "as the largest economy in the world it could carry specialization further than any other country" (1968, p. 158) not only puts the cart before the horses, but has no basis in the evidence. An alternative approach proposed by Burnet (1972, pp. 424–28) maintains that the supply curve is continuously downward sloping, so that the entire growth process is to be viewed as an explosive disequilibrium process. In this way, he suggests, one could lend theoretical legitimacy to Rostow's take-off.[27] But Burnet's theory does not distinguish sufficiently between historical and Marshallian supply curves. The "historical" supply curve contains technological progress, resource discoveries, and capital accumulation, which bring about shifts of the Marshallian supply curve. Burnet's bold statement that "the entrepreneur lucky enough to discover a virgin field of consumer demand can look forward to a golden age of self generating growth" is thus largely based on a misconception, although local gains are of course to be expected.

It appears that the preponderance of the idea that economies of scale were somehow crucial in spite of the absence of evidence is caused by a misunderstanding. In many cases an invention was followed by additional, gradual progress that resolved relatively minor but vital bugs in the application of the new technique (Rosenberg, 1972, esp. pp. 10–14). These subsequent improvements are often mistaken as increasing returns—shifts of the supply curve are likely to be identified erroneously as points lying on a given supply curve when they follow a major invention as aftershocks.[28] It is possible, however, that the opportunities for "learning by doing" type of technological progress were far larger in those industries for which demand was comparatively elastic, and that the learning process was chiefly determined by the quantities produced. "Learning by doing," it appears, is the most convincing prima facie nexus between the structure of demand and the rate of growth of the economy. Whether the correlation between demand elasticity and "learning by doing" potentialities actually existed is an empirical issue.[29]

We return to economies of scale. As Allyn Young noted, it would be wasteful to make a hammer to drive a single nail. But one is hard-pressed to come up with many examples in which the number of nails was so small as to obviate the purchase of at least one hammer. And even when this was the case, could nations not borrow each other's hammers? Perhaps Argentina was too small to found a special school for railroad engineers. For that very reason the Argentine railroad system was built by British engineers and the trains hauled by British locomotives. The Belgian textile industry in the 1840s imported its largest machines, while producing most of the smaller machines itself. The average capacity of a domestically produced steam engine in the East Flanders industry was about 50 percent smaller than that of imported engines. In Verviers the capacity of imported engines was more than three times that of domestic ones (Royaume de Belgique, 1846, p. 48). The one Belgian machine manufacturer who produced largely for export markets, Cockerill's works in Seraing, made machines with a capacity of 145 horsepower. His competitors, who worked largely for the domestic market, made much smaller machines—an average of 20 horsepower (Lévy-Leboyer, 1964, p. 361). Today, Belgium is perhaps too small to build its own civilian airplanes, so it buys them in the United States. Luxembourg, which is even smaller, may not find it profitable to operate its own airlines, so the *Luxembourgeois* fly Sabena.

III.   A Macroeconomic Analysis

An alternative interpretation of the Gilboy thesis maintains that an expansion of demand for industrial goods does not necessarily have to come at the expense of other goods. This would be the case if the preindustrial economy had large amounts of underutilized resources. Indeed, without unemployed reserves of factors, economic expansion initiated by demand would have run into difficulties.[30] If there were large reservoirs of involuntarily unemployed labor, increases in demand would set into motion a multiplier mechanism, which, enforced by induced investment, could have led to the Industrial Revolution.[31] This view is reflected in the famous but infelicitous note on the final page of Hicks's *Value and Capital* that "the whole Industrial Revolution of the last two hundred years has been nothing but a vast secular boom, largely induced by the unparalleled rise in population." It is well known that unemployment and pauperism were widespread in preindustrial societies, and Western Europe was no exception.[32] But unemployment is by no means the same as underutilized resources. The latter would be the case only if aggregate demand were insufficient so that people willing and able to work could not find employment. In a preindustrial or early industrial economy a large amount of "natural" or frictional unemployment is to be expected.[33]

Decisive evidence of whether eighteenth- and early nineteenth-century Europe was in fact in something like Hansen's secular stagnation or Joan Robinson's "limping" golden age is not easily obtained. It is a difficult problem to distinguish in a meaningful way between voluntary and involuntary unemployment of employable workers. But there is one body of evidence that requires scrupulous attention in this context, namely the writings of the so-called mercantilist or "pre-Adamite" school. Between William Potter's *The Key to Wealth* (1650) and James Steuart's *An Inquiry into the Principles of Political Economy* (1767), a long list of political economists expressed opinions which all contain an element of Keynes's theory of aggregate demand. It is unmistakable that many of these writers thought that unemployment could be remedied by an exogenous expansion of effective demand. Keynes cited with enthusiasm Bernard de Mandeville's *Fable of the Bees*, and one could provide much more sophisticated and elaborate illustrations from such eminent writers as William Petty, Nicholas Barbon, and George Berkeley. There can be no doubt that from many points of view these writers should be viewed as precursors of Keynes.[34]

But even if we accept that these writers thought that the unemployment they were witnessing was of the Keynesian type, the issue is not settled. How can we be certain that they actually saw what they thought they saw? Coleman (1955, p. 289) Heckscher (1955, pp. 340–58), and Blaug (1968, p. 15) among others have pointed out that there are powerful alternative explanations to the observed unemployment in the preindustrial economy. One is a high preference for leisure resulting in a backward bending supply curve, which could account for much of the unemployment observed by contemporaries (Ward, 1959; Landes, 1969a, p. 59). High seasonal variance in the demand for labor combined with high adjustment and transportation costs led to widespread seasonal unemployment.[35] The importance of this factor appears to have been diminishing with the increasing availability of nonagricultural employment in agrarian communities.[36]

The above is not meant to imply that shocks and fluctuations did not have a profound impact on the level of economic activity. Harvest failures, fluctuations in exports, political upheaval, tariffs, and wars caused widespread distress and unemployment.[37] But as a *long-run* description of a normal state of affairs, involuntary unemployment in preindustrial Europe seems a dubious proposition. One reason is that in a barter economy Keynesian unemployment cannot occur. While Europe and North America were gradually becoming more monetized in the seventeenth and eighteenth centuries, they still contained large pockets of barter exchange. Moreover, in the seventeenth and eighteenth centuries, both in England and in Europe, long-term investment in capital goods was typically financed out of own funds (family loans, retained profits). This implies that investment cannot exceed *ex ante* savings, but as Heckscher pointed out, the "pure" savers who did not plow their savings back into their business had relatively few alternatives to hoarding. As capital markets improved, the gap between savings and investment narrowed. Heckscher "tests" this hypothesis by looking at secular price movements in the eighteenth and nineteenth centuries (1955, vol. 2, pp. 348–54). The tests are suggestive but not definitive, since the supply of money is not held constant.

One possible answer to the attempts to search for long-run Keynesian unemployment in pre-modern Europe is provided in the *General Theory*. Keynes's rather cavalier description of the pre-modern economy has it that:

> It is impossible to study the notions to which the mercantilists were led by their actual experiences, without perceiving that there has been a chronic tendency throughout human history for the propensity to save to be stronger than the inducement to invest. The weakness of the inducement to invest has been at all times the key to the economic problem. Today the explanation of the weakness of this inducement may chiefly lie in the extent of existing accumulations; whereas, formerly, risks and hazards of all kinds may have played a larger part [Keynes, 1936, pp. 347–48].

What Keynes overlooks is that in order to have continuous involuntary unemployment, hoarding has to exceed dishoarding over prolonged periods of time. In other words, a secular upward trend in the demand for money should be discerned. Why should such a trend occur? Keynes's explanation of "risks and hazards" explains the absolute level of the demand, but it is hard to argue that alternative assets were becoming *gradually riskier* than money. But deflationary pressures could result also if the economy was growing or monetizing, however slowly, and the consequent increment in the demand for money exceeded the growth in the money supply. Such deflationary pressures could have produced unemployment if the price level did not adjust sufficiently.

The absence of unemployment or aggregate output data excludes any direct testing of this hypothesis, but some suggestive facts cast doubt on it. First, if it is true that the demand for money for any reason rose faster than its supply, it is reasonable to suppose that interest rates would have been subject to upward pressure. Available data do not support this hypothesis: on the whole, interest rates declined during the seventeenth century, while in the eighteenth the downward trend tended to be obscured by wartime borrowing after 1740 (Homer, 1963, pp. 133–43, 155–80; DeVries, 1976, p. 211). Second, the evidence indicates that the supply of high-powered money started to grow at an accelerated rate at some point after 1680.[38] Equally important was the emergence of nonmetallic money as a means of exchange. Here one should count as money not only the notes issued by the bank of Stockholm, the Bank of England, and the American Colonies, but also bills of exchange which were increasingly made negotiable. The latter, especially, provided a true source of "inside money," making the money supply more responsive to the needs of the economy.[39] Third, if considerable involuntary unemployment had existed in preindustrial and early industrial economies, it should be expected that sudden expansions of aggregate demand should have affected output and employment in a significant way. It seems, however, that in the one test case for which evidence exists, the Napoleonic Wars, this was not the case.[40] It may thus be inferred tentatively that preindustrial and early industrial economies were as a rule *on* their transformation curves. This is not to say that in no sense were there any under-utilized resources in preindustrial Europe that could be brought into productive activity during the industrialization process. Obvious examples are a better allocation of resources due to increased efficiency of the market mechanism or the formation of additional factors of production complementary to labor. But such movements should be viewed properly as supply and not as demand-related phenomena.

IV.   Conclusions

The intention of this essay has been to examine the Gilboy hypothesis in every possible interpretation, and to decide whether we can assign an important role to demand factors in the explanation of the Industrial Revolution. Few of the various alternative interpretations withstand the scrutiny of *a priori* reasoning or empirical tests. The old schoolboy view of the Industrial Revolution as a "wave of gadgets" may not be far off the mark after all, provided we allow for "more" as well as for "better" gadgets, and we include abstract improvements such as organizational change, changes in workers' attitudes, and so forth, as "gadgets" in a wider sense.

If demand was not a "factor," what exactly was its place in the Industrial Revolution? To start with, we observe that any supply shift will affect the economy in direct proportion to the proportional size of the industry affected relative to the economy as a whole. For a once and for all fall in costs, the demand structure matters only for determining the composition of the increment in national income, but not its size. If the supply shift is a continuous process, however, the shape of the demand curve does matter, because it determines the future pattern of the relative size of the industry in question in the economy. To be more precise: if the own price elasticity is more than unity in absolute value, it can be shown that (a) the overall impact of a constant rate of cost reduction will increase over time, and (b) the spillover effects for all other goods taken together are negative. This casts a peculiar light on the role of so-called "leading sectors," which are supposed to grow due to a very elastic demand curve. Moreover, as output expands, the economy will move down into the inelastic segment of the demand curve. At that point the continuous fall in costs will result in increased demand for all goods (that is, for the good in question and for all other goods taken together), but this impact will slowly peter out over time. Something similar to this process happened in the market for textiles between 1760 and 1860. The elastic demand caused output to grow very rapidly as a response to initial price reductions, so that subsequent price reductions were applied to a much wider base.

Second, there is the stability of demand. While the absolute level of demand for industrial goods cannot be used to explain the timing and speed of the industrialization process, heavy fluctuations in demand had an adverse effect on growth, due to the substantial costs of resource reallocation, the acquisition of new information, and so forth. Wars, revolutions, blockades, tariffs, harvest failures, and other unanticipated catastrophes inhibited growth not so much through the first moments of the demand function parameters as through the second moments.

A third way in which demand-related factors could have been important in determining the speed and timing of the industrialization process is through their determination of the intersectoral terms of trade. As a consequence of a change in the terms of trade, income distribution may change. For example, income may be redistributed from industrial workers and capitalists to landowners. It is, in fact, possible that industrialization could lead to "immiseration" of the modern sector in a way that is analogous to the well-known possibility of "immiseration" of a country increasing its exports. Note, however, that "immiserizing growth" can occur at the level of the economy, but not at the level of the entire world. Similarly, in a closed economy it can occur at the level of a sector, but the economy as a whole is better off. Still, if the modern sector has a higher savings propensity or lower risk averseness than the other sector, such a worsening of the terms of trade may affect the rate of growth (Mokyr, 1976, chap.7).

To summarize, the traditional notion that supply and demand were somehow symmetric in the industrialization process is unfounded. The determination of "when," "where," and "how fast" are to be sought first and foremost in supply, not demand-related processes. Statisticians warn that error can take the form of excessive credulity ("type II") as well as excessive scepticism ("type I"). The wide and uncritical acceptance of the Gilboy thesis is an example of a type II error that has crept into our textbooks and journal articles. It is hoped that the present essay will administer to the demand theory a dose of well-deserved compensating scepticism.

Appendix A

Assume an economy with the following characteristics: (a) It produces two goods, agricultural goods (A) and nonagricultural goods (M). (b) The two goods are consumed by farmers and nonfarmers. (c) The demand for agricultural goods has a price elasticity of less than one in absolute value for both the farmer's and the nonfarmer's demand functions. (d) Both goods are normal; that is, all income elasticities are positive. (e) The supply of manufactured goods is a function of relative prices, but (f) the supply of agricultural goods depends in the short run only on weather conditions.

Proposition: An exogenous decline in agricultural goods due to harvest failures will always result in a fall in the demand for nonagricultural goods.

PROOF

There are four different demand functions in this system. Let the subscript 1 denote the demand of farmers for agricultural goods, subscript 2 the demand of nonfarmers for agricultural goods, subscript 3 the demand of farmers for nonagricultural goods, and subscript 4 the demand of nonfarmers for nonagricultural goods. The demand system can thus be written as

$$Q_i(D) = f_i(Y'_j, P_A, P_M) \qquad i = 1,2,3,4 \tag{1}$$

$$j = A \text{ for } i = 1,3$$
$$M \text{ for } i = 2,4$$

where $Y'_j (j = A,M)$ is nominal income, P_A and P_M the money prices of agricultural and nonagricultural goods, and $Q(D)$ means the quantity demanded. Assuming that all demand functions are homogeneous of degree zero, we divide everything by P_M, thus using nonagricultural goods as our numeraire. Thus

$$Q_i(D) = f_i(Y_j, P, 1) \qquad i = 1,2,3,4 \tag{2}$$

$$j = A \text{ for } i = 1,3$$
$$M \text{ for } i = 2,4$$

where Y_j is income in terms of M-goods and $P = P_A/P_M$.

The price elasticities of the functions described by equation (2) will be denoted by b_i, $i = 1 \ldots 4$. Note that by assumption $-1 < b_1,b_2 < 0$. The *market* demand functions have demand elasticities which are weighted averages of the sectoral elasticities. Let θ_i $(i=A,M)$ denote the proportion of good i consumed by the producing sector. Then

$$\delta = \theta_A b_1 + (1 - \theta_A)b_2 \tag{3}$$

is the overall price elasticity for agricultural goods with respect to P, and

$$\beta = (1 - \theta_M)b_3 + \theta_M b_2 \tag{4}$$

is the overall price elasticity for nonagricultural goods with respect to P, and should be interpreted as a cross elasticity. Finally we note that

$$Y_A = PA \tag{5}$$

denotes agricultural income, where A is exogenous, and

$$Y_M = M(P) \tag{6}$$

denotes industrial income. M is a function of P, that is, the supply of M-goods can have a positive price elasticity. This is expressed in γ, the elasticity of M with respect to P which is negative (since P contains P_M in its denominator), since some agricultural goods are used as inputs into manufacturing.

Let us now define $D = Q_3(D) + Q_4(D)$. We have to show that the elasticity of D with respect to A is positive under the assumptions stated. Using the chain rule, we obtain

$$\frac{dD}{dA} = \frac{\partial f_3}{\partial Y_A} \left[\frac{dP}{dA} A + P \right] + \frac{\partial f_3}{\partial P} \frac{dP}{dA} \tag{7}$$

$$+ \frac{\partial f_4}{\partial M} \frac{dM}{dP} \frac{dP}{dA} + \frac{\partial f_4}{\partial P} \frac{dP}{dA}$$

which can be written in terms of elasticities

$$\frac{dD}{dA} \frac{A}{D} = a_3(1 - \theta_M) \left[\frac{1}{\delta} + 1 \right] + b_3 \frac{1}{\delta} (1 - \theta_M) \tag{8}$$

$$+ a_4\gamma \frac{1}{\delta} \theta_M + b_4 \frac{1}{\delta} \theta_M$$

where δ, b_3, and b_4 are as defined in equations (3) and (4) and the a's are the corresponding income elasticities.[41]

Assume that the theorem is false, that is, equation (8) is negative. By multiplying the right-hand side of (8) by δ, it can be seen that (8) will be negative if

$$a_3(1 - \theta_M) [1 + \delta] + b_3 (1 - \theta_M) + a_4\theta_M\gamma + b_4\theta_M > 0 \text{ (since } \delta < 0). \tag{9}$$

From equation (4) we substitute into (9)

$$a_3(1 - \theta_M)[1 + \delta] + \beta + a_4\theta_M\gamma > 0. \tag{10}$$

The relationship between δ and β can be expressed by using the Cournot aggregation relation.

$$\beta = -(\delta + 1) \frac{PA}{M} \tag{11}$$

Substituting (11) into (10) we obtain

$$(1 + \delta) \left[a_3(1 - \theta_M) - \frac{PA}{M} \right] + a_4\theta_M\gamma > 0. \tag{12}$$

Since γ is negative and $\delta \rangle -1$, this implies

$$a_3 \rangle \frac{PA}{M} \frac{1}{1 - \theta_M} = \frac{PA}{Q_3} \equiv \frac{Y_A}{Q_3} \tag{13}$$

using the definition $1 - \theta_M \equiv \dfrac{Q_3}{M}$.

Equation (13) can be written as

$$\frac{\partial Q_3}{\partial Y_A} \frac{Y_A}{Q_3} \rangle \frac{Y_A}{Q_3} \tag{14}$$

which implies

$$\frac{\partial Q_3}{\partial Y_A} \rangle 1. \tag{15}$$

Equation (15) says that the farmers' marginal propensity to consume manufacturing goods exceeds unity. That means that if their incomes increase by one penny, they will increase their spending on manufacturing goods by more than one penny; in other words, their consumption of agricultural goods will be reduced as their income rises. But we assumed that all goods were normal, and hence there is a contradiction. This completes the proof.

Appendix B

Proposition: All other things equal, population growth will increase the demand of those goods the income elasticity of which is lower than the reciprocal of the elasticity of non-labor in the production function.

PROOF:

Let total national income be denoted as

$$Y = f(L), \ f' \rangle \ 0, \ f'' \langle \ 0 \tag{1}$$

Let y be income per capita, Y/L, and let the demand for any good by one individual be

$$q(D) = g(y). \tag{2}$$

Total demand is thus

$$Q(D) = Lg(y). \tag{3}$$

Differentiating (3) with respect to L yields

$$\frac{dQ(D)}{dL} = g(y) + L\left[g'(y) \frac{dy}{dL}\right]. \tag{4}$$

By using the chain rule and simplifying we obtain

$$\frac{dQ(D)}{dL} = g(y) + g'(y)(f' - y) \tag{5}$$

which can be written in elasticity form

$$\frac{dQ(D)}{dL} \frac{L}{Q(D)} = 1 - g'(y - f') \frac{L}{Q} = 1 - \frac{(y - f')}{y} \frac{g'(y)y}{g} \tag{6}$$

which will be positive if

$$\frac{y}{y - f'} \rangle \frac{g'(y)y}{g}. \tag{7}$$

The left-hand side of (7) is the reciprocal of the share of non-labor in national income, while the right-hand side is the income elasticity of the good under consideration. This completes the proof.

Notes

[1] I would like to express my thanks to Donald N. McCloskey, on whose very elastic supply of knowledge in economics, history, and econography I have liberally drawn. Others who have been of great help with comments and suggestions include Pekka Ahtiala, Reuven Brenner, Karl de Schweinitz, Stefano Fenoaltea, Jonathan Hughes, Eric L. Jones, Glenn C. Loury, Jacob Metzer, F. Michael Scherer, and Richard O. Zerbe.

[2] Very explicit reiterations of Gilboy's thesis can be found, for example, in Eversley, 1967; John, 1967; Deane, 1969, p. 34; and Landes, 1969a, p. 46. A restatement is in Crouzet, 1967a, pp. 113–14. A variation on the same theme is in Georgescu-Roegen, 1971, pp. 246–47. Doubts concerning the demand hypothesis were sounded by Rostow, 1975, pp. 14, 129, 172–73, and in a slightly different context by McCloskey, 1970.

[3] The evidence for France is summarized in Labrousse, 1933, pts.II, III, IV, esp. pp. 137–66. For the nineteenth century, too, the timing does not work. The period usually associated with the most rapid economic growth in France (1840–70) was also one of rising wheat prices. See ibid., 1933, p.141; and B.R. Mitchell, 1975, p.742.

[4] Ippolito's overall conclusion is that the agricultural depression of 1730–50 did not constitute a major source of demand for industrial goods either. It should be emphasized that the estimates do not truly reflect the contribution of the agricultural revolution (i.e., shifts of the supply curve of agricultural goods) to the Industrial Revolution. This would be the case only if the supply curve of agricultural goods were perfectly elastic (as is assumed by Ippolito) or if demand were stationary. Neither of these assumptions seems plausible; hence, what is measured is the impact of price changes only, without further identification of their source.

[5] Let the demand function have the form $Q_M(D) = Y^a P_A^b P_M^c$. This means that we can write the relationship between the demand for industrial goods and the relative price $P = P_A/P_M$ as

$$\frac{\Delta Q_M(D)}{Q_M(D)} = \left[\frac{\Delta P}{P} + 1 \right]^b - 1.$$

An approximate value of b can be estimated by using the so-called Cournot relationship between the own and the cross elasticities of demand:

$$\gamma_A \epsilon_A + (1 - \gamma_A)^b = -\gamma_A$$

ϵ_A is the own price elasticity of demand for agricultural goods, and γ_A is the share of agriculture in total output. A reasonable estimate of γ_A would put it at around $1/3$. The value of ϵ_A is unknown but is generally believed to be less than one in absolute value. Setting it equal to $-.3$ and $-.7$, we obtain estimates of b between $-.35$ and $-.15$.

[6] The relative prices underlying the calculations were obtained and computed from a number of series that overlap to some extent, or which had to be converted to relative prices using some assumptions about weights. The procedure followed was in each case to choose the extreme estimates, thus obtaining upper and lower bounds.

[7] A general discussion of the impact of agricultural fluctuations on the English economy is in Gould, 1962. Gould's attempts to explain the price movement by the operation and later repeal of the Corn Laws in the eighteenth century cannot be viewed as definitive: the export bounties were repealed in 1773, and it is hard to see how that could help raising prices.

[8] According to Freudenberger (1974), the effective labor input per worker doubled during the second half of the eighteenth century.

[9] A longer list of possible links between exports and growth is suggested by Caves, 1971. Some of the mechanisms suggested by Caves work in the wrong direction, however, and other nexuses seem far from easy to test in the case of Europe's industrialization, 1750–1850. For instance, does an expansion in exports stimulate and create *ex nihilo* entrepreneurial talent and initiative, or does it simply divert those resources away from alternative uses? Do increased exports stimulate the formation of overhead capital (e.g., harbor facilities), or should this be viewed as an additional cost imposed on the export-oriented economy?

[10] Exports of woolen goods remained virtually unchanged between 1730–39 and 1780–89, while output of woolen cloth milled in West Riding grew by 396 percent (broadcloth, 1735–85) and 97 percent (narrow cloth, 1739–85). Exports of tin grew by 53 percent (1730/39–1780/89), while output increased by 86 percent. Between 1750 and 1790 exports of coal rose by 60 percent, while coal output more than doubled.

[11] A similar conclusion has been reached by Paul Bairoch, who states flatly that the industrial revolution reached quite an advanced stage in England before seeking foreign outlets. See Bairoch, 1974, p. 569.

[12] The colonial market version of the demand hypothesis is even less convincing for other European economies. Spain, Portugal, and the Netherlands—all late industrializers—had access to substantial colonial markets. Belgium and Switzerland, on the other hand, were confined to the demand structure dictated by the competitive world market, and yet underwent an industrial revolution before 1850. Ireland could have benefited from the enormous demand exerted by Great Britain and its colonial empire, yet Ireland failed to industrialize.

[13] Deane, 1969, p. 34; Murphy, 1971, p. 333. Gilboy herself expressed doubts about the importance of population growth by itself.

[14] Deane and Cole, 1969, p. 255. King's estimates for 1688 indicate that the share of labor income was only 39 percent, which would make the critical income elasticity equal to 1.64.

[15] This is true even in the case of a monopoly in which the industry and the firm are the same. A monopolist will always operate on the elastic segment of the demand curve facing him.

[16] The seminal article is Kennedy, 1964. For a review of the ensuing debate, see David, 1975.

[17] The classic work is Schmookler, 1966, esp. pp. 88–103, 202–9. See also, for example, Habakkuk, 1955, pp. 150–51; Landes, 1969a, pp. 77, 137; and Lilley, 1973. The debate is admirably summed up in Musson, 1972.

[18] The list of inventors who failed to capitalize on their major inventions is very long, with Cort, Crompton, Goodyear, Whitney, W. Kelly, Lenoir, and Ericsson being some of the most notorious examples. Eric Schiff, 1971, has shown that there is little evidence to support the hypothesis that a national patent system makes a significant difference in the rate of industrialization. For a skeptical evaluation of the impact of the patent system in Britain, see Ashton, 1948, p. 11.

[19] Edison, for example, "failed to understand the future of his invention [the phonograph] as part of the world of art and entertainment. He thought of it mainly as a modern dictaphone, [or] a speaking family album, to preserve the speeches of great statesmen, to teach languages" (Hughes, 1973, p. 175). The divergence between the social and the private rates of return on innovations does not seem to have vanished over time. Also see Mansfield, et al., 1977.

[20] For critiques of Schmookler's findings see, e.g., Jewkes, Sawers, and Stillerman, 1969, pp. 210–11; and Musson, 1972, pp. 25–29.

[21] A good illustration is the case of steel. It has been argued that Henry Bessemer's attention was first directed to steel when a cast iron cannon was unable to fire a new projectile he devised, and that the Bessemer process was therefore a result of a "technical imbalance." It is noteworthy that a much more costly imbalance existed in constructing railroad tracks from wrought iron, which had to be replaced frequently. Experiments conducted in England indicated that steel rails could outlast wrought iron rails by a factor of seven. Fogel has estimated that 55 percent of all wrought iron rails laid wore out in the first ten years. Since the life of equipment was much longer and the life of the area-clearing infinite, the inability to produce cheap steel constituted a severe imbalance—which for the first 40 years of the railroad was solved by factor reallocation, not by the invention of cheap steel.

[22] See, e.g., Derry and Williams, 1960, pp. 473–74; Taylor, 1960, p. 58.

[23] Even today, there is considerable difficulty in interpreting the evidence whether national market size conveys a clear-cut advantage or not, although it is likely that in some industries small nations fail to achieve scale economies or sufficient competition. Cf. Scherer, 1970, pp. 93–95.

[24] Jones's results are upper-bound estimates of the importance of scale economies, since he is unable to separate scale effects from technological change. Still, he finds an "observed elasticity" (i.e., the proportional growth of output divided by the proportional fall in price) of about 5 for the Lancashire cotton industry between 1850 and 1870. This implies a degree of homogeneity of 1.25, assuming a Cobb-Douglas production function. Sandberg has disputed the accuracy of Jones's index and insists that costs in the British cotton industry fell substantially between 1885 and 1914. He attributes this decline in costs to technological change, however, not to scale economies. See Sandberg, 1974, pp. 93–119, 131–33. See also Gould, 1972, pp. 229–35.

[25] A summary of these figures, collected from various Parliamentary Papers, is provided in Blaug, 1961, p. 379. The average size of the 1105 cotton manufacturers surveyed in the Horner Report of 1841 was 175 workers, with the median size almost exactly 100 workers. See Gatrell, 1977, p. 98.

[26] See, e.g., Burn, 1940, pp. 191, 194–95; Birch, 1967, p. 205. The number of firms engaged in iron production mentioned in the Coal Commission report was 342, of which 187 engaged in pig iron production. See Kurimoto, 1974. Kurimoto concludes that "small scale firms had not only overwhelming weights in number but also excellent activity in operating equipments [sic]."

[27] Rostow himself is lukewarm about this attempt to formalize his take-off, and notes correctly that Burnet's falling supply curve has to level off somewhere. See Rostow, 1975, p. 141.

[28] An interesting case in point is the debate about the adoption of the reaper in antebellum Midwest grain farming. See Olmstead, 1975.

[29] The one case that has been investigated in this respect is the New England cotton industry. Robert Zevin has found that demand was indeed elastic (the elasticity being between −2 and −3 in the 1820s, falling to about −1.5 after 1833). Paul David has found evidence for "learning by doing," although he views the learning more as a function of time than of accumulated output. See Zevin, 1971, p. 135, and David, 1975, p. 167.

[30] The same point is made by McCloskey, 1970, p. 455.

[31] See, for example, Habakkuk, 1955, p.153; Murphy, 1971, p. 387; de Vries, 1976, pp. 177, 241. The assumption that the early industrial economy was subject to serious Keynesian unemployment is made also by Anderson, 1974.

[32] See esp. Coleman, 1955.

[33] For a view that attributes "unemployment" to dietary inadequacies, see Freudenberger and Cummins, 1976.

[34] See, for example, Pauling, 1951; Grampp, 1952; Hutchison, 1953; Sen, 1957; and Vickers, 1959.

[35] Seasonal unemployment struck agriculture and industry alike, since weather conditions affected water and wind mills, road conditions, bleach fields, and so on. John Law, in his *Money and Trade* (1705), seemed to think that seasonal unemployment could get as high as 50 percent. A 1752 pamphlet cited by Mantoux places the proportion of time in which journeymen tailors were unemployed at about 40 percent. (1961, p. 71n). In the mid-eighteenth century construction workers were idle at least "four or five months in the year" (Campbell, 1747, pp. 103–4, rpt. in George, 1923, pp. 32–33). Seasonal unemployment was particularly severe where rural industry was absent and the crops not diversified, particularly in Ireland. As late as 1836, G.C. Lewis noted that two thirds of the Irish work force was not employed all year round, and that this irregularity was the true cause of poverty in Ireland (p. 312). Other examples are cited by Ashton, 1959, p. 6; Ashton, 1972, pp. 202–3. Wages fluctuated seasonally, so that it is not easy to distinguish between voluntary unemployment (i.e., consumption of leisure) and involuntary seasonal unemployment.

[36] A possible explanation of the widely observed phenomenon of "unemployment" in preindustrial Europe could be built on the idea of structural unemployment. If the marginal productivity of labor was lower than some accepted minimum of subsistence (possibly zero), it follows that people willing to work cannot find employment. For a precise formulation of this idea, see Eckaus, 1958. Under these circumstances a change in the composition of demand could reduce unemployment if demand shifted toward comparatively more labor-intensive goods, thus increasing the total demand for labor. William Petty's recommendation to employ idle workers to "build a useless pyramid upon Salisbury Plain, bring the stones at Stonehenge to Towerhill or the like" sounds reasonable on this background. It is quite clear, however, that such compositional effects were becoming rapidly less important as the Industrial Revolution proceeded and industrial production was becoming more capital-intensive. The argument could, however, go a long way in explaining the rapid expansion of domestic industry before 1750, which was more labor-intensive than factory production.

[37] See, for example, Mokyr and Savin, 1976.

[38] The best indicator is still total output of the silver and gold mines in Mexico and South America collected by von Humboldt and published in 1809 in his *Essai politique sur le Royaume de Nouvelle-Espagne*. These figures were refined and completed by Soetbeer, 1879. Soetbeer's figures show a marked acceleration of bullion output after 1680. Moreover, if his figures are corrected in the ways suggested by W. Lexis (1879), the acceleration is even more marked. The results of applying Lexis's critique to Soetbeer's figures are shown in Table N4.1.

Table N4.1   Total World Annual Output of Bullion (in millions of piastres)

Year	Soetbeer estimate	Revised Soetbeer estimate	Year	Soetbeer estimate	Revised Soetbeer estimate
1601–20	99.9	81.9	1701–20	99.8	89.5
1621–40	94.0	76.9	1721–40	130.8	120.5
1641–60	90.4	74.1	1741–60	164.6	155.3
1661–80	86.5	71.2	1761–80	175.3	162.4
1681–1700	91.6	76.4	1781–1800	207.8	192.4

[39] Braudel and Spooner, 1967, pp. 386–87. It is worth noting that Braudel and Spooner claim, albeit without precise evidence, that not only the supply of money rose considerably in the eighteenth century, but the demand for money in fact declined. Cf. ibid., p. 450.

[40] For details, see Mokyr and Savin, 1976, pp. 210–23.

[41] The parameter δ is not precisely a demand elasticity. Rather, it is the elasticity of an envelope curve of shifting demand curves. An exogenous decline of A causes an initial rise in P as the economy moves up along the demand curve. In a general equilibrium context, however, δ incorporates the secondary effect produced by the decline in M (from eq. 6), causing a leftward shift in the demand for agricultural goods, partially offsetting the rise in P.

5

Industrial Revolution in England and France: Some Thoughts on the Question "Why Was England First?"

N.F.R. CRAFTS[1]

I

A major concern of economic historians since World War II has been to interpret the process of industrialization in now developed countries. One prominent line of approach has been to compare the experience of the European economies in the eighteenth century, and much of the inquiry has been conceptualized along the following lines. "The Industrial Revolution poses two problems: (1) Why did this first breakthrough to a modern industrial system take place in Western Europe? and (2) Why, within this European experience, did change occur when and where it did?" (Landes, 1969a, p. 12).

This comparative approach has been seen as a particularly valuable way of yielding insights into the process of economic growth in general and the causes of the English Industrial Revolution in particular. Thus Crouzet argues that "The economic historian interested in the key problem of growth is bound to find the comparative approach particularly fruitful. A systematic comparison of the eighteenth-century English economy with that of another country—and France as the leading continental power at that time seems the obvious choice—should bring out more clearly what factors were peculiar to England and might have determined what is a unique phenomenon, the English Industrial Revolution of the eighteenth century" (Crouzet, 1967b, p. 139). Since Crouzet wrote, much of the literature has accepted the usefulness of the question "Why was England first?" and the specific question "Why did England experience the onset of the Industrial Revolution before France?" has been promoted to a position of great prominence.[2]

There is by now an extensive literature offering a wide variety of responses to these questions. The answers seem to fall into three types. First, there are studies which

Reprinted from the *Economic History Review*, Vol. 30, No. 3 (August 1977), pp. 421–41. Includes a "Comment" by W.W. Rostow and a "Reply" by N.F.R. Crafts, in *ibid*, Vol. 31, No. 4 (November 1978), pp. 610–14. Reprinted by permission of the Economic History Society.

single out a single crucial reason. To cite just a couple of examples we find views as diverse as those of Kemp ("if one overriding reason can be given for the slower transformation of the continent . . . it must be the continued prevalence of the traditional agrarian structures" (Kemp, 1969, p. 8)) and Hagen ("the differences in personality rather than differential circumstances are the central explanation of Britain's primacy . . . the Industrial Revolution occurred first in England and Wales . . . because British people were inwardly different from those of the continent" (Hagen, 1967, p. 37)).

In reaction against the single factor explanation two positions have commonly been adopted. One is to regard the English Industrial Revolution as the result of a previous period of general economic growth; thus Hartwell argues: "Do we need *an explanation* of the industrial revolution? Could it not be the culmination of a most unspectacular process, the consequence of a long period of slow economic growth? . . . Cannot the industrial revolution be explained more plausibly as the outcome of a process of balanced growth?" (Hartwell, 1965, p. 78). The other is to list a large number of favourable factors, as, for example, does Kranzberg: "In short, there was no single factor which can account for Britain's leadership in the Industrial Revolution. Instead, it was a multiplicity of factors—technological, social, economic, political, and cultural—which came together in the mid-eighteenth century to provide the stimulus for industrial advance. In all these factors, Britain had a slight advantage over France. But the advantage was qualitative rather than quantitative" (Kranzberg, 1967, p. 229).

None of these attempted solutions to the question of why England and not France has been very satisfactory and in their recent book Milward and Saul attacked them all. They argued that "attempts to isolate single factors which can explain the fact that the first industrial revolution occurred where it did . . . tend to break down before the enormous diversity of the continental economies. The more their history in the eighteenth century is considered, the greater appears the difficulty of finding one single factor in the British economy not present in some continental economies" (Milward and Saul, 1973, pp. 32–3). They also pointed out that "most recent research into the French economy in the eighteenth century has demonstrated that the increase in industrial output per head in the eighteenth century was probably faster than that in Britain . . . [so that] this general explanation no longer seems valid." They also maintained that the laundry-list approach typified by Kranzberg is "too tautological to be of much value" (ibid., pp. 31, 33). Milward and Saul went on to suggest a new direction for search for a solution to the puzzling question of England's primacy and contended that "Previous centuries of development determined that the industrial revolution happened not in Europe's wealthiest, most populous, most powerful and most productive country, France, but in an island off its shores" (ibid., p.38).

This article presents a critical reaction to the recent literature on the comparative economic history of England and France in the eighteenth century. In doing so it accepts Milward and Saul's criticisms of the existing attempts to explain England's primacy in experiencing the onset of the Industrial Revolution. However, the position taken below is that the question "Why was England first?" is misconceived and should be discarded rather than new solutions being sought. In particular, it is argued that the question "Why was England first?" should be distinguished from the separate question "Why did the Industrial Revolution occur in the eighteenth century?" and that the failure to do so may have been an important obstacle to an adequate interpretation of the economic history of France in the eighteenth century.

The underlying view of industrialization adopted here is that economic development in general and technological progress in particular in eighteenth-century Europe should be regarded as stochastic processes. The main stages of the argument are as follows. In section II a definition of "industrial revolution" in terms of decisive innovations is adopted as appropriate to the comparison of eighteenth-century England and France. In section III it is maintained that whether a deterministic or a stochastic view of history is adopted the standard question, "Why was England first?" is unanswerable. In section IV a brief review of theories of innovations is presented to suggest that a consensus in favour of viewing innovation as a stochastic process has developed in the literature on technological progress and that accepting this view implies that, although England had the decisive innovations first, *ex ante* it may have been either more or less likely than France to do so. In section V this proposition is used to suggest that the French economy of the eighteenth century has been unfairly and prematurely written off as inferior to the English.

II

To aid our examination of the problems involved in explaining England's primacy, the question will be put in the more specific form found in the literature, "Why did the onset of the Industrial Revolution occur in England not in France?" "Industrial Revolution" will be understood as a period of accelerated structural change in the economy, involving a rapid rise in industrial output, in the share of manufacturing in national product, and in factory-based activity (implying a different kind of economy), based on major technological innovations.

The focus of our attention will be on the transformation of the already existing industrial sector of the economy, not on the overall growth of the economy or the process of primitive accumulation. It will be assumed that in the mid-eighteenth century France and England were both growing economies with significant amounts of small-scale manufacturing activity. Then for our purposes we can follow the lead given by Landes in giving the cotton textiles industry the leading role in precipitating the Industrial Revolution. Landes does so because it met the following specifications: "On the one hand, [the industrial revolution] required machines which not only replaced hand labour but compelled the concentration of production in factories—in other words, machines whose appetite for energy was too large for domestic sources of power and whose mechanical superiority was sufficient to break down the resistance of the older forms of hand production. On the other hand, it required a big industry producing a commodity of wide and elastic demand, such that (1) the mechanisation of any one of its processes of manufacture would create serious strains in the others, and (2) the impact of improvements in this industry would be felt throughout the economy" (Landes, 1969a, p. 81).

The standard question can then be reformulated in the terms adopted by Davis: "The Industrial Revolution had its immediate beginning in the cotton industry ... The events that were decisive were two in number; the invention of the spinning jenny by Hargreaves, and of the water frame by Arkwright ... why ... did the decisive inventions take place in England? " (Davis, 1973, pp. 311–13, original word order amended, but sense the same).

It is as well to make explicit the counterfactual envisaged in this question, namely that if the "decisive innovations" had occurred in France rather than England, France would have had the first industrial revolution. It should be noted now, however, that this formulation does *not* regard "industrial revolution" and the achievement of "modern economic growth" as synonymous, nor is it inconsistent with the view that, the first Industrial Revolution having occurred, France followed a different route to industrialization, an "unobtrusive one."[3]

III

There are two important problems which can be perceived in the current attempts to explain England's primacy: the danger of perpetrating *post hoc ergo propter hoc* fallacies and the failure to assess the relative magnitudes of the impacts of the putative causal factors. In other words there is a need to take into account the *ceteris paribus* and to estimate the partial effects of the supposed independent variables.

This suggests one of two approaches. First, we might seek to invoke a universally applicable "covering law" of the type "whenever, and only if, A then B", i.e. A is a set of conditions necessary and sufficient for B. Rostow's stage-theory approach can be thought of as a (bold but unsuccessful) attempt to proceed in this way by making such a "lawlike statement" (Rostow, 1960). However, solving the problem of the causes of the first Industrial Revolution in this way is impossible since it was a unique event and the outcome of an uncontrolled experiment. The second method would be to make inductive generalizations by looking for empirical associations between various features of economic life and the timing of the "decisive innovations." This would be rather similar to Kuznets's methodology in his examination of modern economic growth. A natural way to proceed would be to run a multiple regression,

$$Y = \alpha + \beta_1 X_1 \ldots + \beta_n X_n + e$$

where Y, the dependent variable, would be the timing of the "decisive innovations," the Xs the proposed "causal factors," and e represents an error term. This methodology would be less ambitious than the former, being concerned with sufficiency, i.e. with attempting to say what changes in conditions in France would have sufficed, *ceteris paribus*, to give France the first industrial revolution. Obviously, this approach is also impossible because we have only one observation. Even if we were prepared to include the imitative follower cases of the nineteenth century we could still expect insuperable problems of interpretation, multicollinearity, and insufficient degrees of freedom.[4]

However, it is helpful to formulate the problem in this way. First, it serves to remind us that some of the βs (the partial derivatives) could be *negative*; it could be that some of the features of the English economy cited as favourable to industrialization were actually *retardative*. Second it draws attention to the error term; its presence implies that for given values of the Xs there are probability distributions of values of

Y. With only one observation, this precludes the use of the result that England was first to infer the favourability of particular conditions of the English economy.

There are two different ways of looking at the error term, based on two quite different philosophical positions with regard to the notion of "chance." One is to attribute it to the difficulty of accounting for a complex event, essentially as an expression of ignorance in a situation where there exists a deterministic relationship between the factors $X_1 \ldots X_n$ plus a further unspecified group of factors $X_{n+1} \ldots X_q$ and Y, which in principle would be knowable but in practice is not. A version of this position appears to be held generally by economic historians. That is to say they believe that the observed result that England had the "decisive innovations" and enjoyed the first Industrial Revolution justifies the contention that the English economy was superior to the others in Europe, including the French even though at present they are unsure exactly how. This would seem to be the position of Milward and Saul, for instance, who are among the sternest critics of existing attempts to explain England's primacy.[5] Unfortunately, this contention that the result demonstrates the superiority easily leads to "explanations of Britain's primacy . . . [which] consist mainly of a not very convincing sort of retrospective inference ('something must have caused Britain's primacy in time, so presumably the earlier conditions overtly observable did')" (Hagen, 1967, p. 37). In other words, the favourability of certain conditions in England has been inferred from the result with the likelihood of *post hoc ergo propter hoc* fallacies.

A different interpretation of the error term is to argue that the relationships between the independent variables and the dependent variable were genuinely stochastic in the sense that randomness rather than ignorance is involved and that the independent variables are related to the dependent variable probabilistically in the true structure. This would imply that even with all the relevant explanatory variables, $X_1 \ldots X_q$ present in the regression there would still be an error term, representing the "irreducible random." This view seems to have no supporters at all in the recent debate over the causes of the Industrial Revolution. As Davis, one of the few to have contemplated such a view, remarks, "It could be argued that no explanation is needed. The events that were decisive were two in number; the invention of the spinning jenny by Hargreaves, and of the water frame by Arkwright . . . These two isolated events may have been fortuitous; the chance of personalities and their good fortune in seeking along the right lines. But the economic historian instinctively recoils from such explanations" (Davis, 1973, pp. 312–13).

Perhaps this is partly because at first sight the idea of randomness has connotations of "lottery" and the abandonment of the idea that there were any causal relationships, i.e. in terms of the regression model this would mean that all the βs were zero and there would be only "noise." This, of course, is not implied by making the second interpretation of the error term. All that need be maintained is that there are probability distributions of values of Y for given values of any X and that the probability distributions of Y are different for different values of X. That is to say that the β coefficients would be *non-zero* and could be interpreted as giving information about the partial effect of an independent variable on the expected waiting time to the "decisive innovations."

So this second view would maintain that it may be, but need not be, that England was superior to France in terms of the probability of achieving the "decisive innovations" in the eighteenth century; i.e. that the result does not reveal the *ex ante* probability of England's winning the race, but is merely one of a distribution which we can conceptualize but never observe. An analogy would perhaps be to ask if Walsall's 2–0 defeat of Arsenal in their 1932 F.A. Cup tie would justify the inference that Walsall was the better team in the sense that they would have emerged victorious a majority of times in a large sample of games.

To summarize section III, then, we conclude that there are no "covering laws" which explain England's primacy; the best we can do is to formulate explanatory generalizations with an error term. Given that the "event" is unique, the tools of statistical inference are inadequate to explain the timing of decisive innovations. Thus it can be fairly claimed that the standard question is unanswerable.

Furthermore, if the Industrial Revolution is thought of as the result of a stochastic process, the question, "Why was England first?" is misconceived: the observed result need not imply the superiority of antecedent conditions in England. However, a different question, "Why did the Industrial Revolution begin in the eighteenth century?" may, within the context of the stochastic view, still be useful. It could be argued that the *ex ante* probability distributions c. 1700 of the "decisive innovations" being made somewhere were such that the cumulative probability of their occurring before 1800, say, was virtually one. Even then the precise timing of those innovations would be of no very great significance.

To clarify these arguments and to gain some idea of their possible relevance the next section looks at theories of inventive activity and innovation in the eighteenth century.

IV

There is, of course, a wide range of hypotheses purporting to explain inventive activity. The "great man" or "heroic" approach holds that "The novelties that constitute the basis of social growth and development are [to be] attributed to the inspiration of genius . . . Such avenues to truth and social change do not admit of explanation or analysis" (Usher, 1954, p. 60). "Social determinist" views see invention, and particularly innovation, as an inevitable result of necessity with "the individual . . . merely an instrument or expression of cosmic forces" (ibid., p. 61). More modestly, there are hypotheses which see innovation and/or invention as induced by the economic environment via the profit motive. A third "response to stimuli" school of thought tends to accept the importance of economic stimuli but stresses the role of factors which affect the ability of economies to react to incentives, such as sociological influences on the quality of entrepreneurship.

All three of these positions have been assumed as the basis of explanations for England's primacy, although the "heroic" view has recently fallen out of favour.[6] There are several reasons but among the most powerful are the demonstration by Merton and others (Merton, 1973, and references therein) of a large number of multiples in scientific discovery generally and the simplicity of the particular "decisive innovations." The result has been a widespread abandonment of the notion that particular individuals are necessary to particular inventions.

Economic inducements are strongly represented by the hypothesis that the "decisive innovations" were the result of the greater pressure of the growth of demand and "factor scarcities" in England than on the Continent (Crouzet, 1967b, pp. 168–73; Habakkuk, 1955, p. 154). Other authors have emphasized instead a superior ability to respond to stimuli; for example, Rostow (1973, p. 270) argues that "What distinguished Britain from the rest as the eighteenth century wore on was the scale of the inventive effort that went into the breaking of crucial technical bottlenecks." Other contributors to the view that the Industrial Revolution was based on a vigorous response are represented by writers such as McClelland (1961, chap. 2), who stress sociological factors, or those like Musson and Robinson (1969), who emphasize the role of science.

However, if the socio-economic theories are regarded as deterministic and examined as to their ability to cope with all the events in eighteenth-century innovation, they appear to be far from satisfactory. Musson has recently mounted a strong critique from this perspective. He suggests that such theories "completely [ignore] the realities of individual achievement, sustained effort, and the mixture of motives involved" (Musson, 1972, p. 49), and continues with reference to a number of eighteenth-century improvements. "If these inventions were simply products of pressing economic and social forces," he writes, "why was there such a long time lag before their widespread application? Surely, if they were sociologically or economically 'determined', 'inevitable', and 'necessary', they should have been brought into widespread use immediately?" (ibid., pp. 22–23). Similarly, it is hard not to sympathize with the point of the following quotation from Hook (1969, p. 311): "Writing in 1880, William James banteringly asked Herbert Spencer whether he believed that if William Shakespeare had not been born at Stratford-on-Avon on April 26, 1564, the convergence of social and economic forces would have produced him elsewhere; and whether if Shakespeare had died in infancy, another mother in Stratford-on-Avon would have delivered a 'duplicate copy' of him?"

As far as traditional economic theory is concerned it is in fact difficult, using neoclassical assumptions, to derive predictions about the rate of technological progress or even to support the assertions of writers such as Crouzet, Habakkuk, and Landes as to the beneficial effect of the "shortages" experienced by the British economy in the first half of the eighteenth century.[7] Indeed, an eminent authority in the field has recently summarized his position in terms of "the extreme agnosticism to which one is led on the subject of technological change by recent theorising" (Rosenberg, 1969).

However, if we look closely amongst all this apparent chaos in the literature, we find agreement among many recent authors on a fundamental point, namely that technological progress is treated as a stochastic process. Writers as apparently diverse in their views as Musson and Merton can be interpreted as sharing a vision of innovations emerging from a search process which is highly uncertain in terms of both the nature and the timing of its outcome, and which is conditioned as to its intensity and direction by social and economic variables and as to its chances of making particular discoveries by scientific knowledge and existing technology.

Thus we find Musson arguing on the one hand that "There seems little doubt . . . innovators or entrepreneurs were certainly very much influenced by economic factors, such as relative factor prices, market possiblities, and profit prospects," (Musson, 1972, p. 23) and on the other hand that "if one studies at first-hand the detailed contemporary evidence—revealing the prolonged thought, experiments, disappointments, and innumerable practical problems involved in producing an invention, from the first original idea to eventual industrial application, not forgetting also the count-less failures and bankruptcies—then a theory of 'inevitability' appears ludicrous" (ibid., p. 49).

The modern version of the "sociological determinist" view in fact is also a proba-bilistic theory, summarized thus by Merton (1973, p. 322): "innovations became virtu-ally inevitable as certain kinds of knowledge accumulated in the cultural heritage and as social developments directed the attention of investigators to particular problems." But Merton takes pains to stress that "I do not imply that all discoveries are inevit-able in the sense that, come what may, they will be made, at the time and the place, if not by the individuals who in fact made them," (ibid., p. 369) and cites evidence of a distribution of lags in discoveries which subsequently turned out to be multiples of Cavendish's (at the time unpublished) work (ibid., p. 364).

The common theme is taken up by Rosenberg, for the "response" school of thought, who stresses the uncertainty of response to economic stimuli, "Many impor-tant categories of human wants have long gone either unsatisfied or very badly catered for in spite of a well established demand . . . a great potential demand existed for improvements in the healing arts generally, but . . . progress in medicine had to await the development of the science of bacteriology in the second half of the nineteenth century"\ (Rosenberg, 1974, p. 97). Elsewhere he argues that "the developed countries never solve more than a fraction of the problems which happen to be formulated and actively pursued" (Rosenberg, 1969).

This view of technological progress has seldom been reflected in the efforts of economic model builders. Recently, though, Nelson and Winter have proposed a model which embodies an evolutionary, conditioned search approach similar to that envisaged by the writers cited above and which was successful in "accounting for" twentieth-century U.S. economic growth. They describe the heart of their model as follows: "Technique changes by individual firms are governed, first of all, by a satis-ficing mechanism. If the firm's rate of return on capital exceeds a target level, the firm retains it with probability one. Otherwise a probabilistic search process generates a possible alternative technique. The probability distribution governing search out-comes is constructed in a manner that reflects the influence of 'closeness' and 'imita-tion' . . . if the technique turned up by the search process is actually less costly, at the prevailing wage rate, than the one the firm currently uses . . . the firm changes tech-nique" (Nelson and Winter, 1974, p. 892). The authors point out that unlike neoclassi-cal theories "there was no production function—only a set of physically possible activities . . . The exploration of the set was treated as an historical incremental pro-cess" (ibid., p. 902).

While this particular model may not be appropriate, its general view of innovation as the result of stochastic search processes, in which both economic inducements and scientific, supply-side considerations play a part, appears to have several advantages in the context of our historical concern. Such a view of the world, which appears to be implicit in, or at least not inconsistent with, the work of Merton, Musson, Rosen-berg, and many others, need not be troubled by a number of the difficulties which have been encountered in the putative explanations of eighteenth-century innovative behaviour. It could accommodate the appearance of inventions which were not used straightaway and also Merton's theme of the "recurrent fact of long delayed discovery" (Merton, 1973, p. 369). Moreover, unlike the neoclassical models reviewed by David (see above), a response to resource "shortages" reflected in changed relative factor prices would be expected and presents no difficulty since the distinction between factor substitution and innovation is blurred in this vision. However, the supply of search inputs need only be an increasing function of economic inducements, not exclusively related to them. The results in terms of innovative outputs would be generally but by no means always related to economic incentives.

We are in no position to specify such a model and that is not the present purpose. What are important here are not the details of such a model but the implications of viewing economic history in this way, where the path of the economy could be thought of as the evolutionary outcome of a contingent sequence of probabilistic events. Two points in particular seem worth emphasizing in relation to the standard question "Why was England first?"

First, in the stochastic world which this view of technological progress embraces, an economy with a lower likelihood *ex ante* of achieving the "decisive innovations," or with features which tended to lessen the chance of achieving them first, may be observed as the winner in a two-country race to achieve the "decisive innovations" that is run just once. Secondly, although at the outset one economy may have a lesser chance of success it is the nature of the process envisaged that if it is "lucky" early on it could evolve into a position with much the higher chance of subsequent success; for example, making a "decisive innovation" first may vastly raise the probability of subsequent innovations being made.

It is held, then, that there is a strong case for the argument that the "decisive innovations" should be seen as the evolutionary outcome of a stochastic process and hence that the standard question "Why was England first?" has been misconceived. This position has several important implications.

(i) The fact that Britain was "more advanced" in 1790 and had a much superior likelihood of further progress in the glamour industries of the period than France does not of itself necessarily imply that *ex ante* (in, say, 1740) Britain had the greater probability of achieving the first Industrial Revolution or that one should feel obliged to seek reasons for Britain's inevitable primacy going far back into her history. This position is in stark contrast with that normally adopted by the contributors to the debate over why England was first.

(ii) Since from the unique observed result we cannot infer anything about the *ex ante* probability of England's beating France to the "decisive innovations," it is otiose to pose the question "Why was England first?" with the hope, à la Crouzet, of gaining insights into growth in general.

(iii) Indeed, if one could construct a simulation model of development during the period embodying stochastic technological progress, one would expect to observe from many runs for each economy a distribution of times for the "decisive innovations". It then seems inappropriate to try to account for the one observable result of history drawn from an unobservable distribution of possible outcomes with a general theory.

V

Two questions immediately arise. First, does this point of view seem absurd in the sense that the British economy was self-evidently superior to the French in, say, the mid-eighteenth century? Secondly, how has the superiority inference been justified?

The answer to the first of these questions would seem to be a resounding "no". In fact, the theme of similarities between the French and English economies is one which from time to time has found a number of friends. For example, Nef, writing in the 1940s, argued that "According to the popular misconception . . . British industrial development was in sharp contrast to Continental throughout the eighteenth century, and not simply at the very end of it. But . . . the rate of industrial change from about 1732 to 1782 was no more rapid in Great Britain than in France, a far larger country with nearly three times as many people. What is striking . . . is less the contrasts than the resemblances between Great Britain and the Continent, both in the rate of economic development and in the directions that development was taking" (Nef, 1943, p. 5).

A rather similar chord has been struck by Rostow in his recent work. His comment on the figures reproduced here as Table 5.1 is that "There is . . . some ambiguity about why Britain and not France was the first nation to move into take-off" (Rostow, 1973, p. 247).

With regard to French innovative potential, Mathias (1972, p. 81) states unequivocally that "The French record of scientific growth and invention in the eighteenth century was a formidable one." We learn from McCloy (1952, chap. 12) that in the first half of the eighteenth century there were more patents granted in France than England, despite a legal situation making it likely that patent statistics understate French relative to English inventiveness. It also becomes clear from a reading of McCloy that the French came very close to pre-empting Hargreaves's invention on at least two occasions in the 1740s and 1720s (ibid.). In retrospect it would hardly seem a great shock if France had succeeded in view of the simplicity of the "decisive innovations," French inventive ability, and the fact that search was evidently taking place. If so, as Rostow (1973, p. 270) puts it, "the French market, with its absolutely larger urban population, was not so poor as to rule out an ample domestic as well as a foreign market for cheap cotton textiles, if French industry had produced them first."

Table 5.1   Population and Output in France and England, 1700 and 1780

	France		Britain	
	1700	1780	1700	1780
Population (million)	19.2	25.6	6.9	9.0
Urban population (million)	3.3	5.7	1.2	2.2
Foreign trade (£ million)	9	22	13	23
Iron output (000 tons)	22	135	15	60
Cotton consumption (million lb.)	0.5	11	1.1	7.4
Agricultural output (1700 = 100)	100	155	100	126
Industrial output (1700 = 100)	100	454	100	197
Total production (1700 = 100)	100	169	100	167
Income/head (1700 = 100)	100	127	100	129

Source: W.W. Rostow (1975), in which the derivation and sources of data are discussed.

The answer to the second question is predictable: it is Britain's ultimate primacy that has, erroneously, been held to justify the presumption that something or other about the preceding conditions was superior, although recent authors have had difficulty in pinpointing the area of that superiority. Thus Davis, having found fault with all the standard arguments, concludes, "The safest thing to say, perhaps, is that although the need for innovation was strong in France as in England, French society offered a less congenial climate to innovation than did English" (Davis, 1973, p. 313). Likewise, Crouzet claims "the explanation for Britain's superior inventiveness . . . [is that] the conditions for innovation seem to have been more favourable than in France . . . [There was] a 'critical mass,' a piling up of various factors favouring England's growth which triggered off a chain reaction—the Industrial Revolution. In France, on the other hand, there was no such critical mass, which is why France did not spontaneously start an Industrial Revolution" (Crouzet, 1967b, pp. 172–3).

But these "explanations" bring to mind Gerschenkron's comment on Rostow: "The question was what made growth start. Rostow would answer that it did so because the preconditions were completed. When one asked how this was known, the further answer was that growth had started" (Gerschenkron, 1962, p. 367). Not surprisingly in the circumstances we find vigorous disagreement over the validity of the assertions of the superiority of particular key features; for example, O'Brien and Keyder (1975, p. 31) would reject Habakkuk's claim (1955, p. 154) of faster growth of demand. Davis rejects Crouzet's diagnosis of labour shortages (Davis, 1973, p. 312; Crouzet, 1967a, p. 168), and Kemp dismisses Landes's claim of greater technical skill and ingenuity (Kemp, 1969, p. 17; Landes, 1969a, p. 61).

An alternative has been to take information from the late eighteenth- and early nineteenth-century progress of the French economy to suggest that the French were less innovative and slower to adopt new methods (e.g., Landes, 1969a, p. 63). Yet this, too, is far from convincing. First, it can be argued that many innovations then made in England should be thought of as consequences of the "decisive innovations." Second, French development took place under the handicaps of an English lead and wartime disruption and does not therefore reveal reliable information concerning the *ex ante* potential of the French economy. In any case, the determinants of diffusion are not necessarily the same as those of initial development, particularly where international diffusion is concerned.

So as with the *a priori* arguments of the preceding section, this discussion leaves us with strong grounds for resisting any automatic inference of British *ex ante* superiority. It is interesting, therefore, to note that some writers have recently begun to criticize what they see as an unjustified condemnation of the French economy of the eighteenth century and have argued for a major re-interpretation of French economic performance.[8] It is the contention of the following paragraphs that the literature of which they complain is, at least partly, an outcome of the misconceived use of the standard question "Why was England first?"

It seems possible to reconstruct one powerful current in the literature as follows. During the retreat from the cataclysmic/exogenous view of the Industrial Revolution,[9] economic historians correctly perceived the need to examine the long-run build-up of conditions in the economy which could have promoted the Industrial Revolution. Ashton (1948), for example, reacted against the earlier "cataclysmic" history and stressed the importance of the long view.

An extension of this argument was the crucial, but misguided, step that, if the first Industrial Revolution was a distinctive feature of the English experience and itself related to prior trends in the economy, then the previous experience of the economy in England must have been more favourable. This also assumed, particularly in the absence of quantitative work, that the course of development up to that point had been much different. This led, on the one hand, to the presumption of English superiority and French inferiority, and, on the other, to attempts to identify, by comparison with other economies, favourable features of the English economy. This stage is well reflected in Habakkuk's work (1955). At this level of comparison, the "inferiority" of the French economy was regarded as established by virtue of England's primacy and non-English features of the French economy were asserted to be retardative of the Industrial Revolution. This process of thought is instanced in Kemp's recent book (Kemp, 1969, chap.1).

The stochastic view of technological progress advocated in this article does not permit this kind of reasoning and suggests a different approach. An appropriate question to have asked, when it was perceived that the long view was important in understanding English developments, would have been, "Were there factors which made the probability of the onset of the Industrial Revolution high in eighteenth-century England?" rather than asking, "What made France inferior?", the comparative economic historians' translation of "Why was England first?"

When the question is put in the new, rather than the standard, form, and when the achievements of the French economy in the eighteenth century are taken into account, it no longer seems obvious that taking the long view should imply seeking reasons for French inferiority. Indeed one might also ask, "Were there factors which made the probability of an industrial revolution high in eighteenth-century France?" and would not presume the probability was necessarily higher in England just because England was first. The adoption of a stochastic view of the development of the two economies naturally leads to the separation of the two questions "Why was the Industrial Revolution likely in the eighteenth century?" and "Why was it likely in England?" Looking at things this way would surely have mitigated against both the "unfair" treatment of France in the literature about which O'Brien and Keyder and Roehl complain, and also the *post hoc ergo propter hoc* fallacies which permeate so much of the literature.

VI

It remains to make a couple of disclaimers. First it is not argued that the Industrial Revolution in England was an entirely fortuitous event. Secondly, it is not argued that the French economy was more likely than the English to have an industrial revolution in the eighteenth century, but simply that the English economy, or particular features of it, has not been proved to be superior in that regard.

Essentially, the argument warns against expecting too much from comparative economic history. Whilst Landes (1969a, p. 39) argues that "if history is the laboratory of the social sciences, the economic evolution of Europe should provide the data for some rewarding experiments," it is unfortunately the case that some of the uncontrolled experiments that history performed were unique, non-repeatable events.

Notes

[1] The author would like to thank Robert Harris, Mark Harrison, Peter Law, Ned Lorenz, Robert Moeller, Stephen Peck, and Gavin Wright for their helpful comments on an earlier version of this paper. They bear no responsibility for errors.

[2] See, for example, Davis, 1973; Kemp, 1969; and Rostow, 1975.

[3] This term is due to Berrill, 1965.

[4] It is noticeable that Kuznets has been able to come up with remarkably little in the way of powerful generalizations about the timing of the onset of modern economic growth as is witnessed by the very brief remarks at the end of his *Economic Growth of Nations*, (1971).

[5] See above.

[6] In notable contrast with the writers of an earlier generation, as seen, for example, by reading the account of the agricultural revolution in Ernle, 1961.

[7] See the extensive review of the "Habakkuk debate" in David, 1975, chap.1.

[8] In particular, O'Brien and Keyder, 1975 and Roehl, 1976.

[9] See Flinn, 1967, chap.1, for this expression and a discussion of the relevant historiography.

No Random Walk: A Comment on "Why Was England First?"

W. W. ROSTOW

Some thirty years ago I allowed myself the following rather grandiose observation: "On occasion it may be proper to regard the course of history as inevitable, *ex post*; but not *ex ante*" (Rostow, 1948, p. 143). I was, therefore, pleased to see Mr. Crafts try his hand at a stochastic explanation of the coming of the first Industrial Revolution (previous essay). In exploring this hypothesis, however, he confronted two lions in his path. It is conceivable that further and deeper research might remove them. He chose to ignore them, rendering his essay unsatisfactory.

The first lion is the marked acceleration in the scale of British relative to French inventions from the 1760s onwards. The presently available statistical data are frail, but, taken at face value, make a powerful case.

If these numbers were all we had, I, at least, would not be wholly convinced. But contemporaries and historians, without the benefit of comparative statistics, were fully aware of the marked absolute and relative acceleration in British inventions, not least contemporary French officialdom. It was after 1760 that the French government became most ardent in trying to acquire British technology. The French

---

Table 5.2   Annual Average Patents Granted and Inventions Approved: Great Britain and France in the Eighteenth Century

	Great Britain		France	Great Britain, comparable years
1702–11	2		6	—
1712–21	5		7	—
1722–31	10		10	—
1732–41	5		6	—
1742–51	9		4	—
1752–61	10		—	—
1762–71	23	(1769–69	7	21)
1772–81	31	(1770–71	10	25)
1782–91	54	(1789–92	22	63)
1792–1801	72	(1796–98	8	69)

Source: W.W. Rostow (1975), p. 176.

became conscious that they were falling behind in this particular respect. It was, for example, sixteen years after the founding of Birmingham's famous Lunar Society that the first private organization addressed to this problem was set up in France: "The Free Society of Emulation for the Encouragement of Inventions which Tend to Perfect the Application of the Arts and Trades in Imitation of that of London."

The British advantage in the scale of inventive activity was noted by a Swiss calico printer as early as 1766, in quoting what was already a proverb (Wadsworth and Mann, 1931, p. 413): "...for a thing to be perfect it must be invented in France and worked out in England." This statement reflects an important distinction between an invention incorporating a principle later proved viable, and an invention refined to the point when production on a cost-effective basis can begin. Working out an invention almost always requires many hands and minds. Present evidence suggests that British society diverted more talents to these tasks of invention and refinement than France. A serious case for a stochastic theory of the British Industrial Revolution must address itself, therefore, to the scale of inventive activity not merely to aggregate data of pre-modern economic expansion, or to the allegation that Frenchmen just missed hitting on the spinning-jenny and water frame.

Now the second lion in the path: innovational zeal. The case against the stochastic hypothesis is heightened if one separates sharply invention and innovation, which Mr. Crafts fails to do. One must, at least, try to get at the relative vigour of private innovative entrepreneurship in the two countries. Here Mr. Crafts is a bit evasive. He uses the work of Shelby McCloy when it appears to fit his thesis but fails to quote McCloy's final conclusion: "Private business of eighteenth-century France thus was more to blame than the government for failure to pursue invention" (McCloy, 1952, p. 191).

In this matter of estimating innovative zeal, one must go beyond Hargreaves's spinning-jenny and Arkwright's water frame. One must look at the full range over which entrepreneurs were seizing on and applying new inventive insights, including agriculture, road and canal building, iron manufacture, and the steam engine, as well as cotton textiles. Here, evidently, we do not have orderly, even imperfect, statistical data. But we do have contemporary judgement and the conclusions of wise and careful scholars. Their universal conclusion that the innovational spirit in the private sector of post-1760 Britain was stronger than in France need not be regarded as sacrosanct. But their cumulative judgement must be altered by equally serious scholarship. It cannot, simply, be ignored.

Nor can the explanation some have offered for this phenomenon be ignored; namely, that for whatever reasons, English non-conformists and Scotsmen, provided a more congenial setting by their society than their French counterparts, played a grossly disproportionate role in innovation as well as invention. This was, after all, what Hagen (inadequately paraphrased by Mr. Crafts) was getting at, on the basis of Ashton's classic analysis.

Was Britain's achievement of the first Industrial Revolution "inevitable?" I would stick with my youthful *obiter dictum* and still say no. But until Mr. Crafts (or others) is prepared to cope with these lions in the path, I would conclude that there were, indeed, "factors which made the probability of the onset of the Industrial Revolution" higher in Britain than in France. Until new and serious research upsets the received findings, the evidence is that the levels of inventive and private innovational activity over a wide front were higher in Britain than in France during the critical quarter-century that preceded the coming of the first Industrial Revolution. The test which took place from, say 1760 to 1783 was not a one-time match between Walsall and Arsenal, but "a large sample of games" in which Britain, with a population about a third that of France, generated sustained processes of invention and innovation on a scale the larger nation could not then equal. This was no random walk.

Entrepreneurship and a Probabilistic View of the British Industrial Revolution: Reply

N.F.R. CRAFTS

Prof. Rostow's comment on my article is very welcome, partly because the intention of my contribution was to be provocative, but also because he has gladly conceded the main part of my case by accepting that it is appropriate to look at the Industrial Revolution in probabilistic terms and that it is therefore not proven that England was a superior economy. Nevertheless there are three points of detail and one of more general significance which require a response.

First, it is not at all clear that the argument that non-conformists played a vital role in innovation is acceptable. Payne (1974, p. 25) has pointed out that there are very serious difficulties in the way of establishing this propositon in terms of differential survival of records.

Second, it is clear that it is *not* acceptable to use patent statistics as comparative indices of inventive activity, or of the elasticity of entrepreneurial innovational response, given the well-known (different) deficiencies of patent legislation in England and France in the eighteenth century. However, as Roehl (1976, pp. 220–21) has argued, it does seem *prima facie* that biases in the patent data would be in the direction of overstating English inventiveness and understating French inventivenness, and hence it is quite possible that one could argue for greater French inventiveness at least prior to 1760.

Third, my article was concerned with the achievement of the decisive innovations that led to structural change in the form of the Industrial Revolution. It is not obvious that the greater innovational zeal which Rostow alleges was present in late-eighteenth-century England reflected a greater likelihood of coming up with and using spectacular and strategic improvements, any more than Germany was guaranteed the invention of the Gilchrist-Thomas process a century later.

In any event, assertions, however widely made, about the quality of entrepreneurship, are notoriously unreliable. It may be revealing, therefore, to ask whether this innovational quality was reflected in rapid acceleration of the rate of growth of total factor productivity in the mid-eighteenth century. On the best, admittedly imperfect, figures available it appears that of the 0.4 percent rise in the growth-rate of the English economy in the period 1740–80 as compared with 1710–40, only 0.06 percent came from an increase in total factor productivity growth (Crafts, 1981). The great innovational zeal which Rostow sees in the British economy for this period seemingly had a very small impact on the growth process.

On the more general content of Prof. Rostow's comment, it seems to me that, although Prof. Rostow has accepted the probabilistic standpoint, he has not fully explored the ramifications of this position. In this view of the world it will not do to talk, as he does, only of the later decades of the century when, as the Industrial Revolution gathers pace in Britain, the relative standing of the two economies is changing. This does not demonstrate that Britain had the greater *ex-ante* chance of making the decisive innovations, which after all had a positive probability of being achieved in one country or the other *earlier* in the century, and, as McCloy (1952, pp. 89–93) shows, very nearly were achieved by France.

If Prof. Rostow follows through the logic of his position, he must agree that we cannot answer the question "Why was England first?" and that earlier hopes for discovering the causes of the Industrial Revolution by comparison of England and France were too optimistic. This was a major thesis of my article. I would hope that he might agree with me, therefore, that it is undesirable to approach eighteenth-century French economic history in a preconceived search for reasons for inferiority.

6

Food Supply in the United Kingdom During the Industrial Revolution

BRINLEY THOMAS[1]

On the occasion of the Silver Jubilee of the British Agricultural History Society in 1977, William N. Parker published an article in which he pointed out that there are still important unanswered questions about the English Agricultural Revolution, 1750–1850. For example:

> By what means was Britain's growing population fed in these critical decades before the massive imports of overseas meat and grain? Could not some balance sheet be constructed to show the relative importance of dietary changes—whether restrictions or improvements (pace Hartwell, Hobsbawm)— increased grain yields and meat supplies at home, Irish and other imports, and finally the new crops and abandonment of fallow? . . . Did turnips or clover or both together feed by way of meat-animals or richer and better tilled soil for the grain crop—30 percent of the population increase or 80 percent of it in the Industrial Revolution? [Parker, 1977, p. 7].

The standard generalization is that in the first half of the nineteenth century, when the population of England and Wales doubled, this substantial addition to numbers, thanks to the agricultural revolution, was fed out of domestic sources. E.L. Jones concluded as follows:

> The total population of England and Wales, which had been 11,004,000 in 1815, reached 14,928,000 in 1836 and this enormous increase was fed. It was fed from home supplies, with no sustained help from imports and clearly without the per capita consumption of foodstuffs falling much, if indeed it fell at all [Jones, 1968, p. 13].

In their well-known textbook, *The Agricultural Revolution 1750–1880*, J.D. Chambers and G.E. Mingay reach a similar conclusion.

> The Agricultural Revolution . . . had performed its role in the process of industrialization. Output had risen almost as fast as population, and as late as 1868 it

Reprinted with major revisions from *Agricultural History*, Vol. 56, No. 1 (January 1982), pp. 328–42. Reprinted by the permission of the Agricultural History Society.

was estimated that no less than 80 percent of the food consumed in the United Kingdom by a highly urbanized and industrialized population had been grown at home.[2]

The questions raised by Parker seem to suggest that the received doctrine on this subject may be overoptimistic. In this paper I propose to examine this issue from a new angle, taking into account recent additions to statistical information on Britain's overseas trade, dietary changes, and cereal consumption in the first half of the nineteenth century. I have also found it instructive to revisit a classic published thirty years ago and somewhat underrated by historians of the agricultural revolution—R.N. Salaman's *The History and Social Influence of the Potato* (1949).

When it is said that the increase in population during the industrial revolution was fed out of domestic supplies, it is necessary to know at what level the people were fed. What kind of subsistence was it? What were the dietary variations in different regions and occupations? The discussion will also be clearer if we specify which area we have in mind. Are we talking about England, Great Britain (England, Wales, and Scotland) or the United Kingdom (Great Britain and Ireland)?

Some English authors slip into the habit of using "England" as short-hand for "Great Britain" and the result is a haze of ambiguity. Just as Trevelyan's *English Social History* (1944) was well described as English history with the politics left out, it would be equally pertinent to say that some books on British economic history are British history with the Celtic fringe left out. The Celtic countries—Scotland, Wales, and Ireland—can be left out simply by burying them in aggregate figures for Great Britain or the United Kingdom. And sometimes these aggregates are used as the statistical basis of a historical work purporting to be about England. A case in point is John Burnett's *Plenty and Want: A Social History of Diet in England from 1815 to the Present Day* (1968), in many ways an admirable study. At the beginning of his first chapter, "England in Transition," it looks as if the author is writing a book about England; we are given population figures not for Britain but for England and Wales (Wales is always lumped in with England). However, later in the chapter when it comes to the consumption of sugar, tea, coffee, and beer in the first half of the nineteenth century, the statistical time series are all averages for Great Britain or the United Kingdom. An examination of the statistical groundwork of the whole book reveals that over a third of the forty-five tables give aggregate figures for Great Britain or the United Kingdom. This seems to suggest that Burnett should have had "Britain" not "England" in the title of his book, and yet the book lacks a systematic account of the history of diet in Scotland and Wales. Surely the proper course would be to base the history of diet in England on strictly English sources.

No doubt for the twentieth century it does not make much difference whether aggregated British or English data are used. However, for the period of the Industrial Revolution it is essential to draw a clear distinction between England on the one hand and the Celtic crescent (Scotland, Wales, and Ireland) on the other. Apart from the cultural differences between the Celtic and English peoples, there are solid economic considerations. First, there was a marked division of labor in the agricultural production network between the two segments of the British Isles economy. The Celtic sector concentrated on the production of foodstuffs, such as the rearing of livestock for export to the fattening areas of England. The significance of the changing balance between grain and pastoral farming under the influence of urbanization and the widening of markets was noted by Adam Smith.

It is not more than a century ago, that in many parts of the Highlands of Scotland, butcher's meat was as cheap or cheaper than even bread made of oatmeal. The Union opened the market of England to the Highland cattle. Their ordinary price at present is about three times greater than at the beginning of the century, and the rents of many Highland estates have been tripled and quadrupled in the same time [Smith, 1904, I, p. 169].

Second, there were striking and long-lasting differences between the bread-eating tastes of the English and the Celts. To be accurate one should say the southern English, for the northern English shared with their neighbors, the Scots, a liking for oats. Until recently the general view was that by 1800 wheat had become the staff of life for virtually the whole population of England and Wales.[3] This is no longer tenable. Recent research has produced strong evidence that in 1801 no less than a third of the population of England and Wales was still dependent on barley, oats, or rye. In Great Britain as a whole the population consuming wheat in 1801 was only 58 percent.[4] The data for England, Wales, and Scotland are set out in Table 6.1. By the end of the eighteenth century the wheaten loaf had triumphed only in southern and eastern England; 94 percent of the 4,284,000 living in those areas were wheat-eaters. In northern England, with a population of 2,092,000, the corresponding portion was 25 percent; in that area, 50 percent consumed oats, 18 percent barley, and 6 percent rye. In the Celtic sector the wheaten loaf was eaten only by a very small minority,

Table 6.1   Wheat and Coarse Grain Consumption in England, Wales, and Scotland in 1801

	Population (1000s)	Wheat-eaters (1000s)	Percent of population	Coarse grain eaters (1000s)	Percent of population
England	8,502	5,890	69	2,612[a]	31
Southern and Eastern England	4,284	4,017	94	267	6
Wales	559	84	15	475[b]	85
Scotland	1,625	163	10	1,462[c]	90
Great Britain	10,686	6,137	58	4,549	42

[a] 1,045,000 of these, 50 percent of the population of northern England, consumed oats.
[b] Mainly barley.
[c] Mainly oats.
Source: Consumption data from Collins, 1975 p. 105. Population data from Mitchell and Deane, 1962, p. 8; Deane and Cole, 1962, p. 103.

10 percent in Scotland and 15 percent in Wales. The Scots went for oats (72 percent), barley (10 percent), and pulse (8 percent), whereas the Welsh went for barley (60 percent), oats (20 percent), and rye (5 percent). It is interesting to notice that the Celtic fringe in Cornwall in southwestern England conformed to the same pattern as Wales; no less than 55 percent of the population of the Southwest were barley-eaters.[5]

The dietary situation in Ireland was entirely different. By the beginning of the nineteenth century the Irish had become heavily dependent on the potato, and in the fifty years between the Union of 1800 and the Great Famine, this dependency grew more intense. Little wheat was produced and less eaten in Ireland. In the early 1850s, when more reliable statistics become available, wheat production averaged 4532 thousand cwts. per annum (1851–55), as compared to an output of 35,037 thousand cwts. of oats.[6] Even oat consumption was comparatively modest, and only in the North and the East did it play a significant role. Elsewhere oats were consumed only in the late summer and early fall, in the weeks before the new potato crop came in. A conservative estimate of the potato consumption in prefamine Ireland puts the average at about 4.5 lbs. per day, which is the equivalent of 1400 calories per capita per day (Mokyr, 1983, p. 7). For the United Kingdom as a whole, J.R. McCulloch's figures for 1821 may not be far off the mark. McCulloch estimated that of the combined populations, 10.3 million depended chiefly on wheat, 7 million on barley and oats, and 5 million (mostly in Ireland) on potatoes.[7]

The third reason why it is important to disaggregate the United Kingdom into the English and Celtic sectors is demographic. In 1801 the distribution of the population was as follows: England 8,502,000, Scotland 1,625,000. Wales 559,000, and Ireland 5,216,000. The three Celtic countries comprise 46 per cent and England 54 percent of the population of the British Isles; the proportions were the same in 1831. Thus, demographically, the Celtic sector was not so much a fringe as a hemisphere. Be that as it may, the role of Ireland must not be underestimated. We shall examine how well England was fed during the industrial revolution and the extent to which she drew on the agricultural resources of the Celtic periphery.

In the second half of the eighteenth century, the scarcity of wood in Britain forced her to change her energy base from wood fuel to fossilized fuel, from the flow of solar energy to the stock.[8] France, with ample supplies of timber, had no such problem.[9] The timber shortage in Britain manifested itself in a sharp rise in the price of charcoal after 1750. She became increasingly dependent on Sweden, Norway, and Russia for bar iron, timber, and naval stores. The price of imported Swedish bar iron rose from £12 per ton in 1763 to £24 per ton in 1795. It has been estimated that in the early 1750s timber cargoes comprised over one-half of the total shipping tonnage entering British ports,[10] and between the 1750s and the 1780s the quantity of timber used in shipbuilding was the equivalent of well over half of the total amount of timber imported. On the eve of the American Revolution one third of the British merchant fleet had been built in the American colonies. A calculation for 1788 shows that over a half of total British iron consumption was dependent on charcoal iron, of which about 75 percent had to be imported (Hyde, 1977, pp. 80, 93–94). There was a long secular fall in Britain's gross barter terms of trade (the volume of exports over the volume of imports) from 1750 to 1788.[11]

One important effect of this stringency was to bring to an end Britain's role as an exporter of food. In the first half of the eighteenth century Britain was the granary of

a large part of Europe. Thanks to the agricultural revolution of the seventeenth century, she had the capacity to export an amount of grain which was the equivalent of
what would feed a quarter of the British population. All this changed after 1750 when
the population explosion was under way. The 1760s and 1770s were hard times, made
all the worse by a succession of bad harvests. The price of wheat went up 40 percent
in relation to other prices; the average price of lambs rose from 4s.4d. in 1732–35 to
7s.1d. in 1761–67 (John, 1960, pp. 153–54). There were frequent violent food riots.
English agriculture, despite the enclosures, was unable to cope. Things must have
been serious to force the English government to repeal the restrictive measures
against imports from Ireland which were known as the Cattle Acts (Cullen, 1968,
p. 33). Inspired by the aim of protecting English breeders, these laws, passed in 1666
and after, totally prohibited the import into Britain of Irish cattle, sheep, beef, butter,
and pork; they had caused considerable dislocation and suffering in Ireland. At the
end of the 1750s when the prices of livestock and livestock products were rising sharply in England, petitions were showered on Parliament from all over the country
demanding the repeal of the Cattle Acts. In 1758 an act was passed permitting the
import of all sorts of live cattle from Ireland free of duty for five years. The same
applied to beef, pork, and butter, and these acts were subsequently renewed, for
example, in 1765 in the case of cattle for another seven years and later they were
made permanent (Macpherson, 1805, Vol. 3, pp. 308, 413). In 1784 the Irish Parliament passed Foster's Corn Law, which consolidated the system of export bounties on
agricultural products, and provided an export subsidy of perhaps 10% of the value of
the product (Crotty, 1966, p. 22). The effect was a big increase of food shipments
from Ireland. The details are given in Tables 6.2 and 6.3.

Between 1760 and 1790 the value of British imports from Ireland rose two-and-
one-half times, from £1,451,000 to £3,696,000. Purchases of beef went up threefold,
butter sixfold, and pork sevenfold. The very high figures for 1795 and 1800 reflect

Table 6.2   Value of Exports from Ireland, 1700 and 1750–1800

Year ending 25 March	To Great Britain (nearest £1000)	To all parts (nearest £1000)	Great Britain as percent of total exports
1700[a]	373	815	45.7
1750	1,070	1,863	57.4
1760	1,451	2,139	67.8
1770	2,409	3,160	76.2
1780	2,385	3,013	79.2
1790	3,696	4,855	76.1
1800	3,483	4,079	85.4

[a] Year Ending 25 December
Source: Cullen, 1968, p. 45.

Table 6.3   Exports of Beef, Butter, and Pork from Ireland to Great Britain, 1760–1800

	Beef (barrels)	Butter (cwts)	Pork (barrels)
1760	24,072	35,162	13,293
1765	20,108	38,022	7,383
1770	31,275	114,363	12,089
1775	36,455	115,100	17,199
1780	89,698	135,465	49,302
1785	43,024	159,526	21,539
1790	51,203	194,748	46,067
1795	95,475	214,962	88,304
1800	123,947	208,683	98,348

Source: Cullen, 1968, p. 70.

the influence of the Napoleonic War. In 1794–1796 Ireland was supplying 44 percent of Britian's imports of grain, meat, and butter.[12] Between 1760 and 1801 the population of Britain increased by 0.83 per cent per annum, while domestic agricultural output grew by only 0.44 per cent per annum (Crafts, 1983, p. 190). It has been estimated that over the eighteenth century as a whole output per head in English agriculture went up by 25 percent, but none of this increase can be attributed to the second half of the century (Deane and Cole, 1962, p. 75). Indeed, the probability is that agricultural productivity fell in the third quarter of the century.

The energy problem in Britain in the second half of the eighteenth century had expressed itself in increasingly strong competing pressures on land use—for bread grains, pastureland for animal products, charcoal for the iron industry, timber for shipbuilding and housing, oak for the Royal Navy, wood ash for alkalies for the textile industry, and land for transport, manufacturing, and urbanization. A major contributing factor was the population explosion. Between 1750 and 1800 the population of Great Britain increased by 46 percent, as against only 9 percent in the previous fifty years. Then, from 1801 to 1851, the population doubled, from 10.7 million to 21 million. How could this unprecedented swarming of numbers on a small offshore island be made compatible with economic growth and a rising standard of living? The answer, which is a major corollary of Malthus's theory, was that Britain would have to obtain the equivalent of a vast extension of her land base. To do that she would need to become the workshop of the world and then exchange her industrial products for abundant cheap food from the continents of new settlement overseas. This is what Britain's Atlantic economy in the second half of the nineteenth century achieved (Thomas, 1973). It was the payoff of her Industrial Revolution. The New World was called in to redress the balance of the Old. Britain's world-wide network based on coal, iron and steel, new technology, capital exports, emigration, and free trade entailed running down home agriculture to 5 percent of national income and in effect endowing the British economy with the equivalent of abundant additional land from overseas.

We now come to the major issue, namely, the feeding of England during the transition—the half century, 1795–1846, which it took to bring into being the industrialized economy that could reap the payoff of the Industrial Revolution. The first part of the period, the years 1795–1815, was dominated by the Napoleonic Wars. Wartime stringencies, the blockade, and a series of bad harvests sent the price of wheat up from an average of 43 shillings a quarter in 1792 to 119 shillings in 1801 and 126 shillings in 1812. The price of a four-pound loaf of bread rose from 6 pence in 1792 to 17 pence in 1812 (Mitchell and Deane, 1962, p. 498). The threat of starvation was avoided by drastic measures to curtail wasteful consumption of grain, a large extension of the area under cultivation, and the subsidizing of imports of food. A crucial factor was the remarkable elasticity of supply from Ireland. In the period 1800–14 no less than 35 percent of the total amount of grains, meal, and flour imported into Great Britain came from Ireland. The various sources of supply are given in Table 6.4. Of the 7,338,000 quarters contributed by Ireland, 5,581,000 consisted of oats and 1,457,000 of wheat (Galpin, 1925, p. 252). Irish exports of foodstuffs to Britain in current values went up almost fivefold from £950,000 in 1784–86 to £4,416,000 in 1814–1816 (Davis, 1978, p. 92). In the crisis years of 1809 and 1810 Napoleon allowed 1.5 million quarters of wheat to be sent to Britain from the French Empire, partly because he had to appease a strong farm lobby in his Empire at a time of bumper crops and partly because he was a good Mercantilist—he demanded payment in gold and hoped in this way to undermine British credit.[13] It is not possible to estimate accurately the increase in domestic output in Britain during the wars; that it was substantial is indicated by the fact that between 1801 and 1815 on an average nearly 53,000 acres were enclosed each year (Olson, 1963, p. 69). However, a heavy price had to be paid. According to Deane and Cole (1962, pp. 74–5), "in the second half of the eighteenth century, and still more at the beginning of the nineteenth, the supply of beef failed to keep pace with the growth of population. . . . During the French Wars . . . a big increase in the output of grain was achieved only by bringing more land under the plough at the expense of the nation's meat supply."

Table 6.4   Imports of Grains, Meal, and Flour into Great Britain, 1800–1814

Country of origin	Quantity (nearest 1000 quarters)	Country of origin	Quantity (nearest 1000 quarters)
Ireland	7,338	United States	1,317
Prussia		Russia	909
(inc. Poland)	4,082	Holland	2,250
Germany	2,961	All other countries	2,300
		Total	21,157

Source: Galpin, 1925, Appendix 8.

When the Napoleonic Wars were over, the landed interest secured the passing of the Corn Law of 1815 which decreed that imports of wheat would be prohibited as long as the domestic price was below 80 shillings a quarter. Barley and oats were much cheaper than wheat, as can be seen from Table 6.5 (Mitchell and Deane, 1962, p. 488). There can be no doubt that the Scots and Welsh, depending on oats and barley respectively, were getting more nutritional value per unit of outlay than the English who consumed white bread. This is underlined by the fact that various adulterants such as alum were added in order to whiten inferior grades of flour used for the bread sold to the mass of the people. In southern England the white loaf had become a necessity which poor people were very reluctant to give up. The flour was very often made out of the worst kinds of damaged foreign wheat.[14] The artificially whitened loaves were sold at the high price of loaves made of the finest white flour.

There is ample evidence that in the first half of the nineteenth century agricultural laborers in the South of England became much worse off than their opposite numbers in the North. The differential had been reversed since 1770 when Arthur Young found that the average weekly agricultural wage in southern counties (7s.6d.) was about 10 percent higher than in northern counties (6s.9d.). By 1850/1851 average wage rates in the North (11s.6d.) were 37 percent higher than in the South (8s.5d.) and the incidence of pauperism was 12.1 percent of the population in the South as against 6.2 percent in the North (Caird, 1852, pp. 510–15). There were pronounced regional differences in the standard of nutrition.

> In the North oatmeal was made palatable by the addition of milk which was rarely available to the southern laborer who had no cow-pasture of his own. Also the conditions of service were quite different. The annual hiring of labor persisted in the North and Scotland—the worker got a part of his wages in meal or grain, irrespective of market prices, and he had cow-pasture or accomodation for pig or poultry [Burnett, 1946, p. 40].

The southern laborers endured the full force of overpopulation, the enclosures, and the Corn Laws.

What was the contribution of the Celtic countries to England's food supply in the thirty years before the Repeal of the Corn Laws in 1846? In seeking to answer this question one is handicapped by the lack of adequate statistics. As of 1826 the British government ceased to keep records of trade with Ireland, except for shipments of grains. Moreover, in this period there are no reliable statistics on British output of

Table 6.5   Comparative Grain Prices in Great Britain, 1810–1840

	Average price per quarter		
	Wheat	Barley	Oats
1810	106s. 5d.	48s. 1d.	28s. 7d.
1820	67s. 10d.	33s. 10d.	24s. 2d.
1830	64s. 3d.	32s. 7d.	24s. 5d.
1840	66s. 4d.	36s. 5d.	25s. 8d.

Table 6.6   Great Britain: Imports of Grains, Meat, and Butter from Overseas and from Ireland, 1804–1806 to 1844–1846 (annual averages at current prices)

	Imports of Grains, Meat and Butter		Total imports (Cols. 1 and 2) (£000)	Col. 2 as % of Col. 3 %	Output of British agriculture, forestry, and fishery (£000)	Irish imports as % of col. 5	Total imports (Col. 3) as % of col. 5[b] %
Period	from overseas (£000) (1)	from Ireland (£000) (2)	(3)	(4)	(5)	(6)	(7)
1804–06	2,573	2,296	4,869	47.1	91,500	2.5	5.3
1814–16	1,714	4,155	5,869	70.1	91,700	4.5	6.4
1824–26	1,846	5,599	7,445	75.2	77,700	7.2	9.6
1834–36	1,512	8,427[a]	9,939	84.8	89,700	9.4	11.1
1844–46	7,377	7,966[a]	15,343	52.0	103,200	7.7	14.9

[a] Estimated on the assumption that imports of meat and butter from Ireland were proportionate to the recorded imports of grains and meal (see Table 6.7).
[b] Allowing for re-exports of grains, the percentages in col. 7 would be 1814–16, 6.2%; 1824–26, 9.5%; 1834–36, 10.5%; 1844–46, 14.6%.
Source: Davis, 1979, pp. 112–19; col. 5: Mid-decade estimate based on Deane and Cole, 1962, p. 166.

wheat and other cereals. Up to 1826 the revised figures of trade in real values compiled by Ralph Davis give a fairly accurate picture which is set out in Table 6.6. Between 1804–06 and 1824–26 the Irish contribution to total British imports of grains, meat, and butter rose from 47 percent to 75 percent; as a proportion of estimated British output in agriculture, forestry, and fishing, these imports from Ireland were 7.2 percent in 1824–26. British imports of these foodstuffs from all countries, including Ireland, in 1824–26 were 9.6 percent of the estimated output in agriculture, forestry, and fishing.

For the years 1826–49 there is a series showing the annual quantity of grains and meal imported from Ireland to Great Britain. G.R. Porter, in *The Progress of the Nation* (1851, p. 344) explained that "when, in order to save the yearly salaries of one or two junior clerks, it was determined to cease keeping any offical record of the commercial intercourse between Great Britain and Ireland, an exception was made as regards grain and flour, that trade being of great personal interest to our legislators." Table 6.7 shows that the quantity of grains and meal supplied to Britain from Ireland almost doubled between 1820–24 and 1835–39 (from an average of 1,493,000 quarters to 2,867,000 annually). Although Porter's series are known to be inaccurate, it is safe to assume that they reflect broad trends. If we assume, furthermore, that meat and butter imports increased in the same proportion, Ireland in the late 1830s was

Table 6.7   Grains and Meal Imported into Great Britain from Ireland, 1815–1849
(annual averages: nearest 1,000 quarters)

Period	Wheat and wheat flour	Barley and barley meal	Oats and oatmeal	Rye, indian corn, beans and peas	Total grains and meal
1815–19	127	32	750	5	914
1820–24	439	51	995	8	1,493
1825–29	458	96	1,605	12	2,171
1830–34	657	165	1,698	21	2,541
1835–39	519	149	2,173	26	2,867
1840–44	290	85	2,345	26	2,746
1845–49	379	72	1,408	22	1,881

Source: Porter, 1851, p. 345.

supplying grains, meal, meat, and butter at a rate at least equal to 10 percent of the output of British agriculture.

A full assessment of the contribution of the Celtic periphery to England's food supply should take into account the movement of livestock from Scotland, Wales, and Ireland. Space does not permit an analysis of this aspect of the subject. Its importance is indicated by the following statement:

> A modern estimate of the output of Scottish farms ... confirms the feasibility of Sir John Sinclair's figure of some 100,000 store cattle exported to England in 1800, 60,000 of which were probably sold at the Falkirk Trysts. This trade via Falkirk probably reached its peak in the 1830s or sometime before mid-century, by which time transport changes were beginning to make an impact on the structure of the cattle trade between Scotland and England [Blackman, 1975, pt. 1, p. 60; also, Symon, 1953–54, pp. 119–21].

G.R. Porter estimated the number of live animals brought from Ireland to Liverpool in 1837 as follows: 84,710 black cattle, 316 calves, 225,050 sheep, 24,669 lambs, 595,422 pigs, 3,414 horses and 319 mules. Their total value was £3,397,760 (Porter, 1851, p. 344). If we add this, the Irish contribution in the late 1830s must have been at least 13 percent of the entire output of English agriculture and over 85 percent of England's imports of grains, meat, butter, and livestock. The figures for 1844–46 are affected by the Irish potato famine and the Repeal of the Corn Laws; they register an enormous increase in imports from overseas—five times the amount in 1834–36—due to the onset of free trade, whereas shipments from Ireland as a proportion of total imports fell to 52 percent. Total imports of grains, meat, and butter in 1844–46 were about 15 percent of the estimated income in agriculture, forestry, and fishing. By 1854–56 imports of grains, meat, and butter from overseas had trebled compared with 1844–46 (£22.3 million as against £7.4 million).

An analysis of wheat imports in relation to English output is given in Table 6.8. The striking change after the repeal of the Corn Laws in 1846 is evident. A quarter of English wheat consumption was supplied by imports in 1847–56 as against about a

Table 6.8   England and Wales: Wheat Imports and Home Output, 1829–1868
(annual averages, nearest 1000 quarters)

	Wheat output	Wheat imports[c]	Total consumption	Imports[d] as percentage of total consumption
1829–36	13,751	634	14,385	4.4
1836–46[a,b]	15,630	1,660	17,290	9.6
1847–56[a]	13,443	4,520	18,063	25.7
1857–64[a]	13,279	7,285	20,264	35.4
1867–76[a]	10,811	10,775	21,586	50.0

[a] These years were chosen in order to minimize possible errors from changes in the composition of the "inspected market" figures, on which the author based her output estimates.

[b] The year 1842 was omitted for statistical reasons.

[c] The author noted that "the imports were admitted officially to the United Kingdom as a whole, but in fact came mostly to England." (p. 102)

[d] Not including imports from Ireland. Adding the recorded imports from Ireland (and ignoring any foreign wheat that went into Ireland before 1845, which was negligible) makes total wheat imports as a proportion of consumption in England 8 percent in 1829–36 and 12 percent in 1837–46.

Source: Fairlie, 1969, p. 102.

tenth in 1837–46 (excluding Irish imports which raise it to 12 percent), and this was long before the New World became the major supplier. In 1854–56 about two-thirds of the grain cargoes entering Britain came from Europe and the Near East and only one-third from the United States. By 1867–76 half the wheat consumed in Britain came from abroad.

The statistics used so far have given an unduly ascetic impression of the British diet—as if the British consumed only bread, butter, and meat. We must be realistic and add tea, coffee, sugar, rice, cheese, fruit, spices, wine, spirits, and other food and drink. All the above items are lumped together under "Food and Drink" in Table 6.9. We find that during the Corn Law regime, 1815–46, Britain's gross imports of food and drink were about one-third of the value of domestic agricultural output; allowing for exports and re-exports the proportion was about one-quarter. In 1814–16, the end of the Napoleonic Wars, re-exports of coffee and sugar to Europe were abnormally large. When the restraints of the Corn Laws were removed in 1846, imports of food and drink, excluding imports from Ireland, doubled in ten years, from £26,691,000 in 1844–46 to £52,769,000 in 1854–56, which was 47 percent of the approximate value of output in British agriculture or 37 percent if we allow for exports and re-exports.

The analysis suggests the following conclusions about the period 1815–46. Notwithstanding the achievements of the agricultural revolution, the supply of grains, butter, meat, and livestock available to the English population would have been

Table 6.9 Great Britain: Imports of Food and Drink (including imports from Ireland) in Relation to the Value of Agricultural Output, 1814–1816 to 1854–1856 (annual averages in current prices)

	Imports of food and drink[a] (£1000) (1)	Income in agriculture, forestry and fishing (£1000) (2)	Col.1 as % of col.2 (%) (3)	Col.1 minus re-exports as % of col.2 (%) (4)	Col.1 minus exports and re-exports as % of col.2 (%) (5)
1814–16	31,127	91,700	34.0	23.2	17.5
1824–26	25,758	77,500	33.2	27.3	25.7
1834–36	28,465[b]	89,700	31.7	27.2	25.5
1844–46	34,657[b]	103,200	33.7	29.9	28.1
1854–56	52,769[c]	112,700	46.7	41.7	36.6

[a]Comprising grains, meats, butter, sugar, rice, cheese, fruit, spices, coffee, tea, wine, spirits, other food and drink.
[b]Including imports from Ireland calculated as in Table 6.2.
[c]Not including imports from Ireland.
Source: See Table 6.6.

smaller by at least one-sixth in the 1830s and early 1840s had it not been for imports, mainly from Ireland. And this indispensable assistance was being drawn from a colony where little was done by English landlords (many of them absentee) to bring about agrarian reform. Although Irish agriculture was far from stagnant in the first half of the nineteenth century, it is clear that there was no agricultural revolution in Ireland. Sluggish capital formation and technological backwardness, coupled to social unrest and the constraints imposed by the heavy dependence on the potato, kept the Irish economy far behind the rest of Western Europe (Mokyr, 1983). The considerable contribution which Irish agriculture made to the Industrial Revolution was expensive: Irish standards of living declined after 1815. As Table 6.10 shows, grain shipments continued throughout the famine years (albeit at a much reduced level) while between 1.1 million and 1.5 million Irish died of famine-related causes and another million fled in panic.

The achievements of the English agricultural revolution in the first half of the nineteenth century tend to be exaggerated. In that period England, as an interim measure, drew heavily on the land resources of her Celtic colony; but, substantial though this input was, it was not enough to alleviate the severe strains, particularly in southern England. Despite the protection given by the Corn Laws, the level of real investment in buildings, improvements, and equipment in agriculture was stationary between 1800 and 1830 when the rate of population growth was at its height (Feinstein, 1978, p. 40). The plight of the agricultural population of southern England, where the vast majority depended on wheat, was very serious. Contemporary

Table 6.10   Irish Exports of Grains to Britain, 1843–1849 (in 1000s of long tons)

	Wheat	Barley	Oats	Wheat meal and flour	Oatmeal
1843–45 (average)	63.8	19.6	264.0	47.3	71.4
1846	46.7	18.6	159.8	36.2	27.7
1847	30.9	9.5	82.2	10.6	16.5
1848	36.2	16.0	158.5	28.0	46.8
1849	25.5	8.9	111.1	23.0	35.9

Source: Donnelly, 1975, p. 82.

witnesses in the 1830s gave plentiful evidence of a shift by consumers away from wheat to the potato, particularly in the South of England (Salaman, 1949, pp. 523–31). In this way many workers were able to survive on the lowest possible wage.[15] At the beginning of the century 94 percent of the people of Southern and Eastern England consumed wheat, but in Scotland 72 percent consumed oats; in Wales 80 percent ate barley or oats, and in the North of England 68 percent ate oats or barley. To interpret wheat consumption trends in the first half of the nineteenth century, we must realize that an increasing number of "converts" were switching from coarse grains to wheat. Between 1800 and 1850 it is estimated that the proportion of the population of Great Britain who consumed wheat increased from 58 percent to 81 percent (Collins, 1975, pp. 105, 114). In interpreting this fact one must recognize that "by the same measure, and with possible implications for the 'cost of living' debate, a disproportionate share of the increase in wheat production during the first half of the nineteenth century was probably absorbed by converts', so that, while overall consumption per head may have been rising, per capita consumption among existing wheat-eaters, who formed the majority of the population, may have been falling" (ibid., p. 115). The "converts" were in Scotland, the North of England and Wales, and the traditional wheat-eaters were in Southern and Eastern England where the white loaf had become a necessity which poor people were very reluctant to give up.

Much against the expectations of English landowners and farmers, the quarter of a century after the introduction of free trade in 1846 turned out to be a "golden age" for British farming, based mainly on a shift to livestock production. There was a long interval before the land resources of continents of new settlement could be fully mobilized. The American Civil War delayed the process; the completion of the first American transcontinental railroad did not occur until 1869. Moreover, during this period up to about 1870 there was increasing scarcity of foods on the continent of Europe caused fundamentally by the population explosion.

Sometime after 1836 north-western Europe became collectively deficient in the bread grains. Britain's traditional suppliers not only ceased to be able to meet her needs, but were to some extent competing for available supplies from elsewhere (that is, principally the Russian Black Sea and Volga Steppes and the United States of America). The Repeal of the British Corn Laws was intimately associated with the coincidence of famine conditions in north-western and central Europe, but also with the need technically to facilitate supplies from new areas [Fairlie, 1965, p. 568].

The supplies of foodstuffs from these new areas overseas began to hit Europe like an avalanche in the 1880s.

Notes

[1] I am grateful to Joel Mokyr for his valuable suggestions, particularly relating to the sections on Ireland.

[2] Chambers and Mingay, 1966, pp. 207–8. No source is given for the 1868 estimate. For a vigorous attack on the received wisdom, see Kerridge, 1969, and the reply by Mingay.

[3] According to Ashley (1932, p. 8), as many as 95 percent of the population were wheat-eaters at the end of the eighteenth century.

[4] See Collins's important article, 1975.

[5] The figures in this paragraph are based on Collins, 1975, p. 105.

[6] Data from Mitchell and Deane, 1971, p. 88. O'Grada (1984) has estimated that in the pre-famine period the value of wheat production was about 4.9 million pounds sterling per annum, barley 1.8 million pounds and oats 8.1 million pounds.

[7] See Collins, 1975, p. 110.

[8] See Thomas, 1980, pp. 1–15.

[9] A specialist on the subject concludes as follows: "On the whole, then, France did not have a fuel crisis similar to the one Britain had faced. An ample supply of wood, particularly for manufacturers, in itself acted as a powerful deterrent to adopting coal. The French were under little pressure to change fuel . . . Ironically, the very lack of a shortage of vegetable fuel, particularly an industrial wood famine, may be considered as one circumstance which caused the economic development of France to lag behind that of Britain during the old regime" (Young, 1976, p. 55).

[10] See Davis, 1972, pp. 184–85.

[11] See Thomas, 1978.

[12] Based on the revised statistics of British overseas trade in Davis, 1978, pp. 87–125.

[13] Galpin, 1925, p. 193. The reserves of the Bank of England fell from £7,855,000 to £3,351,000 between 1808 and 1811 (ibid., p. 193).

[14] The lurid facts were made public in Accum, 1820.

[15] Referring to the low price of potatoes, James Caird in 1852 wrote: "There could be no greater evil befall the English agricultural laborer, than that any circumstance could compel him to depress his standard of comfort so far as to be content for his principal subsistence with the lowest species of food in this country, the potato" (Salaman, 1949, pp. 518–19).

7

Income Elasticities of Demand and the Release of Labor by Agriculture During the British Industrial Revolution: A Further Appraisal

N.F.R. CRAFTS

I

There has been little attention given to the role of the pattern of demand in the transfer of labor from agriculture to industry during the British Industrial Revolution. This is despite the prominence of Engel effects in many economists' models of economic development (Kelley and Williamson, 1974, chap. 10). The few discussions which do exist indicate an expectation that the income elasticity of demand for food in the eighteenth century may have been high (Crafts, 1976; Ippolito, 1975). If this was so, it could be expected to slow down the rate of industrialization, *ceteris paribus*.

On the other hand there has been great interest in the nature of improvement during the so-called Agricultural Revolution. The post-war literature *appears* to deny that agriculture released labor to industry during this period. E.L. Jones sums up one of the best known surveys thus: "It would be tendentious to praise agriculture because its inability to release enough labor prompted inventiveness, but it must be concluded that it was not usually an immediate source of labor for industry" (Jones, 1974, p. 102). Timmer concluded that "The English agricultural revolution increased land, not labor, productivity" (1969, p. 392).

Yet, paradoxically it would seem, Deane and Cole's discussion of structural change in the allocation of the labor force, which has also been a central part of the post war orthodoxy, suggests that the proportion of the labor force in agriculture was between 60 and 80 per cent in Gregory King's time, 36 per cent in 1801 and 22 per cent in 1841, the last census prior to the abolition of the Corn Laws (Deane and Cole, 1962, pp. 137, 142).

Reprinted with revisions from the *Journal of European Economic History*, Vol. 9, No. 1 (Spring 1980), pp. 153–68. Reprinted with permission from the editor of the *Journal of European Economic History*.

This paper re-examines the paradox. Section II discusses and extends the evidence on the income elasticity of demand for food and suggests that it was indeed high, Section III reviews the concept of labor release in terms of the concept of a viable economy and indicates the role which income elasticities play. Section IV pulls together these threads and relates them to the available evidence to suggest that once an appropriate conceptual framework is adopted it is clear that labor was released by agriculture in eighteenth and nineteenth century Britain. Output per worker in agriculture was augmented considerably from at least 1700 on but, given demand patterns, it is not at all surprising that the numbers employed in agriculture grew absolutely between 1700 and 1850. Section V considers some implications of these results and, in particular, argues that it is misleading to regard population growth as sufficient to generate growth of the industrial labor force.

II

Evidence on income elasticities has proved hard to come by for the Industrial Revolution period. Both Crafts (1976) and Ippolito (1975) relied on inferences from twentieth century data. Crafts argued that the income elasticity of demand for agriculture output was likely to be between 0.5 and 0.7 based on FCO data for developing countries (1982), whilst Ippolito suggested 0.5 to 0.75 based on data from Houthakker (1957) and Stone (1954) for Britain.

Two kinds of evidence can be used to glean information on income elasticities during the Industrial Revolution. First, there is cross-section data from budget studies. Very few of these exist but there are three investigations which can be utilized. These were made by Davies (1795) and Eden (1797) for poor, mainly agricultural workers, and Neild (1841) for rather better off Lancashire industrial workers. Secondly, given information over time on the growth of real income and population, on consumption of agricultural products and their prices, we can deduce a time series value for the income elasticity of demand for agricultural output for the economy as a whole.

Let us consider first the budget studies. Results in detail from these studies are presented in Table 7.1, even though in each case the number of observations is small, so that those who wish to make comparisons with the well-known historical budget studies by Houthakker (1957) and Williamson (1966) may do so.

Each of the budget studies was presented with a detailed commentary by the author and it is clear that they were all conducted with great scrupulousness. Nevertheless there are problems with the data which reduce the number of budgets which are usable for present purposes. In particular, care was taken to include in the regressions only those budgets where expenditure was reported on each of the categories rent, fuel, clothing and food, and only those households consisting of man, wife, and children. No attempt was made, however, to consider children in terms of adult equivalents because age information is not generally available.

A more important problem concerns the income variable. Modern investigators usually work in terms of expenditure rather than earnings because it is believed such data are less liable to error and more likely to represent permanent income. Each of the budget studies presented a difficulty. Davies's study gives earnings and expendi-

Table 7.1   Expenditure Elasticities of Demand (standard errors in parentheses)

	Food			Clothing			Housing		
	β	γ	R^2	β	γ	R^2	β	γ	R^2
Neild data	0.668	0.141	0.931				0.633	0.118	0.792
(n=14)[a]	(0.134)	(0.140)					(0.235)	(0.243)	
Eden data	1.003	−0.008	0.972	1.095	−0.181	0.392	0.651	−0.103	0.399
(n=24)[a,b]	(0.043)	(0.046)		(0.330)	(0.354)		(0.194)	(0.208)	
Davies data	0.876	0.132	0.624						
(n=32)[a]	(0.138)	(0.097)							
UK working class	0.594	0.294		1.042	0.143		0.553	−0.072	
1937–38[c]	(0.021)	(0.019)		(0.029)	(0.026)		(0.026)	(0.023)	
UK middle class	0.344	0.386		1.342	−0.111		0.346	0.145	
1937–38[c]	(0.019)	(0.021)		(0.154)	(0.169)		(0.031)	(0.034)	
City dwellers,	0.537	0.261		1.498	0.061		0.913	−0.154	
Germany 1907[c]	(0.018)	(0.015)		(0.045)	(0.038)		(0.026)	(0.010)	
Industrial workers,	0.712	0.158		1.435	0.016		0.839	−0.111	
USA 1901[c]	(0.004)	(0.002)		(0.019)	(0.012)		(0.016)	(0.010)	
Industrial workers,	0.607	0.303		1.821	−0.274		1.436	−0.463	
Mass. 1875[d]	(0.027)	(0.021)		(0.063)	(0.049)		(0.070)	(0.055)	
Skilled workers,	0.570	0.320		1.569	−0.140		1.511	−0.496	
Mass. 1875[d]	(0.069)	(0.040)		(0.109)	(0.074)		(0.133)	(0.091)	
Unskilled workers,	0.730	0.178		1.808	−0.167		1.367	−0.427	
Mass. 1875[d]	(0.038)	(0.040)		(0.118)	(0.123)		(0.124)	(0.129)	

[a] Estimates of the income elasticity of demand for food were also obtained using a semi-log functional form. The point estimates were 0.953 (Davies), 1.069 (Eden), and 0.853 (Neild).

[b] Estimates were also obtained for the sample including households with a deficiency of more than £3 per year. The double-log estimate of the expenditure elasticity of demand for food was 1.000 with a standard error of 0.028 (n = 49).

[c] Reported in Houthakker (1957); double-log functional form.

[d] Reported in Williamson (1966); double-log functional form.

ture on food in detail but does not give details of other expenditures or total expenditures. Earnings were therefore used as the independent variable. Nield's study is similar. He presents evidence for two years: 1836, a "normal year", and 1841, a year of depression. Income elasticities were estimated for 1836 again using earnings as the independent variable. Eden's study mostly concerns 1795–96, a period of high food prices, and budgets reported by him for other years were not used. Expenditure, which is itemized in some detail and for which a total is recorded by Eden, was used as the independent variable. Many of the households, however, reported expenditure far in excess of earnings and Eden himself expressed suspicion of the accuracy of their budgets. The results reported in Table 7.1 therefore used a sample from which were excluded all observations for which expenditure exceeded earnings by more than £3 per year (about one-eighth of the average budget in the sample).

Estimates of the elasticity of demand for food were obtained from the following regression equation:

$$\log F = a + \beta \log Y + \gamma \log N \tag{1}$$

where F is expenditure on food, Y is expenditure (or earnings) and N is the number in the family. β is, of course, directly interpretable as the expenditure (income) elasticity of demand for food. There are two estimation problems to be noted. For the studies based on earnings, if there are errors of measurement of earnings, this can be expected to give a downward bias to the estimate of β. For the study based on expenditure there is the possibility that the regression of a part of expenditure against the whole will impart an upward bias to the estimate of β.

Income and expenditure elasticities of demand for food estimated from the budget studies are reported in Table 7.1, together with results obtained in earlier papers by Houthakker and Williamson. For the Eden study it was possible also to derive estimates of the expenditure elasticity of demand for housing and clothing, and for the Neild study the income elasticity of demand for housing could be obtained. These figures are reported although not a main concern of this paper.

We see from Table 7.1 that the estimated elasticities of demand for food in England during the Industrial Revolution are high, and in the case of the Davies and Eden samples are not significantly different from 1. However, before jumping to the conclusion that the income elasticity of demand for food was high for the economy as a whole two points should be noted. First, although all the estimated coefficients are significantly different from zero at the 1 per cent level, the small sample size has left quite large confidence intervals. For example, the Neild sample coefficient is not significantly different from 0.4 and the Davies sample coefficient not sufficiently different from 0.6 at the 5 per cent level. Second, the samples are drawn from restricted income ranges, indeed from very poor families in two cases. The average yearly earnings for the Davies sample was £4.8 per head and for the Eden sample £5.7 compared with a national income per head in 1801 of £21.7 (Deane and Cole, 1962, pp. 8, 166) when the price level was 55 percent higher as measured by the Schumpeter-Gilboy index (Mitchell and Deane, 1962, p.469). For the Neild sample income per head was £15.2 compared with a national income of £24.4 in 1841 (Deane and Cole, 1962, pp. 8, 166). Naturally the results may not apply to income disposed of by higher-income families.

We can use Lindert and Williamson's (1982) recent revisions of Massie's account of income distribution in 1759 to provide a reasonable guess at the income elasticity of demand for food in the eighteenth century as a whole. Suppose the Eden sample estimate is taken to apply to families receiving up to £40 per year and the Neild estimate is taken to apply to families receiving more than £40 and up to £100 per year. This would leave the top 10% of income receivers to be considered and we might imagine that they would be perhaps a little higher in their income elasticity of demand for food than the middle class of 1937–38 say, 0.4. This procedure would give an estimate of the overall income elasticity of demand for food, with weights based on income shares, as $(0.44 \times 0.4) + (0.37 \times 1.0) + (0.19 \times 0.67) = 0.68$. Obviously, such an estimate has quite wide confidence intervals, although it should be noted that the budget studies of Neild, Eden, and Davies do nothing to indicate that the income elasticity of demand for food was lower than Crafts (1976) or Ippolito (1975) suggested.

Nevertheless, it is useful also to consider time series evidence and this can be done for the nineteenth century. If prices are stable, then the following relationship holds

$$\frac{\dot{Q}}{Q} = \epsilon \frac{(\dot{Y/P})}{(Y/P)} + \frac{\dot{P}}{P} \tag{2}$$

where Q is the supply of agricultural goods, ϵ is the income elasticity of demand for food, Y/P is income per head, P is population and the dot denotes a time derivative. For 1820–40 data exists to give estimates of all terms in (2) except ϵ which can therefore be deduced. The period is a suitable one to infer ϵ from as there were no major disturbances due to war or tariff changes and because relative prices between agricultural and industrial goods probably were fairly stable; certainly, the Rousseaux indices suggest that conclusion (Mitchell and Deane, 1962, p. 471).

Use of equation (2) gives the following results

$$2.10 = \epsilon 1.04 + 1.34$$

which gives an estimate for ϵ of 0.73. The data for the calculation come from Deane and Cole (1962, p. 8) for population and, Deane (1968) and Crafts (1983) for real income growth. For $\dot{Q}/Q$, home agricultural output supply was based on Deane and Cole (1962, p. 166) deflated by a nine year average of the Rousseaux agricultural price index for each year. Net imports were added to home output using Davis (1978, pp. 98, 100, 106, 118, 122) and adjusting for Ireland in a fashion analogous to Thomas (essay 6 in this book).

The time series approach gives a figure which is similar to the result arrived at from budget studies and it is suggested that the income elasticity of demand for food in Britain during the Industrial Revolution was probably around 0.7. Although Britain was an early and rapid industrializer, this was not based on a particularly low income elasticity of demand for food, unlike, for example, Japan for which case it has been claimed that a figure of 0.2 applied during Meiji times (Kelley and Williamson, 1974, p. 160). None of the evidence presented suggests that Britain was anywhere near such a low figure during the Industrial Revolution.

III

It was pointed out in Section I that it has been generally argued that from 1700 on the British economy experienced a rapid industrialization of the labor force. The figures given by Deane and Cole undoubtedly need some revision for the eighteenth century in the light of Lindert's research (1980b). The economy appears to have been somewhat less agricultural than Deane and Cole thought but the share of agriculture in the labor force was probably, nevertheless, around 56% in 1688 and 48% in 1759 (Crafts, 1984, pp. 20–22) and this figure declined to only 22% in 1841 (36% in 1801), Deane and Cole (1962, p. 142). This section briefly considers the role of agriculture in this process of the changing deployment of the labor force.

The focus is on the concept of the "release of labor" from agriculture to industry. The emphasis of the discussion is on agriculture's ability to transfer labor to industry, although, of course, the successful implementation of the transfer required that industry had the capability to employ released labor. The argument is developed in terms of an economy whose food is entirely domestically produced and in which the relative price of food is actually sustained at the same level, although in principle free to vary. This is a helpful, simplifying device but is in any case appropriate for an ex-post view of 1700–60 which will be our first concern in Section IV. The roles of changing prices and imports will be discussed later in Section IV. The model which follows is based essentially on Dixit (1973).

The crux of the industrialization problem for an economy like eighteenth century Britain is as follows. Suppose agriculture is characterised by diminishing returns to labor. Suppose also that food demand grows at the same rate as population. Then, if the relative share of the labor force in agriculture is to fall, i.e. industrialization is to occur, it is necessary that the growth rate of the labor force in agriculture must be less than the growth rate of population (and the labor force) overall. This appears to pose problems, for whilst the demand for food grows with population the food supply grows less rapidly even if all the extra labor is used in agriculture (which would, of course, amount to a deindustrialization). Clearly to home feed all the extra population and also industrialize by having the agricultural labor force growing less rapidly than labor as a whole it would be necessary to have output per worker in agriculture rising. This in fact is the crucial condition for the "viability" of the economy. Obviously, if demand were growing faster than population as a result perhaps of rising per capita incomes, the preceding arguments hold *a fortiori*. Since it is supposed that there are diminishing returns to labor in agriculture, industrialization requires some other force such as technical progress or capital accumulation to raise output per worker in agriculture by more than offsetting the diminishing returns.

The point can be elaborated as follows. The production function in agriculture is assumed to be

$$Qt = Ae^{\mu t}L_t^{\alpha} \quad (0 < \alpha < 1) \tag{4}$$

where μ represents the rate at which capital accumulation and technical progress are augmenting output. The rate of growth of food supply is therefore

$$\frac{\dot{Q}}{Q} = \mu + \alpha\frac{\dot{L}}{L} \tag{5}$$

Since we are assuming constant prices the growth of demand for food is the right hand side of equation (3) and for demand to remain equal to supply we have

$$\mu + \alpha\frac{\dot{L}}{L} = \epsilon(\frac{\dot{Y}}{Y} - n) + n \tag{6}$$

where n is the rate of population growth. This can be rearranged to give the required rate of growth of the agricultural labor force to meet the growth in demand for food as

$$\frac{\dot{L}}{L} = \frac{\epsilon(\dot{Y}/Y - n) + n - \mu}{\alpha} \tag{7}$$

For industrialization, $\dot{L}/L$ has to be less than n. If this condition is met then the economy can be said to be viable in the sense that the food requirements of the extra population can be met by a rate of increase of the labor force in agriculture less than the rate of increase of the labor force and population as a whole. Then some labor is released for use in industry and the food requirements of the population can be met by a lower share of the labor force.

This release of labor requires (using (7))

$$\frac{\epsilon(\dot{Y}/Y - n) + n - \mu}{\alpha} < n \tag{8}$$

which can be rearranged to give

$$\mu - (1 - \alpha)n - \epsilon(\dot{Y}/Y - n) > 0 \tag{9}$$

We can use (9) to consider what is required for the release of labor by agriculture. Even if there is no increase in income per head or zero income elasticity of demand for food, with population growth we need $\mu > 0$ because $\alpha < 1$. Given α, the faster population growth is the higher μ needs to be. That is, industrialization would require that capital accumulation and technical progress in agriculture more than outweighed diminishing returns to agricultural labor so that output per worker in agriculture rises. Inequality (9) also reveals that the necessary μ for industrialization will be raised for faster growth of income per head and/or a higher income elasticity of demand for food.

We can also consider the likelihood of there actually being falls in the absolute size of the agricultural labor force using equation (7). This shows that to get a decline in the agricultural labor force we need $\mu > \epsilon(\dot{Y}/Y - n) + n$. This is a more stringent condition than meeting inequality (9), which merely required

$$\mu > \epsilon(\dot{Y}/Y - n) + (1 - \alpha)n \ .$$

It is therefore quite possible to find (9) is met whilst the agricultural labor force is growing in absolute size.

The (closed economy, constant price) model that we have used suggests the following conclusions. Properly conceived, the release of labor from agriculture to industry is concerned with a decline in the proportion of the labor force in agriculture, not a decline in absolute numbers. The important thing is the ability of the economy to meet the extra food requirements occasioned by growth of population and incomes whilst allowing the share of industry in the labor force to rise. Indeed we might expect to observe that the release of labor implied by a decline in the proportion of labor in agriculture would coincide with a rise in the numbers in agriculture. The achievement of viability or a decline in the numbers in agriculture is made harder by higher income elasticities. To achieve a decline in the proportion of the labor force in agriculture output per worker in agriculture has to be rising and so the economy has to find a way to overcome diminishing returns to labor in agriculture.

· IV

We are now in a position to reconsider structural change during the Industrial Revolution using the results of Sections II and III. We turn first to the period 1700–60. Agricultural prices in relative and absolute terms were about the same at the beginning and end of this period (Deane and Cole, 1962, p. 91) and it is safe to ignore imports (Davis, 1962) so the model of Section III is applicable. Recent research has provided estimates for population growth, agricultural output growth and growth of national income per head (Crafts, 1983). For 1700–60 the estimates are 0.38% per year, 0.60% per year and 0.31% per year respectively, figures which represent significant revisions from the original estimates of Deane and Cole (1962, p. 78).

How was the 0.6 per cent per year growth rate for agricultural output achieved? To give an answer in terms of equation (5) above we need to evaluate α, L/L and μ. Lindert and Williamson's revisions of the social tables of King and Massie can be used to indicate that the growth rate of the agricultural labor force between 1700 and 1760 was about −0.05% (Crafts, 1984, p. 22). Ippolito provided an estimate of 0.36 for α (1975, p. 308); Deane and Cole's data (1962, pp. 152,166) also suggests a share for labor of about 40% in agricultural output in the early nineteenth century and an estimate for α of about 0.4 seems plausible. Substituting these figures into equation (5) gives

$$0.60 = \mu + (0.4)(-0.05) \tag{10}$$

and hence μ is estimated to be 0.62.

Our review of 1700–60 suggests the following. First, it is clear that output per worker in agriculture was rising. Second the proportion of the labor force in agriculture was falling and indeed absolute numbers fell slightly. Thus the economy was viable and labor was released by agriculture during this period prior to the classic Industrial Revolution. Third, the rise in output per worker in agriculture was based on a positive value for μ of 0.62, a considerable achievement for the agricultural sector in augmenting labor productivity.

What factors lay behind this high value for μ? No precise answer can be given but some clues are available. First of all it seems clear that additions to land were not important; Jones estimates that land inputs in agriculture rose by only perhaps 5% in the whole of the eighteenth century (1981a, p. 70). Second, Feinstein argues that until the end of the eighteenth century capital formation in agriculture was quite small and it seems unlikely that the capital stock grew at more than about 0.3% per year or had a share in output of more than about 20% (calculated from Feinstein, 1978, p. 49). Third, recent work does suggest a quite rapid rise in cereal yields based on the use of new crop rotations; cereal yields may have risen by as much as 50–55% between the late 17th century and 1760 (Turner, 1982; Overton, 1979). It thus seems most likely that μ was high because total factor productivity growth was considerable—perhaps 0.5% per year or thereabouts.

We can also examine the role of the income elasticity of demand for food in structural change during this period. Table 7.2 gives illustrations in terms of three cases, the income elasticity of 0.7 believed actually to have applied, the estimate of 0.2 suggested by some writers for Meiji Japan and the case of zero income elasticity of demand for food, i.e. growth of food demand from population growth alone.

The object of Table 7.2 is to consider what would have been required of agriculture to meet different pressures of demand without prices rising and without extra food imports. We see that the level of μ required for viability was virtually double what it would have been had income per head not been growing and that it was raised by over half compared with an economy with a "Japanese" demand structure.

Table 7.2   Release of Labor from Agriculture: Some Permutations of the 1700–60 Experience

i) Estimated values (% per year)

n : 0.38	$\dot{Q}/Q$: 0.60	ϵ : 0.7
$Y/Y - n$: 0.31	$\dot{L}/L$: −0.05	μ : 0.62

ii) Required μ for viability[a]		iii) Required μ for $\dot{L}/L < 0$[b]	
$\epsilon = 0.7$	0.45	$\epsilon = 0.7$	0.60
$\epsilon = 0.2$	0.29	$\epsilon = 0.2$	0.45
$\epsilon = 0.0$	0.23	$\epsilon = 0.0$	0.39

[a]Using inequality (9)
[b]Using equation (7)

The implication of the difference in demand can be shown another way. During 1700–60 the growth of the non-agricultural labor force was about 0.8% per year. Had the income elasticity of demand for food been only 0.2, then given the actual level of μ the economy *could* have had a rate of growth of the industrial labor force 50% higher at 1.2% per year. In other words the British income elasticity emerges as a potentially important retardant of the rate of industrialization. (What *would* have actually happened requires a counterfactual specification beyond the scope of this kind of accounting model, of course).

We can now look at the problems posed for the release of labor from agriculture by the faster growth of incomes and population during the Indsutrial Revolution proper. Table 7.3 gives data from 1760–1800 an 1820–40; 1800–20 is omitted because Deane and Cole's figures for agricultural incomes behave very erratically as do agricultural prices in this period. The data are taken from the same sources as for Table 7.2 and the calculations for equations (3) and (10).

The examples of Table 7.3 are, of course, benchmarks by which to assess demand pressure on agriculture in the absence of trade or price changes and they are constructed in an analogous fashion to Table 7.2. In fact, of course, the economy experienced rapidly rising food prices between 1760 and 1800 where the annual rate of increase of relative agricultural prices was around 0.6% (Crafts, 1983) and imports grew so that by 1840 net imports of all foodstuffs were about 20% of home agricultural output, although by this time relative agricultural prices were close to those of 1760.

A comparison of Tables 7.2 and 7.3 shows that faster population growth alone more than doubled the μ for viability in 1760–1800 and that by 1820–40 the μ value required was more than 3 times that of 1700–60. In 1760–1800, it seems that the economy did *not* pass the viability benchmark and along with this failure there was both a fall in the achieved μ and a rise in the required μ of roughly equal dimensions. The value of μ appears too small even to have passed the benchmark test for a zero income elasticity of demand for food case.

Table 7.3   Pressure of Demand and the Requirements for a Viable Economy
after 1760

1760–1800

i) Estimated values

n : 0.83	$\dot{Q}/Q$: 0.44	ϵ : 0.7
$\dot{Y}/Y - n$: 0.18	$\dot{L}/L$: 0.04	μ : 0.42

ii) Required μ for viability

$\epsilon = 0.7$	0.63
$\epsilon = 0.2$	0.54
$\epsilon = 0.0$	0.50

iii) Required μ for $\dot{L}/L < 0$

$\epsilon = 0.7$	0.96
$\epsilon = 0.2$	0.87
$\epsilon = 0.0$	0.84

1820–1840

iv) Estimated values

n : 1.34	$\dot{Q}/Q$: 1.38	ϵ : 0.7
$\dot{Y}/Y - n$: 1.04	$\dot{L}/L$: 0.28	μ : 1.27

v) Required μ for viability

$\epsilon = 0.7$	1.54
$\epsilon = 0.2$	1.02
$\epsilon = 0.0$	0.81

vi) Required μ for $\dot{L}/L < 0$

$\epsilon = 0.7$	2.07
$\epsilon = 0.2$	1.55
$\epsilon = 0.0$	1.35

By 1820–40, however, circumstances had changed again. The estimated value of μ is now much higher at 1.27% which would easily pass the benchmark test for absolute declines in the agricultural labor force in earlier periods but is not now quite sufficient for viability in the closed economy, constant price case because demand growth has intensified substantially. The economy did pass the benchmark test for viability at zero income elasticity in this period. As this time with output per worker in agriculture rising rapidly it also seems that Britain had relatively high worker productivity by European standards; Bairoch (1972, p. 214) estimated that in 1860 British labor productivity was about 2.1 times that of Continental Europe. Growth of imports during 1820–40 reflected rapid growth of demand and comparative advantage as Britain exported increasing amount of manufactures in return for food imports, it did not reflect slow growth in agricultural labor productivity.

What accounts for the behaviour of μ during 1760–1800 and 1820–40? Again the answers can only be tentative. It seems, however, that after 1760 growth of cereal yields slackened substantially (Turner, 1982) and that until the 1790s agricultural investment was not substantially increased (Feinstein, 1978, p. 40) whilst much of the diffusion of new crop rotations was completed (Jones, 1981a, p. 85). From the 1790s on agriculture became much more capital intensive and the higher levels of investment seem to have been accompanied by a quickening of total factor productivity growth. Calculations based on growth of labor based on Deane and Cole, and capital and land based on Feinstein (1978) suggest that total factor productivity growth whilst perhaps 0.25% per year from 1760 to 1800 was of the order of 0.9% per year by 1820–40.

Thus agriculture's ability to release labor can be seen as follows. In 1700–60 a successful release of labor was achieved based on substantial efficiency growth. During 1820–40 the economy certainly was viable without requiring price rises or extra imports at a zero income elasticity or for $\epsilon = 0.7$ provided that incomes per head rose at no more than 0.66%. In practice, faster growth was obtainable without price rises by exploiting comparative advantage. During 1760–1800 the economy did not, however, pass the benchmark viability test. The symptom of this failure was the rise in agricultural prices and the problem was both that demand pressure grew and the productivity growth in agriculture slackened.

V

The arguments of previous sections have been that the income elasticity of demand for food was high, that the release of labor should be thought of in terms of rises in output per agricultural worker such that extra food requirements can be met with a declining share of the labor force in agriculture and that output per worker rose substantially in the eighteenth and early nineteenth centuries.

Why did the authors cited in Section I appear to deny that agriculture released labor during the Industrial Revolution? It was not because of disagreements over facts, although the present paper uses revised estimates of agricultural output and labor force. In fact, the conventional view has argued that the economy was essentially home fed until the 1840s and has argued also for much greater reductions in the proportion of the labor force in agriculture than would now seem appropriate. Thus Deane and Cole suggest that the share of the labor force in agriculture could have been as high as 80% in 1688 (1962, p. 3) and Deane argues for 60–70% of the labor force being agricultural in 1750 (1979, p. 14). The estimates relied on for this paper are 55.6 and 48% respectively. Also I have suggested in the last section that food imports into Britain were of very substantial importance by 1840.

The answer to the paradox seems to lie in the historiography of the Agricultural Revolution and the conceptualization of labor release rather than in disagreement about fact. Much post war work on the Agricultural Revolution has been enormously influenced by Chambers and all recent work owes a large intellectual debt to him. The analytic lead given by Chambers in his seminal 1953 paper attracted many followers. In reacting to the views of writers like Cole and Dobb, Chambers stressed two points in particular. First, that during the Industrial Revolution the adoption of new farming generated increases in the flows of labor services required in agriculture and that the rural population was rising more or less everywhere. Second, that the source of the supply of the industrial labor force was not agrarian change but population growth (1953, pp. 332–38).

Since Chambers wrote, some discussions have tended to downplay the fact that output per worker in agriculture rose and to stress the rise in the absolute numbers of workers in agriculture (Chambers and Mingay, 1966, p. 99; Jones, 1974, p. 102). Timmer's work, as noted in Section I, suggests that the improvements available to agriculture raised labor inputs proportionately as much as yields. From the perspective of this paper, however, the point that should have been stressed is that the new farming gave the agricultural sector opportunities to raise output per worker by making fuller use of workers previously underemployed for much of the year even in cases where output per worker hour was not raised by improvements.

More fundamental has been the failure to emphasize the decline in the percentage of the labor force in agriculture when thinking of the release of labor. Most authors have readily accepted that the extra population could be fed with a smaller fraction of the workforce in agriculture but have not recognized this as a release of labor, saying rather that population growth led to the industrialization of the labor force. Thus Deane says, "If the agricultural industry did not actually supply the labor which the labor intensive techniques of the new industry demanded, it fed the increasing population from which the industrial labor force was drawn" (1979, p. 48). Jones and Woolf say, "labor was probably not released from agriculture during the first wave of change—mixed farming had heavy labor needs and the absolute number of farmhands actually grew—but the nation's food supply could be secured by an ever *smaller* proportion of the national workforce" (1969, p. 15). The model of Section III shows that this is a release of labor by exposing the counterfactual. The discussion of Section IV indicates that this is perhaps something of an overstatement of agriculture's success.

There is, however, a much more than a terminological difference between the analysis of the present paper and that of Chambers and his followers. Their view argues that population growth provided the labor supply for industry. The model of Section III shows that it is seriously misleading to regard population growth as either necessary or sufficient to generate the industrialization fo the labor force. In particular, if μ had been less than the viability requirement for zero income per head growth, then population growth would generate de-industrialization in the constant price, closed economy, constant living standards case. For example, if 1700–60 had been zero then to preserve constant prices without imports for even the modest population growth of that era would have required an agricultural labor force growth of 1.50% given income per head at 0.31% per year, far above overall labor force growth and thus generating deindustrialization.

Using a result shown by Mokyr (see essay 4 in this book), the point can be made much more explicit. If $\mu = 0$, we have

$$\frac{\dot{Q}}{Q} = \alpha kn$$

where $k = \dot{L}/L \div n$. Industrialization occurs in our definition when $k \langle 1$.

For the economy *as a whole* in the eighteenth century, the elasticity of income with regard to labor was fairly close to the value of α in agriculture, it can be supposed, since labor's share of national income was around 0.45 (Deane and Cole, 1962, p. 301). Mokyr shows that the growth of demand for agricultural goods will be equal to

$$[1 - \epsilon(1 - \alpha]n \quad (\text{essay4}) \ .$$

Equating supply and demand growth we would then have

$$\alpha k n = [1 - \epsilon(1 - \alpha)]n \tag{12}$$

Hence

$$k = \left[\frac{1 - \epsilon(1 - \alpha)}{\alpha} \right] > 1 \tag{13}$$

from which we see that increases in population growth will tend to *raise* the proportion of labor in agriculture given that ϵ and α are less than 1. The intuition of the result is quite appealing, namely that with supply elasticities the same for both sectors population growth tends to raise the relative size of the sector with the low demand elasticity.

Finally we can point to two corollaries of the high income elasticity of demand for food. First, it means that economic growth brought strong demand pressure to bear on agriculture so that faltering supply growth could well generate short term market rises in agricultural prices. Economic growth might well involve, as it did in the late eighteenth century, rapid changes in relative prices. Second, given the well documented sluggish behavior of money wage rates (Flinn, 1974) and the very high share of expenditure on food in lower income budgets (Crafts, 1982) in the short term economic growth might operate to the detriment of lower income groups. The implications for the distribution of gains from industrialization in the early phases of the Industrial Revolution may be worth further consideration.

Note

This is a revised and updated version of a paper originally written in 1977 which was originally published in the *Journal of European Economic History* IX (1980). I am particularly indebted to Joel Mokyr for his insightful suggestions on the revised version and to P.J. Law for comments and to M. Casey for computational assistance on the original paper. I am solely responsible for errors.

8

Industrialization and the European Economy

SIDNEY POLLARD[1]

I

Traditionally, the industrialization of Europe has been viewed as a series of separate "industrial revolutions." Each country has been treated as an "economy" and its progress compared separately with some kind of implied model. There can, for example, be few universities in Britain in which the annual examination ritual does not include some questions about the retardation of the industrial revolution in "France" or its acceleration in "Germany" in the nineteenth century.

There are many good reasons for making the political state, or even a notional country like Germany before 1871, the unit of investigating the process of industrialization. It follows the practice of contemporaries, who were mostly concerned with influencing economic development by the only political authority available, the state. Political historians, too, are wont to see the nineteenth-century world as made up of the individual states of Europe (Bridbury, 1972). And in truth many issues of direct relevance to industrialization operated within political boundaries or were affected by political decisions. These included protection, the currency, access to markets and colonies, and poor laws and factory acts. Other important legal and social data, such as serfdom, the status of the businessman, primogeniture, and guild and staple rights, might in some cases coincide with the political frontiers, but as a matter of fact did not so coincide in some of the leading countries of Europe during the early stages of industrialization.

In recent years yet another reason has emerged for viewing industrialization in national terms: many of the countries attempting to industrialize today have to use the whole apparatus of state power to propel their industrial revolution forward so that it must appear as an act of political will. By analogy, this is then applied to Europe in the nineteenth century.

This article will argue that the traditional view has reached its limit as a method both of exposition and of analysis, and that further advance must come from a new

Reprinted with revisions from the *Economic History Review*, Vol. 26, No. 4 (November 1973), pp. 636–48. Reprinted by permission of the Economic History Society.

starting-point. It will argue that, useful as the "national" approach has been in the past, particularly by evolving testable models, it was based on faulty observation. The industrialization of Europe did not proceed country by country. On a map of Europe in which industrialization was colored, say, red, it would by no means be the case that an area corresponding to a country within its boundary would turn uniformly pale pink, dark pink, and so on to deepest crimson. On the contrary, industrialization would appear as red dots, surrounded by areas of lighter red diminishing to white, and with the spread of industrialization these dots would scatter across the map with little reference to political boundaries. It would also follow that the dynamic of the infection of this rash of red dots, crossing frontiers while by-passing large areas of the home country, must clearly have a largely non-political explanation.

It is this dynamic element, the method of transmission, which should be a major object of study, but has inevitably been lost sight of in the traditional approach. To change the metaphor, we have tended to treat each country like a plant in a separate flower pot, growing independently into a recognizable industrialized society according to a genetic code wholly contained in its seed. But this is not how the industrialization of Europe occurred. Rather, it was a single process: the plants had common roots and were subject to a common climate. Further, the development and chronology of the industrial revolution in each area was vitally affected by its place in the general advance, by those ahead of it as well as those trailing behind it, and this relativist role must form part of any description or analysis.

It should be admitted at once that this article is itself open to the same objection as the traditional single-country approach: the course of the European industrial revolution in turn cannot be explained fully without its mutual interaction with other continents.[2] The story told here, it cannot be stressed too strongly, is therefore still only a partial story. But it is a beginning, and we can at least plead that the necessary and dynamic relationship between the industrialization of Europe and the rest of the world has received some attention recently[3] and is therefore in less need of emphasis. Here we shall try to make the case for a single European economy in the crucial years of industrialization, c. 1815–1914.

II

Before proceeding to consider Europe, an area larger than the nation state, as an appropriate framework for the study of industrialization, it is worth making a digression to a unit smaller than the nation state. It is clear that in the pioneer country itself, Great Britain, we shall miss much of the actual dynamic (Isard, 1949) of industrialization if we neglect the fact that the "industrial revolution" came much earlier, say, to South Lancashire and the Black Country than it did to Lincolnshire or Kent; that even concentrated manufacturing regions like Sheffield with Hallamshire or the West Country woollen areas were revolutionized generations after the cotton areas; and that some of the regions leading in the first phase, like North Wales, the Derbyshire uplands, and even Cornwall (Dodd, 1933; Rowe, 1953; Chapman, 1967), petered out as industrial concentrations in later phases.

Behind the temporal sequences lay functional relationships. Agrarian advances in some areas may have stimulated early industry in other less-favored ones (E.L. Jones, 1968), while in turn an industrial or urban expansion in areas like Lancashire affected agrarian development in surrounding counties. Regional specialization associated with modernization, for example in pottery, in cutlery and toolmaking, or in woollen textiles, was tantamount to de-industrialization elsewhere. Alternatively, the introduction of advanced factories, say cotton mills, in one district, might lead to the extension of an obsolescent system, domestic labor in cotton weaving or framework knitting, in others. And in turn, the concentration of a region on the latter might help to make it miss the bus in relation to machine spinning thereafter (Chapman, 1967, pp. 212–15).

The point is not merely the banal one that the mechanization of one industry has consequences on others, but that around each may be a whole regional society with identifiable features appropriate to a certain stage of the industrialization process differing from the stage reached by other regions. An industrial or commercial concentration transformed its local enonomy and society well before it helped to transform the economic life of the country as a whole. At any given cross-section in time, let us say in 1815, some regions were more advanced than others: ultimately the whole of Britain became modernized and industrialized, but the path followed by each region was different and was determined at each point in time by its inter-relation with the rest. No history of industrialization of any one region in isolation from the others would make much sense: one of the significant features of the industrial revolution in Britain was its complex regional inter-relationships.

So it was on the Continent. A map of c. 1815 would have shown several distinct groups of red dots. One was shaped like a curved dagger pointing from the Channel coast to the heart of Europe, including northern France and Belgium, Rhineland-Westphalia, Alsace, and parts of Switzerland. A second group of dots would be scattered farther east, covering parts of Saxony, Bohemia, and Silesia. As if to prove the vanity of politics, both these main areas happened to straddle several major frontiers. Other secondary centres might be found in and around the large cities such as Paris, Vienna, Berlin, and St. Petersburg.

Even if we agree that "the striking thing about the imitative ventures on the Continent is certainly their spottiness. One modern ironworks went a long way" (Ohlin, 1959, p. 349), the fact remains that when industrialization finally did take its leap forward, these were its jumping-off points. A map of Europe around 1865 would have shown the original areas of dots to have become solid red belts, with new dots scattered thickly all over the north-western half of Europe, and very thinly in its northern, eastern, and southern marches, and in Ireland. If we let another half-century pass and observe conditions around 1914, we note that much of the north-western half of Europe is now solid, while the scatter of dots in the periphery has become much denser. Today, after two world wars, the relative level of industrialization and of incomes across Europe still has basically the same pattern.

Is there anything to be gained by this kind of regional-local approach? Apart from its claim to greater historical accuracy (Thorp, 1926, pp. 103–4; Clough, 1957; Nef, 1950, p. 292; W.G. Hoffman, 1958, pp. 43ff; Wright, 1939, pp. 129 ff.), its merit, if any, must lie in opening up new and potentially fruitful questions (see North, 1955). Two types of question spring immediately to mind. The first is concerned with our concept of industrialization: how do we define, or recognize, the different stages of an industrial revolution? The national framework has left us floundering among proportions of output furnished by manufacturing industry, its share in the labor force, numbers working in factories, provison of capital or horsepower, rate of growth of industrial output, the share of capital goods in total output, and the share working for a market economy or for wages. The regional approach will at least make us wary of such definitions of industrialization as that which uses income per head as an indicator (Hartwell, 1971), since observers from Sismondi to Villerme seem to agree that the industrial centres were noted for their poverty rather than their wealth. There is at least a chance that it may shed some light on our search for a postive identification.

The second set of questions is concerned with favorable settings and preconditions, and therefore, in at least one sense, with causes. What disposed some areas to take more quickly to the new system than others? Was it natural resources? Location and transport facilities? A developed capitalistic commerce or access to foreign technology? Regional advantages in education? (Fohlen, 1971, p. 162). A background of urban handicraft, centers of consumption, or associated external economies? A flourishing domestic industry? Favorable systems of inheritance? (Habakkuk, 1955). Freedom from capricious autocracy, from serfdom, or from guild obstructionism? Again, we see at once that some solutions proffered on a national scale come off badly: such are government policies like protection, subvention, or, on the contrary, free trade, when some early industrializing regions differ so widely from others subject to the same legislation, while showing great similarities to their opposite numbers existing under a very different political framework; or the doctrine of a "critical minimum effort" needed to take an economy out of its traditional balance (Leibenstein, 1957, p. 185 and passim.) which has little persuasive power in a regional context. Perhaps here, too, we may hope to get some positive aid by operating at the microlevel in our search for causes, sequences, and the relative weight of factors.

III

However promising this regional, or for that matter the traditional national, emphasis may be, they must in the end be put into context by treating the whole of Europe as one single macro-development area. Let us begin by considering the period of early European industrialization c. 1815–65.

Paradoxically, whatever economic inter-relationships Europe possessed before the war, and they were many, were reinforced by blockade and counter-blockade, as well as, indeed, by the Napoleonic dream to turn the Continent into one single economic area. From 1815 on, the common distresses of war were followed by the common disasters of peace. First, there was the mass dumping of British manufactures on European markets. The unfortunate timing of the war, which granted the Continent artificial protection from Britain's exports and isolation from her rapid technical progress, followed by the peace, and an abrupt exposure to the full blast of her accumulated commodities and superior skills, undoubtedly constituted a traumatic setback for several continental industrial centres. And this was compounded by the artificial separation of producers from their market, as was the case with the industries of Belgium and Rhineland-Westphalia—divided from the French consumers for whose needs they had been primarily created.

Thus parts of Europe were becoming de-industrialized owing to the expansion of British industry, as East Anglia was becoming de-industrialized owing to the expansion of West Riding industry (Clapham, 1910). The textile and metals industries suffered most, particularly in Austria and parts of Germany. Even centres with well-established export markets, like the Silesian textile manufacture and the Rhineland mills, lost many of them to Britain (Beer, 1891, pp. 312–15; Aegidi, 1865, pp. 40–41). In Italy, French textiles were driven out by the British who, according to Talleyrand, the French ambassador in Naples, "know how to put themselves out to meet the needs, the whims and the imagination of men, making for them fabrics at all kinds of prices according to the level of poverty of the regions for which they are intended".[4]

But some firms, the best and toughest, survived. Their world lay between the more advanced British on one side and the more backward Europe on the other. Belgium was the territory which became keyed first and most successfully into such an intermediary role, and Belgian industrial history can be fully understood only within the context of this dual relationship. Though favored by coal and iron resources, by location and transport, by relative wealth and urban and industrial traditions, Belgium's industrial revolution depended on the British. British entrepreneurs pioneered and founded her major engineering works, above all Cockerill's at Seraing, who boasted in the 1830s that they knew of all inventions within ten days of their appearance in Britain. Others helped to establish some of the leading textile works and, in the early phase of the railways, built and financed large parts of the Belgian railway network, both state-owned and private.

At the same time, Belgium became a centre of diffusion. In the words of one contemporary of 1835:

> John Cockerill travels on the great highways in his coach. Here he builds furnaces and there chimney stacks. He covers fields with his tents and then when all his preparations have been made he erects the steam engines which have followed in his wake . . . and which breathe life into the great pile of bricks. And the next day the peasants hear a loud rhythmical noise coming from the factory—like the breathing of some enormous monster who, once he has begun to work, will never stop. And John Cockerill climbs back into his coach and government officials unsuspectingly sign his passport as if it referred to a consignment of wine and they do not realise that this silent man who seldom puts pen to paper is far more likely to turn their old world upside down than many a revolutionary who has his pockets stuffed with political programmes and manifestoes.[5]

The provenance of steam engines, perhaps representing the most advanced sector of current technology, was characteristic of Belgium's position. In 1830, there were 428 steam engines in the country, of which 74 (21 per cent) were foreign built. By 1844 there were 1,606, of which only 110 (7 per cent) were foreign built. At the same time in the 1830s Belgium exported seven times as much in value of engines than she imported (Lévy-Leboyer, 1964, p. 364).

The French textile industries in the northern *départements* and in Alsace and the French metals and engineering industries similarly had to fit themselves into a world in which the British had established a powerful dominance. Thus, in textiles, as Lancashire-Yorkshire could not be beaten in coarse-quality mass-produced goods, the French developed higher-quality fabrics as their area of strength. Even in cottons, where the British lead was greatest, although the quantity of raw cotton consumed by

Britain in 1836 was at least three times that of France, the output of French fabrics (partly, no doubt, because of higher costs and partly because of higher quality of workmanship) was worth three-fifths of that of the British. The British led in pig iron output, but the French exported large quantities of finished metal goods to the less advanced regions of Europe (ibid., p. 410). At home, the French might have had a protected market. Abroad, at least until the mid-century, the non-industrialized world was still too large for Britain to fill by herself, and here lay the chance for the early continental industrializers.

It was, however, in the German states that awareness of the location between the two worlds was strongest, as indeed it was also the German Confederation in which frontiers were most clearly irrelevant to economic reality. This was, perhaps, made most explicit in the debate surrounding the new Prussian Tariff Act of 1818, and its extension to a large part of Germany through the Zollverein in the course of 1828–33.

The debate of 1815–18 is usually portrayed as a simple clash of sectional interests. Thus Field Marshal H. v. Boyen in a letter to Hardenberg, the Chancellor, in 1819:

> The West, perhaps already over-supplied with manufactures, sees in England its enemy who has to be fought continuously. The East, against which each year another market for corn is being closed, longs for British manufactured products and others like them in order to get rid of its corn by these purchases.[6]

But what is significant here was the extent to which external, rather than internal, relationships were considered. The concern of the eastern landowners (as of the mercantile cities, the other large free-trade lobby) was the relationship with Britain, while western industrialists were concerned partly with Britain and partly with their export markets. In vain did the Prussian bureaucracy protest, truthfully, that the Tariff Bill was intended to deal mainly with internal administrative and taxation problems. Its spokesmen were driven to find justification on the more general grounds of favoring Prussia's prosperity and her industrialization. The decision to go in for free trade in 1818, at a time when Prussia was the only European power to do so, was no doubt ultimately anchored in the power of the Junkers, but the arguments developed in what was a remarkably articulate debate within the hierarchy, were conducted mainly in terms of furthering industry at a stage when Prussia occupied that middle position between British industrial power and the potential markets of her backward neighbors. Here, typically, is Bülow, explaining the proposed Tariff Bill to King Frederick William III in 1817:

> External competition, far from suppressing home industry, tends to perfect manufacture and induce an extension of activity. The Provinces of Lower Rhine, Westphalia and Saxony learnt by these means how to exercise their skills. While they had to stand up to foreign competition without political defences or powers of prohibition, their manufactures rose, and their industriousness [Industriefleisz] prospered to such an extent that they do not now need to worry about sales at home, their goods can stand up to British competition by their high quality and moderate prices.[7]

As another example we may quote the report dated 20 June 1817 by the Taxation Commission of the Prussian Staatsrat which accompanied its vote for the Tariff Bill, an important stage in its progress. Raw material costs were, they noted, much the same all over Europe, though Prussia might have the edge in flax and wool; interest rates were low in Prussia (Silesian 4 per cent stocks standing at 105 being much the same as British 3 per cent stocks at 78 3/4); wages were lower than in England; and only British machinery was superior, but might be copied. Thus many Prussian textile districts (but not the cotton spinners of Berlin and Silesia) should be in a position to beat the British in third (export) markets, as did the unprotected mills of Saxony and Switzerland.[8] Certainly Kunth, travelling in 1817 in the province of Saxony and to Minden and Bielefeld in the west to investigate the textile manufacturers' complaints, reported continuing exports as well as stiff British competition (Rothe and Ritthaler, 1934, pp. 43–44).

Basically, they echoed Silesian provincial President Merckel and the military Governor Maj.-Gen. von Gaudi in their submission of the Silesian demands at the Peace Conference of 1814. These two spokesmen were convinced that the Silesian textiles could hold their own in South America, given fair treatment, and hoped "to ensure in the peace treaty what has never before been achieved: that Silesian linen should not be burdened in Portugal and Spain with any higher duties than French and British linen." They also noted the large markets for Silesian textiles in Russia, Poland, and Austria which should be safeguarded (Treue, 1937, p. 34; Linke, 1899, pp. 193–95, 201–05).

By the time of the debates of 1828–33 which surrounded the formation of the Southern Customs Union, the Central Tax Union, and ultimately the Zollverein, the inter-relation had become much clearer. It was universally expected that within what was now a single free trade area, the more advanced industrial districts—the duchy of Berg, Saxony, Silesia, or Nuremberg, for example—would replace some British manufactures in the less industrialized regions, and these, in turn, would send exports to Switzerland and Italy, while Saxony would continue her smuggling trade into Bohemia (Bab, 1930; Rothe and Ritthaler, 1934, pp. 547, 549–50, 604; Treitschke, 1882, p. 659). As a matter of fact, within a few years the Zollverein had become an importer *and* exporter not only of manufactures, but also of food.[9]

Economic relations with Britain were particularly close in the subsequent twenty years or so. In the dynamic equilibrium established between the two trading areas, both natural resources and labor could be considered immobile, and German wages as a whole could stay below British wages as a whole, as long as German productivity was lower. The ratios of comparative costs (or factor endowment, if the term is preferred) favored Britain where better machinery made British labor more productive, but favored Germany where comparable machinery allowed her lower wages to give her a cost advantage.[10] Thus British yarn and German looms, British iron and German metal goods were added to British ships and Baltic grain and naval stores to form a symbiosis comparable to that of American cotton and Lancashire spindles. Friedrich List (1841) saw part of the truth in the danger threatening the developing German industries from the developed British ones. But he failed to see the other part, the wide open markets available to the industrializing German areas, both inside their own countries, and farther east and south, and the aid they received in their expansion by being able to use cheap British iron, yarn, or machinery. These elastic markets provided the dynamic for German growth, even though British exports were breathing down German necks, and, in principle, that dual relationship became the pattern for European industrialization. It is precisely what is not available to industrializers today.

The analysis cannot be pursued here into the next phase, c. 1865–1914, except for one generalization. As industrialism spread outwards, the original heartlands found the adjacent areas ever less dependent and ever more competitive, so that they had to go farther and farther afield for complementary food, raw materials, and markets, leaving Europe to the later starters. Britain was the first to begin to turn her back on Europe, slowly in the 1840's and more rapidly from the peak of the 1870's on (Hoffman, 1933, pp. 5ff; Condliffe, 1951, p. 208), but the fate of being supplanted by one's earlier industrial dependencies also began to overtake the continental heartlands in their turn in the age of "Imperialism."[11] As for the latecomers, not only is it true that the later they are, the wider the gap in technology and the greater the difference in social structure that have to be bridged; but also the larger the pack of competitors baying at their heels, and the narrower the backward world still open to them (Berend and Ranki, 1982). Somewhere near the outer periphery of Europe there is the watershed between societies which on contact with the new industrialism were capable of imitating it and becoming part of it, and areas which, at least for a long period, were transformed away from it, becoming specialized as "colonial" economies and facing an ever wider gap between themselves and the advanced economies.[12] That line marks the difference between the industrialization of Europe and the industrializers of today.

It is worth repeating that we are describing not merely a sequence but also a mechanism. Looked at from the narrow limits of one country, we may grasp such partial relationships as "export-led industrialization" or "enclave" economy (Berrill, 1960; Froelich, 1936, pp. 58 ff.; Fanfani, 1972, pp. 215 ff.; Hughes, 1959, p. 339; Ohlin, 1959, pp. 350–51; Nurske, 1959, pp. 13 ff.). But the real historical relationships were multilateral and continuously changing. The British industrial revolution took the course it took, because among other reasons, elastic export markets were available for the products of the mills; German weaving could expand because the mills existed in England; and Dutch, Danish, and Swiss agriculture was built up on the nearby existence of large industrial populations. The industrial revolution in Europe was not merely the national repetition of a pattern; it was also the continuous adaptation to a continent-wide opportunity.

IV

So far we have examined industrialization in vertical cross-section, as it were: along the line of chronology. If we turn to the horizontal cross-section, observing Europe at any one point of time, two aspects stand out in importance.

The first is that Europe was not a single market merely for commodities: over much of the nineteenth century it also in effect became a single market for capital, skill, enterprise, ideas, and technical knowledge. The extent of the inter-penetration of capital, whether by the older type of private banker or by the newer joint-stock investment banker (Segal and Simon, 1961; Jenks, 1927; Lévy-Leboyer, 1964; Cameron, 1961; Waltershausen, 1907; Gille, 1959, 1970; Landes, 1969b), has been made clearer by recent work. Similarly there is now no justification for ignoring the transmission of entrepreneurship and technology from the advanced industrial regions to the developing regions across the frontiers of Europe (Cameron, 1956; Henderson, 1954). But their significance and their role have often been misunderstood.

It is sometimes argued that the part played by foreign capital or foreign skilled labor could only have been minimal, since nowhere did it exceed a small fraction of "domestic" capital and labor available at any one time. But that line of reasoning—derived, no doubt, from the experience of present-day industrializers—misinterprets the needs of a European neighbor. European countries were not greatly dissimilar in wealth at the onset of industrialization, and they shared common traditions of settled government, urban culture, and, above all, commercial capitalism. What they required, in different degrees, was not to be pulled up from abroad, but a stimulus or trigger, and some detailed know-how in key sectors so that they could "take-off" by themselves.

It is precisely that which they received from their more advanced neighbors. Thus in the post-1815 period it can be shown that every major iron and engineering works of the modern kind in Belgium and France and every early major railway, beside many textile mills and other enterprises, operated with British help. Similarly, every new German industry used British technology and many used French capital and entrepreneurship. By the mid-century, French capital and engineering skill were to be found in the main railways of Spain and Portugal, Italy, Austria, and Russia. Behind them, their very banks derived from the stimulus and the resources of the French *crédit mobilier* while, it should be noted, most of the chief London investment banks were not of British origin, nor was the Paris *Haute Banque* of French. Among the earlier industrializers at least, the initial stimulus from outside found enough capital, and a sufficiently favorable social environment (pre-existing or created by this process itself), to transfer the main burden to "native" shoulders, as had been the case in the different regions of Britain. But that does not diminish the critical role played by the fuse which in one area after another was ignited without waiting for spontaneous combustion to occur.

Thus, it is the wrong counter-factual question which has often been posed in this regard. It should not be "How long would French main-line railways have been delayed without British help? " in order to prove that British help made little difference: for the British help is known to have occurred and therefore the influence of one industrialized economy upon the other does not need proof. The question should rather be: "If French capital and entrepreneurship had not flowered on the amount of British aid they received, would more have been forthcoming from Britain until they did? " In the light of the quantity of the later transfer of British capital and entrepreneurship overseas, there can surely not be much doubt about the answer.

The second aspect is, in a way, an elaboration of the Gerschenkron concept of backwardness and the different stages of technology which each country has to tackle when it arrives at its "take-off" point (Gerschenkron, 1962; Landes, 1969b, pp. 335–36). Europe was a sufficiently close community for major events to have affected it simultaneously, even while its component industrial regions were at very different stages of development and relationship to each other. This applied, for example, to the impact of war and blockade in 1800–15, to railways in the 1840s and 1850s, socialism in the 1860s, cheap agricultural imports in the 1870s, and the scramble for colonies in the last years of the century.

Thus railways came to England at the end of her industrial revolution, to France as part of hers, to Russia in advance of hers. They used existing engineering talent in Britain, developed such talent in France and Germany, brought in foreign talent in Austria and Russia. And they were the basis of capital exports from Britain and France, internal capital development in Germany, and massive capital imports into Russia. The cheap grain of the 1870s, on the other hand, divided Europe into those areas which could cash in on the boom by exporting grain, like Russia and Hungary, and those which used grain as feedstuff to convert their agriculture to animal husbandry and dairying, like parts of Britain, the Netherlands, Denmark, or Switzerland. Germany was caught out by being still dominated by an anachronistic ruling class, the Junkers, who set out to stem the tide of history. The Junkers, indeed, did not believe their own propaganda about the importance of the German frontier which enclosed the Reich: they knew that the most important German frontier was the one which ran along the Elbe, separating the agrarian Germany from industrialized Germany. And they kept German economic life divided along this line by their victory in the "war of the canals" around 1900, which prevented the obvious link-up of German waterways and preserved a gap, the only such major gap in Europe, running through the middle of Germany, between the linked Danube-Rhine-Rhône-Seine-Ems-Weser system, and the Elbe-Oder system linking up with the east (Marlo, 1908; Hennig, 1913, pp. 82–83). Moreover, they also achieved an unparalleled exploitation of the rest of Germany through the ingenious "export certificate" (Gerschenkron, 1943; Röpke, 1934; Club, 1910), by which the urban consumer was obliged not only to pay more for the bread he consumed, but also to subsidize the eastern rye he did not want to consume.

Thus the structural similarities between the English Corn Law of 1815 and the German tariff of 1879 were also accompanied by vital differences. The timing effect discussed here is another reason why European industrialization should not be seen as the repetition of a model, but as a single, if complex, process.

V

From the 1860s on, the needs of the advanced economies called forth a rapidly growing phalanx of international bodies and forms of collaboration, from the Universal Postal Union and the Berne copyright convention to international railway agreements and international monetary harmonization based on the gold standard. The logic of events fostered an internationalization of economic life, primarily within Europe but ultimately also across the world, which raised the hopes of the Peace Movement, expressed most clearly by Norman Angell's *The Great Illusion* of 1910, that economic interdependence was making European war impossible.

But in the last quarter of the century there began to be found, together with these developments, also those of an opposite tendency. The relationship of the nineteenth-century state, particularly the state based on national revolution, with the industrial revolution with its changing class structure, are complex and contradictory.[13] At an earlier stage the state had been a progressive force, reacting favorably to the elemental needs and pressures of industry by creating large and free internal markets, by abolishing serfdom and feudal tax privileges, by limiting the civil rights of labor or manipulating taxes in favor of capital. But now the tendency of its actions was increasingly to inhibit progress by disrupting the international economy. Barriers between naturally complementary regions were raised even higher, labor migration impeded, and foreign ownership of capital restricted as capital exports became a political weapon. Real costs rose as subsidies encouraged the building of sailing ships in France in the 1890's and the growing of sugar all over Europe. After the brief liberal interlude of c. 1860–79 with its great expansion of international trade, countries turned to Neo-Mercantilism, meaning to become strong by becoming autarkic.

While the positive influence of protection on industrialization is much in doubt, its negative influence on foreign trade and the international division of labor is not in dispute. Given the nature of the political state in its competitive setting in Europe, its obstructive role in the evolution of an integrated European economy is as "natural" as that evolution itself. But it is surely not entirely fanciful, though it would be going much beyond the scope of this article, to see in the opposition of the political authority to the underlying economic logic of European industrial development one of the roots of tensions and wars of the period c. 1865–1945. It may even be that there is a similar link between the astonishing progress of the European economy since that date and the decision of the political authorities, both in the east and the west, to work within rather than against, the integrating tendencies of European industrialization.

VI

It is the argument of this article that the industrialization of nineteenth-century Europe was a single process and had an economic logic of its own. Like an epidemic, it took little note of frontiers, crossing them with ease while leaving the neighboring home territories untouched. The political and legal base in each region was not without influence on it, but it is clear that the factors which made one area more susceptible to infection than another included locational advantages, resources and, above all, preceding economic development bringing in its train a favorable social structure.

It follows that the study of industrialization in any given European country will remain incomplete unless it incorporates a European dimension: any model of a closed economy would lack some of its basic and essential characteristics. These include relationships with economies which were more advanced, with those at similar stages, and with those still awaiting development. They also include differentiation of phasing as various common European experiences touch all economies simultaneously. Finally, they must include an absolute time scale: as the boundary line between industrialized heartland and underdeveloped periphery shifted across Europe, so the basic operative technology and the necessary costs and the nature of social dislocation required for industrialization underwent continuous change. Moreover, the later the start, the larger the existing industrialized world against which the industrial revolution is played out and the farther away the periphery. In the case of today's industrializers, the industrialized heartland is so large as to be in effect uninfluenced by their actions, while the technological gap is so great that government has to play a role that would have been quite inappropriate in Europe (Kenwood and Lougheed, 1971, p. 134; Parsons, 1960, p. 116; Streeten, 1967). But this should not blind us to the mutual inter-actions of the nineteenth-century industrial revolutions in Europe.

This article has discussed only some aspects of these problems. In this sense it is not intended to present a conclusion, but a programme of work. Its object is not to draw on existing research, but to stimulate new study. While it may help towards a more realistic evaluation of some activities which have had the limelight in the past, as for example the policies of government, its main intention is to urge the re-examination of the impact of the total European situation, in each phase, on any given segment of it.

Notes

[1] Thanks are due to the Historische Kommission of Berlin, and to the initiative of Prof. Otto Busch, for providing me with the leisure and the facilities for some of the research on which this paper is based.

[2] "Capitalism itself is, both in the economic and sociological sense, essentially one process, with the whole world as its stage" (Schumpeter, 1939).

[3] E.g. Woodruff, 1966; Thomas, 1972a; Wallerstein, 1974, 1980.

[4] Quoted in Lévy-Leboyer, 1964, p. 151.

[5] Quoted in Henderson, 1954, p. 130.

[6] Quoted in Treue, 1937, p. 220.

[7] Memorandum dated 14 January 1817, reprinted in Rothe and Ritthaler, eds., 1934, pp. 40–41. Among the extensive documentation on the debate about the tariff and the customs union this is the most useful collection.

[8] Rothe and Ritthaler, 1934, pp. 64–68. Also Kunth's reply to the cotton spinners, quoted in Freymark, 1898, p. 82.

[9] E.g. Bülow-Cumerow, 1844, pp. 74–92.

[10] Ashley, 1910, pp. 23–5; Hermes, 1930, esp. pp. 137–39; Shorter, 1967, p. 26. A little later, when the spinning mills of Germany or Switzerland could produce cotton yarn of coarser counts, they still drew the finer counts from Britain, while British coarser yarns went to the peripheral areas of Europe.

[11] See Harms, 1912, p. 200.

[12] Compare Williamson, 1964–65, pt. II.

[13] They are explored brilliantly by Hobsbawm, 1962.

9

English Workers' Living Standards During the Industrial Revolution: A New Look

PETER H. LINDERT and JEFFREY G. WILLIAMSON[1]

The politically charged debate over workers' living standards during the Industrial Revolution deserves renewal with the appearance of fresh data or new perspectives.[2] This essay mines an expanding data base and emerges with a far clearer picture of workers' fortunes after 1750. While optimists and pessimists can both draw support from the enterprise, the pessimists' case emerges with the greater need for redirection and repair. The evidence suggests that material gains were even bigger after 1820 than optimists had previously claimed, even if the concept of material well- being is expanded to include health and environmental factors. Although the pessimists can still find deplorable trends in the collective environment after 1820, particularly rising inequality and social disorder, this article suggests that their case must be shifted to the period 1750–1820 to retain its central relevance.

I

Which occupations and social classes are of the greatest relevance to the debate? It seems unlikely that we would get full agreement from the participants, but there are a few groups whose fortunes have been of prime concern, both to the historical standard of living debate and to the contemporary debate over Third World growth and distribution.[3]

Following established conventions in the literature, each group listed in Table 9.1 refers to adult male employees: the self-employed and permanently unemployed are excluded. Our lowest earnings group consists of hired farm laborers, who represent the bottom two-fifths of all workers. Next comes the non-farm common laborers and

Reprinted from the *Economic History Review*, Vol. 36, No. 1 (February 1983), pp. 1–25. Reprinted by permission of the Economic History Society.

their near substitutes, a low-skilled "middle group". Artisans, whose organizational efforts and sizable wage gains have caused them to be singled out as the "labor aristocracy,"[4] fall roughly between the 60th and 80th percentiles in the overall distribution of earnings. "Blue collar" workers include each of these groups, and define "the working class" most closely, at least within the debate over living standards.[5] The list is completed by the addition of a diverse white-collar group.

These "class" rankings changed little across the nineteenth century, at least between 1827 and 1851. However, since the relative growth of group incomes was rarely the same over the century following 1750, each will be documented in the sections which follow. Furthermore, later in this paper we shall explore just how much of the real wage trends for the blue collar laborer can be explained by shifts into higher paid work and how much by wage gains among all blue collar workers. Table 9.1 simply establishes who the workers were and where they fit in the size distribution of earnings in the early nineteenth century.

II

Quantitative judgements on workers' living standards have always begun with time series on rates of normal or full time pay.[6] This was certainly the starting point for the pioneering contributions by Bowley and Wood, Gilboy, Phelps Brown and Hopkins, and others. We also begin in the same way, adding several new pay series along the way.

An essential first step is to select appropriate annual pay rates. Most pay series are constructed from daily or weekly rates, and we still have only the sketchiest evidence documenting the average number of days or weeks worked per year. It seems sensible to exploit the normal or full-time pay rates first, and then turn to clues about unemployment or underemployment trends (Section V) to infer movements in true annual earnings. Daily and weekly normal pay rates are aggregated up to a 52-week year, using various estimates of normal days per week in different occupations.[7] These annual earnings figures generally exclude payments in kind, but this rule is violated for farm laborers, whose large in-kind payments have been included.

Eighteen nominal pay series are documented in Table 9.2. These series reflect a number of additions and revisions to the time-series literature on wage rates. The most conspicuous additions, though not the most crucial to the conclusions below, are the service occupations (Series 3L, 4L, 1H, and 7H to 12H, inclusive). With the exception of clergy and teachers, our view of service occupation pay leans heavily on the public salary figures reported in the "Annual Estimates" (printed in the House of Commons' Accounts and Papers from 1797 onwards). This is a rich source for consistent time series on well-defined occupations. Annual earnings are reported there for large numbers of employees in each occupational category, spanning the whole earnings distribution over age, tenure, and skill within a given occupational group. The key issue underlying their use is whether trends in public "civil service" salaries replicated trends in the same private sector occupations. Elsewhere we have offered evidence confirming the correlation, at least for the nineteenth century.[8]

Service-sector pay, again for public posts, is also available for 1755 and 1781. For the latter year we have figures reported to the House of Commons.[9] John

Table 9.1   Adult Male Employee Classes and Their Approximate Mean Positions in the Nineteenth-Century Earnings Ranks for England and Wales

Occupational class		"Representative" mean-wage series used here	Approximate mean-wage percentiles positons in the earnings ranks	
			1827	1851
1. Farm labor (Bottom 40%)	(1L)	farm labor	13th	14th
2. Middle group	(2L)	nonfarm common labor	38th	35th
	(5L)	police and guards		50th
	(6L)	colliers	55th	51st
	(5H)	cotton spinners	62nd	58th
3. Artisans ("Labor aristocracy")	(2H)	shipbuilding trades	67th	62nd
	(3H)	engineering trades	77th	77th
	(4H)	building trades	74th	63rd
	(6H)	printing trades	75th	71st
4. Blue-collar workers = (1) + (2) + (3)				
5. White-collar employees	(3L)	messengers and porters	78th	71st
	(4L)	other government low-wage	65th	62nd
	(1H)	government high-wage	87th	80th
	(7H)	clergy	90th	81st
	(8H)	solicitors and barristers	95th	100th
	(9H)	clerks	88th	80th
	(10H)	surgeons and doctors	86th	79th
	(11H)	schoolmasters	75th	70th
	(12H)	engineers, surveyors, and other professionals	89th	94th

6. All workers = (4) + (5)

Note: These size distributions refer to employee earnings only, excluding incomes from property, self-employment, pensions, or poor relief.
Sources: The sources for the group earnings averages are discussed in Section II below, and at greater length in Williamson, 1982b. The overall earnings distributions for 1827 and 1851 on which these group means are ranked are reported in Williamson, 1980, pp. 457–75.

Chamberlayne's estimates supply figures for 1755, though for fewer employees and departments than is true at the later dates.[10] These eighteenth-century public pay data must, of course, be treated with care, since a truly baroque payments system prevailed in the upper echelons.[11]

Table 9.2 Estimates of Nominal Annual Earnings for Eighteen Occupations 1755–1851: Adult Males, England and Wales (in current £'s)

Occupation	1755	1781	1797	1805	1810	1815	1819	1827	1835	1851
(1L) Farm laborers	17.18	21.09	30.03	40.40	42.04	40.04	39.05	31.04	30.03	29.04
(2L) Nonfarm common labor	20.75	23.13	25.09	36.87	43.94	43.94	41.74	43.65	39.29	44.83
(3L) Messengers & porters	33.99	33.54	57.66	69.43	76.01	80.69	81.35	84.39	87.20	88.88
(4L) Other government low-wage	28.62	46.02	46.77	52.48	57.17	60.22	60.60	59.01	58.70	66.45
(5L) Police & guards	25.76	48.08	47.04	51.26	67.89	69.34	69.18	62.95	63.33	53.62
(6L) Colliers	22.94	24.37	47.79	64.99	63.22	57.82	50.37	54.61	56.41	55.44
(1H) Government high-wage	78.91	104.55	133.73	151.09	176.86	195.16	219.25	222.95	270.42	234.87
(2H) Shipbuilding trades	38.82	45.26	51.71	51.32	55.25	59.20	57.23	62.22	62.74	64.12
(3H) Engineering trades	43.60	50.83	58.08	75.88	88.23	94.91	92.71	80.69	77.26	84.05

(4H) Building trades	30.51	35.57	40.64	55.30	66.35	66.35	63.02	66.35	59.72	66.35
(5H) Cotton spinners	35.96	41.93	47.90	65.18	78.21	67.60	67.60	58.50	64.56	58.64
(6H) Printing trades	46.34	54.03	66.61	71.11	79.22	79.22	71.14	70.23	70.23	74.72
(7H) Clergy	91.90	182.65	238.50	266.42	283.89	272.53	266.55	254.60	258.76	267.09
(8H) Solicitors and barristers	231.00	242.67	165.00	340.00	447.50	447.50	447.50	522.50	1166.67	1837.50
(9H) Clerks	63.62	101.57	135.26	150.44	178.11	200.79	229.64	240.29	269.11	235.81
(10H) Surgeons & doctors	62.02	88.35	174.95	217.60	217.60	217.60	217.60	175.20	200.92	200.92
(11H) Schoolmasters	15.97	16.53	43.21	43.21	51.10	51.10	69.35	69.35	81.89	81.11
(12H) Engineers & surveyors	137.51	170.00	190.00	291.43	305.00	337.50	326.43	265.71	398.89	479.00

Note: (4L) = watchmen, guards, porters, messengers, Post Office letter carriers, janitors; (1H) = clerks, Post Office sorters, warehousemen, collectors, tax surveyors, solicitors, clergymen, surgeons, medical officers, architects, engineers; (2H) = shipwrights; (3H) = fitters, turners, iron-moulders; (4H) = bricklayers, masons, carpenters, plasterers; (6H) = compositors.

Source: From Williamson, 1982b, Appendix Table 4.

For clergy and schoolmasters, we have made use of private pay series. Clergymen's mean annual earnings (including the rental value of the vicarage) can be estimated for the greater part of the nineteenth century by using *The Clerical Guide and Ecclesiastical Directory* and *The Clergy List*. A random sample of 550 clergymen, from all patronage sources (royal, ecclesiastical, university, and private) yields their pay for 1827, 1835, and 1851. For earlier benchmark years we had to use public pay rates for clergy, splicing these on to the private series at 1827. This procedure seems to have yielded plausible pay series for the average clergyman back to 1755, judging by the similarity in trend between public and private clergy salaries from 1827 on.

Schoolmasters had low monthly cash earnings, both because much of their income was in kind (rents and fuel), and because they often received supplementary fees and holiday bonuses. We have assumed that income in kind was a stable share of total income, so that the twelve-month cash-income series in Table 9.2 accurately reflects trends in total income. For 1755–1835, our estimates rely on schoolmasters' earnings in several Charity Schools in Staffordshire and Warwickshire. The 1851 figure refers to civilian schoolmasters in public pay, as reported in the Annual Estimates.[12]

For nineteenth-century manufacturing and building crafts (Series 2H to 6H inclusive), the well-known estimates of Bowley and Wood suffice.[13] The available series on eighteenth-century artisans' pay refer only to the building crafts, but Gilboy's data on these crafts offer the advantage of regional diversity. To give proper weight to the well-known regional variance in nominal wages, and to the shift in eighteenth-century populations, we have constructed an earnings average for building craftsmen that reflects changes in the "regional mix" between 1755 and 1797.[14] The result is a steeper rise in earnings in the building trades up to 1797 than that reported by Brown and Hopkins, whose series referred to southern England only (Phelps Brown and Hopkins, 1955, pp. 205–6).

Three very large unskilled occupations remain: colliers, non-farm common laborers, and farm laborers. The colliers' earnings figures refer to underground mining by adult males. The 1851 figure is derived from Wood's wage series.[15] The 1835 figure is from Bowley, as are the 1810–19 estimates, the latter referring to southern Scotland. We have also used figures for 1755 to 1805 inclusive, and (again) 1835 from Ashton and Sykes, referring to colliers' daily wage rates in the northern counties, in Lancashire and Derbyshire (Bowley, 1900; Ashton and Sykes, 1929). These diverse estimates are linked together at various dates and converted into annual earnings rates using the procedures sketched above. Non-farm common laborers' earnings are based on two sources. For the period 1797–1851, we have accepted the Phelps Brown-Hopkins estimates for laborers in the building trades. For 1755–97, their estimates have been set aside in favor of a multi-regional series based on Gilboy data for building labor, using the same procedure described for building crafts above. For farm laborers, the 1797–1851 figures are based on Bowley's wages for a "normal work week", taking account of both income in kind and seasonal wage-rate variation (but not seasonal employment variation).[16] Fifty-two "normal weeks" are arbitrarily assumed in constructing an annual full-time series. The 1781 figure also relies on Bowley, but here it is an unweighted average of the figures for Surrey, Kent, Hertfordshire, Suffolk, Cumberland, and Monmouth, spliced to the national series at 1797. The 1755–81 estimates are constructed from raw earnings data collected by Rogers.[17]

Table 9.2 represents our best interim view of trends in occupational earnings. It is confined to the benchmark years simply because the data are more abundant for these years.

Table 9.3 reports average full-time earnings for the six groups identified in Section I. The employment weights used in the aggregation over our eighteen occupations are very rough. Those for 1811 and earlier are based on work previously published, while those for later years are based on manipulations of the imperfect early census data on occupation.[18] Table 9.3 reveals the earnings history experienced by different classes of workers. The variety is striking. In the latter half of the eighteenth century, farm and non-farm common laborers gained ground on higher-paid workers, the labor aristocracy especially. From 1815 to the middle of the nineteenth century, on the other hand, the gap between higher- and lower-paid workers widened dramatically. Farm wages sagged below, while white-collar pay soared above, the wages for all other groups.[19] Table 9.3 also compares our results with earlier series that have shaped past impressions of wage trends and played a key role in Flinn's recent survey (Flinn, 1974). The new and old series exhibit both conformity and contrast. Where they diverge, we stand by the new series as improvements, and urge other scholars to harvest additional wage series from the archives.[20] The major conclusions of this paper are reinforced by, but not conditional on, our choice of these new nominal pay series.[21]

III

Several scholars have attempted to construct cost-of-living indices to deflate such nominal earning series. The period 1790 to 1850 has attracted particular attention. The four price indices most often cited are those offered by Gayer-Rostow-Schwartz (1953), Silberling (1923), Rousseaux (1938) and Tucker (1936). These pioneering efforts can be criticized on three fronts: (1) the underlying price data; (2) the commodities included in the overall index; and (3) the budget weights applied to each commodity price series.

Wholesale prices are used by Gayer-Rostow-Schwartz, Silberling, and Rousseaux. The former, in fact, used wholesale prices collected by Silberling who, in many cases, chose not to use them. Rousseaux also borrowed from Silberling, as well as from Jevons and Sauerbeck. Silberling's chief source was the *Price Current* lists "issued by several private agencies in London for the use of business men" (1923, p. 224). Tucker's chief sources were the contract prices paid by three London institutions: Greenwich, Chelsea, and Bethlehem Hospitals. Other writers have criticized these series for relying on wholesale and institutional London prices, rather than on retail prices actually paid by workers' families across England and Wales (Ashton, 1949, p. 48; Deane and Cole, 1969, p. 13). As Flinn has argued (1974, p. 402), however, wholesale prices are a fair proxy for consumer prices over the very long term. In most cases, there is no alternative anyway. An exception is clothing, for which we have used a Gayer-Rostow-Schwartz cotton-textile export price series instead of Tucker's institutional London prices, leading to a slightly more optimistic view of the cost-of-living trend between 1790 and 1850.

Table 9.3 Trends in Nominal Full-Time Earnings for Six Labor Groups, Compared with Three Previous Series, 1755–1851 (1851 = 100)

	(1)		(2)		(3)		(4)	(5)	(6)
	Farm laborers	vs. Bowley's farm laborers	Middle group	vs. Phelps Brown-Hopkins building laborers	Labor aristocracy	vs. Tucker's London artisans	All blue collar	White collar	All workers
1755	59.16		42.95	48.5	50.86	69.8	51.05	21.62	38.62
1781	72.62	75.5	54.88	57.6	57.38	69.8	59.64	26.42	46.62
1797	103.41	93.9	72.92	66.7	64.86	81.0	74.42	32.55	58.97
1805	139.12		98.89	83.3	79.44	87.0	96.58	38.88	75.87
1810	144.76		110.95	97.0	92.03	105.6	107.81	43.01	84.89
1815	137.88		105.55	97.0	95.28	112.1	106.18	46.55	85.30
1819	134.47		99.41	97.0	91.92	103.3	101.84	50.77	84.37
1827	106.89	100.8	98.89	97.0	93.55	105.1	97.59	55.09	83.11
1835	103.41	112.3	96.98	97.0	88.68	98.9	94.11	75.03	88.77
1851	100.00	100.00	100.00	100.00	100.00	100.00	100.00	100.00	100.00
52 weeks' earnings in 1851	£29.04	£29.04	£52.95	£42.90	£75.15	n.a.	£52.62	£258.88	£75.51

Note: The indices are aggregated from the finer groups listed in Table 9.1, using wage series from Table 9.2 and employment weights. The employment weights for 1755–1815 draw on Lindert, "English Occupations, 1670–1811," Table 3; while those for 1815–1851 are derived from censuses. The derivations of the employment weights are described in DP, Appendix A.

Source: For the three previous series, see Bowley, 1900, table in back; Phelps Brown and Hopkins, 1955; Tucker, 1936, pp. 73–84. The conversion of the Phelps Brown–Hopkins series from daily to annual wages assumed 312 working days a year.

The commodities included in the cost-of-living index also need revision. We have added more relevant working-class commodities, especially potatoes. Some irrelevant industrial raw materials, included in the Gayer-Rostow-Schwartz series, have been removed. But the most important change is the addition of house rent. While the classic indices all omitted this important part of the cost-of-living,[22] ours includes a rent series based on a few dozen cottages in Trentham, Staffordshire (just outside Stoke-on-Trent). While the data base is narrow, it does apply to a housing stock of almost unchanging quality.[23] The rent series implies that the cost of housing (at a fixed location) rose relative to other consumer items throughout the Industrial Revolution, thus offering some new support to the pessimists.[24]

Finally, the cost-of-living index should use commodity weights which reflect workers' budgets shares. Past series do not fully satisfy this requirement. All exclude any weight for housing, some include industrial inputs, and others are simply vague about their weights. One set of workers' household budgets stems from the pioneering work of Davies and Eden on the rural poor in the late eighteenth century.[25] Another is a miscellaneous group of urban workers' budgets from the late eighteenth and early nineteenth centuries.[26] The urban workers' budgets reveal a lower share spent on food, and a higher share spent on housing, than do the rural poor studied by Davies and Eden.

Choosing the most appropriate set of budget weights could matter a great deal. Goods and services are consumed in different proportions by northern and southern households, by the rural and the urban, or by the poor and rich. Cost of living trends could differ across classes simply because of differences in budget weights, as happened often in American experience (Williamson, 1976; Williamson and Lindert, 1980, chap. 5). This possibility was pursued with four separate cost-of-living indices using weights from the rural north, rural south, urban north, and urban south. As it happens, prices moved in such a way that the choice of weights mattered very little. The reason is that the net rise in the price of food relative to manufactures, which would have impoverished the rural poor more than the better-paid urban workers, was offset by the equally impressive relative rise in house rents, which took a greater toll on urban households. The analysis below continues to use southern urban weights, but we now know that the choice makes little difference.

The resulting "best-guess" cost of living index is displayed in Table 9.4. From 1788–92 to 1820–26, our index falls midway between optimists (Gayer-Rostow-Schwartz, Rousseaux, Silberling) and pessimists (Phelps Brown and Hopkins, Tucker). Between 1820–26 and 1846–50, our index is more optimistic, showing a somewhat bigger drop in living costs than any of the past indices.[27] For the century as a whole, the "best-guess" index supports the middle ground between the optimist and pessimist extremes.

IV

Deflating the nominal full-time wage series from Table 9.3 by the cost of living index in Table 9.4 yields the real wage trends in Table 9.5 and Figure 9.1 below. The results support Michael Flinn's conclusion that "there are relatively few indications of significant change in levels of real wages either way before 1810–14."[28] For later years,

Table 9.4   A "Best-Guess" Cost-of-Living Index, 1781–1850, Using Southern Urban
Expenditure Weights (1850 = 100)

	Index		Index		Index
1781	118.8	1805	186.7	1828	143.2
1782	119.3	1806	178.5	1829	143.2
1783	121.9	1807	169.1	1830	143.9
1784	118.4	1808	180.5	1831	141.3
1785	112.3	1809	204.9	1832	133.9
1786	109.6	1810	215.4	1833	124.7
1787	112.5	1811	204.5	1834	117.6
1788	115.9	1812	235.7	1835	112.8
1789	122.3	1813	230.0	1836	126.4
1790	125.9	1814	203.3	1837	129.2
1791	121.2	1815	182.6	1838	138.3
1792	118.3	1816	192.1	1839	142.3
1793	127.3	1817	197.5	1840	138.4
1794	130.7	1818	192.4	1841	133.3
1795	153.8	1819	182.9	1842	123.4
1796	159.5	1820	170.1	1843	109.6
1797	138.8	1821	150.5	1844	114.5
1798	136.9	1822	139.8	1845	112.0
1799	155.7	1823	146.0	1846	116.4
1800	207.1	1824	154.6	1847	138.0
1801	218.2	1825	162.3	1848	110.9
1802	160.9	1826	144.4	1849	101.2
1803	156.8	1827	140.9	1850	100.0
1804	160.2				

Source: DP, Appendix B.

however, Table 9.5 offers some revisions. Flinn was struck by the concentration of all real wage improvements into a period of only a dozen years of deflation beginning around 1813. Table 9.5 does not conform with Flinn's view.[29] There was general real wage improvement between 1810 and 1815, and a decline between 1815 and 1819, after which there was continuous growth. After prolonged wage stagnation, real wages measured by the evidence presented here, nearly doubled between 1820 and 1850. This is a far larger increase than even past "optimists" had announced.[30] It is also large enough to resolve most of the debate over whether real wages improved during the Industrial Revolution. Unless new errors are discovered or a host of new declining wage series added, it seems reasonable to conclude that the average worker was much better off in any decade from the 1830s on than in any decade before 1820. The same is true of any class of worker in Table 9.5.

Why has this announcement not been made before? One might have expected it from any of several devout optimists. The answer lies partly in the steady accumula-

Table 9.5   Trends in Real Adult Male Full-Time Earnings for Selected Groups of Workers, 1755–1851

Benchmark year	Farm laborers	Middle group	Artisans	All blue collar	White collar	All workers
1755	65.46	47.54	56.29	56.50	23.93	42.74
1781	61.12	46.19	48.30	50.19	22.24	39.24
1797	74.50	52.54	46.73	53.61	23.45	42.48
1805	74.51	52.96	42.55	51.73	20.82	40.64
1810	67.21	51.54	42.73	50.04	19.97	39.41
1815	75.51	57.81	52.18	58.15	25.49	46.71
1819	73.52	54.35	50.26	55.68	27.76	46.13
1827	75.86	70.18	66.39	69.25	39.10	58.99
1835	91.67	85.97	78.62	84.43	66.52	78.69
1851	100.00	100.00	100.00	100.00	100.00	100.00

Percentage change, 1781–1851, under three sets of cost-of-living weights and price assumptions:

Most pessimistic	31.6%	75.1%	68.0%	61.8%	294.5%	103.7%
"Best-guess"	63.6%	116.5%	107.0%	99.2%	349.6%	154.8%
Most optimistic	107.0%	175.3%	164.2%	154.4%	520.3%	220.3%

Note: The indices in the upper panel use the data in Tables 9.3 and 9.4, as does the row of "best-guess" estimates in the lower panel. The most pessimistic and most optimistic variants are based on relatively unrealistic cost-of-living indices, selected as extreme cases from 16 alternatives. The most pessimistic used a cost of living index combining northern urban expenditure weights with Tucker's institutional clothing prices and Trentham cottage rents, while the most optimistic used an index combining northern rural weights with export clothing prices and no rents. Again, we prefer the "best guess" index, combining southern urban weights with export clothing prices and Trentham rents.

Source: The 1755 figures are derived by relying on the Phelps Brown–Hopkins index to extend our 1781–1850 series (Table 9.4) backwards.

tion of data. Yet past findings have also been muted by the belief that trends in real full-time earnings of adult males failed to measure trends in workers' true "living standards". Each time a recent writer has come close to announcing the post-1820 improvement, the report has been disarmed by a confession of ignorance regarding trends in unemployment and in "qualitative" dimensions to life: perhaps health became poorer, work discipline more harsh and degrading, housing more crowded, and social injustice more outrageous, and perhaps these more than cancelled any improvement workers might have gained from rising real wages. These important issues dominate the remainder of this paper.

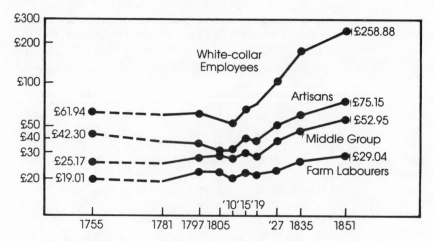

Fig. 9.1 Adult Male Average Full-Time Earnings for Selected Groups of Workers, 1755-1851, at Constant Prices

V

Time and again the unemployment issue has brought discussion of trends in workers' living standards to a halt: lacking national unemployment data before 1851, how can the real wage series be trusted as indicators of annual earnings? Into this empirical vacuum Hobsbawm has injected fragmentary hints about unemployment in the industrial north, suggesting that the depression of 1841–43 was "almost certainly the worst of the century."[31]

Yet no conceivable level of unemployment could have cancelled the near-doubling of full-time wages and left the workers of the 1840s with less than their grandfathers had had. Such a cancellation of gains would require that the national unemployment rate would have had to rise from zero to 50 per cent, or from 10 per cent to 55 per cent—jumps which even the most ardent pessimist would dismiss as inconceivable. Even in the 1930s, unemployment was less than a quarter of the labor force. The 1840s lacked the availability of unemployment compensation, the sharp drop in output, wages and prices, as well as the fall in the investment share that accompanied record jobless rates ninety years later.

We can be more precise about the extent to which the unemployment issue has been overstated in the standard of living debate. We have a number of clues about early nineteenth-century unemployment in Britain that have yet to be exploited. Let us examine these, focusing on the controversial period 1820–50, beginning with the non-agricultural sector before tackling the knottier problem of agricultural underemployment.

We can put an upper limit on non-agricultural unemployment in the 1850s by starting with the share of engineering, metal and shipbuilding union membership who were out of work: in 1851, 3.9 per cent were out at any one time, and the average was 5.2 per cent for 1851–59. This sector had all the attributes to suggest that unemployment would exceed economy-wide rates: early unionization, an unemployment insurance scheme, and business cycle sensitivity typical of all capital-goods industries. Indeed, from 1851 to World War I the unemployment rate in the engineering-metals-shipbuilding sector (EMS) fell below overall unemployment for insured workers in only two years, both of them boom years. Between 1923 and 1939, the EMS unemployment rate exceeded that of all insured workers by far (Mitchell and Deane, 1971, pp. 64–67). Thus, the 3.9 and 5.2 per cent EMS figures clearly overstate unemployment for the non-agricultural sector as a whole. These figures establish upper bounds on the extent to which non-agricultural unemployment cold have worsened.

How much worse could non-agricultural unemployment have been in the "hungry forties" than in the 1850s? That unemployment history can be approximated by appealing to the behavior of other variables. We know that unemployment varies inversely with output over the business cycle. Furthermore, EMS unemployment must have been closely tied to the share of capital formation in national product. There was also a tight nonlinear relationship between unemployment and wage rate increases in Britain between 1862 and 1957, according to A.W. Phillips's classic study of the Phillips Curve (Phillips, 1958). Aside from the influence of these three variables, one might also suspect that the structure of the economy drifted over time in a way that shifted the unemployment rate.

These propositions can all be tested for the second half of the nineteenth century. If they are successful, then they can be used to predict non-agricultural unemployment back into the 1830s. Regression analysis can sort out the determinants of the unemployment rates in engineering-metals-shipbuilding (1851–92) where

U_{EMS} = the EMS unemployment rate (a 1 per cent rate measured as "1.0");

GNP Ratio = the ratio of current nominal gross national product at factor cost to its average level over the immediately preceding five years;

1/GNP = the share of gross domestic captital formation in gross national product at factor cost;

$\dot{w}$ = the rate of change from the previous year in the wage rate for shipbuilding and engineering (a 1 per cent rise is ".01"); and

Time = the year minus 1851.

The regression results on annual data for the United Kingdom are (with standard errors of coefficients in parentheses):[32]

$$U_{EMS} = 32.96 - 16.15 \text{ (GNP Ratio)} - 168.02 \text{ (1/GNP)} - 71.37 \, \dot{w}$$

$$(7.85) \qquad\qquad (63.81) \qquad\qquad (21.83)$$

$$-288.45 \, (\dot{w})^2 - 0.0032 \text{ (Time)} + 0.148 \text{ (Time)}^2$$

$$(121.80) \qquad (0.0036) \qquad\quad (0.151)$$

$$U_{EMS} = 5.78, \text{ SEE} = 2.50, \text{ R}^2 = 0.543, \text{ F} = 9.11, \text{ d.f.} = 35.$$

The results confirm that EMS unemployment was lower when GNP was on the rise, when investment was a higher share of national product, and when engineering and shipbuilding wage rates were rising. The results also fail to reveal any other structural drift over the second half of the century: the coefficients on the time variables are statistically insignificant.

The regression can now predict EMS unemployment rates for the 1840s and late 1830s.[33] It would be unwise to make any predictions earlier than this, given the Poor Law reform of 1834 and other structural changes in the earlier years. For the period 1837–50, the equation generates the estimates shown in Table 9.6.

Table 9.6

Period	Point estimate of U_{EMS}	Bounds for $U_{EMS} =$ estimate $\pm$ two standard errors
1837–1839	2.70%	0–7.70%
1840–1850	4.41%	0–9.41%
(two worst years: 1842–43)	(9.44%)	(4.44–14.44%)

The overall rate of non-agricultural unemployment was probably lower than these estimates. Of the different sectoral output series available for the 1830s and 1840s,[34] only brick output showed as bad a slump in the early forties as did shipbuilding, the latter reflected in the EMS unemployment figures. It is not at all clear that the slump of the early forties was the "worst of the century". The available evidence makes it no worse than the slumps of the late 1870s or mid-1880s. More important to the standard of living debate, industrial depression might have been as bad in the immediate post-war years (1814–19) as in the early forties, given that the earlier wage-price deflation was far more severe. We conclude that non-agricultural unemployment was not exceptionally high in either the 1840s or the 1850s, and even if it did rise after 1820, that unlikely event could have had only a trivial impact on workers' real earnings gains.

How might employment conditions in *agriculture* have affected the unemployment trends for the economy as a whole? Darkness is nearly total on this front. Seasonal unemployment was, of course, a serious problem throughout the eighteenth and nineteenth centuries (Timmer, 1969; Collins, 1976). To guess when underemployment reached crisis proportions, we can be guided by literary evidence, grain yields, and the terms of trade. The literary signs of distress were strongest during the harvest failures of the 1790s and in the the twenty years after Waterloo (Jones, 1974, chap. 10; Richardson, 1976; Hobsbawm and Rudé, 1969). Post-Napoleonic wheat yields were trendless from 1815 to 1840, and then rose (Jones, 1974, chap. 8.) The terms of trade shifted drastically against agriculture only twice in the century surveyed here—by about 20 per cent against wheat from c. 1770 to c. 1780 and by about 10 per cent against agricultural products from 1812–14 to 1822–24 (Deane and Cole, 1969, p. 91; Mitchell and Deane, 1971, chap. 14). The common denominator emerging from this evidence is that the early postwar period, especially the decade 1815–24, probably witnessed exceptional unemployment in agriculture, followed by overall improvement to 1850.

All of this evidence suggests two plausible inferences: first, that unemployment among workers listing non-agricultural occupations was less than 9.41 per cent in the 1840s and 1850s; and second that unemployment among agricultural workers was no worse in the 1840s or 1850s than around 1820. We also know that the share of the

British labor force engaged in agriculture dropped from 28.4 percent for 1821 to 21.7 percent for 1851 (Deane and Cole, 1969, p. 142). This information is sufficient to demonstrate that the (alleged) net rise in unemployment could not have exceeded 7.37 percent, and it may well have fallen.[35]

The trend in unemployment thus could not have detracted greatly from the improvement in workers' real wages, and it may even have contributed to their improvement. Furthermore, even a pessimists's reckoning of the influence of unemployment overstates its relevance by assuming that time spent unemployed has no value as either leisure or non-market work.

VI

Thus far we have taken the orthodox path by focusing solely on adult male purchasing power. Yet questions about work and earnings by women and children have always been working in the the wings througout the standard of living debate. The rise of their employment in mills and mines is deplored as much today as it was during the public outcry prior to the Factory Acts. The increasing dependence of working-class families on the earnings of children, and the shifting of both children and single young women from the authority of fathers to the discipline of captitalists, are thought to have undermined traditional family roles and fathers' self-esteem (Smelser, 1959, chaps. 9–11; Thompson, 1968, chap. 10). Such social side-effects will be treated as part of the larger issue of urban and industrial disamenities in Section VIII below. This section will address the prior question of how trends in the earning power of women and children compared with those in men's real wages.

What data there are suggest the tentative conclusion that the earning power of women and children marched roughly in step with the real wage of unskilled laboring men, a group with whom women and children tended to compete as substitutes. The evidence for this view begins with data on the ratios of women's and children's pay relative to that of adult male laborers, both within sectors and overall. The best single indicator of the relative earning power of a woman's or a child's time is the ratio of their hourly rate to that of men, averaged over all seasons and including home commodity production. Yet such hourly rates are seldom given in historical sources before 1850. We therefore gather clues on some close substitute measures.

Table 9.7 presents the best available evidence on two measures that should serve to bracket trends in the value of women's and children's time. One is the weekly earnings ratio. The other is the ratio of hourly hired-labor wage rates, based on data that do not reflect differences in hours worked per week.

Working women may have gained ground on unskilled men during the century from 1750 to 1850. Our gleanings of data on relative *weekly earnings* hint as much, both for women within rural areas and for a shifting rural-urban average. Yet hints about relative *hourly wages* (the second column in Table 9.7) warn that we cannot be sure that there was any upward trend in the true relative value of women's time. It may simply be that the weekly hours of those working rose, though this seems unlikely. Our tentative conclusion is that the relative earning power of women did not decline. It may have stayed the same or it may have risen.

Table 9.7 Relative Earnings of English Working-Class Women and Children, as Fractions of Those for Full-Time Adult Male Laborers, 1742–1890 (1.000 = earnings or wage rate of full-time adult male laborers)

Data context	Employed wives/women		Employed children (unweighted boy-girl averages)		
	Weekly earnings	Hourly wage rate	Ages	Weekly earnings	Hourly wage rate
(a) 18th-century rural:					
Brandsby, Yorkshire, 1742–51	<.488[a]	<.488	not given	<.495[a]	<.495
Corfe Castle, Dorset, 1790	.202	>.202	13–17	.253–.330	>.253–>.330
English rural poor, 1787–1796	.134	>.134	13–17	.196–.214	>.196–>.214
(b) 19th-century rural:					
Rural England and Wales, 1833	.224	.224–.365	9–15	.130	.130–.253
Norfolk-Suffolk, 1838	.284	>.284	over 10	.172	>.172
(c) 19th-century town:					
Textiles in towns, England and Wales, 1833	.471	>.471	13–17	.233–.413	>.233–>.413
Birmingham, 1839	.327[b]	>.327	13–17	.153–.230	>.153–>.230
Manchester, 1839	–	>.350	14–18	–	>.230
Industrial workers' wives and children, England and Wales, 1889–1890	.407	>.407	13–17	.185–.345	>.185–>.345

[a]Relative daily wages. For this reason, and because the hired-labor data are in this case biased toward the peak-demand season more for women and children than for men, the "weekly" (here, daily) wage ratio overestimates the hourly ratio more than for later observations.

[b]63 working women, ages 21–70.

Note: Two different concepts of an "employed" state are being applied here. The averages for weekly earnings are for persons employed either at or away from home for a significant part of the year. This concept of employment is close to the broad definition of labor force participation. The average hourly wage rates refer to persons hired outside the home, thus excluding any unemployment.

Source: Line a: *Brandsby, Yorkshire* hired women and children: Thorold Rogers, 1902, pp. 499–500. Men: 10,657 days at 9.779d., all seasons; women, 2,061.5 days at 4.772d.; boys: 1,948 days at 5.194d.; girls, 122.5 days at 4.486d. Similar ratios for women's earnings are given for 1770 in Young, 1771. *Corfe Castle, Dorset:* all wives, 20–59, and children with stated occupations including outwork; from the detailed 1790 census at the Dorset Record Office. 261 families. *English rural poor:* 172 poor families with children, calculated from Davies and Eden data as described in Lindert, 1980b.

Line b: *Rural England and Wales,* 1833: Great Britain, 1833, drawing on parishes giving explicit answers to questions about earnings. Similar wage rates for women and children are quoted for 1843 in Great Britain, 1843. *Norfolk-Suffolk farms,* 1838: 64 couples without children, 120 families with one child over 10; from Kay, 1838.

Line c: *Textiles in towns,* England and Wales, 1833: weekly earnings for 1,864 children at age 13, 1,434 children at age 17, and 972 women at ages 26–30; from Dr. James Mitchell's report in Factory Inquiry Commission, in Great Britain, 1834. Birmingham, 1838: by a Local Subcommittee (1840, p. 441). *Manchester,* 1839: hourly wage rates from several industries in Chadwick, 1860. The comparisons used here were biased against our argument somewhat by choosing lower-paid groups of women and children and better-paid adult male laborers. The 1849 ratios from the same source are similar. *Industrial workers' wives and children,* 1889–1890: 857 industrial workers' wives and 159 families with one child over 10; from U.S. Commissioner of Labor, pt. III, 1891 and 1892.

The relative earning power of children probably stayed the same above the age of fifteen or thereabouts, while declining slightly for younger children. This conclusion is derived mainly from the data on relative weekly earnings in Table 9.7. These data again may differ in trend from the true average time values because of changes in relative weekly hours, but relative hours would have had to have risen at an implausibly high rate to reverse the main conclusions advanced here.

Thus, it appears that an employment-weighted average of the wage rates of women and children together would have advanced about as fast as those for adult male farm laborers in the course of the century 1750–1850. This conclusion would not be overturned by noting the decline in overall labor-force participation of both women and children.[36] An optimist might interpret this decline as voluntary, that is as showing that the implicit purchasing power (the "shadow price") of time spent away from work rose faster than the observed wage rates. A pessimist might counter that the trend was involuntary, that women and children were being thrown into involuntary unemployment faster than adult males. The latter position is hard to sustain. Aside from "protective" hours legislation from 1833 on, no institutions compelled employers to pay women and children wage rates that were increasingly above the opportunity cost of their time out of work. The real wage gains documented for men in Table 9.5 were not achieved at the expense of women and children. As for the perceived disamenities of having women and children shift their work from home toward factories, these became part of the net disamenities appraised in Section IX below.

Since wage rates differ between occupations, migration from low- paid to high-paid employment can raise average wages for the working class as a whole, even if wage rates do not change for any one occupation. How much of the wage gains up to 1850 were due to such mobility-induced wage drift? The "blue collar" and the "all worker" wage series in Tables 9.3 and 9.5 already capture this mobility effect. It can be factored back out by applying fixed wage rates to shifting employment numbers. Detailed calculations described elsewhere show that occupational mobility contributed less than 5.3 per cent to the rise in average full-time earnings of all blue-collar workers between 1781 and 1851, using either Laspeyres or Paasche weights.[37] Virtually all of the apparent wage gains were gains within occupations, not wage drifts due to changing occupational weights.

Migration from low-wage to high-wage regions can also raise wages for the average worker even if wages fail to rise in any one region. That nominal wages varied widely across English counties well into the nineteenth century has been well known at least since Arthur Young's late eighteenth-century tours. Elsewhere we have analyzed the causes of the regional differences in wage rates for agricultural labor.[38] It appears that *real* wage gaps persist even after regional adjustments for variation in cost of living and disamenities are made. Furthermore, it has long been appreciated that labor drifted from the low-wage south to the high-wage north during the Industrial Revolution.[39] Since the average "blue-collar" and "all worker" wage series in Tables 9.3 and 9.5 already include most of these regional migration effects, it is now a simple matter to explore their quantitative impact on real wage gains up to 1850.

It appears that regional migration contributed very little to the real wage gains for the average English worker after the 1780s. True, some periods registered far larger regional migration gains than others: 1841–51 was a decade of impressive gains through migration to high-wage regions; and the late eighteenth century records some small positive gains.[40] But over the period 1781–1851 as a whole, regional migration contributed less than 3.6 per cent to the observed real wage gains. It was real wage gains within regions that mattered most.

VII

Most of us care more about people's consumption *per lifetime*, rather than just per year. Conclusions based on trends in real earnings per annum risk grave error if the workers' length of life deteriorated. Alternatively, any improvements in the workers' length of life implies that standard of living gains are understated in Table 9.5, especially if sickness and longevity are inversely correlated. The standard of living debate fails to confront the issue of lifetime incomes. There are exceptions to this characterization of the debate, and surely the most famous is Engels's original broadside on *The Condition of the Working Class in England*, which indicted industrial capitalism for killing workers with unhealthy conditions:

> society in England daily and hourly commits what the working-men's organs, with perfect correctness, characterise a social murder . . . its deed is murder just as surely as the deed of the single individual; disguised, malicious murder against which none can defend himself, which does not seem what it is, because no man sees the murderer . . . [Engels, 1974, pp. 126, 127].

To link workers' early deaths with rising capitalism, Engels drew on several available estimates showing that mortality was worse in the cities than the countryside, appalling in Liverpool and Manchester, and worst in the most crowded neighborhoods of the same cities. A host of studies has since confirmed this spatial pattern of mortality.

Two pitfalls await anyone trying, as Engels did, to infer from such patterns that working-class longevity diminished as the Industrial Revolution progressed. First, it is important to remember that the working classes were not neatly segregated from the upper classes by place of residence. Liverpool was no closer to being purely working-class than was England in the aggregate. On the contrary, census figures show that the socio-occupational group most concentrated in the unhealthy cities was the bourgeoisie, although most bought their way out of the worst sections by paying higher rents in the more salubrious sections of the same unhealthy cities. The rise of centres of bad health gives no more support to the pessimists' view of working-class conditions than the nineteenth-century decline in national mortality gives to the optimists' position.

Thanks to the energies of William Farr and a few other scholars, a fairly clear picture of adult male working-class life expectancy can be put together towards the end of the Industrial Revolution. As we have shown elsewhere, life expectancies did not differ dramatically across occupations for England and Wales as a whole. The occupational differences were far smaller than the spatial differences, though the estimates may be slightly biased toward uniformity by migration effects and by the omission of paupers from the available figures.[41] We are warned that occupational differentials were unlikely to have been as great as stark contrasts between Manchester and rural Norfolk would suggest.

The other pitfall is mistaking a snapshot for a motion picture. Past observers have inferred that mortality must have worsened for city-dwellers (and for the working class) since mortality was higher in fast-growing growing cities. Such inferences are unwarranted. In fact, mortality improved (receded) in the countryside *and* most cities, and did so by enough to improve national life expectancy from about 1800 on. The exceptional cities were Liverpool and Manchester, where crude death rates stayed about the same from 1801 to 1851, while age-adjusted death rates appear to have risen only slightly up to 1820 and declined slightly to mid-century.[42]

In short, while we cannot yet determine trends in working-class infant and child mortality, it can be shown that any tendency of the rising industrial centres to lure adult workers to an early death was fully offset, or more than offset, by the lengthening of life both in the cities and the countryside.[43]

VIII

Where in our measures is the degradation and demoralization associated with the long rigid hours spent at mind-numbing work for an insensitive avaricious capitalist? The disruption of traditional family roles? The noise, filth, crime, and crowding of urban slums? Until we can devise ways of weighing these varied dimensions against material gains, we cannot answer questions about living standards, but rather only questions about real earnings.

In judging the importance of these quality of life factors, we must avoid imposing twentieth-century values on early nineteenth-century workers. We must avoid both facile indifference to past suffering and excessive indignation at conditions that seem much more intolerable now. The workers of that era must themselves be allowed to reveal how much a "good" quality of life was worth to them.

How is their voice to be heard? Most of them lacked the right to vote. Some protested violently, while most remained silent, but we cannot infer a majority view from the either the outcries or the silence. The most satisfactory clue to a worker's view is his response to living and working conditions that offered different rates of pay and different qualities of life.

Employers in the rising industries and cities had to pay workers more to attract a growing share of the labor force. How *much* more is a valuable clue to the importance which the workers attached to quality of life. To err on the side of exaggeration on so sensitive an issue, let us contrast the pay of unskilled common laborers in two extreme settings in the late 1830s: cotton and metal mills in Manchester in 1839 versus year-round farm labor in Norfolk and Suffolk in 1837.[44] Among the better paid unskilled in Manchester were laborers in metal mills and adult male warehousemen in cotton mills. These groups received 18 shillings a week, or £41.4 for a normal 46-week year. Other common laborers generally got less. In healthy East Anglia, a single adult male farm laborer averaged £25.1 in 1837. The extreme Faustian "Satanic mill" wage premium was thus 65 percent.

At some human cost of moving, laborers could choose to suffer the disamenities of Manchester work, even if it looks like a Hobson's choice to us today. And choose they did, in significant numbers. The census of 1851 shows that every county in England,

and even the rural districts of every county, attracted persons born in every other county. Workers also shuttled between the industrial and agricultural sectors on a seasonal basis.[45] They were free to move, and many of them knew enough about conditions in other sectors if they cared to consider moving.

The possibility of migration implies that the wage premium offered in Manchester cannot understate the importance of urban-industrial disamenities and living costs to those workers who were actually near the margin in choosing between Manchester and East Anglia. Indeed, it may well overstate this importance not only because the continued flow toward the cities implied a true gain for movers, but also because we have selected two extreme cases for contrast. Manchester was as "bad" a city as any (except perhaps Liverpool), and farm workers in East Anglia were paid a good deal less than their counterparts in the rural north.

The Manchester-East Anglia "wage gap" must be viewed as an upper-bound on what it took to induce rural labor to modern industry in the second quarter of the nineteenth century. This gap can be viewed as compensation for two closely related costs: the payment necessary to compensate workers (in their own eyes) for a lower quality of life, and the payment necessary to compensate workers for the higher urban cost of living (e.g. expensive housing).

The 65 percent gap in the 1830s and 1850s is wide, but how much long-run deterioration does it reveal? Very little, as it turns out. First, it is a contemporaneous comparison between sectors. Workers did not choose between the living conditions of 1780 and those of 1850. Yet workers' migration behavior in the nineteenth and twentieth centuries shows that they would have chosen the conditions of 1850 overwhelmingly, not only because real wages rose over time but also because the quality of life was *improving* within both the urban and the rural sectors over time. We infer this mainly from trends in mortality, the best single proxy for the disamenities associated with demoralization, bad health, and low resistance to disease. As we have seen in Section VII, mortality was declining within the countryside and within the cities (though it was only stable in Liverpool and Manchester). Thus, disamenities were declining within both sectors, an improvement we have not measured in monetary terms.

What of the impact of population shift from low-density areas of high quality of life to high-density urban areas with unpleasant disamenities? For this implicit spatial migration taking place between generations, the full 65 percent gap might be applied. But it could apply only to that share of the population making the implicit move. An overestimate of this fraction is the rise in the share living in urban places, a measure that generously assumes that all cities were as bad as Manchester. This fractional shift is only 14.89 percent from 1781 to 1851,[46] making the disamenities and living-cost increases for the average worker only $.1489 \times .65 = 9.7$ percent. To repeat, even this is a generous overestimate. Elsewhere, one of the present authors has analyzed the urban-industrial disamenities and cost of living effects in greater detail, and found that the former was probably under 2.5 percent and the latter was probably under 3.3 percent around the 1840s (Williamson, 1981, 1982a).

Many workers did suffer from the higher disamenities and living costs in the rising industrial centres, and many others resisted them by resolving to live and work elsewhere. Yet the value implicitly put on these human costs by the marginal workers, who actually moved into the urban-industrial centres, was not large enough to cancel even a tenth of blue collar workers' real wage gains. Nor should this surprise us. The development process inevitably finds workers and policymakers more intent on basic purchasing power in the hungry early phases of development, as the history of environmental quality in Manchester, Pittsburgh, Manila, and Sao Paulo clearly shows.

IX

We now have a much broader empirical basis for inferring how workers fared in the century between 1750 and 1850. Our tentative findings can be summarized most easily by focusing on the relatively data-rich Industrial Revolution era from 1781 to 1851.

Table 9.8 collects our best estimates of workers' experiences, beginning with our "best-guess" real wage trends and proceeding through several long-needed adjust-

Table 9.8   Revised Measures of English Workers' Standard-of-Living Gains, 1781–1851

| | Overall improvement, 1781–1851 | | |
Source of improvement	Farm laborers	All blue-collar workers	All workers
1. Real full-time earnings ("Best guess," Table 9.5)	63.6%	99.2%	154.8%
a. Due to occupational change (DP, Sec. 6)	(0)	(<5.3%)	(<17.2%)
b. Due to regional migration (DP, Sec. 7)	(<3.6%)	(<3.6%)	(<3.6%)
c. Residual: real wage gains within occupations and regions	(>60.0%)	(>90.3%)	(>134.0%)
2. Diminished by an "upper-bound" rise in unemployment, or <7.4% (see Sec. VI above)	63.6%	>91.8%	>147.4%
3. Diminished by the shift toward higher urban living costs, or<3.3%[a]	63.6%	>88.5%	>144.1%
4. Diminished by urban-industrial disamenities, or <2.5%[a]	63.6%	>86.0%	>141.6%
5. Augmented by adult mortality gains, which were not negative (Sec.VIII)	>63.6%	>86.0%	>141.6%

[a] These figures taken from DP, Section 8. Readers preferring the estimates in Section IX above may wish to substitute the 9.7% figure for Rows 3 and 4 together in the "blue-collar" and "all workers" columns.

ments. Table 9.8 suggests impressive net gains in the standard of life: over 60 per cent for farm laborers, over 86 per cent for blue-collar workers, and over 140 per cent for all workers. The hardships faced by workers at the end of the Industrial Revolution cannot have been nearly as great as those of their grandparents.

The great majority of these human gains came after 1820. Pessimists must retreat to the pre-1820 era, where workers' net gains look as elusive in this essay as in past studies of single occupations. Optimists might feel a temptation to proclaim victory by shifting attention away from the classic Industrial Revolution era, but this inference seems premature. After all, the best measures of industrialization are still so uncertain for the years before 1831 that the timing of the Revolution itself is debatable. Furthermore, the separate influence of the French Wars has yet to be factored out of the longer-run development experience.

Pessimists in tune with larger intellectual currents of the 1960s have called for less attention to conventional measures of real income and more to the environmental aspects of the Industrial Revolution—all of those appalling health conditions and social injustices with which workers were affronted. The shift is certainly welcome. Yet the results presented here suggest that nineteenth-century environmental influences on health—such as crowding, infection, and pollution—could hardly have lowered average quality of life over time.

Research inspired by the pessimists' allegations about the Industrial Revolution will now have to shift to social injustice and social disorder. Reported crime, alcoholism, protest, and illegitimacy appear to have been on the rise in the first half of the nineteenth century. In addition, rising material inequality seems to characterize the period, and these trends were likely to have influenced social disorder. We know from related research, for example, that common laborers failed to experience gains as rapid as those for better-paid employees, as even Table 9.8 shows in comparing three working-class aggregates. Earnings inequality statistics suggest the same between the 1820s and the 1880s. Our preliminary results on probated wealth and land rents also suggest rising inequality between upper and lower-middle classes in the course of the first half of the nineteenth century. Inequality between workers and the very poor may also have widened: we need far better information on the material condition of those below the working classes—vagrants and disabled paupers—than the large literature on poor relief has yet been able to supply. These issues, not trends in absolute living standards, are likely to mark the future battleground between optimists and pessimists about how workers fared under nineteenth-century British capitalism.

Notes

[1] This article is part of a larger research project on "British inequality since 1670," supported by grants from the U.S. National Science Foundation (SOC76-80967, SOC79-09361, SOC79-06869) and the U.S. National Endowment for the Humanities (RO-26772-78-19). The authors gratefully acknowledge the able research assistance of George Boyer, Ding-Wei Lee, Linda W. Lindert, Thomas Renaghan, Ricardo Silveira, Kenneth Snowden, and Arthur Woolf, as well as the helful comments of G.N. von Tunzelmann, Stanley L. Engerman, two anonymous referees, and seminar participants at the University of California (Berkeley, Davis, UCLA), Harvard University, Northwestern University and the University of Wisconsin. Readers are referred to

the fuller display of evidence in the discussion paper "English Workers' Living Standards during the Industrial Revolution: A New Look," September 1980, available either from the Department of Economics, University of California, Davis, 95616 (Working Paper Series No. 144) or from the Graduate Program in Economic History, University of Wisconsin, Madison, 53706. Hereafter the paper is cited as "DP".

[2] The historical literature is too vast to cite here. Readers who want a full bibliography could begin with sources cited below and in Flinn, 1974; Taylor, ed., 1975; O'Brien and Engerman, 1981. For heated eloquence, the best twentieth-century clash is that between Ashton, 1954 and Thompson, 1968.

[3] On the debate over the "bottom 40 percent" in the Third World, see Chenery, et al., 1974; Cline, 1975; Ahluwalia, 1976; and Kuznets, 1979.

[4] See Ashton, 1955 and 1949; Hobsbawm, 1964 , esp. chaps. 15 and 16; and Perkin, 1969, pp. 131, 143, 395–7, 417.

[5] On the changing nuances of the term "working class", see in particular Briggs, 1967 and Morris, 1979.

[6] We follow past authors in referring to earnings as "pay" as though these represented all pre-transfer income, either gross or net of direct taxes. This simplification is valid for English workers before this century. Only a tiny share of blue-collar employees owned their own homes or significant amounts of other non-human property, and only a tiny share paid any direct taxes. The heavier indirect taxes—exercises, import duties, and the local rates on property—were reflected in the prices and rents workers paid, which are measured below.

[7] The choice of numbers of weeks per year is arbitrary and matters little to what follows. Arthur L. Bowley (1900, p. 68) thought that six weeks was the average "lost time" per year. The choice of weeks per year matters only if the number of weeks "lost" varied greatly over time, due to movements in true involuntary unemployment and not just due to marginal shifts in employment rates by persons valuing their time about the same in and out of work. We doubt that the work year shifted in ways altering the conclusions of this paper, to judge from the unemployment evidence in Section V below and from M.A. Bienefeld's exploration of trends in normal annual industrial hours (1972, chaps. 2 and 3).

[8] See Williamson, (1982b).

[9] Report of "Commission Appointed to Examine, Take, and State the Public Accounts of the United Kingdom," House of Commons Papers, 1782 and 1786.

[10] John Chamberlayne, *Magnae Britanniae Notitia, Or the Present State of Great Britain*, 17th ed. (1755). Earlier editions begun by Edwin Chamberlayne, date back to the 1680s. We are indebted to David Galenson for alerting us to the Chamberlayne almanacs.

[11] For example, department heads and high titled clerks were part of a patronage system. Often extremely high reported salaries were gross salaries out of which the recipient had to maintain his staff of clerks. We have ignored the pay of all officials for which this seemed to be the practice. In other cases, salaries surely understated earnings. Customs officials, for example, received a portion of the taxes collected in addition to the reported incomes. These were excluded from our estimates. Also excluded were officials for whom the stated stipends were but partial political side-payments and heraldic perquisites. For example in an earlier edition of *Magnae Britanniae Notitia* (1694 ed. p. 238), Edwin Chamberlayne listed the Lancaster Herald's pay as only £26 13s. 4d. per annum. The Herald in this case was Gregory King. Were this his only income, King would have been no better paid than a common seaman, a messenger or a porter.

[12] For a fuller discussion of all schoolmaster pay series, with comparisons to other available series on benchmark dates, see Williamson, 1982b.

[13] Bowley, 1900, and the series of Bowley-Wood articles that appeared in the *Journal of the Royal Statistical Society* between 1898 and 1906.

[14] For the London area we used an unweighted average of wage series from Westminster, Greenwich Hospital, Southwark and Maidstone. The London area series is then combined with

series from six counties: Oxfordshire, Gloucestershire, Devon, Somerset, the North Riding, and Lancashire. These county earnings are combined using the regional population weights reported in Deane and Cole, 1969, Table 24, p. 103.

[15] As reproduced in Mitchell and Deane, 1971.

[16] Bowley (1898). Alternative estimates for the period 1790–1840 are also available for Kent, Essex, Dorset, Nottinghamshire, Lincolnshire, Hampshire, and Suffolk in Richardson, 1977. Richardson's nominal daily wages for "fully employed agricultural day laborers" show somewhat less steep rises across the 1790s than do Bowley's national averages. The discrepancy may reflect the more rapid rise in wages in the north, an area given its due more fully in the Bowley averages. In any case, the Bowley and Richardson averages conform rather closely between 1805 and 1840.

[17] Once again, we have tried to build an earnings average for England and Wales that reflects shifts in population between regions across the eighteenth century, this time for farm labor. The task is complicated by the paucity of time series data, and the resulting average is hardly definitive. Our average wage for southern England is a weighted average of Cambridgeshire and Gloucester, the only two counties for which Rogers supplies continuous daily wage series for adult male farm laborers. The north is represented only by Brandsby, Yorkshire, though the number of observations for this location is large. The northern and southern averages were weighted by population estimates from Deane and Cole, where the "south" is defined by the twenty counties including, or south of, Gloucester, Oxford, Northampton, Cambridge, and Norfolk. The "north" in this case consists of Lancashire and the three Ridings. The resulting average daily wage is then linked with the 1781 annual earnings estimate.

[18] The occupational numbers for 1811 and earlier are estimated, with comparisons to contemporary estimates by Massie and Colquhoun, in Lindert (1980).

[19] For more details on these distributional changes, see Williamson, 1982b, and 1980.

[20] Bernard Eccleston (1976) has assembled a new series on Midlands wage rates for building craftsmen, building laborers, estate workers and road laborers. Consistent with our findings in Table 9.3, for common laborers Eccleston finds the Phelps Brown–Hopkins series rising too slowly between 1755 and 1815, and agrees that the Phelps Brown–Hopkins series misses the slight postwar deflation as well. Eccleston finds faster wage advances for craftsmen between 1755 and 1815 than Phelps Brown–Hopkins or the present estimates, which also show faster nominal gains than Tucker's sluggish series. Eccleston's results serve to emphasize a geographic contrast already suggested by past writers: nominal wage gains were considerably greater in the midlands and north than in London and the south, at least up to 1815. Past impressions about the late eighteenth century and the war years have underestimated nominal wage gains by relying too heavily on southern series.

[21] For fuller documentation of the points made in this section, see DP, Section 4 and Appendices B and C.

[22] House rents have been measured for parts of England covering slightly shorter or more recent periods: see Barnsby, 1971; and Neale, 1966, p. 606 giving rents for Bath, 1812–1844.

[23] We were able to hold the quality of the cottages virtually constant by (a) splicing together subseries that followed fixed sets of cottages and (b) conducting hedonic rent regression tests on detailed Trentham cottage surveys of 1835, 1842, and 1849. The regressions quantified the impact of cottage qualities and attributes of the tenants on the rent charged. It turned out that the rents fetched by the best and worst cottages differed very little for given types of tenants. See DP, Appendix C.

It has not been possible to pursue the issue of quality variation for other consumer items. Perhaps the quality of clothing and bedding rose, and perhaps the quality of meat declined, in ways not revealed by prices. The quantitative relevance of such possible quality drifts is doubtful given what we know about expenditures among workers' households. If, for example, the quality of meat fell by half between 1780 and 1850, the hidden extra cost to workers would still be only $.50 \times .111 = 5.5\%$, since .111 is the share of meat expenditures in the average budget (DP, Appendix B). The true net drift in quality was almost surely far less than this.

[24] The importance of adding rents, and of replacing institutional prices with market prices for clothing, can be seen from the following calculations, using "southern urban" budget weights (see Table 9.4 and DP, Section 4 and Appendix B). The net effect of the two cost-of-living revisions is to tip the trend toward optimism (towards declining living costs), but the inclusion of rents by itself adds 11 percent to the net cost-of-living increase between 1790 and 1850.

Cost of Living	Percentage change		
	1790–1812	1812–1850	1790–1850
With Tucker's institutional clothing prices, and without rents	96.4	−56.0	−13.0
With export price of clothing, without rents	81.0	−62.3	−31.7
With export price of clothing, with rents (Table 9.4, "Best guess")	87.2	−57.6	−20.6

Readers should be warned, however, that the small Trentham sample may give too pessimistic an impression about trends. Across the nineteenth century the Trentham series has the same trends as two urban series (Barnsby, 1971, p. 236; and Singer, 1941, p.230). If rural cottage rents rose more slowly across the nineteenth century, then the Trentham series overstates the rise in a national average residential rent index using fixed locational weights. (As for the migration from low- to high-rent locations, see Section VI below). From about the 1770s to about the 1840s, the Trentham series rises much faster than two other rural series (Richardson, 1977, pp. 245–58; and Caird, 1967, p. 474). The difference in trend is so great as to imply an unreasonably rapid rise in urban rents if Trentham were taken as a national (rural-and-urban) average index. So for both the Industrial Revolution era and the nineteenth century, the Trentham series rose faster than the most likely trends in national residential rents.

[25] Rev. David Davies, 1795; and Eden, 1797, II and III. Phelps Brown and Hopkins also used budget weights from Eden, though without house rents (1955, pp. 296–314).

[26] Five urban budgets for 1795–1845 are presented by Burnett, 1969. Neale, (1966, pp. 597–99) gives a laborer's budget for Bath in 1831. Tucker (1936, p. 75) ventured two non-farm household budgets as averages of some underlying studies' budgets.

[27] To wit:

	Percentage change in prices		
	1788–92 to 1809–15	1809–15 to 1820–26	1820–26 to 1846–50
Silberling	74.1	−31.2	−16.7
Tucker	85.2	−24.5	−10.0
Rousseaux	–	−34.8	−16.4
Gayer-Rostow-Schwartz	65.7	−30.7	−19.4
Phelps Brown–Hopkins	84.6	−23.5	−10.5
Table 9.4, Best Guess	72.5	−27.3	−26.0

(see Flinn, 1974, p. 404.)

[28] Flinn, 1974, p. 408. There would be clearer signs of deterioration between about 1800 and 1820 if the earnings of weavers and other non-spinning cotton workers were added to the overall averages, as could be done from 1806 on. Using our "best-guess" deflator, Bowley-Wood wage rates for all cotton workers (Mitchell and Deane, 1971, pp. 348–9) yield the following real wage

indices: 1806, 78.62; 1810, 66.57; 1815, 75.43; 1819, 54.67; 1827, 66.96; 1835, 78.62; and 1851, 100.00. Compared with blue-collar earnings in Table 9.5, these real earnings of all cotton workers fell sharply from 1806 to 1819, but kept pace thereafter.

Even the famous handloom weavers may not have suffered any further net losses after 1820. Bowley's data on piece rates for handloom weavers in the Manchester area (1900, opp. p.119) imply a real wage gain of 15.3 per cent between 1819 and 1846, with most of the gain achieved by 1832. All cotton weavers, handloom plus power loom, gained an apparent 58.0 per cent from 1819 to 1850. Even the piece rate series probably have a pessimistic trend bias. They fail to reflect rising productivity of weavers of given age and sex, and the dwindling group of handloom weavers whose pay seemed to plummet before 1820 appears to have been increasingly dominated by women and children, as adult males fled to better-paying trades (Bythell, 1969, pp. 50–51, 60–61). On women and children's earnings, see Section VII.

[29] Flinn's dating of the real-wage upturn has also been questioned by von Tunzelmann, 1979, esp. p. 48.

[30] The closest approach to the present finding for the first half of the nineteenth century is the guarded conjecture by Deane and Cole that "real wages [improved by] about 25 per cent between 1800 and 1824 and over 40 per cent between 1824 and 1850" (1969, pp. 26–27).

Some readers of an earlier draft have wondered whether the apparent upturn after 1820 is not dependent on our use of the 1827 and 1835 benchmarks instead of nearby years. Some prefer to follow pessimist tradition by stressing the depression of 1842–43, while others choose the peak-price year 1839. Yet even these extreme choices do not remove the post-1820 gains, as evident from these available real-wage data and unemployment estimates:

	1819	1835	1839	1843	1851
Real wage index, farm laborers	73.52	91.67	80.04	103.91	100.00
Real wage index, middle group	54.35	85.97	68.17	88.50	100.00
Estimated EMS unemployment rate (Sec. VI)	n.a.	3.9%	2.2%	10.0%	3.9%

In the real-wage trough year 1839 fewer workers were denied income by unemployment. The depression year 1843 was a time of high real wages, thanks to cheap provisions. Neither of these extreme benchmarks looks as bad as 1819.

[31] Hobsbawm, 1964, p. 74. We have checked Hobsbawm's discussion of unemployment against the materials he drew from Finch, Adshead, *Facts and Figures*, Ashworth, and the Leeds Town Council. In all cases we found the primary materials shaky enough to make them unreliable even as testimony on purely local unemployment, let alone as national averages. The sources repeatedly counted persons not fully employed in a particular trade as unemployed, a procedure that ignores the widespread shifting of individual workers between sectors over the year. Thus a worker employed 40% of the time as a carpenter and 50% of the time in harvesting and assorted odd jobs is simply counted as a carpenter who can find work only 40% of the time (and who may also be counted as an underemployed harvest worker). Many of the sources include as unemployed those who have left for other towns or America. Some, especially Ashworth, ignore newcomers who came to town recently and found jobs, while taking a very generous definition of the unemployment of those previously at work. In one case, Hobsbawm (p. 75) cites figures showing that about 11% of the town of Leeds had *average* weekly incomes of 11 pence as evidence that "15–20 per cent of the population of Leeds had an income of less than one shilling per head per week", a conclusion that ignores the obvious difference between a group average and a group upper bound. Two final difficulties: all of the sources were designed

to influence Parliament with pleas of special distress, and at no time does Hobsbawm compare these scraps from the 1840s with similar materials for earlier periods.

[32] The EMS unemployment rates are from Phillips, 1958, pp. 64–65; the GNP ratio and 1/GNP are from Deane, 1968, pp. 104–5; the rate of nominal wage increase in engineering and shipbuilding is the Bowley-Wood series from Mitchell and Deane, 1971, pp. 348–51.

[33] Serial correlation would imply that the text is too generous in setting an upper bound on unemployment in the 1840s and late 1830s. The Durbin-Watson statistic was 1.40, suggesting the possibility of serial correlation. A first-order Cochran-Orcutt transformation was performed (rho = 0.30). The altered regression had a lower standard error of estimate (2.33), but still had a Durbin-Watson statistic of only 1.59, far enough from 2.00 to encourage the suspicion of continuing serial correlation.

In the spirit of seeking overestimates of likely unemployment, we have reverted to the original equation, unadjusted for serial correlation, instead of pursuing successive iterations to push the Durbin-Watson statistic up toward 2.00. This yields inefficient estimates, overstating the standard error of the unbiased estimates presented here. (The fact that serial correlation also causes underestimation of the standard errors of the coefficients has little bearing here, since we seek accurate predictions rather than significance tests on coefficients.)

[34] For sectoral output series, see Mitchell and Deane, 1971, passim, and Pollard, 1980, pp. 212–35.

[35] The proof runs as follows. Let the ^{0} superscript denote 1820, and the ^{1} denote 1850. Further, let the $_a$ subscript refer to agriculture and $_n$ to the rest of the economy. Let "a" be the share of the labor force in agriculture, and U the rate of unemployment. The national unemployment rate (no sectoral subscript) is linked to the sectoral rates by definition as follows:

$$U^0 = a^0 U_a^0 + (1 - a^0) U_n^0 \text{ and } U^1 = a^1 U_a^1 + (1 - a^1) U_n^1 .$$

Since a^0 is .284 and $a^1 = .217$, the net change in the unemployment rate becomes

$$U^1 - U^0 = (.217 U_a^1 - .284 U_a^0) + .783 U_n^1 - .716 U_n^0.$$

Given that $U_n^1 < .0941$, and that $U_a^0 \geqslant U_a^1$, it follows that only the second of these right-hand terms can be positive, and its value must be below $.783 \times .0941 = 7.37\%$. This exercise for Britain can be repeated with the same results for England and Wales.

[36] On rates of labor-force participation, see DP, Section 3.4, and the sources cited in Table 9.7.

[37] For all workers, the Paasche measure of the mobility effect was as high as 17.2 per cent between 1781 and 1851, but this was again a very small share of the overall real wage gains. These are improvements over the estimates discussed in DP, Section 6, due to slight revisions in the employment weights.

Some additional shift toward higher-paying occupations after 1811 has eluded our measures. We could include only those occupations that supplied pay proxies, and the excluded groups (about a third of the labor force) shifted from a low-skill mix dominated by domestic servants to a high-skill mix dominated by new occupations created by the Industrial Revolution. More complete measures would show faster average wage gains between 1811 and 1851.

[38] See DP, Section 7.

[39] In this section, "migration" is defined as changes in the labor force distribution across regions. There is, of course, an extensive literature which debates the demographic source of the population and labor force shift to high-wage areas over the period which bounds the standard of living debate. This section is not concerned with whether the observed shift can be attributed to natural increase (and whether to birth or death rate differences) or to actual migration.

[40] But hardly of the size suggested by the qualitative literature. See, for example, Deane and Cole, 1969, chap. 3.

[41] See DP, Table 20. "Migration effects" could bias the life expectancy measure toward uniformity because persons whose health had been damaged by high-mortality environments (e.g., mining or Manchester) may have migrated to healthier environments to no avail, dying there (e.g., recorded rural laborers) and raising rural mortality rates for misleading reasons.

[42] On national life expectancy, see Wrigley and Schofield, 1981, esp. Table A3.1. For crude death rates by county and city, see Deane and Cole, 1969, p. 131, and Great Britain, 1801–02, vols. VI and VII, 1849, vol. XXI, and 1865, vol. XIII, pp. 14ff. For London, we have calculated the following infant mortality rates as percentages of live births, using the bills of mortality plus the third English life table up to 1830 and annual reports of the Registrar General thereafter: 1729–39—.3746, 1750–9—.3322, 1780–89—.2406, 1800–09—.1864, 1820–30—.1428, 1851–60—.1548.

[43] See DP, Table 21 and the accompanying text.

[44] The earnings data come from Chadwick, 1860; and Kay, 1838. Both estimates posit some partial unemployment. This took the form of lower winter earnings in the Norfolk-Suffolk farm data and a 46-week year for Manchester.

[45] On migration countercurrents, see also Ravenstein, 1885, esp. pp. 187–89.

[46] Urban populations for 1801–51 were taken from Mitchell and Deane, 1971, pp. 24–27. Deane and Cole, (1969, p. 7) suggested that the urban population share in the mid-eighteenth century was about 15–16 per cent, and we extrapolated between 1751 and 1801 using this figure for the former date.

10

The Standard of Living Debate and Optimal Economic Growth

G.N. von TUNZELMANN[1]

The recent spate of work reassessing real wage trends during the Industrial Revolution (e.g., Lindert and Williamson, essay 9 in this volume; Flinn, 1974; von Tunzelmann, 1979) has produced a substantial consensus. Roughly speaking, the period from around 1790 to 1850 can be divided into two parts, with real wages fairly constant for the working class as a whole between 1790 and 1820, then rising in a sustained fashion after about 1820. There are minor disagreements over the dating of the turning point(s)[2] and rather more significant ones over the scale of improvement between 1820 and 1850, but the general story holds good. Moreover, the result accords in both degree and timing with what has emerged from the alternative "macro" approach, attempting to derive average per capita consumption from national income data, especially in view of recent suggestions that the existing estimates of the latter overstate the rate of economic growth (Crafts, 1980, 1983; Harley, 1982).[3] I shall argue below that most of the serious participants in the debate, *whether optimists or pessimists*, have accepted this general pattern. Then why should the debate have been so bitter and so protracted?

One obvious answer is that real wages need not measure the standard of living sufficiently reliably. In the first place, real wage rates may diverge from average real earnings, e.g., through varying participation rates (changing rates of unemployment, changing levels of employment of women and children, changes in the number of hours worked per annum, etc.), or changes in the structure of employment (such as shifts towards higher-paying occupational groups). In principle these can be quantified, as Lindert and Williamson have tried to do in the preceding chapter. Secondly there may be discrepancies between pre-tax and post-tax earnings. It is well-known that taxation was highly regressive, but whether it was becoming more or less so is unknown. It is not clear in what degree the price series used to deflate money wages are picking up tax changes. And the incidence of public expenditure according to social class is unexplored. Thirdly, pessimists have long insisted that real earnings ought to be adjusted for changes in environmental conditions, in the belief that these were deteriorating, given urban mortality rates, pollution, hard and degrading conditions of factory work, etc., etc. The neoclassical framework utilised by Williamson (1982a; also Lindert and Williamson, essay 9 in this volume), while a constructive advance, does not really begin to grapple with the pessimist case. In supposing that working-class response to environmental deterioration can be assessed by migration in response to wage differentials, it assumes that the migrants are "free to choose"—it thus ignores the traditional pessimist view that migrants were pushed out of agriculture by enclosure, etc., rather than being pulled into industry. Fourthly, optimists and pessimists agree that a rise in the average consumption of commodities does not necessarily betoken an improvement in "happiness" (e.g., Clapham, 1930, pp. viii, 114; Hartwell, 1971, p. 345; E.P. Thompson, 1968, pp. 231, 485); whilst pessimists, at least, regard the latter as the object of the study. The natural interpretation for economists of "happiness" is "utility", which immediately alerts one to the possibility that there can be no answer to the debate, since interpersonal comparisons of utility will evidently arise (Mokyr and Savin, 1978, p. 518; also, Thompson, 1968, pp. 256–57).

If we are prepared to settle for some assessment of "economic welfare" (and there are grounds for contending that this is what "the standard of living" is properly about), the potential outcome nevertheless seems fairly clear. Through adjusting the real wage indices we shall no doubt find a decline in the standard of living from 1790 to about 1820, followed by a rise which though less than that in real wages will still be very perceptible.

The contention of this chapter is that, although the matters surveyed above have been in the forefront of recent debate, they are not the most important issues and indeed over the whole course of the debate since the Industrial Revolution the major issues have lain elsewhere. For "the standard of living debate" has really been two debates (at least): one that can be described as "factual" debate, over what actually happened to the standard of living; another that can be called the "counterfactual," over what might have happened to the standard of living. The former I shall call the "meliorist vs. deteriorationist" debate, the latter the "optimist vs. pessimist" debate proper.[4]

Those who disdain counterfactuals cannot, however, rest content with the meliorist/deteriorationist debate. For one thing, to use the observed results as a measure of welfare can be justified only if the distribution of income is unchanging (barring certain freakish possibilities—see Sen, 1979), whereas the recent quantitative evidence affirms a major increase in income inequality between the middle of the eighteenth and the middle of the nineteenth centuries (Williamson, 1982b; Lindert and Williamson, 1983b). Secondly, if the kinds of goods being consumed in 1850 differed from those of, say, 1760, then as Samuelson (1950) and Elster (1978, Ch. 2) showed we have to entertain the possibility of a double counterfactual, not only redistributing 1850 income according to 1760 patterns (or whatever), but also redistributing 1850 production in accord with production possibilities. If goods are aggregated by characteristics (providing nutrition, shelter, etc.) this might not be especially problematic for our historical case. But thirdly, it has so far been assumed that the consumers of 1850 are the same people as those of 1760, with fixed social preferences, etc., which is patently absurd. Since interpersonal comparisons of utility are formally debarred, the best we may be able to do is to ask whether the people of 1760 would have preferred the basket of goods consumed by people in 1850 or not (Elster, 1978, chap. 2). Fourthly, to evaluate many of the aspects of the standard of living for which market prices are not immediately available may involve counterfactual computations, e.g., for the value of changes in hours of work, rates of unemployment, displacement into "dishonourable" trades, the incidence of taxation, and so forth. Fifthly, even supposing that suitable adjustments can be effected on all these accounts, we will be left with a number that will still have to be classed as "big" or "small"—to assert that it is "big" will involve a counterfactual comparison with another number that is subjectively deemed to be "small," and vice versa.

The "counterfactual" debate between optimists and pessimists therefore differs in degree rather than in kind from the "factual" debate between meliorists and deteriorationists. The question becomes: Which particular counterfactual? The critical choices are set out lucidly by Hartwell and Engerman (1975, pp. 193–94):

> "Thus in evaluating the consequences of the industrial revolution the question should be *whether, given some set of exogenous changes, the working classes were better off than they would have been in the absence of industrialization.* And this question should be distinguished conceptually from the question *whether, given the Industrial Revolution, it would have been possible for there to have been some set of policies which would have permitted the working classes to have been better off than they actually were.* And these questions are different again from the question *whether the working classes improved their standard of living over the period of the Industrial Revolution, say from 1750 to 1850"* [emphasis added].

What is wrong with the Hartwell-Engerman formulation is that, in plumping for the first counterfactual, their arguments are irrelevant to their intention of combatting the pessimist case, which is in fact the second of these counterfactuals. Thus one answer to the question of why the debate has so long remained open and unresolved is that the two sides have been arguing past each other.

There is, of course, no unique pessimist case, just as there is no unique optimist case, and on both sides some writers have attacked others ostensibly in their own camp. The pessimist arguments considered here can loosely be grouped in the "liberal" and the "socialist" pessimist cases. The socialist counterfactuals would have required major changes in the structure of society and especially in the pattern of ownership of capital and land: these considerations go far beyond the scope of this chapter which thus focusses on the "liberal" or "reformist" case. The essence of the pessimist counterfactual can nevertheless be obtained by conflating the views of the "liberal" Hammonds and the "socialist" E.P. Thompson.[5]

The first point to emphasise about the argument of the Hammonds, particularly, is that it is *explicitly* counterfactual.[6] They are concerned specifically about political alternatives to the regime in power, which could and should have allowed the working classes to attain higher standards of happiness. Chronologically they are concerned about English politics between the French Revolution and (the Hammonds in the *Labourer* trilogy) the time of the Reform Bill of 1832, when Britain was governed by what Thompson (following Cobbett) calls "Old Corruption," i.e. a domination by great landowners and large commercial interests with only the occasional "popular" candidate for Parliament. Both the Hammonds and Thompson are incensed by the advent of a much more repressive administration in the backlash of response to the

French Revolution, implementing for instance the Treason and Sedition Acts and later the Six Acts; in the economic sphere implementing the Combination Acts of 1799 and 1800 and repealing the wage-fixing and apprenticeship clauses of the Elizabethan Statute of Artificers in 1813–14. The Industrial Revolution was therefore accompanied by a political counter-revolution (e.g., Hammonds, 1925, p. 251; Thompson, 1968, pp. 215–16). The ruling classes coalesced in fear of Jacobinism and the working classes at large (e.g., Hammonds, 1917, p. 68; Hammonds, 1925, p. 206; Thompson, 1968, pp. 12, 194–95; Thompson, 1978; Toynbee, 1884, p. 148; Cunningham, 1912, p. 739). The economic regime thus brought about is often described as laissez-faire capitalism: the links have often been drawn, perhaps unfairly, with the contemporaneous rise of political economy (Berg, 1980, pp. 16–17, 35; Coats, 1971). Whether it is appropriate to describe the economic and social policy of governments during the Industrial Revolution as "laissez-faire" is a debate in its own right (see Taylor, 1972, and references therein). For present purposes it is enough to note that the term "laissez-faire" may give just the wrong impression: part of the point is that the government was taking on a much more actively repressive policy in regard to labor and the working class. Inglis (1972, pp. 31–33) adroitly observes that "laissez nous faire" (in regard to the ruling classes in their private capacity) may be a more adequate description (the term dates from Colbert's days; see Gaskell, 1833, 1836).

The Hammonds' *Labourer* trilogy aimed not just to chronicle the experience of, but to suggest better alternatives for, the village, town, and skilled laborer. Their counter-factuals are unusually clearly specified, and carry the additional advantage of being both "small" and "assertable".[7] (i) For the village (i.e. agricultural) laborer, they would have had the government curb the more deleterious effects of enclosure, possibly by implementing earlier rather than later drafts of the General Inclosure Bill. The effects are not studied here because they raise wider questions of property rights, but it may be noted that much recent research (e.g., Allen, 1982) could be used in their support. On wages they would have wished to see Samuel Whitbread's proposed Bill of 1795–6 for the regulation of wages in husbandry enacted, to give rural laborers a fairer share in the soaring agricultural prices of the French Wars period. (ii) For the town (i.e. unskilled) laborer, the Hammonds believed in the necessity of a minimum wage, to prevent competitive undercutting of wages in times of depression. In their view, the supply schedule of labor in unskilled trades was backward-bending at income levels only fractionally above subsistence: workers desperate for work were compelled as wages were reduced to work inhuman hours just to achieve the most basic standards of subsistence (Hammonds, 1917, pp. 202–3; Hammonds, 1919, pp. 96, 172; Thompson, 1968, pp. 306–7, 309; Berg, 1980, p. 245; Hilton, 1964, p. 168). (iii) For skilled laborers the Hammonds believed in wage-fixing along the lines of the celebrated Spitalfields Act of 1773 for London silk-weavers. Such wage-fixing would have differed from the minima for the unskilled in two main ways: first, the magistrates responsible (acting under the advice of both employers and employees) would be setting not minimum wages but "fair wages"—under the Spitalfields Act fines were levied for excessive as well as insufficient wages. Second, the practice required relatively strong trade unions or equivalents, in order to be able to negotiate with employers on the semblance of an equal footing. The latter had to be squared with the operation of the Combination Laws from 1799 to 1824.

The first general point to emphasise is that the pessimists' objection is not to *industrialization* but to *capitalism* (or more precisely to the forms that capitalism took over these years). As the late E.H. Carr (1964, p. 80) said in his splendid lectures, published as *What is History?* : "Nor have I ever heard of a historian who said [of British industrialization 1780–1870] that, in view of the cost, it would have been better to stay the hand of progress and not industrialize; if any such exists, he doubtless belongs to the school of Chesterton and Belloc, and will—quite properly—not be taken seriously by serious historians." This is why Hartwell and Engerman (1975) and other optimist writers who plump for the counterfactual of no-industrialization are simply not meeting the pessimists' case. Under a different political system, pessimists' would have welcomed industrialization and economic growth (for the Hammonds, see 1917, pp. 9, 172; 1930, p. 34; 1939, pp. 228, 247–49; also Thomis, 1974, p. 1). As it was the putative benefits of machinery and innovation were sadly wasted by a system which unduly directed them to the few rather than to the many. The simultaneous approval of machinery and disapproval of profit-making is a consistent line that can be followed from the time itself (e.g., on Robert Owen, see Thompson, 1968, pp. 884–5, 915; on William Cobbett, see Williams, 1983, p. 61; on William Morris, see Thompson, 1977, pp. 643–54). The objection to industrialism as opposed to capitalism has been overwhelmingly a *conservative* (Tory) desire to return to preindustrial, aristocratic ways (e.g., Hilton, 1977; Berg, 1980, chap. 11).

Furthermore, many pessimists have not been deteriorationists, at least at the level of real wages rather than happiness. It is well known that the Hammonds were prepared to accept, with some sharp qualifications, Clapham's case that real wages were rising. Peter Clarke (1978, p. 245), who has combed the Hammonds' letters as well as their books, writes: "In the *Town Labourer*, there is a sentence, the first half of which is often quoted: 'For the revolution that had raised the standard of comfort for the rich had depressed the standard of life for the poor; it had given to the capitalist a new importance, while it had degraded the work-people to be the mere muscles of industry.' This is, rather surprisingly, virtually the only categorical statement made by the Hammonds which would be vulnerable to Clapham's riposte." J.L. Hammond himself (1930, pp. 215–16) thought Clapham was attacking Toynbee, but Toynbee's conclusions about agricultural wages are actually identical to Clapham's (Toynbee, 1884, p. 69; Clapham, 1930, pp. 129, 131).[8]

By the same token, the frequent criticism of the pessimist case—that it ignores the probability that conditions were even worse before the Industrial Revolution—is evidently beside the point once the argument is seen to be a counterfactual one—unless perhaps one were to argue that there were still greater counterfactual possibilities of improving living standards before and after the days of "laissez-nous-faire" capitalism. Equally, the focus of optimists on industrialism (or its hypothetical absence) and of pessimists on varieties of capitalism explains why the former pay most attention to wages in factory industry whereas the latter give much greater weight to those groups who they consider were first expanded and then annihilated by capitalism, such as the handloom weavers.

*   *   *

The substantive objections to the pessimist case—by substantive I mean those which *do* attempt to grapple with it as outlined above—have been both political and economic. The former have constituted the main line of attack by the leading optimists, arguing that state intervention on the scale contemplated by the pessimists was beyond the administrative competence of early nineteenth-century governments (Clapham, 1916, p. 475; 1918; 1930, pp. 335–36; Usher, 1921, pp. 387–88; Ashton, 1948, pp. 112–13; Hartwell, 1966, xix–xxi; Clark, 1962, p. 94). The objection in my view is misconceived, as the Hammonds, for instance, wanted their policies to be implemented by the existing organs of local government, which had indeed traditionally carried out such functions. Moreover, the objection is a weak one, for—as Clapham (1912) in his review of *The Village Labourer* came close to admitting—it tacitly concedes that there may be an economic advantage in wage-fixing; the problem being that political circumstances were not yet sufficiently ripe to execute it.

The economic objections are less easily brushed aside. First, there is the possibility that higher wages would have increased unemployment: supposing the demand schedule for labor to be exogenously given, and less than perfectly elastic, then as the supply curve shifts upward because of successful wage-fixing, the level of employment falls (e.g., Mingay, 1978, p. xvi). The effects may be particularly strong on the relatively defenceless, such as the aged (Cunningham and McArthur, 1910, p. 91; Clapham, 1916). At its broadest, this raises the old Mercantilist chestnut about whether high or low wages are more in the national interest. Secondly, higher wages could restrict (Lovell, 1978, pp. ix–x)—or alternatively accelerate (Cunningham, 1912, pp. 667–68; Taylor, 1975, p. li)—the rate of innovation. Finally one comes to the point of the analysis to follow: that a higher share for wages meant a lower one for profits, as in the Ricardian model (Pollard, 1978; Lovell, 1978; Hobsbawm, 1964, pp. 352–3; Perkin, 1969, p. 139; Marglin, 1978, p. 35). To the extent that profits were ploughed back into capital formation, and capital formation was crucial to industrialization, such increases of wages could be expected to slow down the whole pace of industrialization (Pollard, 1958, p. 216; Taylor, 1960, p. 26; Hartwell and Engerman, 1975, p. 213; Mokyr and Savin, 1978, p. 518; Rule, 1979, p. xv). At its most extreme the point has been stated thus: "in the state of society as it existed in the eighteenth century, the question arises as to whether if industrialization had to take place on the Hammonds' terms it would have taken place at all?" (Lovell, 1978, p. x). In my estimation, this general issue is much the most intractable that the pessimist case has to face. Given the apparent plausibility of the Ricardo argument (accepted in the empirical work below), the objection cannot be dismissed by pat counter-argument. Over time it raises what I construe as the most fundamental welfare issue in economic development: that is, whether to adopt the strategy that Stalin did in Soviet Russia in the 1930s of cutting real wages, in the expectation of getting much higher capital formation and much faster growth, or instead to raise wages from the outset and accept the risk that growth would be substantially slowed down. In other words, in an industrializing nation, should the first generation bear the brunt of the agony for later generations to benefit, or should the burden be spread out more evenly across time, in the likelihood that by so doing the industrialization process will take much longer?

* * *

The specific answers attempted to these questions in this chapter rest critically upon the data employed, and the research of a bevy of quantitative economic historians underlines the need for care and revision. At a future date I intend to conduct sensitivity tests; here I can simply list the procedures employed for obtaining Table 10.1.

Table 10.1 Investment, Employment, and Output in England and Wales, 1761–1770 to 1841–1850, in 1788–1792 Prices

Decade	Capital stock (£m)	Repairs and renewals (£m)	Capital for- mation (£m)	Gross invest- ment (£m)	Labor force (000s)	Wage bill (£m)	Land rents (£m)	Land stock (£m)	Total output
(A) Agriculture									
1761–70	260	22.5	0.9	23.4	874	23.5	19.8	374	66.7
1771–80	276	24.4	1.8	26.2	908	23.8	19.7	395	69.7
1781–90	299	27.0	2.1	29.1	894	23.6	20.3	423	73.0
1791–1800	326	30.0	2.4	32.4	842	23.9	21.2	453	77.5
1801–10	351	30.8	1.8	32.6	768	24.1	24.5	435	81.2
1811–20	373	33.3	1.9	35.2	770	27.1	21.0	418	83.4
1821–30	396	35.9	1.9	37.8	820	27.3	22.0	680	97.0
1831–40	421	38.3	2.2	40.5	805	28.6	32.3	739	101.3
1841–50	455	42.3	3.5	45.8	809	29.6	37.0	886	112.4
(B) Industry									
1761–70	198	6.6	1.8	8.4	447	16.5	0.3	6	25.2
1771–80	219	7.5	2.3	9.8	504	18.6	0.3	7	28.7
1781–90	248	8.9	3.7	12.5	594	21.9	0.4	8	34.8
1791–1800	292	10.8	5.0	15.8	789	27.6	0.5	10	43.8
1801–10	341	11.1	4.9	16.0	988	33.7	0.6	12	50.2
1811–20	403	13.7	7.4	21.2	1204	46.0	0.7	15	67.9
1821–30	501	17.6	12.4	29.9	1473	75.6	0.9	19	106.4
1831–40	664	21.6	20.2	41.7	1862	97.0	1.8	37	140.6
1841–50	887	29.0	24.3	53.3	2217	128.3	3.9	79	185.5

Notes: All figures assume full employment (hence some agricultural series have been revised upward to allow for actual unemployment). Gross investment = Repairs & renewals + Capital formation. Labor force measured as numbers of families (thousands). Labor force and Wage bill figures take into account earnings by some members of chiefly agricultural families in industrial employment. Rents for industry are "urban rents," derived from Feinstein (1978). Total output (= Gross Investment + Wage Bill + Land Rents) is exclusive of transfer payments, of which the most important were interest payments. Services, etc. excluded (see text).

(1) Capital. All figures on capital and investment used here are based on the recent estimates of C.H. Feinstein (1978), and without them the present task would be impracticable. For present purposes Feinstein's figures had to be adjusted in three main ways. (a) His data are for Britain (i.e., including Scotland) mine are for England and Wales alone. (b) The base for his constant-price series is 1851–60, a decade of no direct concern here, so the base was revised to 1788–92 for compatibility with the wage series. (c) Feinstein is careful to extract and eliminate expenditures on repairs, wear and tear, etc., other than renewals, from his series. As such expenditures are essential for the upkeep of the capital stock, and are evident deductions from expenditure available for private consumption, they are written back into capital costs for this problem. The land stock was calculated in the same manner as by Feinstein and from his series for gross rentals and the value of improvements.

(2) Labor. To cope with the problem of underemployment, endemic in English agriculture in the period, I have chosen to work with the number of *families* rather than the number of *persons*. Wives of agricultural laborers and their children frequently obtained work for some part of the year, e.g., during weeding or the hay harvest, or the corn harvest, or in hop-picking; but whether they are counted in with the number of persons recorded as being in the agricultural labor force in the early Censuses is almost impossible to know. Though it is true that the boundaries of a "family" are vague, in fact considering individuals as economic beings raises similar problems (weighting child against adult, etc.). Some members of families "chiefly employed in agriculture" were employed in non-agricultural activities, and the labor estimates in Table 1 are adjusted for this on the basis of findings drawn from the 1834 Poor Law Queries. The breakdown between agricultural and industrial families in the late eighteenth century (before the existence of the Census) was based on extrapolations from county populations for "agricultural", "industrial", and "mixed" counties (from Deane and Cole, 1962, chap. 3). The most striking feature of the resulting series of agricultural families (Table 10.1, Panel A, col. 5) is that it reaches a maximum in the 1770s (or 1780s if different sources are used), and never regains such levels—contrary to the common belief that agricultural employment rose slowly throughout the Industrial Revolution. The pattern in the early nineteenth century is open to a variety of interpretations; my impression is one of fluctuations around a fairly stable mean. If instead of families, best-guess estimates of numbers of individuals were used, much the same would hold good. The counterpart of the fall in agricultural employment from the 1770s is a Rostow-like takeoff of industrial employment from the 1780s.[9] But the eighteenth-century results derive from some fierce extrapolations, and need buttressing by local demographic studies before they could be more confidently asserted. It should be particularly noted that the agricultural and industrial categories in Table 1 do not exhaust total employment—various types of services (e.g., domestic, professional, government) are excluded.

(3) Wages. Agricultural wages, county by county, were extracted from the voluminous replies to the Poor Law Commissioners' Inquiry for the year 1833, broken down by demographic status. To aggregate into county-level wage bills I conjectured the following life-history for males in 1833: from 16 to 25 he is a single man; at 25 he marries; at 27 he has children and up to the age of 44 he averages 3 children (the eldest of whom will be obtaining some work at the end of this period); after 44 he is again married without children; at 60 he retires. Females follow the same pattern except that

they marry and have children two years earlier. "Excess" females (or occasionally males) for whom there are insufficient partners in the county earn as single women-men. And so on. Naturally the categorization immensely simplifies the actual situation, but one way or another I feel that everybody involved in agricultural employment is accounted for, and that it is overwhelmingly likely that up to a trivial level of error any biases in the calculation cancel out. Unemployment, differentiated between summer and winter, is also obtained from the replies to the Poor Law Commissioners. The resulting grossed-up figures for agricultural earnings for England and Wales are extrapolated from 1833 to all other years using the Bowley-Wood series of agricultural wages from 1781 onwards and data from Gilboy (1934) for 1760–80.

The principal source for an industrial wage bill was the survey conducted by Dr. James Mitchell across the country in 1831–32. Mitchell averaged wages according to age and sex for over 28,000 employees in England and Wales, not counting 21,000 in Scotland and 1270 in Northern Ireland. Mitchell's data are heavily biased towards the textile industries, and comparison with other occupations suggests that if anything the resulting aggregates are too low. Expressed as family-equivalents, the results are extrapolated forwards and backwards using the preferred principal-components series for industrial wages and for prices generated in von Tunzelmann (1979).

(4) Consumption. I assume a Cambridge-type savings function, i.e., no savings out of wage incomes. Savings can come out of rents or profits, but in the later calculations I suppose that savings are equal to profits, so that rents can be thought of as equal to consumption of luxuries (the Feinstein figures for land and rents assume that the stock of land cultivated was constant, an assumption that is obviously false but difficult to correct). There is much material in the replies to the 1834 Poor Law Inquiries that support the assumption that savings out of wages were negligible, so long as payments to sick clubs, friendly societies, etc., are regarded as actuarially based on average.[10] (Studies have shown that deposits by the industrial working class in savings banks were very limited, e.g. Fishlow, 1961; Supple, 1974). Hence, working-class consumption is here equal to the wage bill. Any weakening of the assumption that working-class savings were zero is likely to strengthen the results derived below, because capital becomes a less binding constraint (cf. W. Thompson, 1827, p. 87).

The major difficulty that arises on the score of consumption is that it cannot be permitted to fall below a subsistence minimum in any counterfactual state of the world. The concept of such a minimum is a most slippery one. As is well known, all practical attempts to define an absolute standard for poverty ("primary poverty") carry with them implicit *relative* standards, i.e. relative to the customs and habits of the day or place, as indeed the classical economists recognised. Thus wheat bread could have been considered an absolute minimum in southern England of the time, even though the cheaper option of oatmeal or rye bread was available, and more widely consumed in the northern counties. To estimate the minimum in each county I used actual payments for poor relief in each reporting parish in 1833, in the belief that these payments corresponded quite closely to subsistence needs. In many areas the reliefs were explicitly tied to the cost of an important subsistence component (the price of bread in the celebrated Speenhamland system and its mutations—note that the bread scale had been substantially reduced since the war years). Comparison with the cost of workhouse diets, as well as with more general budget studies, underlines the low level at which these payments were usually set, though relative rather than absolute poverty standards probably dictated their levels in most cases. To correct for discrepancies between the average cost of living and that of low-paid workers, I made use of the observations of T.L. Richardson (1976) on the relationship between expenditure on bread and the price of bread for Kentish agricultural workers.

* * *

For one-period optimization, the obvious course of action to maximize consumption is to consume the whole of output by "eating up" the capital stock. The inapplicability of this tactic to an industrializing nation is transparent—it gets a lot of jam for today but leaves little for tomorrow. Jam today has therefore to be balanced against jam tomorrow. Consider the problem from the point of view of production. If the country tries to increase its jam ration for today by lowering investment then it runs the risk of having to produce for tomorrow with a more labor-intensive endowment of resources, exposing it to diminishing returns as other resources contract relative to labor. Conversely, if the country devotes all its energies to sacrificing jam today in order to benefit the future (as might be asserted for the U.S.S.R. in the early 1930s), it may be faced tomorrow by an unduly capital-intensive endowment of resources. I say "unduly" because—unless there is offsetting technical progress, which there might well be—diminishing returns may again set in, this time from expanding capital relative to other resources. Thus the trade-off between today's and tomorrow's jam hinges critically upon the conditions of production and the circumstances of technical progress. The production functions are accordingly written as:

$$Y_t = z_t K_t^{a_t} L_t^{b_t} T_t^{d_t} \tag{1}$$

Where: Y = Output;

K = Capital Stock;

L = Labor Force;

T = Land Stock;

z is a factor of proportionality ($\dot{z}/z$ is the rate of technical progress);

a, b, and d are elasticities of output with respect to the factors; and

t subscripts refer to particular time periods (generally decades).

The rather clumsy subscripting of the variables is to draw attention to the fact that the parameters change from one period to the next. A case can be made for supposing competitive conditions *within* each sector at the time of the English Industrial Revolution, but to suppose competition across sectors is at odds with usual historical presumptions and with my own findings about relative factor prices in each sector. The aggregate production function for the whole economy [equation (1)] is therefore difficult to justify historically, and the main focus below is on the disaggregation to agriculture and industry considered separately (obviously further disaggregation should also be considered—recall that services are not included in the aggregate figures). For the whole economy and for the agricultural sector I specify the elasticities of output to sum to unity, i.e. there are constant returns to capital plus labor plus land. Since a large amount of land is used in agriculture, sharply diminishing returns to capital-plus-labor are implied for that sector: if capital and labor had both been doubled in the 1760s, agricultural output would have risen less than 63 percent; if in the 1840s, less than 60 percent. For the industrial sector I have set a + b = 1. Since a small amount of land was used in industry, the relevant equation implies slightly increasing returns to scale in that sector, amounting to 1.2 percent in the 1760s, rising to 2.4 percent by the 1840s. These various results accord with intuition, but I have attempted to go further and estimate elasticities of substitution empirically, by relating changes in capital-labor ratios to changes in wage-rental ratios. In the case of industry, the assumption of unitary elasticity of substitution between capital and labor squares reasonably well with the actual observations for the second half of the eighteenth century and the second quarter of the nineteenth, but for the intervening period the calculation provides an elasticity of substitution close to zero, perhaps because of the impact of "exogenous" shocks like the French Wars.

The immediate task is to derive the highest sustainable level of consumption through the period of industrialization (1760 to 1850). This objective is defined here as consumption *per head* over the period—if alternatively one wanted to maximize aggregate consumption, one would patently do much more for the later generations, when population growth had swollen the size of the consumption bill.[11] In order for the industrialization process to make sense, the capital stock in the terminal year (1850) is required to be not less than that actually observed in 1850, to prevent the "eating up" of capital accumulation that was in historical practice bequeathed to subsequent generations. The problem is launched from the situation actually observed at the outset in 1760, a situation which is taken to be the outcome of accretionary growth over the preceding centuries. In the initial calculations, which are all that are reported formally in this chapter, the following are taken to change exactly as they did historically: land and land rentals, the labor force in each sector, the parameters of the production functions in each sector, and the amount of foreign trade and investment. Some comment will be made later on these assumptions—the basic point being that they tightly constrain the range of counterfactual alternatives.

Two concessions to reality common to many optimal growth models are not initially allowed for here. All generations are in the first instance treated evenhandedly, so I do not yet discount one generation's earnings as against another's. As I shall intimate, relaxing this assumption considerably strengthens the results. Furthermore, I do not at this juncture express any normative evaluation of one level of per capita consumption as against another: so long as consumption is above the minimum of subsistence as defined earlier, £40 per family is simply twice as good as 20.[12]

The problem is then written as:

$$\max_{(c(t))} J = \int_{t=1760}^{t=1850} c(t)dt \tag{2}$$

$$\text{Subject to: } \dot{k} = y - qk - c - r \tag{3}$$

$$\bar{c}(t) \leqslant c(t) \leqslant y(t) - r(t) \tag{4}$$

$$k_{1760}, k_{1850} \text{ both given} \tag{5}$$

Where: J = the stream of per capita consumption through time;

c = consumption per capita ($=$ family);

$\bar{c}$ = subsistence consumption per capita;

k = the capital-labor ratio ($\dot{k}$ dk/dt);

y = output per capita;

$q = m + n$;

m = the rate of depreciation of the capital stock;

n = the rate of growth of the labor force;

r = land rentals per capita.

This problem can be solved using the production functions (1) above, since the latter can all be expressed in the form $y = f(k)$, given the assumption of a constant land-labor ratio. Fig. 10.1 sets it out graphically, with output per head (and consumption per head) on the vertical axis and the capital-labor ratio on the horizontal one. The curves are drawn for any one arbitrarily chosen decade within the period. The curve $y = f(k)$ is the rewritten production function, say for the whole economy, its curvature reflecting diminishing returns to capital alone. The ray qk is drawn as a straight line since it is supposed that in any one decade the rate of depreciation is constant and so is the rate of growth of the labor force. The lower curve, $y - qk$, is simply the subtraction of this ray from the production function, $f(k)$. The horizontal lines display the given data on rentals and subsistence per head. If investment per capita is constant, the feasible levels of consumption per head are given by the shaded area lying between k_L (the lower feasible bound for the capital-labor ratio) and k_U (the upper bound), because of the accounting constraint (3) and the inequality constraints (4). Maximum consumption per capita (i.e. family) is evidently at the capital-labor ratio k^*, where the slope of the production function is equal to q. This latter relationship (the "Golden Rule") will help us to identify the optimal level of consumption in each decade. It may be noted that the factors responsible for altering k^* and thus c^* through time comprise: changes in the rate of depreciation (m); changes in the output elasticities with respect to capital (a_t—altering the curvature of the production function); changes in the rate of technical progress (z); and changes in the rate of growth of the labor force (n). In practice the latter two are much the most important. *Ceteris paribus*, a rise in the rate of growth of the workforce will steepen the ray qk and hence lead to a fall in k^*—this is because a greater amount of capital has to be diverted from raising the capital-labor ratio to simply equipping the enlarged labor force at existing standards.

Obtaining numerical values for the balanced growth path (c^*, k^*) is less straightforward than Figure 10.1 might imply. High-school calculus will not serve to obtain J, which is defined as a stream of consumption per family through time, because the optimal values at any point of time must take into account the values at all other points of time. The standard mathematical procedure for obtaining J is the calculus of variations, but in general it can produce results that are not "attainable", in the sense of satisfying constraints like the end-point conditions (5) or the restriction to the k_L–k_U range (4). With some effort the calculus of variations can be extended to cover end-point conditions but it is not really satisfactory for inequality constraints like (4).

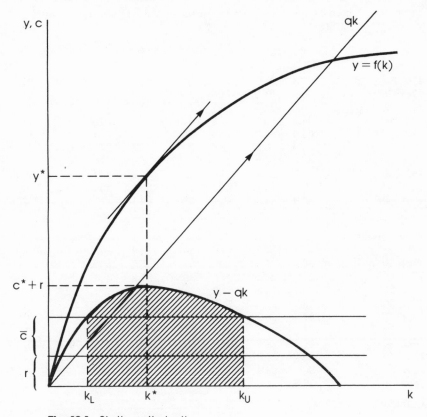

Fig. 10.1. Static optimization

Two methods developed in the context of the "space race" in the late 1950s and 1960s have proved most satisfactory in similar applications. In the U.S.S.R. Pontryagin et al. developed the "maximum principle" (see Appendix), while in the U.S.A. Bellman, et al. developed "dynamic programming." Both are utilised here: the maximum principle to obtain what I denote the static intertemporal optimum (k^* in Table 10.2), and dynamic programming for the dynamic optimum (c^0, k^0). The former represents the optimum that would obtain if the parameters of the various production functions had remained constant at the levels attained in the relevant decade. In actuality of course they were changing all the time, whence, as already mentioned, the subscripting of time on the parameters in equation (1); in these circumstances the maximum principle helped point the way to results that were derived by dynamic programming. The latter is what is required to solve the problem but identifying the static intertemporal path helps to pin down the explanation for the results achieved; the subject to which I now turn.

The first point to make about the results, set out in Table 10.2, is the obvious one that they depend entirely on the data and the model employed, and that the optimization procedures just discussed are to be regarded as no more than technical

Table 10.2 Optimal Growth Paths for the Economy, Agriculture, and Industry, 1760–1850

	c	c̄	c^0	k^0	$y^0 - r$	k*	c**	+%	IMP
A. Whole economy									
1760	30.8	24.7	51.9	313	51.9	298	51.9	69	3
1761–70	30.9	24.6	24.6	224	45.7	308	52.6	70	3
1771–80	30.6	24.6	25.7	283	51.2	333	53.7	75	4
1781–90	31.2	24.6	24.6	344	57.3	341	56.1	80	5
1791–1800	31.9	24.9	24.9	424	64.5	346	58.1	82	6
1801–10	33.0	25.2	66.8	500	66.8	345	57.0	72	8
1811–20	37.2	25.4	25.4	255	55.2	319	62.0	67	12
1821–30	45.7	24.8	74.4	381	74.4	339	71.3	56	16
1831–40	47.8	24.8	24.8	184	58.8	408	47.8	0	0
1841–50	52.9	24.9	92.1	550	92.1	472	–	–	–
1850	59.2	24.9	62.7	403	88.2	481	–	–	–
B. Agriculture									
1760	27.2	24.7	24.7	301	53.2	307	35.6	31	0
1761–70	26.9	24.6	24.6	315	55.2	280	27.1	1	0
1771–80	26.2	24.6	24.6	326	57.0	346	29.9	14	0
1781–90	26.4	24.6	24.6	368	62.0	400	32.3	22	0
1791–1800	28.3	24.9	24.9	424	70.4	553	52.7	86	0
1801–10	31.4	25.2	35.5	570	83.6	570	62.4	99	0
1811–20	35.3	25.4	25.4	587	90.1	439	51.7	47	0
1821–30	33.3	24.8	24.8	651	94.0	537	42.8	29	0
1831–40	35.5	24.8	24.8	769	106.8	597	35.5	0	0
1841–50	36.6	24.9	123.7	916	123.7	598	–	–	–
1850	38.9	24.9	37.0	577	92.9	546	–	–	–
C. Industry									
1760	36.3	24.7	55.0	452	55.0	420	55.0	52	6
1761–70	36.8	24.6	24.6	365	52.2	364	55.7	51	5
1771–80	36.9	24.6	58.2	476	58.2	493	56.4	53	7
1781–90	36.8	24.6	24.6	318	52.4	262	57.9	57	7
1791–1800	34.9	24.9	55.8	386	55.8	309	54.9	57	8
1801–10	34.1	25.2	25.2	214	43.1	283	50.2	47	9
1811–20	38.2	25.4	53.2	287	53.2	338	55.8	46	13
1821–30	51.3	24.8	59.1	173	59.1	341	71.6	40	19
1831–40	52.1	24.8	27.1	97	50.3	438	52.1	0	0
1841–50	57.9	24.9	89.0	530	89.0	621	–	–	–
1850	65.1	24.9	72.5	428	91.5	674	–	–	–

Note: c^0, k^0, y^0 = values on optimal-growth path; k* = Golden Rule capital/labor ratio, i.e., ignoring constraints (4) and (5); c** = maximum per-family consumption in each decade without lowering aggregate consumption through time; +% = percentage increase of c** over c; IMP = percentage improvemnt of c** path over c path for remainder of period to 1850. For evaluating the paths in the dynamic-programming calculations of optimal growth and c**, the decades 1761–70 to 1841–50 were weighted equally at 10 units each, 1760 at 5 units, and 1850 at zero (consumption in the final year is essentially arbitrary). The values for k^0 in 1760 and 1850 in each case are actual historical values, because of constraint (5).

apparatus. The complexity of the procedures helps explain why nobody else has attempted numerical solutions to the optimist/pessimist debate, but that complexity arises out of the nature of the problem rather than the choice of model, etc. The model adopted is in fact extremely simple—too simple, as we shall soon see.

The feasible optimal path is that given as c^0 and k^0 in the table, with the Golden Rule value k^* as well as actual per capita consumption c shown for comparison. For the purposes of this table, and implied by equations (1), industry and agriculture are treated as separate economies, to be individually maximized—a highly unrealistic assumption that is made at the outset purely to gesture towards differences between the sectors. The gain of the optimal path over actual consumption is 17.8 percent for agriculture, 11.9 percent for industry, and 14.7 percent for the whole economy. The nature of the problem—requiring an economy or sector to shift its path of capital accumulation around between two historically-given end-points, with no feedback effects or whatever—makes higher gains improbable, particularly where subsistence is not too far below actual average levels of consumption.

Agriculture gives the kind of result often expected in these calculations—an agonisingly long period of crawling along on the minimum of subsistence (broken only in 1801–10), before giving way to a *"grande bouffe"* in the 1840s. Only in the sense of the strong assumptions so far employed can this be thought of as "optimal." The result for industry is much more interesting—it also has a splurge in the 1840s, but in many preceding decades it would have paid to increase consumption and thus wages in the quest for the maximum stream.

Table 10.2 also shows a limitation of optimal paths, in the tendency to generate "bang-bang" paths (either k_L or k_U in Fig. 10.1; see Appendix). The instability involved is especially marked in Panel A, for the whole economy: there c^0 tends to alternate between the maximum possible $(y^0 - r)$ and the minimum $(\bar{c})$, and this could not have been politically acceptable. My unreported further research, still in progress, is trying various ways to obviate this problem, but of course at the cost of being much more subjective. But whatever the "social optimum" that is decided upon, it is evidently not difficult to generate hypothetical paths that yield both more consumption and more capital formation than the actual path. The model of "unproductive investment" that has been popular with many pessimists (e.g., Pollard, 1958; Williams, 1966) has previously been criticized on empirical grounds (e.g., Hartwell and Engerman, 1975), but here I show that, up to the limitations of the present model, it is conceptually misleading, in that there was no simple tradeoff of more consumption versus more investment.

The results provide a much stronger attack on the optimist position. The thesis of the Hammonds that a suitably enlightened government could have brought about higher living standards without necessarily sacrificing economic growth is vindicated. The optimal-growth path (c^0, k^0) is not the best way of demonstrating this, because though it shows the maximum amount of extra consumption that could have been squeezed out, subject to the above assumptions and parameters, it sometimes involves lowering consumption standards to the subsistence minimum in particular decades. Accordingly, I have estimated, for each decade *taken separately*, the extent to which consumption per family could have been increased without needing to reduce aggregate living standards up to 1850. There are several ways in which this counterfactual could be run. For the one chosen here, c^{**} in Table 10.2, the condition has been imposed that in every preceding decade c and k should take on their actual values (implying that for the decade in question k would continue to take on its actual value, though c would change); only in subsequent decades could c and k both be altered to suit the demands of optimal growth.[13] As can be seen from the next column of the table, headed " +%", c^{**} is always at least 40 percent higher than actual c without detriment to long-run growth in industry, and at least 56 percent higher for the economy, up till the 1820s.[14] In all of these cases, the upper-bound constraint on consumption turns out to be binding (i.e., $c^{**} = y^{**} - r$), with the result that there is still some overall advantage in the c^{**} path as compared with the c path—the residual percentage gain is shown in the final column, headed "IMP." Even for agriculture, a large increase would have been possible without necessarily reducing long-term living standards over the years from 1791 to 1820, so that if Whitbread had been successful in his attempt to increase the wages in husbandry in the mid-1790s, there could have been a particularly marked gain in equity without loss of efficiency.

To the present writer, the most notable result to emerge from Table 10.2, and especially from the c^{**} calculation, is the potentiality for raising living standards even in the "deteriorationist" period before about 1820. Several commentators on my earlier paper have pointed out that there were other ways in which the government could have benefited the working classes beside varying the redistribution from investment activities—most apparently by reducing military and similarly "wasteful" expenditures during the French Wars. I would be the last to deny this, and intend evaluating the argument in a subsequent assessment of the optimist case. The point here is that, even taking such other possibilities to be exogenous and irreducible (e.g., for strategic reasons), redistribution of the kind that *is* contemplated in this chapter could have been advantageous. Of course, if war expenses and the like could have been cut, the gain to the working classes could have been considerably larger.

The explanation for the results obtained, and especially those for industry, is that both statically and dynamically the economy and its sectors were operating at suboptimal levels. In a static sense, as a comparison of k^* with actual k would show, industry was generally excessively capital-intensive—it would have done better to lower the capital-labor ratio and gained some consumption for so doing. In a dynamic sense, the capital-labor ratio in industry was *falling* down to about 1820, and even by 1850 had not regained its initial level of the 1760s, contrary to much popular belief (cf. von Tunzelmann, 1981).

The results are only as good as the assumptions and data underlying them, and the assumptions are clearly very restrictive. I offer no justification for them here, other than that they are the simplest available for use, but I am currently working on relaxing those that seem to me most binding. These can be listed as follows: (a) the assumption that the marginal utility of consumption is constant, rather than diminishing; (b) the lack of discounting of the welfare of different generations; (c) the treatment of laborers as an aggregate, rather than considering different groups within the labor force; (d) regarding Agriculture and Industry as separate and independent "economies," to be individually maximized, rather than constituting interactive parts of a two-sector model; (e) the assumption that land rentals are given and unavailable for redistribution; (f) the assumptions that technical progress is disembodied and that higher wages do not involve further substitution of capital for labor; (g) taking population to be fixed and its rate of growth given, instead of relating to (earlier) hypothetical rises of wages; and (h) supposing international flows of goods and factors to be unaffected by the results.

As I say, no justification can seriously be given for any of these as they stand, but the issue is how the outcomes will be affected by moving toward greater historical realism. My strong belief is that, taking all in all, the results reported so far are likely to prove quite robust. The reasons I would advance (possibly prematurely) for this assertion are as follows. In the first place, the model reflects "supply-side economics" in that problems—say of a Keynesian kind—on the demand side do not exist. The neglect of demand is another ahistorical assumption, for in the real world there were problems of underemployment in agriculture and short-time working in industry. But the point is that hypothetically raising wages would boost aggregate demand, as many contemporaries saw, especially in the troubled years following Waterloo. The supply-side gains from higher wages reported here should thus be augmented by the likelihood of benefits on the demand side, but to show these explicitly would require much more complex models. Second, to revert to a point made at the beginning of the chapter, I do not look beyond consumption to the broad range of environmental, demographic, social and psychological factors that ought to constitute the "quality of life." Some of these could be investigated only by taking up the "socialist" rather than the "liberal" pessimist counterfactual, e.g., alienation, and this remains to be undertaken in future research. Yet though a materialist criterion may be only a small part of the whole issue, real consumption standards might be expected to influence a great many of the other constituents (e.g., Taylor, 1975, pp. xviii–xix). Third, and related to this last point, higher consumption standards leading to higher nutritional standards might have led to higher levels of economic efficiency, and hence ultimately to further rounds of increase in consumption, along the lines of the efficiency-wage argument in development economics. The well-known work of Blaug (1963, 1964) on the productivity effects of the Speenhamland system represents an application of this model to the period, though note the criticisms of McCloskey (1973) and especially Williams (1981, pp. 29ff.). More recently, work on the heights of working-class children by R.C. Floud and others (e.g., Floud and Wachter, 1982) has indicated a close relationship to living standards. Fourth, and most important, most of the above restrictive assumptions in my view limit rather than exaggerate the advantages of higher wages. One of the clearest examples is the restriction that increases in wages have to come out of profits rather than rents—in a model in which rents are defined as containing no component for investment—so that rents are thought of as luxury consumption. Indeed, as the earlier discussion shows, by not examining hypothetical shifts from rents to wages, say during the Napoleonic Wars, the model fails to test an important component of the orthodox pessimist case. Leaving demand to one side for a moment, it is evident that if higher wages can come from sacrifices of luxury consumption then there is no need for a growth/equity tradeoff. More generally, the point to be made is that relaxing the assumptions permits a wider range of counterfactual possibilities to be attainable, and thus the likelihood of greater counterfactual gains.

The fly in the ointment is probably the data rather than the model. Above all, the figures for technical purposes (the z's in the production functions) are implausible. Revisions to the currently accepted data as they become available, along the lines intimated by recent research (e.g., Crafts 1983), bid fair to produce more plausible data, and once again first impressions are that such revisions will strengthen rather than weaken the conclusions of the chapter.

I conclude that, though much remains to be done on both data and model, the fundamental pessimist argument should stand: that a more interventionist government could have raised real wages without endangering long-term growth. Though in principle this should suffice to refute the optimist case, in practice it does not, because as I intend to show elsewhere most optimists have been more pragmatic about the fields which they presume to have warranted earlier deregulation. For instance, wage regulation could have been stepped up and the law of settlement abolished in the early nineteenth century, with both conceivably being advantageous.

Still more fundamentally, it is clear that it is perfectly possible to be a meliorist, in the "factual" debate, and a pessimist, in the "counterfactual" debate; as I have tried to show, many pessimists have taken this stance, at least at the level of real wages rather than "happiness." Arguably one could be simultaneously an optimist and a deteriorationist—living standards would have risen but fell thanks to meddling governments. This position was quite common at the time (for an extreme example see Gaskell, 1833, 1836), but subsequently became rare as data on real wages began to be collected—though it was the view of Thorold Rogers (1884). What was widely interpreted as an optimist vs. pessimist debate in twentieth-century historiography was really a meliorist vs. pessimist debate. It is therefore no wonder that both sides claimed victory, and that the debate has remained so inconclusive as everybody talked past one another.

Appendix

THE APPLICATION OF THE "MAXIMUM PRINCIPLE"

To maximize the consumption stream through time according to the objective (2) and the accounting constraint (3), the maximand can be written as $H = \{c + p[f(k) - qk - c - r]\}$, where as before $f(k) = y$ from the production function, and p is a multiplier akin to the Lagrange multiplier of static optimization (though note that k does not appear explicitly in H). H is known mathematically as the Hamiltonian expression, and can be thought of here as national income per capita. In this model, the Hamiltonian, H, is linear in c $(H = c(1 - p) + p[f(k) - qk - r])$; and the maximum principle of Pontryagin et al. dictates that in these circumstances the solution is of the "bang-bang" type. If the inequalities (4) are strict inequalities—in other words, if consumption lies somewhere between the minimum of subsistence and the maximum of total output minus rents—then the maximum principle requires $\partial H / \partial c = 0$; i.e., $(1 - p) = 0$, or $p = 1$. If k^* is feasible in the sense of lying between k_L and k_U in Figure 10.1, then this will occur—p is the shadow price of additional capital per working family (k), and for a k^* falling within such bounds it provides no premium for or against any additional capital. The inequality constraints (4) can be written into an expanded Hamiltonian by means of further Lagrange multipliers; for the situation just described these multipliers will equal zero. However, if k^* falls below k_L or above K_U such multipliers will take on non-zero values as these constraints become binding. Consumption will fall to the subsistence minimum if k^* lies below k_L or rise to output less land rents if k^* lies above k_U ("bang-bang"). In the former case p will be greater than unity, meaning that there is a premium on increasing capital per worker-family; in the latter case p will be less than 1, implying a premium on consumption per worker-family. Only by sheer coincidence would the economy find itself on the balanced-growth path (c^*, k^*) at the initial and terminal dates, 1760 and 1850, but the conditions (5) dictate that the optimal solution must incorporate these actual circumstances. The so-called turnpike theorem of growth theory argues that if initial and terminal time are sufficiently far apart, the optimal growth path will lie in the vicinity of the balanced-growth path (c^*, k^*)—assuming it is feasible—for as long as possible, regardless of the end-point conditions (5). This assumes the parameters to be unchanging, which as noted in the text is not the historical situation we find ourselves in.

Notes

[1] This is a substantially revised and extended version of a paper submitted to the panel on "Technical Change, Employment and Investment" at the Eighth International Economic History Conference at Budapest, 1982; that paper is hereafter referred to as von Tunzelmann, 1982. In various forms the drafts have been submitted to seminars at the University of Warwick, St. Antony's College (Oxford), and the University of Sussex; my thanks to the participants for their helpful and constrictive remarks. My particular thanks go to Joel Mokyr and Stanley Engerman for their comments on the Conference paper, and to Gene Savin for many discussions.

[2] Flinn (1974) opts for a major upturn around 1815 and a slackening-off about a decade later. My 1979 article contends that in part this conclusion is drawn from a confusion of trend with cycle, as well as from an excessive concentration on years of turning-points in *prices*.

[3] It should however be noted that one of Harley's two methods for revising the macro data is drawn in part from wage trends, so this is not a fully independent confirmation.

[4] I use these terms in preference to those of Elster, 1978, pp. 196, 220, developed in the course of making similar points, of optimism vs. non-optimism and pessimism vs. non-pessimism, partly because I at least find my terms slightly easier to remember and slightly more euphonious (though hardly pretty), and partly because, as Elster admits, his category of "optimism" is an empty set—nobody has taken the Panglossian view that during the Industrial Revolution all was for the best.

[5] The Hammonds have often been mistakenly identified with the Fabians; indeed Thompson errs in this fashion. In fact the Fabians were their nearest political enemies (see Clarke, 1978; Sutton, 1982).

[6] In an extended critique of one of the Hammonds' works, Thomis (1974) objects to their use of counterfactuals as not being the practice of recent historians. This simply betrays an ignorance of modern historiography.

[7] The significance of these terms, and the merits of designing such counterfactuals in historical work, are argued—persuasively in my view—in Elster (1978).

[8] This is less surprising when one reflects that their source (Caird) was the same. For manufacturing wages, Clapham had the benefit of the Bowley-Wood research, but Toynbee too emphasised song-term improvement above all else, though he was vague on the dating of the turning-point.

[9] This makes an interesting parallel with the takeoff in capital formation observed in Feinstein's data, though my findings on productivity referred to later in the paper suggest basic faults somewhere in the data.

[10] In practice, the clubs and societies erred on the side of being overgenerous (e.g., Clapham, 1930 p. 298; Supple, 1974).

[11] Hayek (1954, pp. 14–17) has claimed that the increased population could be regarded as a form of consumption gain; in which case, as Elster (1978, pp. 198–99) has pointed out, one should adopt consumption rather than consumption per head as the maximand. Elster provides

some reasons for rejecting this approach; in addition I would note that many optimists have deemed population growth to be one of the most important "exogenous" forces keeping down per-capita gains in the earlier part of the Industrial Revolution.

[12] In research in progress I am working with a utility function of the form $U = (c - \bar{c})^x$. At the time of writing I have results only for $x = 0.75$, and they turn out to be scarcely different from those set out in Table 10.2, (implying $U = c$), except that with the different specification of consumption as $(c - \bar{c})$ it never quite falls to the minimum of subsistence.

[13] These calculations are made for a more tightly constrained path than the often highly unstable ones in Table 10.2; see von Tunzelmann (1982) for further details.

[14] In each case $c^{**} = c$ for the 1830s, because in conjunction with the value of k^* for the 1840s the end-point conditions turn out to be binding—in other words, the result for the 1830s is a product of artificially terminating the whole problem in 1850. More realistic assessments of the scope for increasing consumption in particular decades from about the 1820s would require later terminating dates for the full calculation.

11

Literacy and
the Industrial Revolution

E.G. WEST

I

Sharp differences of judgement appear to persist on the precise extent and timing of literacy changes in eighteenth- and nineteenth-century Britain and their relationship to economic growth. This essay will explore the exact nature of the differences and will attempt to resolve some of the main issues.

Recent research among British historians seems to have been sensitive to the seminal work of the American economists M.J. Bowman and C.A. Anderson (1963, pp. 247–79). From statistics of cross-sectional comparisons of literacy rates in the 1950s they generalized that a literacy rate of 30–40 per cent was a necessary condition for a country to make a significant breakthrough in *per capita* income. Several British historians seem to have been uneasy about Bowman and Anderson's inclusion of eighteenth- and nineteenth-century Britain as one of the many "industrial and literacy success" examples. Their critical response to the American authors has included the following three arguments: first, that literacy deteriorated in the Industrial Revolution; second, that growth produced literacy, not vice versa; and third, that private educational activities were inadequate.

This response has probably been conditioned by the long-established tradition in British history that the Industrial Revolution, especially in its early stages, was generally inimical to reasonable *material* comforts, let alone educational improvements, among the working class. Typical of the originators of this tradition, for instance were the Hammonds. Their conclusion was that in the new manufacturing towns of the Industrial Revolution:

> . . . all diversions were regarded as wrong, because it was believed that successful production demanded long hours, a bare life, a mind without the temptation to think or remember, to look before or behind [J.L. Hammond, and B. Hammond, 1925, p. 229].

Reprinted from the *Economic History Review*, Vol. 31, No. 3 (August 1978), pp. 369–83. Reprinted by permission of the Economic History Society.

The ruling class argued . . . that with the new method of specialization, industry could not spare a single hour for the needs of the man who served it. In such a system education had no place [ibid., p. 231].

. . . politicians were prepared to leave the nation to a hopelessly inadequate provision made by voluntary societies, and it was not until 1833 that education received any help from the public funds [ibid.].

Richard Altick, a more recent upholder of this tradition, summed it up in one sentence:

The occupational and geographical relocation of the people—the total disruption of their old way of life, their conversion into machine-slaves, living a hand to mouth existence at the mercy of their employers and of uncertain economic circumstances; their concentration in cities totally unprepared to accommodate them, not least in respect to education; the resultant moral and physical degradation—these, as we shall see, had significant consequences in the history of the reading public [Altick, 1957, p. 207].

The supporters of this traditional view, nevertheless, have had to face the challenge not only of Anderson and Bowman but also of the new empirical work of writers (including the present author) who claim that education did not decline (Webb, 1955; Neuberg, 1971 who argues that there was a "mass reading public" by 1800; Robson, 1966; Laqueur, 1976; Stone, 1969; West, 1965, 1975; Hartwell, 1971). The response to this challenge has been interesting. Some historians, whether traditionalists or not, have reacted by concentrating on intensive surveys of particular localities that suggest apparent exceptions to the rule of progress. Sometimes, too, the "new sceptics" have challenged the reliability of the statistical sources used in recent work, but then they have proceeded regardless of the inconsistency, to rely themselves on the same sources, but with their own particular interpretation.[1] More important, the sceptics have concluded that the verdict that the Industrial Revolution period (which most participants in the debate seem to take to be 1760–1840) was favorable to educational growth is, at best, appropriate only for the last few years of the period.[2] They base their main argument on large-scale sample data on eighteenth-century marriage-register signatures, first published in 1973. Previously scholars had been limited to national figures from 1839 in the Registrar's annual reports, and to one or two small local samples.

This essay takes the opportunity to examine the new data. I shall argue that, on correct interpretation, they do not support the sceptics.[3] I shall also consider the claim of the sceptics that wide regional variations in nineteenth-century literacy throw doubt on any generalized conclusion on the relationship between industrialization and educational growth. The main focus will be on the regional example that is so often cited, the case of Lancashire. It will be argued that here some important variables have been missing from the discussion. Finally, it will be shown that, in reaching their conclusion, the sceptics have gone from figures of literacy to figures of schooling, and that, in this latter field, their argument is equally unconvincing.

The discussion begins in section II with a re-examination of the Lancashire case. Section III analyses the new data on eighteenth-century literacy and discusses the current interpretation of it. Section IV links the evidence of changing literacy with that of changing educational institutions, and especially the innovations of "free", "compulsory", and publicly approved schools, in a way that tests hypotheses about such linkage that are commonly employed by the sceptics but not efficiently tested by them.

II

It is generally agreed by all participants that people were more literate at the end of the Industrial Revolution period, 1760–1840, than they were at the beginning. Michael Sanderson's survey of Lancashire, however, has suggested to him initial decline or stagnation that only reversed itself after over one-half of the period was over (Sanderson, 1972). Sanderson based his survey on a selection of what he believed to be fairly representative instances of the industrializing centres in the country.

After adding further data, Thomas Laqueur, using the same measure as Sanderson—marriage-register signatures—also pointed to an early decline in literacy in Lancashire. The low point was 48 percent of men and 17 percent of women able to sign their names in 1814–16 (Laqueur, 1974). Laqueur, however, rejected Sanderson's suggestion that the low point might have been *caused* by the introduction of large-scale factories using steam- power in the 1790s which, according to Sanderson, was the beginning of real social dislocation. This is unproven, Laqueur insisted, because the downward literacy trend had by then already been in progress for forty years. Sanderson's argument, moreover, could not explain the beginning of a long-term rise in the literacy rate which Laqueur placed at around 1800, when the full influence of the factory system was beginning to be felt.

> In fact, it appears that the Industrial Revolution reversed a downward spiral of working-class literacy which began in the mid-eighteenth century . . . By the time the full effects of the factory system came to be felt, literacy was once again on the rise [Laqueur, 1974].

Laqueur emphasized that the marriage literacy test reflected an education that ended about twelve to fifteen years before, as, for instance, with a marriage age of 25 and a school-leaving age of ten. It was for this reason that the correct date for the improvement in literacy was around 1800. Laqueur's article also stressed that the adult literacy rates in the same Lancashire towns were below the national averages just *before* the Industrial Revolution.

In his reply in 1974, Sanderson did not satisfactorily meet Laqueur's point that the downward trend in literacy had been in progress for forty years before the introduction in the 1790s of steam-powered factories, and that the latter were not therefore the obvious cause of the low point in literacy in 1800. Instead, Sanderson shifted the debate to the latter end of the period. He argued that his own figures of literacy in Lancashire at the time of marriage did not show a "consistent" upturn before 1820 (Sanderson, 1974).

The graph of his data (Sanderson, 1972, p. 87) shows that there *was* a distinct upturn before 1820, as Laqueur argued. First, Sanderson's nine-point moving average curve rises steadily from its first point in the year 1817. Second, and much more importantly, his graph needs an adjustment lag to account for the interval between school and marriage. Sanderson (1974) accepted Laqueur's argument that literacy records in marriage registers reflected a schooling of twelve to fifteen years earlier. On the assumption that schooling creates literacy (which all participants accept), his nine-point average curve of literacy should, on his own concession, start twelve to fifteen years before 1817, that is in 1802–5. Third, neither Laqueur nor Sanderson gives the source for his belief that the lag was twelve to fifteen years. My own research (1965, p. 133) suggests that on the average it was about seventeen years. On this estimate, Sanderson's graph reveals the rise in literacy starting in 1800, as Laqueur argued on the basis of his own data. Notice that the argument that the full effects of the large-scale factories in 1800 caused a social dislocation that was inimical to education requires evidence that literacy *declined* at this time. Sanderson's evidence shows instead that the period around 1800 was the beginning of an *increase*.

The question whether industrial change in the past hindered or helped literacy is much more complex when other substantial changes were occurring. The most dramatic change in the late eighteenth and early nineteenth centuries, apart from the Napoleonic War, was the unprecedented expansion of population. The true test of the question is whether literacy rates would have fared better if the same late eighteenth-century population explosion had occurred in the pre-factory environment. Even if we ignored the previous criticisms, this consideration would make Sanderson's argument much more hypothetical. Laqueur mentions a 60 per cent increase in the Lancashire population between 1781 and 1800. Not only was the natural increase well above the national average but so was the rate of immigration. The combined (natural plus migration) increase in population was four times the national average. According to rough estimates, just under half of the increase between 1781 and 1800 was by immigration (126,319 increase by immigration and 146,852 by natural increase—from Deane and Cole, 1962). This means that if the typical immigrant family consisted of two adults and two children, then for every two "local-born" children there was about one immigrant child needing education over this period. The more that immigrants consisted of young single adults, the more the early marriage signatures would be represented by them. Also relevant is that between 1801 and 1831 population increase reached its peak in absolute numbers, 637,543, as did the natural increase, 474,009, and immigration, 183,543 (ibid.). The ratio of immigrants to natural increase, however, was evidently falling by this time.

Because a considerable proportion of the immigrants were low-income Irish, and since by all accounts they had the poorest of educations (West, 1965, pp. 113–14), the growth of Irish arrivals relative to the local-born Lancashire population must have had a significantly depressing effect on the local literacy records, especially between 1781 and 1800. According to Arthur Redford, Lancashire contained a greater number of Irish settlers during the period than any other county, and the majority of them settled in the Industrial Revolution towns (Redford, 1964, p. 154). In 1835, Dr. J.P. Kay estimated that the Irish and their immediate descendants in Manchester had grown to about 60,000. This was between one-quarter and one-third of the town's total population (Mitchell and Deane, 1962, p. 24).

It is surprising that, in the works cited above, neither Sanderson nor Laqueur connects the Irish immigration with the relatively low literacy rates in the Lancashire of the Industrial Revolution. Indeed, Laqueur argues the possibility that the immigrants were typically the more accomplished and literate. Clearly, the data produced by

Sanderson and Laqueur would benefit by a re-examination and search for a correlation between Irish settlement and literacy rates in the various parishes so far studied. Their investigations are surely significantly incomplete without it.

If the explanation of a depressant effect by immigrants holds up, the view that literacy had no major connexion with economic growth in the period would be even weaker.[4] The quickening of economic activity in the Industrial Revolution stimulated the demand for new construction of houses, port facilities, canals, and roads. This in turn increased the demand for general laborers, the literacy among whom, it is generally agreed, is not of the strongest relevance to their particular productivity. As Redford (1964, p. 154) observes:

> Much of the work done by the Irish in Great Britain was of the same general manual nature as their harvesting and agricultural labor ... An immense number of Irish were employed as hodmen in Lancashire ... By 1833 there were at least seven hundred Irish hod-carriers working in Liverpool, and two years later it was said that four-fifths of the bricklayers' laborers in Stockport were Irish.

Such a picture is quite consistent with a situation of significant "threshhold" literacy among the indigenous population enabling them better to concentrate in "key" growth areas, like manufacturing, where literacy *was* of more consequence. But even if this were not the case, insofar as the literacy of the immigrant Irish improved, compared with its normal attainment at their place of origin, we can still speak of this as a growth in education, and one that was associated with industrialization. The positive association could still prevail despite the stagnation or even decline shown in Lancashire marriage signatures in particular localities. This kind of explanation too could give its own kind of support to a "threshold"-type argument similar to Bowman and Anderson's. And it is noteworthy that, at the end of his recent debate, even Sanderson came to reconcile his position with theirs: "Yet I find credible the notion that pre-industrial Britain had already crossed a threshold of literacy sufficient for industrialization and that, however much it fell during early industrialization, it did not regress beyond that threshold" (Sanderson, 1972).

III

One other modern specialist, R.S. Schofield, still rejects the "threshold" theory. After referring to Bowman and Anderson's association of literacy with growth he observes:

> Inferences sometimes drawn from this association are that an illiteracy rate of about 60 per cent is a threshold above which economic growth is unlikely ... Although it is true that the national male illiteracy rate had crossed the 60 per cent threshold before 1750, the female rate only crossed it definitely around 1795, and female illiteracy was very high in areas of high female industrial employment; for example, it was still 84 per cent in Oldham in 1846 [Schofield, 1973, pp. 437–51].

These objections do not stand up. First, the threshold described by Bowman and Anderson is not 60 per cent, but between 60 and 70 per cent (Bowman and Anderson,

1963, p. 252); and it is relevant that these authors also suggested from their data that within the range from 30 to 70 per cent literacy there was "remarkably little" increase in income with rising literacy rates.[5] Schofield's figures show that the national rate for women was about 37 per cent in 1755, rising steadily to 40 per cent around 1795, and still rising thereafter. Clearly, this was well within Bowman and Anderson's relevant threshhold.

Second, Bowman and Anderson's figures refer in any case to the *adult* literacy rate (men and women combined). In England according to Schofield's figures, this rate started well above the limit at about 50 per cent (in 1755), and rose to about 60 per cent in 1840. Finally, Schofield is misleading when he supports his argument that female industrial illiteracy was very high in areas of high female industrial employment by taking "for example" the case of Oldham with a 16 per cent female literacy rate in 1846. This was an extreme instance. The figure for industrial Lancashire as a whole, which is the more relevant one, was about 31.1 per cent (Laqueur, 1974, p. 99).

Schofield's article has the distinction of offering the strongest defence hitherto of the marriage-signature measure of literacy. His main point is that it is the most standard, direct, and inclusive. One can agree with this up to a point;[6] and one can accept, as reasonably representative, the national estimates from his random sample of 274 parishes (out of a total of 10,000) relating to the pre-1839 years, the period before the Registrar-General recorded aggregate literacy. What is debatable is his interpretation of these figures.

Schofield argues that the "long period of stability" in literacy in the eighteenth century suggests that "for England, at least, the usual causal relationship between literacy and economic growth might profitably be reversed." But taking the conventional dates of the first Industrial Revolution to be between 1760 and 1840, and assuming, as Schofield does, that entry into the labor force may be taken to be fifteen years prior to marriage (i.e. at school leaving), then 1790 is the date when the long-term stability in male literacy changed to one of definite improvement.[7] It follows that, despite the unprecedented population growth after 1760, England was not only able to maintain the male literacy rate that had been constant for twenty years preceding the industrial revolution, but well before half the "revolution" period was over, and at a time when the population explosion was in full force, it managed to begin an upward trend. It is interesting again to notice that the date of the upturn, 1790, coincided with the beginning of the large-scale factory system and the widespread commercial use of steam power.

The influence of the British tradition on educational history[8] might be one factor inhibiting Schofield from drawing the central attention to the 1790 "take-off" point, and from making reference to the enormous handicap of the sudden growth of population. For such an early year suggests a growth in the *means* of literacy improvement such as private schools for all classes, while the tradition argues the impossiblity of any progress (or avoidance of decline) until *public* action was taken.[9] Interestingly enough, Schofield eventually moves from his major data, on literacy, and into the evidence on schooling. Since the evidence he uses refers to the post-1830 years, we must, for the moment, shift our focus from the early (eighteenth-century) Industrial Revolution period, and from literacy, to schooling.

Schofield starts by rejecting the "rash of educational surveys" in the 1830s as being too restricted in date span to be useful for study of trends over a long period. Yet, inconsistently, he himself eventually leans heavily on one of them; and he does this to demonstrate that schooling (over a long period) was seriously deficient. More significantly still, he here makes serious errors in interpretation and reporting.

Referring to the period 1750–1850, he argues, "All schools had great difficulty in securing attendance (Schofield, 1973, p. 439, my emphasis)." He supports the statement about this "long period" from one example of the "in-period" survey of the 1830s, the survey of education in Westminster in 1837–38. According to Schofield (ibid.), this reported "that school attendance in winter was down to between a quarter and a half of the number enrolled." But, to be precise, the Committee of the Westminster Statistical Society was reporting, in 1838, on a total of eight different types of school. Its comments on decreased attendance in the winter months related to only two of them; and these contained 29 per cent of the total scholars in the area.

With respect to this sub-set the Committee reported: "*In some instances* the decrease thus caused was stated to amount to one-fourth, to one third and even to one half."[10] If we take a quarter to be the proportion of scholars absent in the whole of this sub-group of schools this would amount to an absence rate of about 7 per cent of the total school population of the area—although to be realistic we should add some small rate of absence in the other schools outside the sub-group. Even this absence rate referred to part of the year (the winter) only. The annual rate of absence would have been smaller.

Next, the winter of 1837–38 was not typical. There were three causes of absence reported by the Committee. One was "the sickness of the children", the second, "the unwillingness of the parents to expose their children to the inclemency of the weather." The Committee added: "This was particularly the case during last winter, which was remarkable for its great and long-continued severity." The third cause of school absence in the sub-group was unemployment. This factor, which could have been related to the severity of the winter, obviously prevented some parents paying the fees.

Schofield mentions neither the sickness nor the severe winter. He simply deduces the general statement that the fees in most schools were an important barrier; and he does this in a way that gives the impression that they prevented the average family from buying education in the typical school. But whatever the balance of causes, the real absence rate reported by the Westminster Committee for 1837–38 would not look unusual in the English state schools of the 1970s especially in the winter months, and more especially when sickness epidemics (like influenza) occur. Schofield switches from his literacy figures into schooling statistics in order to support his hypothesis that education was more the effect than the cause of economic growth. His argument is that if schooling was of economic value the parents would have invested in it widely and voluntarily. Because the education that really promoted productivity was related to more practical skills, the schools, which provided literary skills only, were not well patronized. First, parents did invest in education widely and voluntarily. Second, Schofield's argument does not explain satisfactorily how the literacy rates did manage to improve so strikingly. Third, he makes errors in his numerical estimates of schooling. The latter he gathers from the same single example from the independent surveys of the 1830s (apparently having forgotten that he warned readers that this route is "fraught with danger"). Referring once more, and exclusively, to the survey education in Westminster to show that the parents wanted a practical not a literary education, Schofield concludes: "Consequently, few children were regular in attendance, and few remained at school for more than 1½ years" (Schofield, 1973, p. 452).

The incorrectness of his estimates of attendance has already been explained. The next issue is school duration. Nowhere in the Committee's report is there any statement about the typical child receiving in his lifetime a schooling of not more than one and a half years. What *is* included is an investigation of each of the eight prevailing types of school and a reference to the fact that, in three types of school, the entrances within the course of the year exceeded the number of children upon the books. This suggested, at most, a high turnover in these particular schools. But in those days of high mobility and competition between schools, the children typically accumulated several years of schooling from several schools, having relatively short stays at each (West, 1975, p. 83). Schofield's estimate of one and a half years neglects this fact and is therefore far too low.

The Newcastle report for 1858 found that on the average for the whole country the children of the working class alone were receiving an education of 5.7 years. Horace Mann (1861), the compiler of the special education extension to the national census of 1851, stated that for that year working-class children over the whole country were receiving a schooling that was "more than four years, and more than four and a half years" (Great Britain, 1861, XXI). For these reasons it is difficult to accept Schofield's judgement that "the prospect of upward mobility for their children did not lead many working-class parents to invest heavily in education" (Schofield, 1973, p. 415). The four and above years of schooling on the average for working-class children in 1851, reported by Horace Mann, were paid for substantially by the parents.

Both Schofield and Sanderson venture the arguments that fee paying was a significant barrier to the working class and that accordingly they had to wait for public action to provide nearly free schooling. Neither of these arguments can be accepted. According to the Manchester Statistical Society, 80 per cent of the school-children's education in Manchester in 1834 was paid for entirely by parental fees (West, 1975, p. 86). The same study suggests that at least four out of five Manchester children were being schooled. Neighboring Pendleton (Salford) schooled 97 per cent of its children in 1838 and, according to the particularly intensive survey of this township by the Manchester Statistical Society, one-third of the school-goers remained for three to five years, one-third above five years, and one-third less than three years (West, 1975, p. 18) (figures that are fairly consistent with the national estimate of Horace Mann).

E.J. Hobsbawm has recently given the opinion that the quantitative study of education that has made so much progress since 1963 is largely due to the study of parochial records of marriage signatures. *School* statistics (attendance and availability), Hobsbawm adds, have also been scrutinized for "optimistic" purposes, "but their value remains in serious doubt" (Hobsbawm, 1975, p. 83). If their value is in such doubt then this would reduce confidence in much of the reasoning of Schofield and Sanderson who themselves ultimately rely on them. In the context of the precise facts reported in the Westminster statistical report, Hobsbawm presumably might describe Schofield as selectively scrutinizing the school statistics for "pessimistic" purposes.

The truth is that there are dangers in using all sources, including the parochial returns, as the earlier discussion has shown. Consider Hobsbawm's own conclusions. He argues that the marriage-signature studies suggest a halt or even a reversal in the long-term progress of literacy during the early industrial period, at least in industrial Lancashire up to the late 1820s. Schofield's figures, however, show that average literacy rates (males plus females) measured at the school-leaving stage were slowly rising throughout. Second, the same figures point to 1790 as a significant improvement point for men (1800 in Lancashire). Third, in all cases the trend of the *early* industrial period was about the same as the two decades that preceded it. The new industrialism therefore cannot be argued to have had a depressing effect.

It is too hasty, however, immediately to dismiss any data, whether of literacy or of schooling, the moment a difficulty or complexity arises. Usually, after some sensible expressed qualification, the information from most sources can be employed, tentatively at least; and confidence will be increased if a consistent pattern from the various sources seems to emerge.

Now, a general pattern does emerge from the various sources on schooling. Such as the case, for instance, concerning national statistics of school population, attendance, and years of duration. It is not persuasive to argue against them that, in contrast, the literacy figures are preferable because they derive from an official government source, and one therefore that provides the most standard and disinterested test of education. The 1851 figures of Horace Mann on schooling also came from a central government official source and indeed from the same office—the Registrar-General's. Moreover, this was an all-inclusive universal census. The marriage-signature test of literacy, in contrast, was not all-inclusive, but related only to the 90 per cent or so of the population who were ever married. And for the years before 1839 we have to rely on samples of parishes. The 1851 census figures reported 2.14 million scholars with an average of four years' schooling. Further confidence in these figures is encouraged when we look at their consistency with those of the Newcastle Commission for the year 1859 (with its larger population) which reported 2.54 million scholars. Horace Mann, who completed the 1851 figures for the Registrar-General, encourages the same view with his statement that "the estimate of 1859 [Newcastle Commission] is supported by the results of the previous and more extensive [1851 census] inquiry" (Mann, 1869). And the Newcastle Commission reported that over 90 per cent of children were receiving a schooling; and this long before schooling was "free" and compulsory.

When we consider the 1760–1840 period we certainly have to "reach back" from the 1851 census and rely on a great variety of education surveys and circumstantial evidence. But if the marriage-signature specialists do the same, they cannot simultaneously object that these sources are completely "unreliable". All sources should be carefully sifted for what threads they have to offer, despite initial difficulties. Even the marriage-signature evidence is often ambiguous, at least in the first instance. This is clear, for example, when we remember the questions or assumptions one has to make about migration before one can use the parochial returns.

Obviously, the evidence on literacy and schooling is interdependent. Those who set out to be "pure" specialists in the one invariably succumb to the temptation to merge their findings with information they obtain about the other. Literacy specialists usually describe figures of schooling as "indirect evidence" of literacy. Schooling specialists, meanwhile, regard literacy as "indirect evidence" of schooling. Surely the two specialisms or approaches can converge. And this should be welcomed, for total knowledge will progress better with competition and cross-checking from both sides.

IV

The remaining part of this essay will attempt to ilustrate this by showing how the data on *literacy* can be used to check speculations or hypotheses about *schooling*. Schofield offered the hypothesis that a substantial number of parents did not school their children when "very few genuinely free places were available" (Schofield, 1973, p. 439). Similarly, Sanderson (1972, p. 80) argued that fees were a strong barrier to the lower orders. Schofield's second hypothesis stated that compulsion of the law was even more important in obtaining universal investment in education and therefore literacy. A third hypothesis, which is more explicit in Sanderson, but is at least hinted at in Schofield, is that the supply of education was largely an "exogenous" event to industrialism and to individual (family) self-help; that is, it came largely from the initiative of "public agencies" whose task it was eventually "to combat . . . those adverse effects of industrialization" (Sanderson, 1972, p. 80).

Consider now the latest data on nineteenth-century literacy. Schofield plotted national annual illiteracy rates (percentages unable to sign) on a semi-logarithmic scale showing percentage of illiteracy on the vertical ordinate and on two horizontal ordinates—marriage dates and school-leaving. His diagram is reproduced here as Figure 11.1.

Schofield (1973, p. 443) argues that "the fastest rate of improvement was amongst those . . . leaving school after about 1870." In Figure 11.1 he is referring to the graph that relates to the bottom horizontal axis that refers to schooling. Schofield assumes that marriage signatures reflect on the average school-leaving fifteen years before marriage. Whether he intended it or not, 1870 will trigger off in most minds the famous Forster Education Act of the same year, the most vigorous, ambitious and celebrated piece of Victorian educational legislation, which eventually made "public agencies" supersede private in school provision. When we refer exclusively to the bottom (school) axis, both curves in Figure 11.1 do indeed show a distinct point of inflexion (or kink) in the later part of the century. But Schofield is wrong in locating it at 1870. Rather it is in 1867, three years *before* the Forster Act.

The first time Forster's legislation could have had any significant influence on schooling must, in any case, have been some few years after 1870. The legislation did not pass through Parliament until after the middle of the year in 1870. It then took some time to establish school boards. When they were elected their time was initially taken up electing chairmen, vice-chairmen, finance committees, school sites and building committees, school staffing committees, and education committees. The boards then had to make extensive inquiries about educational deficiencies in their areas, and this often resulted in protracted correspondence with the Registrar's Office. Where a deficiency was found, the private schools were given a period of grace to give them a chance to "fill the gaps."

After this period and, where "deficiencies" remained, the school boards had next to draw up and debate various plans, negotiate loans from the Public Works Commission, and eventually appoint architects and builders. To illustrate, the various procedures took two years to carry out, while the first (newly built) board school was not opened until October 1874.[11] On the assumption that an efficient schooling lasts six years at minimum, the Act's effects on education and literacy in Northampton would

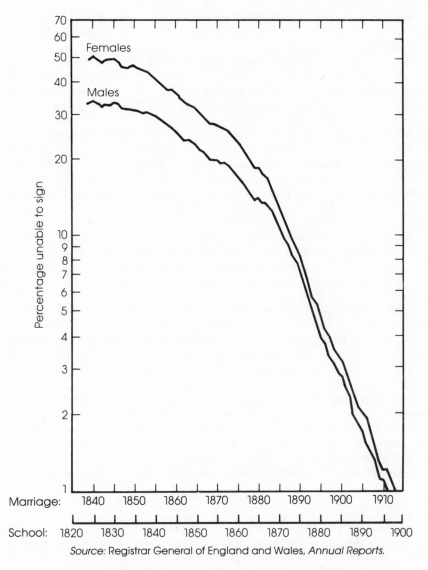

Source: Registrar General of England and Wales, Annual Reports.

Fig. 11.1 Annual Percentage of Males and Females Unable to Sign at Marriage, England and Wales, 1839-1912

not, therefore, begin to show until the school-leavers of 1880 who, of course, were married several years later.

Return to Schofield's assumption that the marriage registers reflect school-leaving fifteen years before marriage. (I shall not press my own preference, explained above, for a lag of seventeen years). The point on the graph, for instance, for 1870, reading from the bottom (school) axis, represents the marriage-signature rates in 1885. This must next be qualified. If individuals were married on the *average* fifteen years after school, there would be a certain number on either side of the average. We must therefore make some qualification.

Throughout these years individuals who married under 20 years of age were under a half of 1 per cent of the total population.[12] For practical purposes, therefore, I shall take the 20-year-old grooms and bridegrooms as being "the first of the few" to appear in the nineteenth century who could possibly have benefited from Forster's Act. To give the Act the fullest chance I shall also assume that those who married youngest needed education most. But even supposing that *all* school-leavers were in this category (all married ten years after school), and assuming building time lags similar to Northampton's, the first school-leavers to benefit from the Forster schooling (as in Northampton) would not appear until well to the right of the kink in the curve, say 1876 at the earliest. This point is indicated in Figure 11.2. This figure is identical with Figure 11.1 except for the addition of my vertical arrows with associated explanations.

If we now extrapolate the curve onwards to the late 1890s from that part of the curve between the turning-point of 1867 to 1876, the latter year, to repeat, being the first possible influence of the 1870 Act, we obtain an almost linear trend result. This pre-Forster trend shows approximately the same "success rate" as that in Figure 11.1. The data in the diagram therefore do not, at least at first sight, support the third hypothesis that major literacy improvement had to wait for *public* (government) initiative. We should remember, however, that *some* intervention was operative before 1870. This was a system of subsidies to all kinds of private schools. More precisely, the diagram suggests that this mixed private and public system (dating from 1833) was just as efficient as the new apparatus of "nationalized" school intervention introduced by Forster.[13]

With respect to making education "free", the extrapolation of the trend established between 1867 and 1876 suggests that it made no difference. And even if it did, its maximum effect shown in the diagram is merely an improvement in the national literacy rate of 1 per cent—from 98 to 99 per cent. Similarly, the extrapolated trend suggests that compulsion had negligible effect. And even if it did, it could have affected literacy at most by making only 3 per cent of the total population literate.

V

I conclude that the recent attempts to reject Bowman and Anderson's "threshold theory" of literacy, as it applies to England and Wales, have not been successful; second, that available national estimates do not demonstrate that the Industrial Revolution depressed literacy—even if we consider the rate for males or females exclusively; third, that the date of distinct improvement in the national literacy trend coincided with the beginnings of the large-scale factory system; and fourth, that the apparent local exception of Lancashire is closer to the national trend than has been believed, and that in any case when we take Irish immigration into account, the association between education and economic growth is considerably strengthened. Finally, I have shown that, despite the attempts by historians of *literacy* and historians of *schooling* to keep their studies separate, this is not easily achieved in practice.

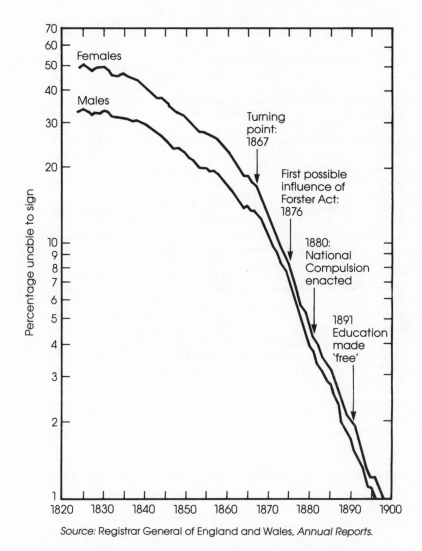

Source: Registrar General of England and Wales, *Annual Reports*.

Fig. 11.2 Annual Percentages of Illiterate Male and Female School Leavers as Determined by their Inability to Sign the Marriage Register Fifteen Years Later

The convergence of the two approaches nevertheless is necessary, although it is still important for the one specialist carefully to cross-check the use of his sources by the other. Evidence on literacy has its difficulties and problems, just as does evidence on schooling. But, if properly handled, both can still yield the *truest*, rather than the most "pessimistic" or "optimistic" view of eighteenth- or nineteenth-century educational progress.

Notes

[1] This was a central point in my reply to J.S. Hurt (West, 1971).

[2] See, for instance, Sanderson's review (1976) of my 1975 book.

[3] These were not available at the time of writing my 1975 book. On the same reasoning the opinion of Sanderson, ibid. that "the recent debates on literacy" render some of the conclusions of my book "seriously outdated", will be rebutted.

[4] See the view of Schofield in section III.

[5] More precisely this was the case in 27 out of 32 countries studied.

[6] I gave almost as strong support for the marriage-signature test of literacy, but from different arguments, (West, 1965, p. 134).

[7] Schofield (1973, p. 446) agrees with this timing.

[8] See section I.

[9] The government did not intervene until 1833, and even then only with very modest subsidies to private schools, (West, 1975, p. 75).

[10] "Second Report of a Committee of the Statistical Society of London, Appointed to Enquire into the State of Education in Westminster," *Journal of the Statistical Society of London*, I (1838), 193–215 (my emphasis).

[11] *Northampton Mercury*, 25 Nov, 1876. I am grateful to Victor A. Hatley of Northampton for supplying me with this source. I am aware that some boards opened schools earlier, but these were usually existing private schools that were soon taken over by them. I am only concerned here with *net* improvements in school supply which would show up in entirely new buildings.

[12] Mitchell and Deane, 1962, Table 5, p. 151. The average marriage age was nearly 28 years in 1881 according to the Registrar-General's Report (Vol. IV) for that year.

[13] This finding supports a central argument in my *Education and the Industrial Revolution*, an argument that Sanderson, in his review of it (1976), seems strangely to have overlooked; for he presents me as arguing simply that "state intervention was of doubtful necessity."

Bibliography

Accum, F.C. 1820. A Treatise on Adulterations of Food and Culinary Poisons. Philadelphia.

Aeigidi, L.K. 1865. *Aus der Vorzeit des Zollvereins.* Hamburg.

Ahluwalia, M. 1976. "Inequality. Poverty and Development." *Journal of Development Economics,* II, Vol. 3, no. 4, December, pp. 307–42.

Allen, R.C. 1982. "The Efficiency and Distributional Consequences of Eighteenth Century Enclosures." *Economic Journal,* XCII, no. 368, Dec., pp. 937–53.

Altick, R.D. 1957. *The English Common Reader.* Chicago.

Anderson, J.L. 1974. "A Measure of the Effect of British Public Finance, 1793–1815." *Economic History Review,* XXVII, no. 4, Nov., pp. 610–19.

Ashley, P. 1910. *Modern Tariff History.* 2nd ed. London.

Ashley, Sir W. 1932. *The Bread of Our Forefathers.* London.

Ashton, T.S. 1948. *The Industrial Revolution, 1760–1830.* New York.

_____. 1949. "The Standard of Life of the Workers in England, 1790–1830." *Journal of Economic History.* Supplement IX. Reprinted in A.J. Taylor, ed. *The Standard of Living.* London, pp. 36–57.

_____. 1954. "The Treatment of Capitalism by Historians." In *Capitalism and the Historians,* ed. F.A. von Hayek, Chicago, pp. 33–63.

_____. 1955. *An Economic History of England: The 18th Century.* London; reprinted 1972.

_____. 1959. *Economic Fluctuations in England, 1700–1800.* Oxford.

_____. 1968. *Iron and Steel in the Industrial Revolution.* 4th ed. (orig. published 1924), Manchester.

Ashton, T.S. and Sykes, J. 1929. *The Coal Industry in the Eighteenth Century.* Manchester.

Atkinson, A.B. and Stiglitz, J.G. 1969. "A New View of Technological Change." *Economic Journal,* Vol. 79, no. 3, Sept., pp. 573–78.

Bab, B. 1930. *Die offentliche Meinung über den deutschen Zollverein zur Zeit seiner Entstehung.* Berlin doctoral dissertation.

Bairoch, P. 1972. "Free Trade and European Economic Development in the Nineteenth Century." *European Economic Review,* III, no. 3, Nov. pp. 211–45.

_____. 1974. "Geographical Structure and Trade Balance of European Foreign Trade from 1800 to 1970." *Journal of European Economic History,* III, Winter.

Barnsby, G.J. 1971. "The Standard of Living in the Black Country during the Nineteenth Century." *Economic History Review,* 2nd ser., XXIV, no. 2, May, pp. 220–39.

Beer, A. 1891. *Die Österreichische Handelspolitik im 19. Jahrhundert.* Vienna.

Berend, I.T. and G. Ranki. 1982. *The European Periphery and Industrialization 1780–1914.* Cambridge.

Berg, M. 1980. *The Machinery Question and the Making of Political Economy 1815–1848.* Cambridge.

Berrill, K.E. 1960. "International Trade and the Rate of Economic Growth." *Economic History Review*, 2nd ser., XII, no. 3, April, pp. 351–359.

_____ . 1965. "Historical Experience: The Problem of Economic 'Take-Off'." in K.E. Berrill, ed. *Economic Development with Reference to South East Asia*. New York.

Bienefeld, M.A. 1972. *Working Hours in British Industry*. Trawbridge.

Birch, A. 1967. *The Economic History of the British Iron and Steel Industry*. London.

Blackman, J. 1975. "The Cattle Trade and Agrarian Change on the Eve of the Railway Age." *Agricultural History Review*, XXIII, Part I, pp. 48–62.

Blanqui, J.A. 1837. *Histoire de l'Economie Politique*. Paris.

Blaug, M. 1961. "The Productivity of Capital in the Lancashire Cotton Industry during the Nineteenth Century." *Economic History Review*, XIII, no. 3, April, pp. 358–81.

_____ . 1963. "The Myth of the Old Poor Law and the Making of the New." *Journal of Economic History*, XXXIII, no. 2, June, pp. 151–184.

_____ . 1964. "The Poor Law Report Reexamined." *Journal of Economic History*, XXIV, no. 2, June, pp. 227–245.

_____ . 1968. *Economic Theory in Retrospect*. Homewood, Ill.

Boserup, E. 1981. *Population and Technological Change*. Chicago.

Bowley, A.L. 1898. "The Statistics of Wages in the United Kingdom. Part I. Agricultural Wages." *Journal of the Royal Statistical Society*, LXI, Part IV, December, pp. 702–22.

_____ . 1900. *Wages in the United Kingdom in the Nineteenth Century*. Cambridge.

Bowman, M.J. and Anderson, C.A. 1963. "Concerning the Role of Education in Development," in C. Geertz, ed. *Old Societies and New States*. New York.

Boyer, G.R. 1983. "An Economic Model of the English Poor Law, 1780–1834." Cornell University, Dept. of Labor Economics Working Paper no. 49, Ithaca, N.Y.

Braudel, F. and Spooner, F. 1967. "Prices in Europe from 1450 to 1750" in *Cambridge Economic History of Europe*, vol. IV, Cambridge, pp. 386–87.

Briavoinne, N. de 1839. *De l'industrie en Belgique, causes de décadence et de prosperité sa situation actuelle*, 2 vols., Brussels.

Bridbury, A.R. 1972. *Historians and the Open Society*. London.

Briggs, A. 1967. "The Language of 'Class' in Early Nineteenth-Century England," in A. Briggs, and J. Saville, eds. *Essays in Labour History*, Hamden, Conn.

Brown, W. 1957. "Innovation in the Machine Tool Industry." *Quarterly Journal of Economics*, LXXI, Aug., pp. 406–25.

Bülow-Cummerow, 1844. *Der Zollverein, sein System und dessen Gegner*. Berlin.

Burn, D. 1940. *The Economic History of Steelmaking, 1867–1939*. Cambridge.

Burnet, I.D. 1972. "An Interpretation of Take-Off." *Economic Record*, XLVIII, no. 123, Sept., pp. 424–28.

Burnett, J. 1968. Plenty and Want: *A Social History of Diet in England from 1815 to the Present Day*. Harmondsworth.

_____ . 1969. *A History of the Cost of Living*. Harmondsworth.

Bythell, D. 1969. *The Handloom Weavers*. Cambridge.

_____ . 1978. *The Sweated Trades*. New York.

Caird, Sir. J. 1852. *English Agriculture in 1850–1851*. London. Reprinted 1967, New York.

Cameron, R.E. 1956. "Some French Contributions to the Industrial Development of Germany, 1840–1870." *Journal of Economic History*, XVI, no. 3, Sept., pp. 281–321.

_____ . 1961. *France and the Economic Development of Europe*. Princeton.

_____ . 1967. *Banking in the Early Stages of Industrialization*. New York.

Campbell, R. 1747. *The London Tradesman*. London.

Cardwell, D.S.L. 1972. *Turning Points in Western Technology*. New York.

Carr, E.H. 1961. *What is History?* (G.M. Trevelyan Lectures, 1961), Pelican Books, Harmondsworth, 1964.

Carus-Wilson, E.M., ed. 1962. *Essays in Economic History*. 3 vols. London.

Caves, R.E. 1971. "Export-led Growth and the New Economic History," in J.N. Bhagwati, ed. *Trade, Balance of Payments, and Growth*, Amsterdam, pp. 403–42.

Chadwick, D. 1860. "On the Rate of Wages in Manchester and Salford . . . 1839–59." *Quarterly Journal of the Statistical Society*, XXIII, pp. 1–36.

Chambers, J.D. 1953. "Enclosure and Labour Supply in the Industrial Revolution." *Economic History Review*, 2nd ser., V, no. 3, pp. 319–43.

Chambers, J.D. and Mingay, G.E. 1966. *The Agricultural Revolution, 1750–1880*. London.

Chapman, S.D. 1967. *The Early Factory Masters*. London.

Chenery, H.B. 1960. "Patterns of Industrial Growth." *American Economic Review*, L, no. 4, September, pp. 624–54.

Chenery, H.B. et al. 1974. *Redistribution with Growth*. London.

Church, R.A., ed. 1980. *The Dynamics of Victorian Business: Problems and Perspectives to the 1870s*. London.

Cipolla, C.M. 1969. *Literacy and Development in the West*. Harmondsworth.

Clapham, J.H. 1910. "The Transference of the Worsted Industry from Norfolk to the West Riding." *Economic Journal*, XX, no. 78, June, pp. 195–210.

_____ . 1912. "Review of *The Village Labourer* and Gonner's *Common Land and Inclosure*," *Economic Journal*, XXII, no. 86, June, pp. 248–55.

_____ . 1916. "The Spitalfields Acts, 1773–1824." *Economic Journal*, XXVI, no. 104, December, pp. 459–71.

_____ . 1918. "Review of *The Town Labourer*." *Economic Journal*, XXVIII, no. 110, June, pp. 202–205.

_____ . 1926–38. *An Economic History of Modern Britain*, 3 vols., Cambridge.

_____ .1930. *An Economic History of Modern Britain: the Early Railway Age 1820–1850*. 2nd revised ed. Cambridge.

Clark, G.K. 1962. *The Making of Victorian England* (Ford Lectures, 1960) London. Reprinted in 1970.

Clarke, P. 1978. *Liberals and Social Democrats*. Cambridge.

Cline, W.R. 1975. "Distribution and Development: A Survey Article." *Journal of Development Studies*, II, pp. 359–400.

Clough, S.B. 1957. "The Diffusion of Industry in the Last Century and a Half." *Studi in Onore di Armando Sapori*, II Milan.

Club, C. 1910. *The Influence of Protection on Agriculture in Germany*, London.

Coats, A.W. 1958. "Changing Attitudes to Labour in the Mid-Eighteenth Century." *Economic History Review*, 2nd ser., pp. 35–51. Reprinted in M.W. Flinn and T.C. Smout, eds. 1974. Essays in Social History. London.

_____ . 1971. *The Classical Economists and Economic Policy*. London.

Cohen, J.S. 1981. "Managers and Machinery: An Analysis of the Rise of Factory Production." *Australian Economic Papers*, Vol XX, no. 36, pp. 24–41.

Cole, W.A. 1973. "Eighteenth-Century Economic Growth Revisited." *Explorations in Economic History*, X, Summer, pp. 327–48.

Cole, W.A. and Deane, P. 1965. "The Growth of National Incomes," in *Cambridge Economic History of Europe*, VI, Cambridge, pp. 1–55.

Coleman, D.C. 1955. "Labour in the English Economy of the Seventeenth Century." *Economic History Review*, VIII, no. 3, April, pp. 280–95.

_____ . 1983. "Proto-Industrialization: A Concept too Many." *Economic History Review*, 2nd ser., XXXVI, no. 3, Aug., pp. 435–48.

Collier, F. 1964. *The Family Economy of the Working Classes in the Cotton Industry, 1784–1833*. Manchester.

Collins, B. 1981. "Irish Emigration to Dundee and Paisley During the First Half of the Nineteenth Century," in J.M. Goldstrom and L.A. Clarkson, eds. *Irish Population, Economy, and Society, Essays in Honour of K.H.Connell,* Oxford, pp. 195–212.

Collins, E.J.T. 1975. "Dietary Change and Cereal Consumption in Britain in the Nineteenth Century." *Agricultural History Review,* XXIII, pt. 2, pp. 97–115.

_____. 1976. "Migrant Labour in British Agriculture in the Nineteenth Century." *Economic History Review,* 2nd ser., XXIX, pp. 38–59.

Collins, M. 1983. "Long-Term Growth of the English Banking Sector and Money Stock, 1844–80." *Economic History Review,* 2nd ser., XXXVI, no. 3, Aug., pp. 379–95.

Colquhoun, P. 1815. *Treatise on the Wealth, Power, and Resources of the British Empire.* London. 1st ed. 1814.

Condliffe, J.B. 1951. *The Commerce of Nations.* London.

Coppejans-Desmedt, H. 1962. "De Statistieken van E.C. Van der Meersch over de Katoenindustrie in *Oost Vlaanderen,*" *Bulletin de la Commission Royale d'Histoire,* 128, pp. 121–181.

Cottrell, P.L. 1980. *Industrial Finance, 1830–1914.* London.

Crafts, N.F.R. 1976. "English Economic Growth in the Eighteenth Century: A Re-Examination of Deane and Cole's Estimates." *Economic History Review,* XXIX, no. 2, April, pp. 226–235.

_____. 1980. "National Income Estimates and the British Standard of Living Debate: A Reappraisal of 1801–1831." *Explorations in Economic History,* XVII, no. 2, April, pp. 176–88.

_____. 1981. "The Eighteenth Century: A Survey," in R.C. Floud and D.N.McCloskey, eds., *The Economic History of Britain Since 1700,* vol. I, Cambridge, pp. 1–16.

_____. 1982. "Regional Price Variations in England in 1843: An Aspect of the Standard of Living Debate." *Explorations in Economic History,* XIX, pp. 51–70.

_____. 1983. "British Economic Growth, 1700–1831: A Review of the Evidence." *Economic History Review,* 2nd ser., XXXVI, 2, May.

_____. 1984. *Economic Growth During the British Industrial Revolution.* Oxford.

Craig, G. 1980. *Germany, 1860–1945.* New York.

Crane, C. 1983. "The Industrial Revolution and the Effect on the Market for Child Labor." Unpublished paper, Northwestern University, Dec.

Crotty, R.D. 1966. *Irish Agricultural Production.* Cork.

Crouzet F. 1965. "Capital Formation in Great Britain During the Industrial Revolution," in *The Proceedings of the Second International Conference of Economic History,* The Hague 1965. Reprinted in F. Crouzet, ed. 1972. *Capital Formation in the Industrial Revolution,* London, pp. 162–222.

_____. 1967a. "Western Europe and Great Britain: Catching up' in the First Half of the Nineteenth Century," in A.J. Youngson, ed. *Economic Development in the Long Run.* New York.

_____. 1967b. "England and France in the Eighteenth Century: A Comparative Analysis of Two Economic Growths," in R.M. Hartwell, ed. *The Causes of the Industrial Revolution in England.* London.

_____. 1972. "Editor's Introduction," in F. Crouzet, ed. *Capital Formation in the Industrial Revolution,* pp. 1–69, London.

_____. 1980. "Toward an Export Economy: British Exports During the Industrial Revolution." *Explorations in Economic History,* XVII, no. 1, Jan., pp. 48–93.

Cullen, L.M. 1968. *Anglo-Irish Trade, 1660–1800.* New York.

_____. 1969. "Irish Economic History: Fact and Myth," in L.M. Cullen, ed. *The Formation of the Irish Economy,* Cork, pp. 113–24.

Cunningham, W. 1912. *The Growth of English Industry and Commerce in Modern Times. Part II: Laissez Faire.* Cambridge, 5th ed. (1st ed. 1882.)

Cunningham, W. and McArthur, E.A. 1910. *Outlines of English Industrial History.* Cambridge, (1st ed. 1895.)

Dallas, K. 1974. *One Hundred Songs of Toil*. London.

David, P.A. 1975. *Technical Choice, Innovation and Economic Growth*. Cambridge.

Davies, Rev. D. 1795. *The Case of Labourers in Husbandry*. Bath.

Davis, R. 1962. "English Foreign Trade, 1700–1774." *Economic History Review*, XV, pp. 285–303.

_____ . 1972. *The Rise of the English Shipping Industry in the Seventeenth and Eighteenth Centuries*. England.

_____ . 1973. *The Rise of the Atlantic Economies*. Ithaca and London.

_____ . 1978. *The Industrial Revolution and British Overseas Trade*. Leicester.

Deane, P. 1955. "The Implications of Early National Income Estimates For the Measurement of Long-term Economic Growth in the United Kingdom." *Economic Development and Cultural Change*, IV, pp. 3–38.

_____ . 1957. "Contemporary Estimates of National Income in the Second Half of the Nineteenth Century." *Economic History Review*, 2nd ser., IX, pp. 451–61

_____ . 1961. "Capital Formation in Britain Before the Railways Age." *Economic Development and Cultural Change*, IX, pp. 352–68.

_____ . 1968. "New Estimates of Gross National Product for the United Kingdom, 1830–1914." *Review of Income and Wealth*, XIV, pp. 104–5.

_____ . 1969. *The First Industrial Revolution*. Cambridge.

_____ . 1962. "The Role of Capital in the Industrial Revolution." *Explorations in Economic History* Vol. X, no. 2, Summer, pp. 349–64.

Deane, P. and Cole, W.A. 1969. *British Economic Growth, 1688–1959*. Cambridge. 2nd ed. 1st printing 1962.

Denison, E.F. 1967. *Why Growth Rates Differ*. Washington.

_____ . 1969. "Some Major Issues in Productivity Analysis: A Review of Estimates by Jorgenson and Griliches." *Survey of Current Business*, XLIX, no. 5, May, pp. 1–27.

Derry, T.K. and Williams, T.I. 1960. *A Short History of Technology*. Oxford.

Dixit, A.K. 1973. "Theories of the Dual Economy: A Survey," in J.A. Mirrlees and N.H. Stern, eds. *Models of Economic Growth*. New York.

Dodd, A.H. 1933. *The Industrial Revolution in North Wales*. Cardiff.

Domar, E.D. 1961. "On the Measurement of Technological Change." *Economic Journal*, LXXI, pp. 709–29.

Donnelly, J.S. 1975. *The Land and the People of Nineteenth Century Cork*. London.

Eccleston, B. 1976. "A Survey of Wage Rates in Five Midland Counties, 1750–1834." Ph.D. diss. University of Leicester.

Eckaus, R. 1958. "The Factor-Proportions Problem in Underdeveloped Areas," in A.N. Agarwala and S.P. Singh, eds. *The Economics of Underdevelopment*. London.

Eden, Sir F.M. 1797. *The State of the Poor*. London.

Edwards, M.M. 1967. *The Growth of the British Cotton Trade*. Manchester.

Ellison, T. 1886. *The Cotton Trade of Great Britain*. London.

Elster, J. 1978. *Logic and Society: Contradictions and Possible Worlds*. Chichester.

Engels, F. 1974. *The Condition of the Working Class in England*, translated from the 1845 German edition, with an introduction by E.J. Hobsbawm, London.

Engerman, S.L. 1972. "The Slave Trade and British Capital Formation in the Eighteenth Century." *Business History Review*, XLVI, no. 4, Oct, pp. 430–443.

Ernle, Lord 1961. *English Farming Past and Present*. London.

Eversley, D.E.C. 1967. "The Home Market and Economic Growth in England, 1750–1780," in E.L. Jones and G.E. Mingay, eds. *Land, Labour and Population in the Industrial Revolution*. Cambridge, pp. 206–59.

Fairlie, S. 1965. "The Nineteenth Century Corn Law Reconsidered," *Economic History Review*, 2nd ser., XVIII, no. 3, Dec., pp. 562–75.

Falkus, M.E. 1982. "The Early Development of the British Gas Industry, 1790–1815." *Economic History Review*, XXXV, no. 2, May, pp. 217–34.

Fanfani, A. 1972. "Considerations on the Industrial Revolution," in M. Kooy, ed. *Studies in Economics and Economic History: Essays in Honour of H.M. Robertson*, pp. 212–58.

Feinstein, C.H. 1978. "Capital Formation in Great Britain," in P. Mathias and M. M. Postan, eds. 1978. *Cambridge Econ. History of Europe*, vol. 7, part 1, Cambridge, pp. 28–96.

_____ . 1981. "Capital Accumulation and the Industrial Revolution," in R.C. Floud and D.N. McCloskey, eds. *The Economic History of Britain since 1700*, Cambridge, pp. 128–42.

Field, A.J. 1979. "Occupational Structure, Dissent, and Education Commitment: Lancashire, 1841," in P. Uselding, ed. *Research in Economic History*, vol. 4. Greenwich, Conn., pp. 235–88.

Findlay, R. 1982. "Trade and Growth in the Industrial Revolution," in C.P. Kindleberger and G. di Tella, eds. *Economics in the Long View, Essays in Honor of W.W. Rostow*, New York. Vol. I, pp. 178–88.

Fishlow, A. 1961. "The Trustee Savings Banks, 1750–1850." *Journal of Economic History*, XXI, no. 1, March, pp. 27–40.

Flinn, M.W. 1966, 1967. *Origins of the Industrial Revolution*. London.

_____ . 1974. "Trends in Real Wages, 1750–1850." *Economic History Review*, 2nd ser., XXVII, 3 , pp. 395–413.

_____ . 1981. *The European Demographic System, 1500–1820*. Baltimore.

Floud, R.C. and Wachter, K.W. 1982. "Poverty and Physical Stature: Evidence on the Standard of Living of London Boys, 1770–1870." *Soc. Science History*, LXIV, 4, Fall, pp. 422–452.

Fogel, R.W. 1983a. "Scientific History and Traditional History" in R.W. Fogel and G.R. Elton, *Which Road to the Past?* New Haven and London, pp. 7–70.

_____ . 1983b. "Secular Changes in American and British Stature and Nutrition." *Journal of Interdisciplinary History*, XIV, no. 2, Autumn, pp. 445–82.

_____ . 1984. "Growth as a Measure of the Economic Well-Being of Populations in the Eighteenth and Nineteenth Centuries." Unpublished paper, University of Chicago.

Fohlen, C. 1971. *Qu'est-ce que la revolution industrielle?* Paris.

Fores, M. 1981. "The Myth of a British Industrial Revolution." *History*, LXVI, no. 217, June, pp. 181–198.

Freudenberger, H. 1966. "The Mercantilist Proto-Factories." *Business History Review*, XL, Nov., pp. 167–89.

_____ . 1974. "Das Arbeitjahr," in I. Bog et al. eds. *Wirtschaftliche und Soziale Strukturen im saekularen Wandel*. Hanover, pp. 307–20.

Freudenberger, H. and Cummins, G. 1976. "Health, Work and Leisure Before the Industrial Revolution." *Explorations in Economic History*, 2nd ser., XIII, no. 1, Jan. pp. 1–12.

Freymark, H. 1898. *Die Reform des Preussischen Handels- und Zollpolitik von 1800–1821 und ihre Bedeutung*. Jena.

Froelich, O. 1936. *Die Wirkungen der Industrialisierungjunger Länder auf ihre Einführ*. Dresden.

Galpin, W. F. 1925. *The Grain Supply of England during the Napoleonic Period*. New York.

Gaskell, P. 1833. *The Manufacturing Population of England*. London.

_____ . 1836. *Artisans and Machinery: the Moral and Physical Condition of the Manufacturing Population*. Reprinted 1968. London.

Gatrell, V.A.C. 1977. "Labour, Power and the Size of Firms in Lancashire Cotton in the Second Quarter of the Nineteenth Century." *Economic History Review*, XXX, no. 1, Feb, pp. 95–139.

Gayer, A., Rostow, W.W. and Schwartz, A.J. 1953. *The Growth and Fluctuations of the British Economy, 1790–1850*. Oxford.

George, M.D., ed. 1923. *English Social Life in the Eighteenth Century*. London.

Georgescu-Roegen, N. 1971. *The Entropy Law and the Economic Process*. Cambridge, Mass.

Gerschenkron, A. 1943. *Bread and Democracy in Germany*. Berkeley.

_____. 1962. *Economic Backwardness in Historical Perspective: A Book of Essays.* Cambridge, Mass.

_____. 1967. "Discussion," in W.W. Rostow, ed. *The Economics of Take-off into Sustained Growth.* New York.

Gilboy, E.W. 1932. "Demand as a Factor in the Industrial Revolution," in A.H. Cole, eds. *Facts and Factors in Economic History.* Reprinted in R.M. Hartwell, ed. 1967. *The Causes of the Industrial Revolution in England.* London, pp. 121–38.

_____. 1934. *Wages in Eighteenth Century England.* Cambridge, Mass.

Gille, B. 1959. *Le crédit en France, 1815–1848.* Paris.

_____. 1970. *Banking and Industrialization in Europe, 1730–1914,* in C. Cipolla, ed. *Fontana History of Europe, III.*

Goldstone, J. 1981. "The Origins of the English Revolution: a Demographic Approach." Unpublished Ph.D. dissertation, Harvard University.

Good, D.F. 1973. "Backwardness, and the Role of Banking in Nineteenth-Century European Industrialization." *Journal of Economic History,* XXXIII, no. 4, Dec., pp. 845–50.

Gould, J.D. 1962. "Agricultural Fluctuations and the English Economy in the Eighteenth Century." *Journal of Economic History,* XXII, no. 3, Sept., pp. 313–33.

_____. 1972. *Economic Growth in History.* London.

Grampp, W.D. 1952. "The Liberal Elements in English Mercantilism." *Quarterly Journal of Economics,* LXVI, Nov., pp. 465–501.

Great Britain 1801–02 vol. VII. Abstract of the Answers and Returns Made Pursuant to "An Act for Taking Account of the Population of Great Britain, and the Increase or Diminution Thereof."

_____. 1818, vol. VI. "Report from the Select Committee Appointed to consider the Effect of the Laws which regulate or restrain the Interest of Money."

_____. 1833, XXX–XXXIV. Poor Law Commission, *Rural Queries.*

_____. 1834, XIX. Factory Inquiry Commission, "Supplementary Report of the Central Board . . . as to the Employment of Children in Factories."

_____. 1843, XII. Special Assistant Poor Law Commissioner, *Reports on the Employment of Women and Children in Agriculture.*

_____. 1849, XXI. *Appendix to Ninth Annual Report of the Registrar General of Births, Deaths and Marriages.*

_____. 1861, XXI. Commissioners on Popular Education, *Minutes of Evidence.*

_____. 1865, XIII. "Mean Population 1851–61 and Deaths from Different Causes of Males and Females at Different Ages in the 10 years 1851–60."

Griffiths, R. 1979. *Industrial Retardation in the Netherlands, 1830–1850.* The Hague.

Habakkuk, H.J. 1955a. "Family Structure and Economic Change in Nineteenth Century Europe." *Journal of Economic History,* XV, no. 1, pp. 1–12.

_____. 1955b. "The Historical Experience of the Basic Conditions of Economic Progress," in L.H. Dupriez, ed. *Economic Progress.* Louvain.

_____. 1962. *American and British Technology in the Nineteenth Century: the Search for Labour-Saving Inventions.* Cambridge.

_____. 1963. "Population Problems and European Economic Development in the Late Eighteenth and Nineteenth Centuries." *American Economic Review,* LIII, no. 2, May, pp. 607–618.

Habakkuk, H.J. and Deane, P.M. 1962. "The Take-off in Britain," in W.W. Rostow, ed. *The Economics of Take-off into Sustained Growth.* London.

Hagen, E.E. 1962. *On the Theory of Social Change: How Economic Growth Begins.* Homewood, Illinois.

_____. 1967. "British Personality and the Industrial Revolution: the Historical Evidence," in T. Burns and S.B. Saul, eds. *Social Theory and Economic Change,* pp. 35–66.

Hammond, J.L. 1930. "The Industrial Revolution and Discontent." *Economic History Review,* II, no. 2, January, pp. 215–228.

Hammond, J.L. and B. 1911. *The Village Labourer*. London. Reprinted 1978.

―――――. 1917. *The Town Labourer*. London. Reprinted 1978.

―――――. 1919. *The Skilled Labourer*. London. Reprinted 1979.

―――――. 1925. *The Rise of Modern Industry*. London, reprinted 1939.

―――――. 1930. *The Age of the Chartists, 1832–1854: a Study of Discontent*. Hamden, Conn. Reprinted 1962.

Harcourt, G.C. 1969. "Some Cambridge Controversies in the Theory of Capital." *Journal of Economic Literature*, VII, no. 2, pp. 369–405.

Harley, C.K. 1982. "British Industrialization Before 1841: Evidence of Slower Growth During the Industrial Revolution." *Journal of Economic History*, XLII, no. 2, June, pp. 267–90.

Harley, C.K., and McCloskey, D.N. 1981. "Foreign Trade: Competition and the Expanding International Economy," in R. Floud and D.N. McCloskey, eds. *The Economic History of Britain Since 1700*, vol. 2, Cambridge, pp. 50–69.

Harms, B. 1912. *Volkswirtschaft und Weltwirtschaft: Versuche der Begründung einer Weltwirtschaftslehre*. Jena.

Hartwell, R.M. 1965. "The Causes of the Industrial Revolution: An Essay in Methodology." *Economic History Review*, 2nd ser., XVIII. Reprinted in R.M. Hartwell, ed. *The Causes of the Industrial Revolution in England*. London, pp. 53–79.

―――――. 1966. "Introduction" to J.L. and B. Hammond 1937, 1966 ed. *The Rise of Modern Industry*, London.

―――――. 1967. *The Causes of the Industrial Revolution in England*, London.

―――――. 1971. *The Industrial Revolution and Economic Growth*. London.

Hartwell, R.M. and Engerman, S. 1975. "Models of Immiseration: the Theoretical Basis of Pessimism," in A.J. Taylor, ed. *The Standard of Living in Britain in the Industrial Revolution*. London, pp. 189–213.

Hatton, T.J., Lyons, J.S. and Satchell, S.E. 1983. "Eighteenth Century British Trade: Homespun or Empire Made?" *Explorations in Economic History*, XX, no. 2, April, pp. 163–182.

Hawke, G.R. 1970. *Railways and Economic Growth in England and Wales, 1840–70*. Oxford.

Hayek, F.A. ed. 1954. *Capitalism and the Historians*. London.

Heaton, H. 1937. "Financing the Industrial Revolution." *Bulletin of the Business Historical Society*, XI, no. 1, Feb., reprinted in F. Crouzet, ed. 1972. *Capital Formation in the Industrial Revolution*. London, pp. 84–93.

―――――. 1948. *Economic History of Europe*. New York.

Heckscher, E. 1955. *Mercantilism*. 2nd rev. ed., vol. II, London.

Henderson, W.O. 1954. *Britain and Industrial Europe, 1750–1870*. London, 3rd ed., 1972.

Hennig, R. 1913. *Die Hauptwege des Weltverkehrs*. Jena.

Hermes, G. 1930. "Statistische Studien zur Wirtschaftlichen und gesellschaftlichen Struktur des Zollvereinten Deutschlands", *Archiv für Sozialwissenschaft und Sozialpolitik*, vol. 63, pp. 121–62.

Heuschling, X. 1841. *Essai sur la statistique générale de la Belgique*. 2nd ed., Brussels.

Hicks, J.R. 1946. *Value and Capital*. London.

―――――. 1969. *A Theory of Economic History*. London.

Hilton, B. 1977. *Corn, Cash, Commerce: the Economic Policies of the Tory Governments, 1815–1830*. Oxford.

Hilton, G.W. 1964. "The Controversy Concerning Relief for the Handloom Weavers." *Explorations in Entrepreneurial History*, 2nd ser., I, no. 2, Winter, pp. 164–86.

Hirsch, F. 1976. *Social Limits to Growth*. Cambridge, Mass.

Hobsbawm, E.J. 1962. *The Age of Revolution: Europe, 1789–1848*. London.

―――――. 1964. *Labouring Men*. New York, London.

―――――. 1975. "The Standard of Living Debate," in A.J. Taylor, ed. *The Standard of Living in the Industrial Revolution*. London, pp. 179–88.

Hobsbawm, E.J. and Hartwell, R.M. 1963–4. "The Standard of Living During the Industrial Revolution: A Discussion." *Economic History Review*, 2nd ser., XVI, pp. 119–46.

Hobsbawm, E.J. and Rudé, G. 1969. *Captain Swing*. New York.

Hoffman, R.J.S. 1933. *Great Britain and the German Trade Rivalry, 1875–1914*, Philadelphia.

Hoffmann, W.G. 1955. *British Industry 1700–1950*. Oxford.

_____. 1958. *The Growth of Industrial Economies*. Manchester.

Homer, S. 1963. *A History of Interest Rates*. New Brunswick, N.J.

Honeyman, K. 1983. *Origins of Enterprise: Business Leadership in the Industrial Revolution.* New York.

Hook, S. 1969. "The Hero in History" in R.H. Nash, ed. *Ideas of History*, II, New York.

Hopkins, E. 1982. "Working Hours and Conditions During the Industrial Revolution: A Re-Appraisal," *Economic History Review*, 2nd ser., XXXV, no. 1, Feb., pp. 52–66.

Houston, R.A. 1982a. "The Development of Literacy: Northern England, 1640–1750," *Economic History Review*, 2nd ser., XXXV, no. 2, May, pp. 199–216.

_____. 1982b. "The Literacy Myth: Illiteracy in Scotland 1630–1760," *Past and Present*, no. 96, Aug., pp. 81–102.

Houthakker, H.S. 1957. "An International Comparison of Household Expenditure Patterns Commemorating the Centenary of Engel's Law." *Econometrica*, XXXIII, pp. 532–551.

Hueckel, G. 1973. "War and the British Economy, 1793–1815: A General Equilibrium Analysis." *Explorations in Economic History*, X, pp. 365–396.

Hughes, J.R.T. 1959. "Foreign Trade and Balanced Growth: The Historical Framework." *American Economic Review*, XLIX, Supplement, no. 2, May, pp. 330–37.

_____. 1969. "Henry Mayhew's London." *Journal of Economic History*, XXIX, no. 3, Sept., pp. 526–36.

_____. 1970. *Industrialization and Economic History*. New York.

_____. 1973. *The Vital Few*. London.

Hurt, J.S. 1971. "Professor West on Early Nineteenth-Century Education." *Economic History Review*, 2nd ser., XXIV, pp. 624–32.

Hutchison, T.W. 1953. "Berkeley's Querist and its Place in the Economic Thought of the Eighteenth Century." *British Journal for the Philosophy of Science*, IV, May, pp. 52–77.

Huzel, J.P. 1969. "Malthus, the Poor Law, and Population in Early Nineteenth Century England." *Economic History Review*, 2nd ser., XXII, no. 3, December, pp. 430–52.

_____. 1980. "The Demographic Impact of the Old Poor Law: More Reflections on Malthus." *Economic History Review*, 2nd ser., XXXIII, no. 3, Aug., pp. 367–81.

Hyde, C.K. 1973. "The Adoption of Coke-Smelting by the British Iron Industry, 1709–90." *Explorations in Economic History*, 2nd ser., X, pp. 397–418.

_____. 1977. *Technological Change and the British Iron Industry, 1700–1870*. Princeton, N.J.

Imlah, A.H. 1958. *Economic Elements in the Pax Britannica: Studies in British Foreign Trade in the Nineteenth Century*. Cambridge, Mass.

Inglis, B. 1972. *Poverty and the Industrial Revolution*. Rev. ed., London 1st ed., 1971.

Ippolito, R.A. 1975. "The Effect of the 'Agricultural Depression' on Industrial Demand in England, 1730–1750." *Economica*, XLII, Aug., pp. 298–312.

Isard, W. 1949. "The General Theory of Location and Space Economy." *Quarterly Journal of Economics*, LXIII, no. 4, pp. 476–506.

Jenks, L.H. 1927. *The Migration of British Capital to 1875*. London.

Jeremy, D.J. 1977. "Damming the Flood: British Government Efforts to Check the Outflow of Technicians and Machinery, 1780–1843," *Business History Review*, LI, no. 1, Spring, pp. 1–34.

Jewkes, J., Sawers, D. and Stillerman, R. 1969. *The Sources of Invention*. 2nd ed. New York.

John, A.H. 1960. "The Cause of Agricultural Change, 1660–1760," in L.S. Pressnell, ed. *Studies in the Industrial Revolution*. London, pp. 125–55.

_____. 1967. "Agricultural Productivity and Economic Growth in England," in E.L. Jones, ed. *Agriculture and Economic Growth in England 1650–1815*. London, pp. 172–93.

Jones, E.L. 1968. "Agricultural Origins of Industry." *Past and Present*, XL, July, pp. 58–71.
————. 1968. *The Development of English Agriculture 1815–1873*. London.
————. 1974. *Agriculture and the Industrial Revolution*. New York.
————. 1981a. "Agriculture, 1700–80," in R.C. Floud and D.N. McCloskey, eds. *The Economic History of Britain since 1700*, vol. I, pp. 66–86. Cambridge.
————. 1981b. *The European Miracle*. Cambridge.
Jones, E.L. and Woolf, S.J. 1969. "The Historical Role of Agrarian Change in Economic Development," in E.L. Jones and S.J. Woolf, eds. *Agrarian Change and Economic Development*. London.
Jones, G.T. 1933. *Increasing Returns*. Cambridge.
Jorgenson, D.W. and Griliches, Z. 1967. "The Explanation of Productivity Change." *Review of Economic Studies*, XXXIV, no. 99, pp. 249–83.
Kay, J.P. 1838. "Earnings of Agricultural Labourers in Norfolk and Suffolk." *Journal of the Royal Statistical Society*, 1, July, pp. 179–180.
Kelley, A.C. and Williamson, J.G. 1974. *Lessons from Japanese Development*. Chicago.
Kemp, T. 1969. *Industrialization in Nineteenth Century Europe*, London.
Kendrick, J.W. 1961. "Some Theoretical Aspects of Capital Measurement." *American Economic Association, Papers and Proceedings*, LI, no. 2, 1st supplement, May, pp. 102–11.
Kennedy, C. 1964. "Induced Bias in Innovation and the Theory of Distribution." *Economic Journal*, LXXIV, no. 295, Sept., pp. 541–47.
Kenwood, A.G. and Lougheed, A.L. 1971. *The Growth of the International Economy 1820–1960*. London.
Kerridge, E. 1969. "The Agricultural Revolution Reconsidered." *Agricultural History*, XLIII, no. 4, October, pp. 463–75.
Keynes, J.M. 1936. *The General Theory of Employment, Interest, and Money*. New York.
Kindleberger, C.P. 1964. *Economic Growth in France and Britain 1851–1950*. New York.
Kranzberg, M. 1967. "Prerequisites for Industrialisation," in M. Kranzberg and C.W. Pursell, Jr., eds. *Technology in Western Civilisation*, Vol. I. New York.
Kravis, I.B. 1970. "Trade as a Handmaiden of Growth: Similarities between the Nineteenth and Twentieth Centuries." *Economic Journal*, LXXX, no. 320, Dec. pp. 850–872.
Kriedte, P. 1981. "Proto-Industrialization between Industrialization and de-Industrialization," in P. Kriedte, H. Medick and J. Schlumbohm, *Industrialization Before Industrialization*. Cambridge, pp. 135–160.
Kurimoto, S. 1974. "A Statistical Arrangement of the Royal Commission on Coal in 1871." *Quarterly Review, Nara Prefectural College*, XXII, Aug. pp. 65–93.
Kuznets, S. 1957. "Quantitative Aspects of the Economic Growth of Nations: II." *Economic Development and Cultural Change*, Supplement to vol. 5, no. 4, July, pp. 1–110.
————. 1966. *Modern Economic Growth: Rate, Structure and Spread*. Cambridge, Mass.
————. 1971. *Economic Growth of Nations*. Cambridge, Mass.
————. 1979. *Growth, Population, and Income Distribution*. New York.
Labrousse, C.E. 1933. *Esquisse du mouvement des prix et des révenus en France au XVIIIe siècle*. Paris.
Laqueur, T.W. 1974. "Literacy and Social Mobility in the Industrial Revolution in England." *Past and Present*, LXIV, pp. 96–107.
Laqueur, T.W. 1976. *Religion and Respectability: Sunday Schools and Working-Class Culture, 1780–1850*. New Haven.
Landes, D. 1950. "The Statistical Study of French Crises." *Journal of Economic History*, X, no. 2, Nov., pp. 195–211.
————. 1965. "Factor Costs and Demand: Determinants of Economic Growth." *Business History*, VII, no. 1, Jan., pp. 15–33.
————. 1969a. *The Unbound Prometheus*. Cambridge.

_____. 1969b. "The Old Bank and the New: the Financial Revolution of the Nineteenth Century," in F. Crouzet, W.H. Chaloner, and W.M. Stern, eds. *Essays in European Economic History, 1789–1914.* New York.

Langer, W.L. 1969. *Political and Social Upheaval, 1832–1852.* New York.

Law, J. 1705. *Money and Trade.* London.

Leibenstein, H. 1957. *Economic Backwardness and Economic Growth.* New York and London.

Lévy-Leboyer, M. 1964. *Les banques européenes et l'industrialisation internationale dans la première moitié du XIXe siècle.* Paris.

Lewis, G.C. 1836. *On Local Disturbances in Ireland.* London.

Lexis, W. 1879. "Beitrage zur Statistik der Edelmetalle." *Jahrbücher fur National-ökonomie und Statistik,* XXXII, pp. 361–417.

Lilley, S. 1973. "Technological Progress and the Industrial Revolution," in C.M. Cipolla, ed. *The Fonata Economic History of Europe,* vol. 3. London.

Lindert, P.H. 1980a. "Child Costs and Economic Development," in R.A. Easterlin, ed. *Population and Economic Change in Developing Countries.* Chicago, pp. 5–79.

Lindert, P.H. 1980b. "English Occupations, 1670–1811." *Journal of Economic History,* XL, no. 4, pp. 685–712.

Lindert, P.H. and Williamson, J.G. 1982. "Revising England's Social Tables, 1688–1812." *Explorations in Economic History,* XIX, no. 4, pp. 385–408.

_____. 1983a. "English Workers' Living Standards during the Industrial Revolution: a New Look." *Economic History Review,* 2nd ser., XXXVI, no. 1, Feb, pp. 1–25.

_____. 1983b. "Reinterpreting Britain's Social Tables, 1688–1913." *Explorations in Economic History,* XX, no. 1, January.

Linke, O. 1899. "Schlesiens Wünsche bis den Friedensverhandlungen 1814." *Zeitschrift des Vereins für Geschichte und Altertumskunde Schlesiens.*

List, F. 1841. *Das nationale System der politischen Oekonomie.* English translation 1885, London.

Local Subcommittee 1840. "Contribution to the Economic Statistics of Birmingham." *Journal of the Royal Statistical Society,* 2.

Lovell, J. 1978. "General Introduction" to J.L. and B. Hammond (1917) *The Town Labourer.* 1978 ed. London.

Lyons, J. 1979. "Family Response to Economic Decline: English Cotton Handloom Weavers in the Nineteenth Century." Unpublished paper, Washington, D.C.

McClelland, D.C. 1961. *The Achieving Society.* Princeton.

McCloskey, D.N. 1970. "Did Victorian Britain Fail?" *Economic History Review,* XXIII, no. 3, Dec., pp. 446–59.

_____. 1973. "New Perspectives on the Old Poor Law." *Explorations in Economic History,* X, no. 4, Summer, pp. 419–36.

_____. 1980. "Magnanimous Albion: Free Trade and British National Income 1841–1881." *Explorations in Economic History,* XVII, no. 3, July, pp. 303–20.

McCloy, S.T. 1952. *French Inventions of the Eighteenth Century.* Kentucky.

MacFarlane, A. 1978. *The Origins of English Individualism.* New York.

McKendrick N. 1974. "Home Demand and Economic Growth: a New View of the Role of Women and Children in the Industrial Revolution." in N. McKendrick, ed. *Historical Perspectives. Studies in English Thought and Society in Honour of J.H. Plumb.* London, pp. 152–210.

McNeill, W.H. 1982. *The Pursuit of Power.* Chicago.

Macpherson, D. 1805. *Annals of Commerce Manufactures, Fisheries and Navigations,* 3, London.

Mann, H. 1861. *Commissioners on Popular Education, Minutes of Evidence,* Parl. Papers, XXI, pt. VI, Q. 833.

_____. 1869. "National Education." *Transactions of the British Association for the Promotion of Social Science, Bristol Meeting, 1869.*

Mansfield, E., et al. 1977. "Social and Private Rates of Return from Industrial Innovation." *Quarterly Journal of Economics*, XCI, no. 2, May, pp. 221–40.

Mantoux, P. 1961. *The Industrial Revolution in the Eighteenth Century*. Rev. ed. New York and Evanston: First English ed. 1928, first French ed. 1905.

Marglin, S.A. 1974–75. "What Do Bosses Do?" *Review of Radical Political Economy*, VI, no. 2 (summer 1974) and VII, no. 1 Winter 1975. Also 1978 reprinted in A. Gorz, ed. *The Division of Labour: the Labour Process and Class Struggle in Modern Capitalism*. Hassocks.

Marlo, L. 1908. *La politique allemande et la navigation interieure*. 2nd ed., Paris.

Marriner, S. 1980. "English Bankruptcy Records and Statistics before 1850." *Economic History Review*, 2nd ser., XXXIII, no. 3, Aug., pp. 351–366.

Marshall, T.H. 1929. "The Population Problem during the Industrial Revolution." *Economic History*, I, pp. 429–56.

Mason, S.E. 1962. *A History of the Sciences*. Rev. ed., New York.

Mathias, P. 1969. *The First Industrial Nation: An Economic History of Britain, 1700–1914*. Cambridge.

————. 1972. "Who Unbound Prometheus? Science and Technical Change, 1600–1800," in A.E. Musson, ed., *Science, Technology, and Economic Growth*. London.

Mathias, P., and Postan, M.M., eds. 1978. *The Cambridge Economic History of Europe*. Vol. VI: *The Industrial Economies: Capital, Labour and Enterprise*. Cambridge.

Mayshar, J. 1983A. "On Divergence of Opinion and Imperfections in Capital Markets." *American Economic Review*, March, LXXIII, no. 1, pp. 114–128.

————. 1983B. "Financial Constraints on Investment by the Firm." Dept. of Finance, KGSM, Northwestern University, unpublished paper.

Medick, H. 1981. "The Proto-Industrial Family Economy," in P. Kriedte, H. Medick, and J. Schlumbohm, *Industrialization Before Industrialization*. Cambridge.

Merton, R.K. 1973. *The Sociology of Science*. Chicago.

Mill, J.S. 1929. *Principles of Political Economy*, edited by W.J. Ashley, London.

Millward, R. 1981. "The Emergence of Wage Labor in Early Modern England." *Explorations in Economic History*, XVIII, no. 1, Jan., pp. 21–39.

Milward, A.S. and Saul, S.B. 1973. *The Economic Development of Continental Europe, 1780–1870*, Vol. I, London.

Minchinton, W.E., ed. 1969. *The Growth of English Overseas Trade*. London.

Mingay, G.E. 1978. "General Introduction" to J.L. and B. Hammond 1911. 1978 ed., London.

Mitch, D. 1982. "The Spread of Literacy in Nineteenth Century England." Unpublished Ph.D. dissertation, University of Chicago.

Mitchell, B.R. 1975. *European Historical Statistics*, New York.

Mitchell, B.R. and Deane, P. 1962. *Abstract of British Historical Statistics*, Cambridge. Reprinted 1971.

Mokyr, J. 1975. "Capital, Labour and the Delay of the Industrial Revolution in the Netherlands." *Economic History Yearbook*, (Amsterdam), XXXVIII, pp. 280–99.

————. 1976a. *Industrialization in the Low Countries, 1795–1850*. New Haven.

————. 1976b. "Growing-Up and the Industrial Revolution in Europe." *Explorations in Economic History*, XIII, no. 4, Oct., pp. 371–96.

————. 1980. "Industrialization and Poverty in Ireland and the Netherlands: Somes Notes Toward a Comparative Case Study." *Journal of Interdisciplinary History*, X, no. 3, Winter, pp. 429–59.

————. 1982. "Prosperous Interlude." *Economic Development and Cultural Change*, XXX, no. 4, July, pp. 863–69.

————. 1983. *Why Ireland Starved*. London.

————. 1984. "Consumption and the Standard of Living: Is There Still Life in the Pessimist Case." Unpublished working paper, Evanston, Ill.

Mokyr, J. and Savin, N.E. 1976. "Stagflation in Historical Perspective: the Napoleonic Wars Revisited," in P. Uselding, ed. *Research in Economic History*, vol. 1, pp. 198–259.

_____ . 1978. "Some Econometric Problems in the Standard of Living Controversy." *Journal of European Economic History*, VII, nos. 2–3, Fall-Winter.

Morris, R.J. 1979. *Class and Class Consciousness in the Industrial Revolution 1780–1850*. London.

Murphy, B. 1971. *A History of the British Economy, 1740–1970*. London.

Musson, A.E., ed. 1972. *Science, Technology and Economic Growth*. London.

Musson, A.E. and Robinson, E. 1969. *Science and Technology in the Industrial Revolution*. Manchester.

Nadiri, M.I. 1970. "Some Approaches to the Theory and Measurement of Total Factor Productivity." *Journal of Economic Literature*, VIII, Dec., pp. 1137–77.

Nardinelli, C. 1980. "Child Labor and the Factory Acts." *Journal of Economic History*, XL, no. 4, Dec., pp. 739–755.

Neale, R.S. 1966. "The Standard of Living, 1780–1844: A Regional and Class Study." *Economic History Review*, 2nd ser., XIX, no. 3, Dec., pp. 590–606.

Nef, J.U. 1943. "The Industrial Revolution Reconsidered." *Journal of Economic History*, III, no. 1, May, pp. 1–31.

_____ . 1950. *War and Human Progress. An Essay on the Rise of Industrial Civilization*. Cambridge, Mass.

Neild, W. 1841. "Comparative Statement of the Income and Expenditure of Certain Families of the Working Classes in Manchester and Dukinfield in the Years 1836 and 1841." *Journal of the Statistical Society*, IV, pp. 330–34.

Nelson, R.R. and Winter, S.G. 1974. "Neoclassical vs. Evolutionary Theories of Economic Growth: Critique and Prospectus." *Economic Journal*, LXXXIV, no. 336, Dec., pp. 886–905.

Neuberg, V.E. 1971. *Popular Education in Eighteenth-Century England*. London.

North, D.C. 1955. "Location Theory and Regional Economic Growth." *Journal of Political Economy*, LXIII, no. 3, June, pp. 243–258.

_____ . 1968. "Sources of Productivity Change in Ocean Shipping, 1600–1850." *Journal of Political Economy*, LXXVI, pp. 953–70.

_____ . 1981. *Structure and Change in Economic History*. New York.

Nurske, R. 1959. *Patterns of Trade and Development*. Stockholm.

O'Brien, P.K. 1982. "European Economic Development: The Contribution of the Periphery." *Economic History Review*, 2nd ser., XXXV, no. 1, pp. 1–18.

O'Brien, P.K. and Engerman, S.L. 1981. "Changes in Income and its Distribution," in R. Floud and D.N. McCloskey, eds., *The Economic History of Britain Since 1700*, Vol. I, pp. 164–181.

O'Brien, P.K. and Keyder, C. 1975. "Economic Growth in Britain and France from the Revolution to the First World War." mimeographed, Oxford.

_____ . 1978. *Economic Growth in Britain and France*. London.

O'Grada, C. 1984. "Irish Agricultural Output Before and After the Famine," *Journal of European Economic History* 13, vol. 1, Spring, pp. 149–65.

Ohlin, G. 1959. "Balanced Economic Growth in History." *American Economic Review*, XLIX, Supplement, no. 2, May, pp. 338–353.

Olmstead, A.L. 1975. "The Mechanization of Reaping and Mowing in American Agriculture, 1833–1870." *Journal of Economic History*, XXXV, no. 2, June, pp. 327–52.

Olson, M., Jr. 1963. *The Economies of Wartime Shortage*. Durham, N.C.

_____ . Jr. 1982. *The Rise and Decline of Nations*. New Haven.

Overton, M. 1979. "Estimating Crop Yields from Probate Inventories: An Example from East Anglia, 1585–1735." *Journal of Economic History*, XXXIX, no. 2, June, pp. 363–378.

Parker, W.N. 1972. "Technology, Resources and Economic Change in the West," in A.J. Youngson, ed. *Economic Development in the Long Run*. New York.

_____ . 1977. "From the Colonies: A Tempered Tribute." *Agricultural History Review*, XXV, pt. 1, Silver Jubilee Issue, pp. 6–13.

_____ . 1979. "Industry," in P. Burke, ed. *The New Cambridge Modern History*, vol. XIII (companion volume), Cambridge.

Parsons, T. 1960. "Some Reflections on the Institutional Framework of Economic Development," in *Structure and Process in Modern Societies*. Glencoe, Ill.

Pauling, N.G. 1951. "The Employment Problem in Pre-Classical English Economic Thought." *Economic Record*, XXVII, no. 52, June, pp. 52–65.

Payne, P.L. 1974. *British Entrepreneurship in the Nineteenth Century*. London.

Perkin, H.J. 1969. *The Origins of Modern English Society, 1780–1880*. London.

Phelps Brown, E.H. and S.V. Hopkins 1955. "Seven Centuries of Building Wages." *Economica*, XXII.

Phillips, A.W. 1958. "The Relationship between Unemployment and the Rate of Change in Money Wage Rates in the United Kingdom, 1862–1957." *Economica*, XXV, pp. 283–99.

Polanyi, K. 1944. *The Great Transformation*. Boston.

Pollard, S. 1958. "Investment, Consumption, and the Industrial Revolution." *Economic History Review*, 2nd ser., XI, no. 2, Dec., pp. 215–26.

_____. 1964. "Fixed Capital in the Industrial Revolution." *Journal of Economic History*, XXIV, September, no. 3. Reprinted in F. Crouzet, ed. *Capital Formation in the Industrial Revolution*, London, pp. 145–161.

_____. 1965. *The Genesis of Modern Management*. London. Penguin ed. 1968.

_____. 1978. "Labour in Great Britain," in Mathias and Postan, eds. *The Cambridge Economic History of Europe*, Vol. 6, Cambridge.

_____. 1980. "A New Estimate of British Coal Production, 1750–1850." *Economic History Review*, 2nd ser., XXXIII, no. 2, May, pp. 212–35.

_____. 1981. *Peaceful Conquest: the Industrialization of Europe 1760–1970*. Oxford.

Porter, G.R. 1851. *The Progress of the Nation*. London.

Post, J.D. 1974. "A Study in Meteorological and Trade Cycle History: The Economic Crisis Following the Napoleonic Wars." *Journal of Economic History*, XXXIV, no. 2, June, pp. 315–49.

Postan, M.M. 1935. "Recent Trends in the Accumulation of Capital." *Economic History Review*, VI, no. 1, October, 1935. Reprinted in F. Crouzet, ed. *Capital Formation in the Industrial Revolution*. London, pp. 70–83.

Pressnell, L.S. 1956. *Country Banking in the Industrial Revolution*. Oxford.

Ranis, G. and Fei, J.C.H. 1969. "Economic Development in Historical Perspective." *American Economic Review*, LIX, no. 2, May, pp. 386–400.

Ravenstein, E.G. 1885. "The Laws of Migration." *Journal of the Royal Statistical Society*, Series A, XLVIII, pp. 167–235.

Redford, A. 1964. *Labour Migration in England 1800–1850*. Manchester. American ed. 1968, New York.

Reid, D.A. 1976. "The Decline of Saint Monday, 1766–1876." *Past and Present*, no. 71, May, pp. 76–101.

Richardson, T.L. 1976. "The Agricultural Labourer's Standard of Living in Kent, 1790–1840," in D. Oddy and D. Miller, eds. *The Making of the Modern British Diet*, pp. 103–16, London.

_____. 1977. "The Standard of Living Controversy, 1790–1840," University of Hull. Unpublished Ph.D. thesis, pt. II.

Robinson, J. 1953–4. "The Production Function and the Theory of Capital." *Review of Economic Studies*, XXI, pp. 81–106.

Robson, D. 1966. *Some Aspects of Education in Cheshire in the Eighteenth Century*. Manchester.

Roehl, R. 1976. "French Industrialization: A Reconsideration." *Explorations in Economic History*, XII, pp. 230–81.

Rogers, J.E. Thorold 1884. *Six Centuries of Work and Wages: the History of English Labour*. 1909 ed., London.

_____. 1902. *A History of Agriculture and Prices in England*, VII, London.

Röpke, W. 1934. *German Commercial Policy*. London.

Rosenberg, N. 1963. "Technological Change in the Machine Tool Industry 1840–1910." *Journal of Economic History*, XXXIII, no. 4, Dec., pp. 414–43.

_____. 1967. "Anglo-American Wage Differences in the 1820s." *Journal of Economic History*, XXVII, no. 2, June, pp. 221–229.

_____. 1969. "The Direction of Technological Change: Inducement Mechanisms and Focusing Devices." *Economic Development and Cultural Change*, XVIII, no. 1, Part 1, Oct., pp. 1–24.

_____. 1972. "Factors Affecting the Diffusion of Technology." *Explorations in Economic History*, X, no. 1, Fall, pp. 3–34.

_____. 1974. "Science, Invention, and Economic Growth." *Economic Journal*, LXXXIV, March, pp. 90–108.

_____. 1976. *Perspectives in Technology*. Cambridge.

Rossman, J. 1931. *The Psychology of the Inventor*. Washington.

Rostow, W.W. 1948. *The British Economy of the Nineteenth Century*. London.

_____. 1960. *The Stages of Economic Growth*. Cambridge.

_____. 1973. "The Beginnings of Modern Economic Growth in Europe: An Essay in Synthesis." *Journal of Economic History*, XXXIII, no. 3, Sept., pp. 547–80.

_____. 1975. *How It All Began*. New York.

Rothe, W. von E. and Ritthaler, A. eds. 1934., *Vorgeschichte und Bergruendung des deutschen Zollvereins 1815–1834*, Berlin.

Rousseaux, P. 1938. *Les mouvements de fond de l'économie anglaise*. Louvain.

Rowe, J. 1953. *Cornwall in the Age of the Industrial Revolution*. Liverpool.

Royaume de Belgique, Ministère des Travaux Publiques 1846. *Statistique de la Belgique: Mines, usines minéralurgiques, machine à vapeur, 1839–44*. Brussels.

Rudé, G.E. 1953–4. "Prices, Wages and Popular Movements in Paris during the French Revolution." *Economic History Review*, 2nd ser., VI, no. 2, pp. 246–267.

Rule, J. 1979. "General Introduction" to J.L. and B. Hammond, 1919. *The Skilled Labourer*. 1979 ed. London.

_____. 1983. *The Experience of Labour in Eighteenth-Century English Industry*. New York.

Salaman, R.N. 1949. *The History and Social Influence of the Potato*. Cambridge.

Samuelson, P.A. 1950. "Evaluation of Real National Income." *Oxford Economic Papers*, n.s., II, no. 1, Jan. pp. 1–29.

Sandberg, L.G. 1974. *Lancashire in Decline*. Columbus.

_____. 1979. "The Case of the Impoverished Sophisticate: Human Capital and Swedish Economic Growth before World War I." *Journal of Economic History*, XXXIX, no. 1, March, pp. 225–242.

Sanderson, M. 1972. "Literacy and Social Mobility in the Industrial Revolution in England." *Past and Present*, LVI, no. 56, Aug., pp. 75–104.

_____. 1974. "Literacy and Social Mobility in the Industrial Revolution in England: A Rejoinder." *Past and Present*, LXIV, no. 64, Aug., pp. 108–112.

_____. 1976. Review of West, 1975 in *Economic History Review*, 2nd ser., XXIX, no. 2, May, pp. 323–324.

Saul, S.B. 1970. *Technological Change: The United States and Britain in the Nineteenth Century*. London.

Scherer, F.M. 1970. *Industrial Market Structure and Economic Performance*. Chicago.

Schiff, E. 1971. *Industrialization without National Patents*. London.

Schlöte, W. 1952. *British Overseas Trade from 1700 to the 1930s*. Oxford.

Schmookler, J. 1966. *Invention and Economic Growth*. Cambridge, Mass.

Schofield, R.S. 1973. "Dimensions of Illiteracy, 1750–1850." *Explorations in Economic History*, vol. X, no. 4, Summer, pp. 437–51.

Schöller, P. 1948. "La transformation économique de la Belgique de 1832 a 1844." *Bulletin de l'Institut des Sciences Économiques*, XIV, Dec., p. 585.

Schumpeter, J.A. 1934. *The Theory of Economic Development*. Cambridge, Mass.

_____ . 1939. *Business Cycles*. New York.

Scitovsky, T. 1971. *Welfare and Competition*. Rev. ed. Homewood, Illinois.

Scott, I.O., Jr. 1952. "The Gerschenkron Hypothesis of Index Number Bias." *Review of Economics and Statistics*, XXXIV, November, pp. 386–87.

Segal, H.H. and Simon, M. 1961. "British Foreign Capital Issues, 1865–1894." *Journal of Economic History*, XXI, no. 4, Dec., pp. 566–77.

Sen, A.K. 1979. "The Welfare Basis of Real Income Comparisons: A Survey." *Journal of Economic Literature*, XVII, no. 1, March, pp. 1–45.

Sen, S.R. 1957. *The Economics of Sir James Steuart*. Cambridge, Mass.

Shorter, E.L. 1967. "Social Change and Social Policy in Bavaria, 1800–1860, (unpublished Ph.D. thesis, Harvard University).

Silberling, N.J. 1923. "British Prices and Business Cycles, 1779–1850." *Review of Economics and Statistics*, V, pp. 223–61.

Singer, H.W. 1941. "An Index of Urban Land Rents and House Rents in England and Wales, 1845–1913." *Econometrica*, IX, nos. 3 and 4, July–October, pp. 221–30.

Smelser, N.J. 1959. *Social Change in the Industrial Revolution*. Chicago.

Smith, A. 1759. *Theory of Moral Sentiments*. London.

_____ . 1776. *An Inquiry into the Nature and Causes of the Wealth of Nations*. London.

Smout, T.C. 1978. "Famine and Famine-relief in Scotland," in L.M. Cullen and T.C. Smout, eds., *Comparative Aspects of Scottish and Irish Economic History 1600–1900*. Edinburgh, pp. 21–31.

Soetbeer, A. 1879. *Edelmetallproduktion und Wertverhaltnis zwischen Gold und Silber seit der Entdeckung Amerikas bis zur Gegenwart*. Gotha.

Solar, P. 1983. "Poor Relief and Economic Development in Britain and Ireland until the mid-Nineteenth Century." Unpublished manuscript.

Solow, R.M. 1957. "Technical Change and the Aggregate Production Function." *Review of Economics and Statistics*, XXXIX, pp. 312–20.

Soltow, L. 1968. "Long Run Changes in British Income Inequality." *Economic History Review*, 2nd ser., XXI, no. 1, April, pp. 17–29.

Stigler, G. 1968. "The Division of Labor is Limited by the Extent of the Market," reprinted in W. Breit and H.M. Hochman, eds. *Readings in Microeconomics*. New York.

Stone, L. 1969. "Literacy and Education in England, 1640–1900." *Past and Present*, XLII, Feb., pp. 69–139.

Stone, R. 1954. *The Measurement of Consumer's Expenditure and Behaviour in the United Kingdom, 1920–38*. Cambridge.

Streeten, P. 1967. "The Frontiers of Development Studies: Some Issues of Development Policy." *Journal of Development Studies*, IV, no. 1, Oct., pp. 2–24.

Styles, P. 1963. "The Evolution of the Law of Settlement." *University of Birmingham Historical Journal*, IX, no. 1, pp. 33–63.

Supple, B.E. 1974. "Legislation and Virtue: An Essay on Working-Class Self-Help and the State in the Early Nineteenth Century," in N. McKendrick, ed. *Historical Perspectives: Studies in English Thought and Society in Honour of J.H. Plumb*. London.

Sutton, D. 1982. "Radical Liberals, Fabianism, and Social History," in Centre for Contemporary Cultural Studies, *Making Histories: Studies in History-Writing*. Birmingham.

Symon, J.A. 1953–4. "The Falkirk Trysts: a Gauge to Highland Stock Output." *Scottish Agriculture*, Winter.

Taylor, A.J. 1960. "Progress and Poverty in Britain, 1780–1850: A Reappraisal." *History*, XLV, no. 153, Feb., pp. 16–31.

_____ . 1961. "Labor Productivity and Technological Innovation in the British Coal Industry, 1850–1914." *Economic History Review*, XIV, 2nd ser., no. 1, Aug., pp. 48–67.

_____ . 1972. *Laissez-Faire and State Intervention in Nineteenth Century Britain*. London.

_____. 1975. editor, *The Standard of Living in Britain in the Industrial Revolution*. London.

Taylor, J.S. 1969. "The Mythology of the Old Poor Law." *Journal of Economic History*, XXIX, no. 2, June, pp. 292–297.

Thomas, B. 1972a. *Migration and Urban Development*. London.

_____. 1972b. "The Rhythm of Growth in the Atlantic Economy of the Eighteenth Century," in P. Uselding, ed. *Research in Economic History*, vol. 3, Greenwich, Conn., pp. 16–22.

_____. 1973. *Migration and Economic Growth: A Study of Great Britain and the Atlantic Economy*. 2nd ed., Cambridge.

_____. 1978. "The Rhythm of Growth in the Atlantic Economy of the Eighteenth Century," in P. Uselding ed. *Research in Economic History*, Vol 3. Greenwich, Conn., pp. 16–22.

_____. 1980. "Towards an Energy Interpretation of the Industrial Revolution." *Atlantic Economic Journal*, VIII, 1, March, pp. 1–15.

Thomas, R.P. and McCloskey, D.N. 1981. "Overseas Trade and Empire 1700–1860," in R.C. Floud and D.N. McCloskey, eds. *The Economic History of Britain Since 1700*, vol. I, pp. 87–102.

Thomis, M.I. 1974. *The Town Labourer and the Industrial Revolution*. London and Sydney.

Thompson, E.P. 1963. *The Making of the English Working Class*. Harmondsworth. Reprinted 1968.

_____. 1967. "Time, Work-Discipline and Industrial Capitalism." *Past and Present*, XXXVIII, Dec., pp. 56–97. Reprinted in M.W. Flinn and T.C. Smout, eds. 1979. *Essays in Social History*, Oxford.

_____. 1977. *William Morris: Romantic to Revolutionary*. Rev. ed. London. 1st ed. 1955.

_____. 1978. "Eighteenth-Century English Society: Class Struggle Without Class?" *Social History*, III, no. 2, May, pp. 133–165.

Thompson, W. 1827. *Labour Rewarded: the Claims of Labour and Capital Consolidated*. London.

Thorp, W.L. 1926. *Business Annals*. New York.

Timmer, C.P. 1969. "The Turnip, the New Husbandry and the English Agricultural Revolution." *Quarterly Journal of Economics*, LXXXIII, no. 3, pp. 375–95.

Toynbee, A. 1884. *Lectures on the Industrial Revolution*. T.S. Ashton, ed. 1969, New York.

Trebilcock, C. 1969. " 'Spin-off' in British Economic History: Armaments and Industry, 1760–1914." *Economic History Review*, 2nd ser., XXII, no. 3, Dec., pp. 474–90.

von Treitschke, H. 1882. "Die Anfange des deutschen Zollvereins, I." *Preuszische Jahrbücher*, XXX, nos. 4, 5, and 6.

Treue, W. 1937. "Wirtschaftszustande und Wirtschaftspolitik in Preuszen 1815–1825." Supplement 31 to *Vierteljahrschrift für Sozial und Wirthschaftsgeschichte*.

Trevelyan, G.M. 1944. *English Social History: A Survey of Six Centuries, Chaucer to Victoria*. London.

Tucker, R.S. 1936. "Real Wages of Artisans in London, 1729–1935." *Journal of the American Statistical Association*, XXXI, no. 193, March, pp. 73–84.

von Tunzelmann, G.N. 1978. *Steam Power and British Industrialization to 1860*. Oxford.

_____. 1979. "Trends in Real Wages, 1750–1850, Revisited." *Economic History Review*, 2nd ser., XXXII, no. 1, Feb., pp. 33–49.

_____. 1981. "Technical Progress during the Industrial Revolution," in R.C. Floud and D.N. McCloskey, eds. *The Economic History of Britain since 1700*, vol. I, Cambridge, pp. 143–63.

_____. 1982. "The Standard of Living, Investment, and Economic Growth in England and Wales, 1760–1850," in L. Jörtberg and N. Rosenberg, eds. *Technical Change, Employment and Investment*. Stockholm, Sweden.

Turner, M.E. 1982. "Agricultural Productivity in England in the Eighteenth Century: Evidence from Crop Yields," *Economic History Review*, XXXV, no. 4, Nov., pp. 489–510.

U.S. Commissioner of Labor. 1891. *Sixth Annual Report*. Washington.
_____. 1892. *Seventh Annual Report*. Washington.
Usher, A.P. 1921. *An Introduction to the Industrial History of England*. London.
_____. 1954. *A History of Mechanical Inventions*. London.
Vickers, D. 1959. *Studies in the Theory of Money, 1690–1776*. Philadelphia.
DeVries, J. 1976. *The Economy of Europe in an Age of Crisis, 1600–1750*. Cambridge.
Wadsworth, A.P. and Mann, J. de L. 1931. *The Cotton Industry and Industrial Lancashire, 1600–1780*. London.
Wallerstein, I. 1974. *The Modern World System*, vol. 1. New York.
_____. 1980. *The Modern World System*, vol. 2. New York.
Waltershausen, Sartorius von 1907. *Das volkswirtschaftliche System der Kapitalanlage im Auslande*. Berlin.
Ward, I.D.S. 1959. "George Berkeley: Precursor of Keynes as Moral Economist on Under-development." *Journal of Political Economy*, LXVIII, Feb., pp. 31–40.
Webb, R.K. 1955. *The British Working-Class Reader*. London.
Weiss, T.J. 1976. "Economies of Scale in Nineteenth-Century Economic Growth." Summary of Research Workshop. *Journal of Economic History*, XXXVI, no. 1, March, pp. 39–41.
West, E.G. 1965. *Education and the State*. London.
_____. 1970. "Resource Allocation and Growth in Early Nineteenth-Century British Education." *Economic History Review*, 2nd ser., XXIII, pp. 68–95.
_____. 1971. "The Interpretation of Early Nineteenth-Century Education Statistics." *Economic History Review*, 2nd ser., XXIV, P. 633–42.
_____. 1975. *Education and the Industrial Revolution*. London.
White, L. 1978. *Medieval Religion and Technology*. Berkeley.
Wiener, M.J. 1981. *English Culture and the Decline of the Industrial Spirit, 1850–1980*. Cambridge.
Williams, E. 1944. *Capitalism and Slavery*. Chapel Hill, North Carolina.
Williams, J.E. 1966. "The British Standard of Living, 1750–1850." *Economic History Review*, 2nd ser., XIX, no. 3, Dec., pp. 581–589.
Williams, K. 1981. *From Pauperism to Poverty*. London.
Williams, R. 1983. *Cobbett*. Oxford.
Williamson, J.G. 1964–5. "Regional Inequality and the Process of National Development: A Description of the Patterns." *Economic Development and Cultural Change*, XIII, pt. II, no. 4, July, pp. 1–82.
_____. 1966. "Consumer Behaviour in the Nineteenth Century: Carroll D. Wright's Massachusetts Workers in 1875." *Explorations in Entrepreneurial History*, IV, pp. 98–135.
_____. 1976. "American Prices and Urban Inequality since 1820." *Journal of Economic History*, XXXVI, no. 2, June, pp. 303–33.
_____. 1980. "Earnings Inequality in Nineteenth-Century Britain." *Journal of Economic History*, XL, no. 3, pp. 457–76.
_____. 1981. "Urban Disamenities, Dark Satanic Mills, and the British Standard of Living Debate." *Journal of Economic History*, XLI, no. 1, pp. 75–84.
_____. 1982a. "Was the Industrial Revolution Worth It? Disamenities and Death in Nineteenth Century British Towns." *Explorations in Economic History*, XIX, no. 3, July, pp. 221–45.
_____. 1982b. "The Structure of Pay in Britain, 1710–1911," in P. Uselding, ed. *Research in Economic History*, Vol. 7. Greenwich, Conn.
_____. 1984. "Why Was British Growth so Slow during the Industrial Revolution," *Journal of Economic History*, XLIV, no. 3, Sept., pp. 687–712.
Williamson, J.G. and Lindert, P. 1980. *American Inequality; A Macroeconomic History*. New York.

Wood, G.H. 1910. *The History of Wages in the Cotton Trade During the Past Hundred Years.* London.

Woodruff, W. 1966. *Impact of Western Man. A Study of Europe's Role in the World Economy, 1750–1960.* New York.

Wright, C.M. 1939. *Economic Adaptation to a Changing World Market.* Copenhagen.

Wrigley, E.A. 1962. "The Supply of Raw Materials in the Industrial Revolution." *Economic History Review,* XV, no. 1, pp. 1–16.

_____ . 1967. "A Simple Model of London's Importance in Changing English Society and Economy 1650–1750." *Past and Present,* XXXVII, no. 37, pp. 44–70.

Wrigley, E.A. and Schofield, R. 1981. *The Population History of England, 1541–1871: A Reconstruction.* Cambridge.

Young, A. 1771. *A Six Months' Tour of the North of England.* London.

Young, D.B. 1976. "A Wood Famine? The Question of Deforestation in Old Regime France." *Forestry,* XLIX, no. 1.

Zevin, R.B. 1971. "The Growth of Cotton Textile Production After 1815," in R.W. Fogel and S.L. Engerman, eds. *The Reinterpretation of American Economic History.* New York.

Index

About the Contributors

Nicholas F.R. Crafts is a fellow of University College, University of Oxford. He is the author of *Economic Growth During the Industrial Revolution*.

Peter H. Lindert is Professor of Economics at the University of California at Davis. He is the author of *Fertility and Scarcity in America* and *American Inequality: A Macroeconomic History* (with J.G. Williamson).

Donald N. McCloskey is Professor of Economics and History at the University of Iowa. He is the author of *Enterprise and Trade in Victorian Britain* and *The Rhetoric of Economics*.

Joel Mokyr is Professor of Economics and History at Northwestern University. He is the author of *Industrialization in the Low Countries* and *Why Ireland Starved*.

Sidney Pollard is Professor of History at the University of Bielefeld. He is the author of *The Genesis of Modern Management* and *Peaceful Conquest: The Industrialization of Europe, 1760–1970*.

Robert M. Solow is Professor of Economics at the Massachusetts Institute of Technology. He is the author of *Capital Theory and the Rate of Return* and *Growth Theory And Exposition*.

Peter Temin is Professor of Economics at the Massachusetts Institute of Technology. He is the author of *The Jacksonian Economy* and *Causal Factors in American Economic Growth in the Nineteenth Century*.

Brinley Thomas is a former Professor of Economics at the University of Wales in Cardiff and at present is Visiting Professor of Economics at the University of California at Davis. He is the author of *Migration and Economic Growth: A Study of Great Britain and the Atlantic Economy* and the editor of *The Economics of International Migration*.

G.N. Von Tunzelmann is Reader in Economic History at the University of Sussex. He is the author of *Steam Power and British Industrialization to 1860*.

E.G. West is Professor of Economics at Carleton University. He is the author of *Education and the Industrial Revolution*.

Jeffrey G. Williamson is Laird Bell Professor of Economics at Harvard University. He is the author of *Late Nineteenth Century American Development: A General Equilibrium Analysis* and *Did British Capitalism Breed Inequality?*